CHRISTIAN

Christian

THE POLITICS OF A WORD IN AMERICA

Matthew Bowman

Harvard University Press

Cambridge, Massachusetts
London, England
2018

First Printing

Library of Congress Cataloging-in-Publication Data
Names: Bowman, Matthew Burton, author.
Title: Christian : the politics of a word in America / Matthew Bowman.
Description: Cambridge, Massachusetts : Harvard University Press, 2018.
Identifiers: LCCN 2017045116 | ISBN 9780674737631 (alk. paper)
Subjects: LCSH: Christianity and politics—United States—History—20th century. |
Christianity and politics—United States—History—21st century. | Republican Party
(U.S. : 1854–)—Religion—20th century. | Republican Party
(U.S. : 1854–)—Religion—21st century.
Classification: LCC BR115.P7 B6675 2018 | DDC 261.70973—dc23
LC record available at https://lccn.loc.gov/2017045116

For Penny, Jack, Hazel, and Henry

CONTENTS

CHRISTIAN

Prologue

O N JANUARY 18, 2016, presidential candidate Donald Trump visited the campus of Liberty University, an evangelical Christian college in southern Virginia, to give a speech. "Two Corinthians, 3:17," the real estate mogul and television celebrity declared. "That's the whole ballgame. 'Where the Spirit of the Lord is, there is liberty,' and here there is liberty." His biblical reference was met with combined laughter and applause, because while his audience appreciated the sentiment, Trump had flubbed the citation; the Pauline epistle is commonly referred to as Second Corinthians.[1] Soon, the worries that some Christian leaders held about Trump's fitness for office escalated beyond his simple religious illiteracy. In October a recording of Trump bragging about aggressive sexual behavior came to light, and he was accused of mistreatment by a number of women. Many Christian leaders shared the opinion of prominent evangelical public-affairs consultant Mark DeMoss, who said of his refusal to endorse Trump, "I didn't think this candidate represented the values that Liberty had spent 40 years trying to instill in its students."[2]

And yet, Liberty's president, Jerry Falwell Jr., son of the founder of the Moral Majority, a conservative Christian political advocacy group which upended American politics in the 1970s and 1980s, endorsed Trump anyway. On the night of the 2016 presidential election, Trump secured a majority of self-identified American Christians, winning 52 percent of Catholics and 58 percent of Protestants, including an overwhelming 81 percent of white evangelicals—more than the Mormon Mitt Romney had won four years before.[3]

To Christians like Falwell and those who applauded the sentiment of Trump's garbled biblical reference even as they chuckled at it, the candidate seemed the best option despite his moral failings. The reasons why indicate what Christianity had come to mean to them. While to many of Trump's critics, the candidate's evident unfamiliarity with Christian ideas disqualified him from claiming the faith, for some white Christians, the way Trump spoke about the relationship between Christianity and the nation reflected a long tradition of identifying Christianity with the concept of "Western civilization," which they associated with democratic government, individual liberty, and a white, European heritage. Indeed, many white evangelicals believed that America was afflicted with a non-Christian elite whose lack of faith was degrading these values. The evangelical leader James Dobson, a Trump supporter, warned that there was a clear connection between what he called a "massive assault on religious liberty" and the rise of "tyranny" in the United States. Rick Scarborough, a Baptist leader in Texas, warned, "We are living in a growing age of secularism that is forcing itself on people who hold traditional values," and praised Trump as "a champion to the common man, a guy who says to Christians: 'I'm going to take care of you.'"[4] Trump may have lacked basic knowledge of the Bible, but his Liberty speech gave evangelicals hope that despite his moral failings, he understood the crucial link between Christianity and American democracy.

That link was rooted in a particular geographical, historical, and ethnic vision of what constituted Western civilization. Throughout his campaign, Trump warned that American freedom was threatened by a range of peoples he labeled un-American, particularly Muslims and Latin American immigrants. After he was inaugurated as president in early 2017, Trump issued a series of executive orders attempting to slow migration from Islamic-majority countries and cracking down on undocumented immigrants from Latin America. In a March 2017 television interview, Trump supporter Steve King, a member of Congress from Iowa, argued that "Western civilization itself" was defined as "every place where the footprint of Christianity settled the world." King went on to defend the Trump administration's restrictive immigration policies, later writing that "we can't restore our civilization with somebody else's babies."[5] For King and other Christians who sympathized with him, Northern Europe and North America, what they called "Western civilization," had been uniquely blessed with Protestant Christianity and hence with free, democratic government. To these Christians, Trump's personal behavior paled next to his willingness to defend Christian civilization, which they understood to be closely identified with the West. Latin America, which to King was neither white nor Protestant, and the Muslim world, neither white nor Christian, stood outside those categories.

In the 1980s and 1990s, conservative Christians who identified with these values had formed lobbying groups like the Christian Coalition and the Moral Majority and had achieved a series of triumphs, gaining the ear of presidents and fueling Ronald Reagan's two elections as president and the Republican Party's takeover of Congress in the 1994 elections. The impressive organizational successes of these groups aside, perhaps the movement's most enduring accomplishment was to shape what Americans thought of when they thought of "Christianity."[6] This rhetorical revolution was a conscious effort. Leaders of the Religious Right worked hard and ceaselessly to define Christianity in their own image. In August 1980, some 15,000 evangelicals gathered to hear Reagan, then a candidate for president, speak at the National Affairs Briefing, a forum organized to allow conservative evangelical Christians to express political opinions. Before the candidate spoke, the televangelist James Robison drew as clear boundaries around what was and was not Christian as King had. "I'm sick and tired of hearing about all of the radicals and the perverts and the liberals and the leftists and the Communists coming out of the closet. It's time for God's people to come out of the closet," Robison declared, arguing that Christians were by definition not members of any of the groups listed in his first sentence. He and his allies dismissed welfare programs, the sexual revolution, crime, and Carter's policies on the family as manifestations of "secular humanism." Defining such things as "secular," and therefore not Christian, allowed Robison to assert that they had no place in the United States, just as King invoked Christianity as a reason to restrict immigration.[7]

Robison's and King's insistence that Christianity was synonymous with cultural conservatism and ethno-nationalism was not inevitable. Rather, it has a historical genealogy that reveals the ways in which the raw material of the term *Christian* and the host of ideas and language historically associated with it can be fused to political theory. Because of that malleability, the term always resists collapse into a single definition; though American Christians ceaselessly invoke the word, it has no essential, normative meaning. Rather, Christianity is an example of what philosopher W. B. Gallie calls "essentially contested concepts."[8] Such ideas are simultaneously central to human functioning and frustratingly hard to pin down. Like other essentially contested concepts—such as "justice" or "art"—the notion of "Christianity" lies near the primal level of the American imagination, and yet different people emphasize various elements, interpret it differently based upon particular social or political circumstances, or offer definitions that seek to establish the supremacy of their own uses. This book takes as a premise that talk about Christianity in America is essentially diverse and disputed. And yet, it is foundational. The word *Christian* provides Americans with metaphysical justification for political belief. It allows them to root notions as diverse as human equality and white supremacy in supernal claims about human nature and divine will. But because there is no single definition of *Christianity*, there is also no single consensus about which of those values are most important or precisely how they are to be applied.

The form of Christianity which Donald Trump pledged allegiance to has its roots in something historians have called "Christian republicanism." Through the nineteenth and twentieth centuries, many American Christians, particularly white Protestants, subscribed to it, cloaking Protestant virtues like individual liberty and the priority of ethical behavior in the broader category of "Christianity."[9] Christian republicanism had perhaps its most enduring exponent in Alexis de Tocqueville, a French nobleman and observer of America. He wrote that the European settlers who peopled the British colonies "brought with them into the New World a form of Christianity which I cannot better describe than by styling it a democratic and republican religion." For him, American democracy thus grew from Christian principles. Tocqueville observed that the British Puritans who colonized the American Northeast had egalitarianism embedded in their theology: they believed that human beings were possessed of innate worth derived from divine creation. But that worth was tempered with moral stricture. Their Christianity demanded rigorous ethics that prevented selfishness and inculcated duty. Tocqueville argued that taken together these values provided the intellectual and cultural foundation of the American Revolution and the Constitution, but also underlay the structure of American society. In the United States, he claimed, Christianity's "influence over the mind of woman is supreme, and women are the protectors of morals." American women were dutiful protectors of the home, and American men were hardy individualists, for Protestantism, Tocqueville said, "tends to make men independent."[10] Religion thus gave the United States a gendered order that fostered democratic liberty.

Tocqueville's argument has certainly been contested by historians, but it has also been long embraced by white American Protestants in particular. The Revolutionary and Protestant leader Benjamin Rush believed that Protestantism and democracy were coincident; as he claimed of the American political system, "Republicanism is a part of the truth of Christianity." For Rush, both Protestant Christianity and self-government required moral discipline and respect for individual liberty, and hence they needed each other.[11] More recently, Tocqueville's argument has been embraced by a number of American Christian commentators. The evangelical scholar Mark Noll dubbed Christian republicanism a "compound of evangelical Protestant religion, republican political ideology and commonsense moral reasoning" that Noll believed had come to dominate American politics in the nineteenth century.[12] Similarly, commentators Hugh Heclo and Ross Douthat maintain that some variety of Christianity provides Americans with confidence that the individual is the foundational unit of society and is endowed with unique worth, balanced with the conviction that American democracy flourishes when this commitment to liberty is conditioned with moral discipline. Heclo lauds the Protestant insistence on human worth that served as the basis of moral reform efforts from abolitionism to the black-freedom movement; Douthat, a Catholic, condemns the degeneration of what he calls "Christian orthodoxy's" demand for self-discipline into "an un-Christian worship of the individual."[13] For both, Tocqueville's arguments essentially hold firm.

In the twentieth century, during the cultural crises of two world wars and the Cold War, Christian republicanism became increasingly linked to the imagined idea of Western civilization and hence to Europe, to middle-class sexual and economic norms, and to whiteness. American politicians, universities, and other cultural leaders emphasized that Christianity promoted individual autonomy and moral responsibility, linked these values to the sustenance of American democracy, and denounced as secular those forces that seemed to unduly restrict individual liberty or promote moral laxity. Because their vision of Christianity was implicitly in debt to Protestantism, for them Christian republicanism was premised upon the superiority of the Northern European and American civilization that produced and extended the Protestant Reformation. In the late nineteenth century, the nations of Europe and the United States were ascendant in military and economic strength, and they used the concept of "civilization" to distinguish themselves from the peoples of Africa, South Asia, and other places they were in the process of conquering, and to justify those conquests. In 1877 the American anthropologist Lewis Henry Morgan defined *civilization* as the end point of human progress from "savagery" through "barbarism" to ethical behavior in three major areas of life: government, the family, and the economy.[14] In government, ethical behavior would be manifest as democracy and equality; in the family, it would be manifest in the presence of monogamy and a gendered division of labor; in the economy, it would be manifest in respect for private property. Morgan and many of his contemporaries saw civilization as the endpoint of an evolutionary process, something which a society developed, and he believed that some societies had achieved it while others were unlikely to.

Many Americans and Europeans seized upon these definitions, believing that the sum total of political, economic, and social institutions a society constructed—its civilization—was an expression of its values. To American Christians, the virtues of the civilization Morgan described derived from their faith, and thus their domination of non-Christian and presumably uncivilized nations was a blessing. Robert Speer, a prominent Presbyterian layman and leader of the Student Volunteer Movement, the largest Protestant mission effort of the late nineteenth century, showed how such Protestants could link a whole host of social virtues to the presence of Christianity. "Western civilization is disintegrating both the customs of savage nations and the more stable civilization of the east," he said, because it provided a society superior to "the old and effete orders." Those civilizations lacked manly individualism and hence the sort of vigorous democratic government Christian civilizations enjoyed. "There are three great elements in religion: the element of fellowship, the element of dependence, and the element of progress," Speer declared. Only Christianity provided all, and democracy required all.[15]

For many white Christians, then, the virtues of their religion and the superiority of their Western heritage were inseparable. By the early twenty-first century, many American Protestants like Donald Trump and Steve King drew on Christian republicanism to promote a sort of Christian nationalism. But others who treasured the values of Christian republicanism—moral virtue, selflessness, public-spiritedness—worked hard to disentangle that legacy from support of Donald Trump. In April 2016 a number of Christian leaders issued a statement entitled "Called to Resist Bigotry: A Statement of Faithful Obedience." It denounced nationalist declarations as un-Christian, asserting that "messages of racial, religious, and nationalist bigotry compel confessional resistance from faithful Christians who believe that the image of God is equally within every human being." It offered an alternative way to understand the relationship between Christianity and the United States, deeming "the growing racial and cultural diversity" in the United States "a blessing" representative of the true nature of the "body of Christ."[16] After the election, the prominent Methodist minister and activist Jim Wallis worried, "Racism and misogyny needed to be clearly resisted and were generally not in white churches." Too many white Christians, Wallis said, had failed to be "faithful to Christian principles about loving our neighbors and welcoming the stranger."[17] For him, Christian republicanism demanded inclusion and equality.

And yet, Trump's victory confirmed to many Americans that his version of the faith was triumphant. In April 2017, the *Washington Post* reported that a poll of 957 Americans revealed that 14 percent of those who regularly attended church services in 2016 left their congregations after the election. The *Post*'s story on the poll ascribed this leave-taking to distress over widespread Christian support for Trump.[18] Indeed, the election seemed only to confirm a long-standing frustration Christians like Wallis held: that, prompted by the publicity the Religious Right won, Americans tended to associate Christianity with conservative politics. A few years before, Wallis had mourned that too many Americans assumed that "religious voters," or voters who supported "moral values," were simply "voters who are against abortion and gay marriage." More strikingly, the best-selling novelist Anne Rice, raised Catholic, announced, "I remain committed to Christ as always but not to being 'Christian' or to being part of Christianity. . . . In the name of Christ, I refuse to be anti-gay. I refuse to be anti-feminist. I refuse to be anti-artificial birth control. I refuse to be anti-Democrat. I refuse to be anti-secular humanism. I refuse to be anti-science. I refuse to be anti-life."[19]

These subjective impressions are backed with remarkable raw data. In 2008, David Kinnaman and Gabe Lyons reported that their research firm, the Barna Group, found that among Americans between the ages of sixteen and twenty-nine, 91 percent associated the term *Christian* with hostility toward LGBT Americans. Eighty-seven percent said that Christians were judgmental, and 85 percent that they were hypocritical. Moreover, it seemed that Anne Rice was not alone. Half of active churchgoers agreed that these criticisms applied to "Christians," and Kinnaman, himself a believer, confessed that he regularly used the label "Christ follower" to avoid calling himself a "Christian."[20]

The fracturing of Christian republicanism's dominance in the twentieth century is one of the stories this book tells. Over the course of the twentieth century some groups of American Christians, including liberal Protestants, African American Christians, and new Christian groups began to sever the link between Christianity and Western civilization that many Christians took for granted. Many of these groups had all along found Christian republicanism lacking, and had always offered alternative visions of the relationship between Christianity and democracy. Roman Catholics, whose faith prized community and institution, found themselves in a precarious relationship with Protestant Christian republicanism's insistence upon individual liberty. The black-freedom movement blasted Christian republicanism's identification with a Western heritage that had long embraced African slavery. During the 1960s, new religious movements that drew on Asian Christianity and the counterculture found the Christian republican consensus hollow and useless, dismissing its identification with capitalism, the cultural status quo, and Cold War militarism. In response, a group of academics promoted an interpretation of something called "civil religion," an attempt to revive traditional Christian republicanism without its older commitments to explicitly Christian theology, and conservative evangelical Christians formulated the Religious Right to promote their own version of that same tradition. Through the mid-twentieth century, debates among these groups splintered the public meaning of Christianity in America.

This book uses the theme of "materialism" to unify these various narrative strands. As American Christians began enunciating the relationship between Christianity and American democracy, they also began fearing its corruption. The word they used to describe that corruption was *materialism,* a force which denied the metaphysical claims of Christianity and hence threatened to corrupt the civilization Christianity had built. Like *Christian* itself, the term is nebulous enough to mean many things, but its specter and explanatory power have often proven a rallying point for American Christians seeking to defend the relationship between their faith and their politics. In defining their opponent, they define themselves. If the word *Christian* has meant what American Christians value, the term *materialism* means whatever American Christians fear. The war on materialism has also been an attempt to define the boundaries of the religious and the secular in American politics. As long as American Christians have been convinced that the preservation of those things they deem Christian is essential to sustaining American democracy, materialism becomes to them the threat of democracy's collapse.[21]

Just as the late nineteenth century saw the forging of new links among Christianity, democracy, and civilization, it was also a transformative moment for the concept of materialism. Influenced by the rising prestige of science, American philosophy was moving away from the loose conglomeration of ideas that had dominated American thought since transcendentalism. Thinkers like Emerson emphasized transcendence and the spiritual, privileging ideals over the tangible world. But by the end of the century, grappling with Americans' new respect for the empirical and tangible, philosophers like George Santayana had begun to use the term *naturalism,* a word that gave primacy to the tangible while making some room for the reality of ideas. In the early twentieth century the problem of the relationship between the material and the ideal became dominant in American thought.[22]

William James, uneasy with such formulations, put his finger on why many American Christians found materialism distressing. In *Pragmatism* he drew a distinction between "materialism" and "spiritualism," observing that "the laws of physical nature run things, materialism says. The highest productions of human genius might be ciphered by one who had a complete acquaintance with the facts, out of their physiological conditions, regardless whether nature be there only for our minds." Against materialism he placed "spiritualism," which he said contended that "the mind not only witnesses and records things but also runs and operates them." Either the world was made up of the material, and human beings were nothing more than a series of chemical reactions, or the human mind and will were distinct from the morass of matter around them. James noted, correctly, that this was largely an "aesthetic" dispute, but he grasped why many found materialism distressing: "Materialism denies reality to the objects of almost all the impulses which we most cherish. The real meaning of the impulses, it says, is something which has no emotional interest for us whatsoever."[23] To James, the threat of materialism was an entirely mechanical universe in which human values lacked meaning.

If materialism denied the higher reality of the divine and humanity's relationship to it, many Christians wondered on what grounds morality, the necessary foundation of democracy, could survive. Alexis de Tocqueville had warned that "materialism . . . is more especially to be dreaded amongst a democratic people," because it denied the transcendence of moral law and hence permitted degeneracy.[24] And indeed by the late nineteenth century many Christians feared that the theory of evolution would lead to a materialist conception of humanity and thus a general collapse of the social order.

Joseph LeConte, son of a Presbyterian minister, graduate of the Lawrence Scientific School at Harvard, and eventually professor at the University of California, did much to show that evolution and Christianity might be reconciled. But he also admitted in an essay published in 1880, "I have sometimes wrestled in an agony with this fearful doubt, with this demon of materialism." LeConte worried that evolution might demonstrate "there is no such thing as spirit," and therefore that "life is only transformed physical and chemical force," rendering human existence no different in kind than rain, combustion, and the decay of dead plants or animals.[25] For many Protestants LeConte's reconciliation was successful, but for many others it was not: evolution remained a marker of essentially atheistic materialism, and hence the gateway to a society which placed no value on individual liberty.

Many American Christians, less philosophically sophisticated than James or LeConte, shared these fears, and after the Civil War they saw the materialist tide rising faster than ever. To them, living in a world of rapid industrialization, rising smoke stacks, and a yawning gap between the gilded mansions of the wealthy and the splintered tenements of the poor, the word *materialist* took on a Marxist cast. Marx and other theorists of the late nineteenth and early twentieth century, such as Max Weber and Emile Durkheim, were convinced that the material conditions of modern industrial society limited and corrupted humanity's higher possibilities. Marx blamed industrial capitalism for poverty, for the destruction of traditional kinship and cooperative relationships, and particularly for the subordination of the individual to the machine. As he and Friedrich Engels declared of the rise of industrial capitalism in the *Communist Manifesto,* "The work of the proletarians has lost all individual character and consequently all charm for the workman. He becomes an appendage of the machine."[26] Weber and Durkheim both drew distinctions between "organic" societies and "mechanical" or "rationalized" societies, theorizing that industrial materialism might obliterate society's religious imagination.

Though only a few American Christians evinced sympathy for Karl Marx, as the industrial era progressed, their fears mirrored his. Marxist thinking was filtered into the United States through American social critics like Henry George, and Americans soon began to echo his critique of capitalism's impact on the traditional fabric of society.[27] Aesthetes like the professor Edward Woodberry and the educator and journalist Charles Eliot Norton used the word *materialism* to combat the capitalist decadence they perceived in Gilded Age America, pressing instead for a renewed spiritual life focused on human virtue. The architect Ralph Adams Cram advocated a renewal of the world of the medieval era. In such a realm, human beings would live in an organic social order vitalized by religious faith, a healthy replacement for the grim impersonality of the industrial age. Others, like supporters of the Knights of Labor workingman's movement and some populist leaders, advocated similarly for small self-sufficient communities which would resist the centralizing forces of industrial capitalism. They believed that the spiritual vitality of Christianity would enervate personal workmanship and intimate human relationships against an increasingly mechanized economy. "Christ must have been a true Knight of Labor, being a carpenter's son. And this proves that all Knights of Labor should be Christ like," said the movement's journal.[28]

The late nineteenth century thus saw the appearance of new dimensions of materialism—new threats it might pose and guises it might take. Standing against materialism as the only bulwark against the ruination of democracy was Christianity. But just as Christianity itself had a variety of forms, depending on which Christian one asked, so did Christians' fears of materialism. Indeed, the ways in which Christians defined *materialism* illustrated as much about what they believed regarding Christianity itself as about the seeming threat of the world. In the early twentieth century Protestant fundamentalists saw materialism in the theory of evolution. Roman Catholics saw it in the looming strength of consumer capitalism. By the second half of the twentieth century, hippies and other advocates of the counterculture saw materialism in the overweening power of the state, and African Americans saw it in the inhumanity of Jim Crow laws. The Religious Right saw it in the rise of social changes they labeled "secular humanism" and launched a defense of the religious nature of American democracy. All these groups mounted Christian language to press for a form of politics they found humane and, ultimately, religious. Placing the Religious Right in this longer tradition of Christian antimaterialism reveals that the narrative that Anne Rice accepted and Dave Kinnaman documented has, in fact, a more complex history than might be imagined, and that the easy identification of Christianity with the Religious Right is too simple.

The story told here is not *the* history, or an exhaustive history, of the use of the language and idea of Christianity in twentieth-century American politics. Rather it is a narrative constructed from a series of case studies that illustrate certain spans of the broad arc of Christian involvement in American politics. It is *a* history that shows how some Americans have used the language of Christianity to assert the transcendent authority of their democracy against threats they labeled materialistic. As Christianity itself might take a number of forms, so too can the concepts of democracy, civilization, and materialism. The story told here, then, is of an ongoing argument, a struggle to control one of the key legitimating terms in American history.

CHAPTER ONE

Reconstruction, Spiritualism,
and the Shape of
an Argument

·┼·

A T TEN A.M. in the morning of January 11, 1871, a woman in a simply cut black velvet dress waited in the hallway outside the meeting room of the House Judiciary Committee of the United States Congress. Victoria Woodhull was thirty-two years old and already famous. She was a medium whose contact with the spirits had earned her and her patron, the railroad magnate Cornelius Vanderbilt, improbable wealth after the stock market crash of autumn 1869. Vanderbilt, overjoyed with his new riches and enamored with Woodhull's sister Tennessee Claflin, welcomed the young woman into his circles, which transformed her into a noted socialite and earned her connections to politicians and activists like the journalist Theodore Tilton and the Civil War veteran Congressman Benjamin Butler.

Woodhull had also found her way into the women's movement. In May 1870, she and Tennessee started a newspaper designed to offer commentary on the problems of the day. Their early issues, vehemently in favor of women's suffrage, had attracted a visit to their offices from Susan B. Anthony. The previous month Woodhull had announced her intentions in a widely re-printed newspaper notice: "I therefore claim the right to speak for the unfranchised women of the country and . . . I now announce myself as a candidate for the Presidency."[1] She was the first declared candidate in the 1872 presidential election. Several months later, at the invitation of Butler, she stood waiting to testify before Congress on behalf of a proposed law to grant women the right to vote. She made her case not only before Congress but to the country as a whole. Her newspaper, *Woodhull & Claflin's Weekly*, was popular enough that she received widespread attention and speaking invitations across the nation.

For many Gilded Age Americans, Woodhull's candidacy made the 1872 election interesting. She ran as a protest candidate, declaring her support for the advancement of both women's suffrage and African American rights. Her political party, the Equal Rights Party, nominated Frederick Douglass, the noted African American abolitionist, as her running mate. But Douglass ignored his selection, finding Woodhull insufficiently respectable due to her spiritualism, her flamboyance, and rumors of her sexual adventures. Others agreed. "Can any Christian woman sanction in any way the efforts of such a woman?" demanded Catharine Beecher, scion of one of America's leading Protestant families. In response to such attacks Woodhull shook her head. "I fear the hearts of such Christians are still far away from Jesus," she noted. "Give heed to the truths to which I shall call your attention, and they will help bring you all nearer to Him."[2] To Beecher and the pious Republican Party she supported, Woodhull's improprieties voided her claim to Christianity and called into question her capacity for leadership. Yet Woodhull insisted that such critics misunderstood the nature of Christianity itself. Jesus was no prude. To Woodhull he was a social radical.

The argument Woodhull and her adversaries had in 1872 about the relationship between Christianity and democracy foreshadowed many of the issues Christians would grapple with as they engaged with American politics through the twentieth century. In the era of Reconstruction, Americans argued about what might qualify or exclude new religious movements for participation in the public sphere, about persistent and painful issues of race, about industrialization, capitalism, and government corruption—and about the relation of all these things to the materialism emergent in American philosophy and economics. However bitter the disputes between Beecher and Woodhull, between North and South, within the Republican Party, and even among reformers like Woodhull and Douglass, the definition of Christianity was not settled, and therefore nor were the political issues it was invoked to resolve.

Woodhull's radicalism showed the transformative social and political potential Christian language might invoke. But the Catharine Beechers of the nation, respectable moralists, rallied behind Ulysses S. Grant and the Republican Party. They fancied themselves the heirs of the Christian republican tradition, arguing strenuously that the survival of democracy required disinterested moral commitment. They worked hard to present Grant, a gloomy military strategist, as a man of great piety and moral probity because Grant was the champion of the Radical Republican movement that controlled Congress well into the 1870s. For the Radicals, Christianity taught human equality and hence demanded that the formerly enslaved people of the South be made equal citizens of the Union. It also required that the South repent for its crimes and that Americans be instilled with virtue through law and education. Although they shared Victoria Woodhull's commitment to at least theoretical equality for all, these people looked at Woodhull and saw debauchery, a form of self-indulgent materialism that belied her claims to Christianity and would wreck the nation.

But other Christian moralists deserted the Republican Party for the Liberal Republican movement, eventually aligning with the Democratic Party to nominate journalist Horace Greeley for president. Greeley's surrogates defended him as the "Christian candidate" for president. To them, Christian republicanism meant freedom from corrupt centralized power of all sorts. As George Julian, a leading Liberal Republican, declared, "The rights of man are sacred, whether trampled down by Southern slave drivers, the monopolists of the soil, the grinding power of corporate wealth, the legalized robbery of a protective tariff, or the power of concentrated capital in alliance with labor saving machinery."[3] To Julian and other Liberal Republicans, power was by definition materialism—associated with wealth, profit, and gain—and the Grant administration was its prisoner. The Liberal Republican movement, which denounced wealth, industrialization, financial corruption, and autocratic government alike, used Christian language generated a powerful Christian language of protest. Long after Greeley's loss, American Christians would continue to invoke Christian language to rail against centralization, industrialization, and commercial modernity.

Victoria Woodhull and the Freedom of the Soul

Neither the partisans of Greeley nor the partisans of Grant could tolerate Woodhull, who stubbornly insisted that Christianity impelled her to defy social norms, not defend them. She offered a Christian politics counter to that of either the Radical Republican pious moralism or the Liberal Republican suspicion of corruption. More than anything else, her notoriety derived from her embrace of "free love": her position that the "stupidly arbitrary law" of marriage in the United States, and the Western world more broadly, restricted the natural sentiments of human beings, forcing passionate people like herself into artificially limited lives. (She was long estranged from her abusive first husband, Canning Woodhull, whom she had abandoned for James Blood, a Civil War veteran who left his wife for Victoria.) "Law cannot change what nature has already determined. Neither will love obey if law command," Woodhull cried to a roaring crowd in New York's Steinway Hall on November 20, 1871. The spectators' responses were peppered with both shouts of "Hurrah" and hisses. Woodhull held that human beings naturally possessed the liberty to live as they would, and that those rights should not be constrained. "Every living person has certain rights of which no law can rightfully deprive him," she offered the New York audience, and those rights included "political, religious, and social freedom" alike. When an audience member interrupted her, crying out, "Are *you* a free lover?" Woodhull cast her written speech to the ground and declared, "Yes! I am a free lover! I have an inalienable, constitutional, and natural right to love whom I may."[4] The crowd buzzed.

Some spiritualists like Woodhull called themselves "Christian spiritualists," claiming that their beliefs were closer to Jesus's teachings than were the sermons of America's ministers and priests. Andrew Jackson Davis, nineteenth-century spiritualism's greatest exponent, declared that "the good and truth and beauty of the doctrines of Jesus have been deformed and placed in unnatural juxtapositions." He insisted that modern Christian leaders suffered the same problem he believed the leaders of Judaism in Jesus's time had: Jesus "did not teach the doctrines which they had resolved could only be orthodox."[5] Woodhull was no exception to this sort of spiritualist restorationism, and the idea allowed her to press back upon accusations of impiety with her own religious authority. Typical was her speech before a "tremendous" audience in Detroit in November 1873, which left not even standing room in the hall. "She apologized for what she had said that might be construed into a lack of veneration for Christ," wrote a newspaper reporter. "She was a religious woman and revered Him and His doctrines. But she despised the hypocrites who had His name for ever on their lips but had none of His principles in their hearts."[6]

For Woodhull, as for other spiritualists, Christianity should be read as a radically optimistic ideology of human potential, which demanded liberation from artificial restraints of all sorts. Thus she labeled the mores and expectations of Victorian society "materialist," for they were not attuned to the living reality of human existence. Woodhull claimed that human beings were uniquely gifted with freedom; as she stated, "as God is eternal man created in His image must likewise be eternal." Furthermore, she believed that the expansion of freedom in modern America meant that the nation was moving toward true Christianity. She supported the policies of the Radical Republicans in Congress who were pushing for increased rights for African Americans, because to her the abolition of slavery and the progress made in the early years of Reconstruction demonstrated that "the general love of freedom, because it is an inherent right, is one of the first evidences the soul presents that it is growing from the boundaries and control of the material from which it sprang into those of the spiritual toward which it tends."[7] This language was typical for American spiritualists. Andrew Jackson Davis synthesized what he called a "harmonial philosophy," which maintained that the universe was, in realms beyond this earth, in perfect equilibrium with itself—a series of spheres linked through common affection and mutual exchange. He taught that human beings could cultivate "harmonial relations" with each other and the universe and thus gain eternal progress.[8]

While Davis was primarily a thinker and writer, Woodhull embodied spiritualism's activist tendencies and its desire to combat the social norms of its day. Spiritualists in the Civil War era called for a sweeping reconstruction of American society to promote freedom, the Christian virtue they placed above the moralism of Christians like Catharine Beecher. To Woodhull, Christianity was essentially a call for the destruction of "boundaries and control," freeing the human from artificial constraints. She bent the harmonial interpretation of Christianity, which had for Davis and other midcentury leaders been resolutely male, toward women's suffrage and sexual liberation. Her advocacy of free love was therefore in her view Christian, as was her insistence on women's suffrage and equal rights. As she stated in Boston in December 1872, "The impending revolution, then, will be the strife for the mastery between the authority, despotism, inequalities and injustices of the present, and freedom, equality, and justice in their broad and perfect sense, based on the proposition that humanity is one, having a common origin, common interests and purposes, and inheriting a common destiny, which is the complete statement of the religion of Jesus Christ, unadulterated by his professed followers."[9] For Woodhull, Christianity was necessarily revolutionary, tearing down existing power structures. She looked at American patriarchy and American politics and saw "the great of the world," who forgot that the "promulgators of the new truths have ever been, and probably ever will be, Nazarenes; that is, will be the despised people of the world . . . it was in this sense that Jesus was a Nazarene."[10] For her, the truth of Christianity foreshadowed a more egalitarian future, "when those who now cry out 'Can any good thing come out of Nazareth?' will bow with becoming humility before the later day fishermen, for these will then occupy the places of public trust, and spirit telegraphy having superseded material wires will convey the commands of God's accredited ministers from the central seat of Power throughout the world."[11] Her Christian society was an effortlessly egalitarian utopia.

Ulysses S. Grant as Christian Republican

Victoria Woodhull's assertion that Christianity demanded an ever-expanding sphere of human freedom and a radical transformation of American institutions collided with another view gaining ascendancy in the 1872 election: the Christian republicanism ascribed to Ulysses Grant. His followers assailed Woodhull for licentiousness and depravity. And yet on the face of it Grant seemed an odd tribune for any sort of religion. He was not much of a churchgoer. To the extent that he held any Christian faith at all, it was the stoic moral discipline of his New England ancestors. Thus, lacking much evidence in the way of Grant's own faith, but possessed of a good deal of evidence of his rectitude, biographers attempting to sell their audience on his piety placed Grant in the starched and civic-minded Christian republican tradition praised by Tocqueville and descended from New England Puritanism.

Ulysses was the eldest child of Jesse and Hannah Grant, reasonably prosperous farmers and tanners in Ohio, and he was the only child they never baptized. Eventually, near death, he feebly protested baptism at the hands of John Philip Newman, a family friend and Methodist minister. In his personal memoirs, the only sentiment of faith he expressed was the first line of the preface: "Man proposes, and God disposes." Indeed, Grant was decidedly modest throughout the book, chastising himself for his lack of "moral courage" and downplaying his own character.[12] That modesty, though, was enough for his followers. Though his parents did not always insist on church attendance, in Jesse and Hannah Grant's home there was no swearing, no alcohol, no dancing, and very little expressed emotion. Ulysses grew up reticent, stern, and talented at self-castigation, traits frequently noticed by those around him. He never danced; his telegrapher observed that he rarely used profanity beyond "Confound it!" One friend noted, "I have seen him freeze a man up instantly with a look when a vulgar story was started."[13]

Many Republicans, particularly New Englanders and those of the Puritan outmigration into Ohio and the rest of the Midwest, found Grant's rectitude the logical descendent of the New England strain of piety they were born to. For many of them, abolitionists and moralists, the Unitarian ex-president John Quincy Adams was patron and saint. To abolitionist Charles Sumner, Adams was the model of a "Christian statesman." Though he doubted Jesus's divine origins, Sumner found Unitarian language about human equality and moral seriousness irresistible. The word *Christian* meant for him "love to my neighbor, namely my anxiety that my fellow-creatures should be happy, and disposition to serve them in their honest endeavors . . . Certainly, I do feel an affection for everything that God created, and this feeling is my religion."[14] John Sherman, another Republican senator from Ohio, wrote that as a young politician assailing slavery, "I fortified myself by the opinions of John Q. Adams." Rutherford B. Hayes, a colleague of Sherman's who followed Grant into the White House, said he took John Quincy Adams's presidency as a model for his own—both men being one-termers who stoically endured their time in office as a duty to the nation.[15]

The primary principle these men took from Adams was his insistence that moral discipline was a universal human imperative. "Among the Grecian systems of moral philosophy, that of the Stoics resembles the Christian doctrine in the particular of requiring the total subjugation of the passions," Adams instructed his son. He understood that this was difficult; he knew human nature was weak. But he also lacked much sympathy for those who succumbed to failure. "The weakness and frailty of our nature it is not possible to deny; it is too strongly tested by all human experience as well as by the whole tenor of the Scriptures, but the degree of weakness must be measured by the efforts to overcome it and not by indulgence to it," he instructed. "Exertion, therefore, is virtue." This concept of moral struggle lay at the heart of Unitarian moral theology, which taught that human beings were born with moral and rational faculties but that these faculties were often clouded or thrown into imbalance by the "passions"—a word the Unitarians who taught Adams and hundreds of others at Harvard invoked to describe emotions and affections which, if left unregulated, would disrupt a person's ability to comprehend and execute what was good. Passions had to be disciplined if a human being was to become a productive member of society.[16]

This was the tradition that animated what historian David Sehat calls the "moral establishment" of nineteenth century America, in which pious Protestants sought to legislate moral expectations across the United States. It was also the tradition Grant's followers sought to make him heir to. His campaign biographers characteristically insisted that Grant was the fruit of a good vine, his family notable primarily for its Puritan faithfulness and moral probity. His father, Jesse, was descended from New England Puritans; his mother, Hannah, was, as her husband described her in an often-cited quotation, a member of the Methodist church, "and I can truthfully say that it has never had a more devoted and consistent member." Many a campaign biographer insisted that Grant's character was shaped by this inheritance; as Albert Richardson claimed, "If leading ancestral qualities are inherited, the infant son of these young parents had fallen heir to inflexible Puritan integrity."[17]

In 1868 and 1872, when Grant was aspiring to the presidency, Republicans linked the achievements claimed by their party—triumph in the Civil War, the liberation of the enslaved people of the South—to Grant's righteousness. Of Methodist Ohio, Grant's homeland, biographer Edward Mansfield declared, "Here universal freedom began," crediting the Ohio territory as the first place in the United States where slavery was never legal because of its Christian inheritance.[18] The *New York Times* published a long profile of Grant on July 4, 1868, taking as its thesis that Grant's rise evidenced the "progression of civilization and Christianity round the circle of the world." According to the *Times*, Grant's middling performance as a student at West Point and his undistinguished career in business before the Civil War were evidence that he did not imagine himself a "man of destiny." He was not proud. Rather, the *Times* claimed, he came from "good old Puritan sires" and eschewed entitlement. Grant's religion was obscure for the same reason: "He has never said anything about it." But it could be seen in "the rectitude of his conduct and the purity of his life." All this, the *Times* claimed, meant Grant would be an ideal president because he had formed his "moral nature" in the service of "republican plainness"; he respected "the right of man to be free" because he had labored so much for freedom himself.[19]

Not only did the moral exactitude of Christian republicanism serve to exalt Grant; it helped to form the Republican Party's expectations for Reconstruction during his campaigns and presidency. Republicans insisted over and over that the South must embrace moral rigor; it had to repent, reform, and do good works before it could be fully forgiven and reunited with the Union, because without true Christianity, Southerners could not participate in democracy. At the 1868 Republican convention, the Ohio delegate Friedrich Hassaurek declared that the South needed "a new Moses, to lead a people unfitted for self-government to and fro in the wilderness, until the old generation, with its prejudices and vices, has died away." Hassaurek declared the South "unfit" to govern itself because it had rejected the principles of true religion. Indeed, until it embraced equal rights for the freed slaves and abjured the violence of the Ku Klux Klan and other white-supremacist groups, the South would remain unfit. Only then, after Christian righteousness became established, could "true democracy be the groundwork of reconstruction."[20] Other Republicans agreed, using the language of repentance and reform to argue that the South was neither truly Christian nor truly democratic as long as it resisted a moral purge. A journalist for the Cincinnati *Commercial* observed after a trip through the South that he embraced "moderate Republicanism," but that "six months down there, I fear, would have made me a Radical." He was disgusted at Southerners' moral indifference. "They feel no repentance, and no regret, unless it be for failure." Consequently, "The Southerner . . . is not yet a good citizen for a republic," he warned the North. "They are fighting against God to-day."[21]

Many Radical Republicans, steeped in this Christian republicanism, saw the reform of the South as an uncompromisable imperative. They understood the fundamental implication of Christianity for American democracy to be the lesson of human equality. Through the 1860s the Radicals were intent on enacting that truth into law, let the consequences fall as they may. The Radical senator Charles Sumner declared to Congress in 1862, "God in his beneficence offers to nations as to individuals opportunity, opportunity, opportunity. Never before in history has he offered such as is ours here. Do not fail to seize it." As the war thundered on, Sumner and his fellow Radicals offered resolution after resolution attacking Southern social organization: laws ending slavery in the District of Columbia, emancipating slaves who served in the Union army, and proclaiming African American suffrage in the conquered Southern states of Louisiana, Arkansas, and Missouri.[22] In 1866 Congress voted to end racial restrictions on voting in the District of Columbia. In 1868 the Fourteenth Amendment, guaranteeing equal protection under the law, was ratified. In early 1869, Congress passed the Fifteenth Amendment, guaranteeing the right to vote to African American men.

The Unitarian-flavored arguments the Radicals advanced in defense of these bills went as follows: all human beings were created in God's image, so they were fundamentally equal. Acknowledgment of that truth led to the necessary conclusion that democracy was the only moral form of government—and, therefore, the freed slaves should have the vote. Any failure to recognize this principle was, to them, a moral crime, a rejection of Christianity itself. The Indiana representative George Julian addressed the presiding officer of the House in favor of the bill to grant equal suffrage in Washington, DC. "Sir, on this broad ground, coincident with Christianity itself, I plant my feet," he declared. "I simply demand the national recognition of Christianity, which is the root of all democracy, the highest fact in the rights of man."[23] Henry W. Barry, a Republican congressman from Mississippi, declared on the floor of Congress, "The American people have willed the incorporation of manhood suffrage into their organic law. They have accepted the great law of Christian civilization propounded upon Mars Hill by the Apostle Paul: that God hath made of one blood all the nations of men."[24]

Further, Radicals did not deal well with disagreement. They were convinced that because human nature was fundamentally uncorrupted, the moral righteousness of their position should be obvious to anyone who contemplated it. Sumner, who had been taught Enlightenment political theory at Harvard, declared that humanity could not hide behind pleas to "imperfect human nature" to support an evil like war or slavery. Rather, he said, "They must see clearly that it is a monster of their own creation born with their consent whose vital spark is fed by their breath and without their breath must necessarily die."[25] John Bingham, the Ohio representative who was the primary author of the Fourteenth Amendment, declared that the amendment simply enacted the basic principle of Christianity and thus should be uncontroversial to those who recognized it. "Is it objected to by any Christian man," he asked, "to embody in your Constitution at least the simple golden rule you learned at your mother's knee: Whatsoever ye would that others should do unto you, do ye even so unto them?"[26]

Since the Radicals believed that human nature tended toward morality, they also believed that history was essentially progressive. Human beings could ultimately not resist the moral imperatives built into their souls, and thus racism, dictatorship, and other forms of inequality would inevitably fade. In Charles Sumner's famous speech on "caste" (which he defined as "claim of power founded on any unchangeable physical incident derived from birth"), he argued that the spread of Christianity was inexorably destroying castes around the world. Describing the presumed fading of the caste system in India, he claimed that due to "the growing influence of Christianity, the system is so far mitigated that according to an able writer whose soul is enlisted against it, the distinctions are felt on certain limited occasions only."[27] Radicals thus tended to understand their own role in history as providential, divinely ordained to prick the nation's conscience and bring about the moral rebirth it required. Henry Wilson, the Radical senator from Massachusetts who became Grant's vice president, declared that the Republican Party was "created by no man or set of men, but brought into being by almighty God to represent the higher and better sentiments of Christian America . . . the enduring interests of the regenerated nation, the rights of man, and the elevation of an emancipated race."[28]

But by 1872 many of these Radicals had abandoned Grant in disgust. The Radicals' record after the end of the war was somewhat mixed. They had failed to remove President Andrew Johnson, who had replaced the martyred Abraham Lincoln and whose leniency toward the South many found intolerable, but they had succeeded in wrenching control of the region away from him with a series of laws assuming military authority over the South. But Johnson had fought the Radicals every step of the way, and in several states Republicans had grown hesitant about proposals to extend suffrage to African Americans, using the same language of moral discipline the Radicals had applied to the South. George Julian complained that the governor of his home state of Indiana, the Republican Oliver Morton, gave speeches that "made a dismal picture of the ignorance and degradation of the plantation negroes of the South and scouted the policy of arming them with political power." Julian viewed this as demagoguery on the part of a man who should have known better; he speculated that the governor's motivations were entirely political, in that he feared a Democratic challenge for his office. Morton urged "a probation of fifteen or twenty years to prepare for the ballot," but Julian excoriated him because "his moral vision failed to discern anything amiss in his own ghastly policy of arming the white Rebels with the ballot and denying it to the loyal negroes." He noted, however, that when he began to speak against Governor Morton's campaign, "I found the people steadily yielding up their prejudices and ready to lay hold of the truth when fairly and dispassionately presented." He had no other phrase for Morton's behavior than "inexpressible bitterness."[29] Julian's vision of human nature is laid bare in the story. He ascribed to selfishness Morton's opposition to the clearly moral right of suffrage, characterizing his own stance as self-evidently correct, if only viewed fairly.

But other Republicans soon began to express concerns similar to Governor Morton's, turning the language of moral discipline upon African Americans and worrying that the freed peoples of the South lacked the piety, vigor, and strength to fully participate in American democracy. Historian Edward Blum has described the transformation of the Beecher siblings, including famed preacher Henry Ward Beecher and abolitionist author Harriet Beecher Stowe, whose wartime denunciation of the South gradually morphed into worry that African Americans lacked the moral fortitude to become democratic citizens. The freed slaves, Stowe fretted, suffered from the "inevitable defects of imperfect training, ignorance, and the negligent habits induced by slavery." She urged the government to set a program of "education" before African Americans would be fit to be "freemen and voters."[30] Henry Ward Beecher, for his part, described Pete Sawmill, the African American character in his 1868 novel *Norwood,* as one who "can never be organized into society, but live as marmots do, by burrowing in the neighborhood of men without living among them." Sawmill was thus incapable of political participation or leadership, "strong" but "idle," with "no purpose in life . . . no trade or calling."[31]

Republicans like Beecher and his sister—and even radicals like George Julian and Charles Sumner—began in the early 1870s to grow disillusioned with the efforts of Reconstruction in general and Grant's leadership in particular. While Radical Republicans understood that Southern slavery was a moral violation of Christianity and thus an iron chain bound around democracy, many also believed that slavery was just one manifestation of a larger threat to the religious foundations of American democratic government. They worried that the Republicans' inordinate focus on it neglected other dangers. The human autonomy they believed Christianity protected was under threat from, more than anything else, dominating authority, whether it be through the mechanism of slavery or of capital.

The Expanding Threat of Materialism

In May 1872, a group of Republicans disaffected with Grant gathered in Cincinnati. Calling themselves the Liberal Republican party, they nominated the journalist Horace Greeley for president. Though many were not delighted with Greeley's nomination, considering him something of a flake, they despised Grant even more. The party's core was a group of intellectuals dismayed with the same thing that alarmed George Julian: the corrupting influences of centralized power, whether political or economic. Such centralization, they believed, jeopardized the moral underpinnings of American democracy. While Ulysses Grant's presidential campaigns illustrate the power of the Christian republican synthesis, and Victoria Woodhull's protest shows how effectively Christian language could be marshaled against that synthesis, the Radical Republicans illustrate a third aspect of the ways American Christians have thought about the relationship between Christianity and democracy: the threat of materialism.

The Radical Republicans saw Grant's cabinet overrun with businessmen and bureaucrats intent on expanding their own financial gain at the expense of human rights. They turned on Grant's Reconstruction program, using Christian language to assail corruption in business as much as in politics. In 1869, the old abolitionist Horace White, editor of the *Chicago Tribune*, declared that divinely given human rights faced a new challenge from the power of big business, which he believed was establishing a monopoly in the American economy. "Slavery is abolished and impartial suffrage established [but] the right of every man to exchange the products of his labor freely is as sacred as any right that God had given him," White asserted. The *Tribune* began to beat the drum against Grant, arguing that wealthy businessmen and their allies were drowning that right in a steady rain of corruption. In August 1872, White ticked off Grant's corruptions: "his mal-appointments to office . . . his misuse of the patronage as a corruption fund . . . the corruptions of his Cabinet," and the influence of numerous railroad magnates, financiers, and other businessmen over Grant's administration. White argued that Christianity demanded "repentance" and "good government."[32]

One of the most vocal of Grant's opponents was Asa Mahan, a former abolitionist and president of the Methodist Oberlin College, a leading abolitionist stronghold. In August 1872, Mahan delivered a heavily publicized speech blasting Grant's presidency. He identified as a Greely supporter and declared that Grant's pretenses to personal morality had been proven false by his administration. Mahan quoted the King James Version of Exodus 23:8: "A gift blindeth the wise and perverteth the words of the righteous." He then condemned Grant's administration for saturation in bribery and argued that this failure, as Scripture promised, led the Grant administration into tyranny and the obliteration of freedom. To vote for Grant, Mahan stated, "is to vote for National demoralization."[33] The links between the materialism of wealth and industry and the failure of Christian democracy was clear to all Grant's opponents.

Many such Republicans, who had been abolitionists before the Civil War, feared that the Grant administration signaled the return of the sort of materialist power they had before the war located in the "slave power," a Southern conspiracy to undermine representative government. The abolitionist Theodore Parker denounced the slave power's ambitions as "offensive materialism" by which "we copy the vices of feudal aristocracy abroad."[34] Another abolitionist denounced the Kansas-Nebraska Act as the result of "a gross materialism, the success of trade, the progress of gain . . . preferred to the lofty ideal aspirations and spiritual truth."[35] They also denounced the slave power in religious terms. At one 1848 meeting, eventual Liberal Republican Charles Francis Adams, the son of John Quincy, sat presiding and pled with his hearers to make the United States a "Christian commonwealth." Doing so, another delegate said, required rejection of the "all-grasping, over-reaching, and never-satisfied power of slavery."[36]

Twenty-five years later, Grant to them seemed no better. "The Kingly Grant," as Mahan called him, sought "costly fabrics [and] a crown on his head," while each Union official Grant sent South "manages politics for his own pecuniary benefit."[37] Mahan could not restrain himself; a month later he sent an open letter to various newspapers, declaring that the "doctrine of human rights" required all "Christian editors and Christian ministers" to join the movement against Grant, whose Reconstruction policies left him standing "with one foot trampled on the Constitution and the other upon the neck of each of these States."[38]

When Greeley managed to engineer for himself the Liberal Republican nomination for president, however, many in the party were dismayed. Greeley was hardly an advocate for Liberal Republicans' preferred positions: he had very little to say about civil service reform and had long been a booster for American business. Instead, Greeley took up the single issue upon which he and most Liberal Republicans seemed to overlap: protesting Grant's treatment of the South. Greeley's guiding issue became, as Mahan put it, "peace and reconciliation . . . can we, as American citizens, as Christian men, vote [for it]?"[39] Both Greeley and the Liberal Republicans who remained behind him emphasized that forgiving the South, in contrast to other Republicans' seeming harsh demands for discipline and repentance, was not simply an act of benevolence. Rather, doing so would preserve the essential dignity of human nature against the corrupt and increasingly dehumanized institutions that Liberal Republicans feared: the authoritarian nature of Grant's government and the corrupt profiteering of the federal officials the Grant administration sent South. For them, Greeley's position represented the triumph of human personality against the machine that Grant's administration had become. Greeley insisted, for instance, that Southern secession was not the desire of most Southerners, whom he called "good and true"; rather, he blamed the collapse of the Union on "the machinery of the Democratic party" and the conspiring Confederate government. Greeley proposed what he called a true "National Reconstruction" based on "peace, fraternity, and mutual good will," and defended it as an acknowledgment of the divine right to human freedom.[40]

However, Greeley's opponents leveled accusations of immorality at him. Grant supporters attempted to link him to the moral debauchery of Woodhull. The *New York Times*, observing that Theodore Tilton was campaigning for Greeley in September 1872, claimed, "It is tolerably well known, that like many others who go for Greeley, Theodore Tilton does not support the philosopher as his first choice for the presidency." Rather, the *Times* stated, "the person honored" with Tilton's preference was "Victoria Woodhull-Blood, née Claflin."[41] Attempting to shock its readers, the paper insisted that Tilton, certainly, and Greeley, likely, were supporters of Woodhull's radical violations of traditional morality and gender norms. Similarly, Grant partisan Everett Chamberlain painted Greeley as a degenerate opponent of traditional gender norms. Citing Greeley's antebellum interest in the utopian Oneida community, Chamberlain accused the candidate of favoring "the cause of the Socialists, they who sought to reorganize society on a far better plan than that which the Creator ordained, to abolish in great measure the sacred ties of family and to substitute the Community in its place." All this proved to Chamberlain that Greeley "has a morbid laxity of conduct toward evil," because he "is ignorant of the qualities and capacities of human nature."[42]

Similarly, a number of African American writers argued that although Greeley claimed to be defending the interests of humanity against the corrupt forces of institutions, his platform in fact favored another sort of corrupt power: white supremacy. The Democratic Party eventually endorsed Greeley for president, despite the fact that the Liberal Republican platform demanded that the South accept the Reconstruction Amendments that defended the rights of African Americans. Many Democratic leaders hoped that Greeley would not enforce the platform and would be easier than Grant to work with. Some African American leaders indeed were inspired to question Grant's leadership. But many more defended the general. Frederick Douglass declared, "The Democratic Party of late has become very Scriptural, and preaches the doctrine of forgiveness. I don't know but that I am prepared to act on the principle inculcated by the parable of the Prodigal Son." He elaborated: "The prodigal said he had sinned, and asked to be taken back as a hired servant." If the South evidenced repentance and reform, as Grant had called for, Douglass was willing to entertain forgiveness. Douglass's conception of Christianity, then, more closely resembled the justice of the Grant campaign than the lenience of the Liberal Republicans.[43]

African Americans also pointed out that there were many self-professed Christians in the United States who took Greeley's "scriptural" rhetoric as justification for slavery. The *San Francisco Elevator*, an African American newspaper, reported on a number of Greeley supporters who believed that "laws of God" required "a prompt disenfranchisement of the African race."[44] In New Orleans in April 1872, a national convention of African Americans affirmed these conclusions. There, Douglass exhorted them to remain with Grant, and speakers overwhelmingly supported the president, voting on a motion to "repudiate any sympathy or connection whatsoever with . . . the convention of liberal Republicans." Opinions generally held that, as P. B. S. Pinchback said, "We are a free people and we must defend ourselves."[45]

The Afterlife of the 1872 Election

Grant won, and it was not particularly close. Greeley died only weeks after the election, and Reconstruction slowly ground to a halt. African Americans supported Grant yet steadily lost ground to the sort of white Christians the *Elevator* had warned of. Victoria Woodhull fled New York City for Great Britain in 1876 and never lived for long in the United States again. Within a matter of years the election seemed to have vanished from American memory.

And yet, the election of 1872 is worth examining because the debates over Christianity it exhibited set a useful paradigm for the next century of American politics. Woodhull and Douglass, Grant and Greeley offered different versions of Christianity, with different emphases, and they disagreed vehemently about why precisely Christianity mattered to American government. To moralist supporters of Grant, Woodhull lacked any morals whatsoever and so was obviously inadequate to provide guidance on national issues. To Greeley's campaign, suspicious of elites, the Grant administration was too enamored of wealth and power to effectively legislate human brotherhood. And to African Americans like Douglass, any form of Christianity that did not acknowledge fundamental human equality was a misnomer.[46] Still, they all agreed that Christianity, properly understood, lent critical support to American democracy.

Many of these debates continued to matter to American Christians well into the twentieth century. George Julian's equation of "Southern slave drivers" with "the grinding power of corporate wealth" and "the power of concentrated capital in alliance with labor saving machinery" as oppressors of the "sacred rights of man" signaled a growing conviction among many Christians, particularly northern Protestants, that the expanding power of industry threatened the Christian republicanism they believed in. Many Protestants began to join what came to be called the "social gospel" movement, warning that the materialism of American industry threatened to reduce spiritual democracy to corruption. Walter Rauschenbusch, the loudest voice of the movement, stated flatly, "The power of capitalism over the machinery of our government and its corroding influence on the morality of our public servants, has been revealed within recent years. . . . The spiritual force of Christianity should be turned against the materialism and mammonism of our industrial and social order."[47] Frequently, as Horace Greeley had, advocates of the social gospel and other Christians who feared the growing consolidation of American capital and political power used the language of materialism and machinery to express anxiety that the spiritual aspects of American democracy were being destroyed. Rauschenbusch employed the word *machine* to describe both the American capitalist system and the political order that upheld it, warning of the "overheated machine of our commercial and political life."[48] He and other progressives feared that materialism was overtaking American life in the form of industrial and political regimentation.

These fears of centralized power frequently coincided with the worries of those who shared the Christian republican sentiment that materialism eroded American morality. Often, as the revulsion inspired by Woodhull shows, that concern was cast in gendered language: materialism, by threatening the sanctity of the individual, would blur or collapse gender norms, leading to violations of sexual taboos and hence the collapse of a moral democracy.

Rauschenbusch warned that the "industrial machine has absorbed the functions which women formerly fulfilled in the home. . . . They are made to compete with the very men who ought to marry them."[49] These changes, he said, would invariably lead to declining marriage rates, fewer children, and the breakdown of American society. Other progressives concurred: the social reformer Jane Addams, for instance, argued that prostitution was the result of modern American industrial capitalism. "For the first time in history multitudes of women are laboring without the direct stimulus of family interest or affection," she warned. Addams insisted further that the modern economy was ill-suited for women's natural condition. Women were "unable to proportion their hours of work and intervals of rest according to their strength." All this, Addams believed, led to moral decay. "The effort to obtain a livelihood fairly eclipses the very meaning of life itself." No one, she said, "can assert how far the superior chastity of women . . . has been the result of her domestic surroundings and certainly no one knows under what degree of economic pressure the old restraints may give way." The answer, Addams said, was a revived moral vigor. Echoing the Christian republican synthesis, she observed that "many young people living in our cities at the present moment have failed to apprehend the admonitions of religion and have never responded to its inner control." Renewed attention to the moral demands of Christianity was the only way to tame prostitution.[50]

But Christians outside the generally white Christian republican synthesis also feared materialism and argued that American democracy would subsist with greater health should its spiritual nature be maintained. African Americans did not cease using Christian language to agitate for greater equality. They consistently argued that American racism gave the lie to white Americans' claim to Christianity, marking white Americans' pretensions to democracy as indelibly flawed. To many African American Christians, racism itself was the product of materialism: evidence that white Americans saw African Americans as things, not human beings. Carter G. Woodson, a pioneering African American academic, lambasted the churches of the United States in the years after World War I. "The church has surrendered to the materialistic system," he declared, denouncing white Christian churches' unwillingness to promote the cause of African American rights for fear of losing followers. Those churches may have once "championed the cause of the Negro [but] are today working indirectly to promote racial distinctions. . . . Churches dominated by abolitionists soon yielded to the temptation of sacrificing the principles of Jesus for dollars and cents."[51] To Woodson and other African American leaders, materialism enabled racism and thus made American democracy conditional rather than universal. Over the course of the twentieth century, American Christians both black and white questioned the relationship between their faith and their democracy in the light of world wars, African American protests, and the rising wealth of their nation. These problems raised issues of morality and of the nature of democracy—and, thus, of the meaning of Christianity itself.

CHAPTER TWO

Creating Western Civilization
at Columbia University

I N T H E F A L L O F 1917, a few months after the United States entered the
First World War, a representative of a joint project between the Young
Men's Christian Association (YMCA) and the U.S. Army knocked on
John Erskine's office door on the fifth floor of Hamilton Hall, where the
English department of Columbia University was headquartered. Erskine, a
professor known for passion in both his writing and his classroom, welcomed the man in. The man explained that the American Expeditionary
Force, sent to break the back of the German army, had established an educational institution for soldiers in tandem with the YMCA. It was a sudden
university to be built with all speed in Beaune, France, a small city located
halfway between Paris and Switzerland. The army wanted Erskine for its
de facto president and charged him with constructing a curriculum to
serve the soldiers. Erskine recalled sitting in his office for a time after the
man departed, uncertain about what to do. He finally resolved to take the
job because he worried that in the rush to war Americans faced a moral
hazard.[1]

The origins of World War I were irreducibly complex, but to many
Americans at the time they seemed quite simple: the war was the fault of
Germany. A heavily Protestant nation whose once progressive and spiritual
culture Americans thought not so dissimilar from their own, Germany had
decayed into militaristic authoritarianism and acquired the pathology of
conquest, a distressing development. Erskine worried that the problems of

32

Germany might spread in the United States as well, and he located their origins in a disregard for humanity's spiritual life. Americans were "driving unconsciously into that same admiration for creature comforts and that same trust in mechanical substitutes for character which perverted modern Germany," he observed.[2] American soldiers, he was convinced, needed spiritual fortification to avoid this fate, and he did not trust the YMCA to deliver it alone.

This was not because he worried that the YMCA or the American military lacked religion. When the YMCA committee aiding the project interviewed Erskine, they asked him about his faith. He told them he was Episcopalian, a regular churchgoer, and a vestryman at New York's Trinity Church. It was true; Erskine's faith was that of a conventional upper-class American liberal Protestant, but it was also long-standing and heartfelt. He worried, for instance, about secularizing trends he saw on campus. "Chapel services were instituted when the spiritual life of the student was thought important, and they are declining now that outward well-being comes first and inner states are ignored. Yet teachers know that the life of what used to be called the soul is still present," he mused. "If this craving is thwarted . . . [students] settle down to the career of a trained animal." The threat that Erskine perceived was often labeled "materialism": the subordination of the individual to the great machinery of modern technology, modern capitalism, and modern bureaucracy.[3]

The confrontation between Germany and the United States provided the liberal Protestant establishment of the United States, of which Erskine was a devoted member, occasion to revisit its strength in the light of this new materialist threat. In the years between the election of 1872 and the First World War, liberal Protestants had gained dominance over American government and culture. They were America's well-educated, largely white, upper classes. They could be liberal Protestants in belief or in genealogy or both, and they cultivated fears of Germany specific to their orientation. First, while they clung to Christian republicanism, they did so with a particularly optimistic and ecumenical twist. Liberal Protestants emphasized human autonomy, were suspicious of what they called "sectarian" devotion to specific creeds or denominations, and believed that morality was cultivated through education, not dogma or diktat. They thus saw in Germany a moral reversion. Second, they became during World War I promoters of a certain notion of American civilization based on faith in progress. They believed the American military, cultural, and political resources marshaled against Germany emerged from a long process of cultural and religious refinement linked to the rise of Protestantism. In response to the war, Erskine and his fellows at Columbia University synthesized these ideas into a historical narrative that rooted American democracy in the progress of European Christianity and explained German failure as abandonment of that progress. The First World War thus bound American democracy to the history of Christianity more tightly than it ever had been before.[4]

The Religion of Democracy

A central trait of early twentieth-century white liberal Protestants was optimism. Like Erskine, they had great faith in the soul's capacity for moral progress given sufficient autonomy, great faith that education would lead to moral refinement and hence a healthier civilization, and great faith that this process, more central to their version of Christianity than what they believed to be the dogmatics of traditional theology, was the moral bedrock of American democracy. Indeed, for many liberal Protestants the distinctions between *Christianity* and *democracy* or *religion* and *civilization* were invisible; liberal Protestantism seemed to them simply what a democratic society was.[5] Erskine once wrote a fierce jeremiad against the Prohibition movement, warning that it marked a willingness to surrender spiritual freedom for material success. The idea of banning alcohol, he said, was "contradictory to the Christian doctrine of temperance." Rather, Erskine claimed that the central principle of Christianity as he understood it was "the virtue of self-control in conditions of freedom. To the early church as to the ancient world there could be no credit for virtue or blame for vice if the virtue or the vice was compulsory."[6] For Erskine, democratic liberty and moral duty were inexorably intertwined, bound to the republican politics of self-sacrifice and rectitude that he and the rest of the liberal Protestant establishment associated with their faith.

These beliefs were so deeply integrated into the world of the early twentieth-century white American establishment that they were shared even by the many intellectuals who had abandoned orthodoxy—including some of Erskine's colleagues. A few Columbia professors shared his commitment to institutional Christianity. The day the United States entered World War I, for instance, the young philosophy professor John Coss wrote to his mother that he had attended chapel as he regularly did, and that "it makes one think to realize war is declared on Good Friday. I hope the sacrifices the country will be called upon to make will come nearer to bringing universal brotherhood."[7] Many other of Columbia's faculty were not church-goers, though still marked by their upbringing. They were post-Protestants, born and raised in Protestant environments, no longer typical believers, but subscribers nonetheless to the essential assumptions of Erskine's genteel liberalism. They took for granted historical narratives that associated Protestant Christianity with the rise of democracy and belief in the value of the individual person. They recoiled from "sectarianism," believing instead that the value of religion was its capacity to inspire morality and commitment to human autonomy. In all of this, they were not so far from an establishment churchgoer like John Erskine.[8]

For instance, when the philosopher John Dewey, who also taught at Columbia, was young, he sounded much like Erskine: "Democracy has a spiritual meaning which it behooves us not to pass by."[9] When he grew older he abandoned faith in Jesus, but he remained committed to the notion that democracy needed the metaphysical undergirding that religion might provide. "The future of religion is connected to the possibility of developing faith in the possibilities of human existence and human relationships," he wrote.[10] Similarly, the sociologist Franklin Giddings, son of a minister, quit attending church as an adult. Yet he credited early Christianity for its embrace of "like-mindedness," the notion that the healthiest governments developed when a population was able to recognize the commonalities of all its members.[11] Irwin Edman, a friend of Coss's and another philosopher, was a genteel ecumenicist who valued religious practice primarily for its aesthetic qualities; he fondly remembered sitting in Erskine's class as an undergraduate and marveling at how skillfully the professor evoked the romance of the ancient Christian church.[12] But Edman insisted that democracy was "spiritual" because it was the form of politics most in consonance with humanity's innate moral autonomy.[13]

Though these men had left traditional belief behind, they still clung to an essentially liberal Protestant notion of politics, a commitment to what William James called the "religion of democracy." It taught them that while Christian sectarianism and fixation on doctrine were objectionable, Christianity conceived as an ethical faith in humanity's divine origins was worthwhile because it promoted individual worth, inculcated morality, and lent metaphysical support to democracy.[14] In Beaune, Erskine told his students that Christianity was an essential predicate to properly understanding human achievement. "Neither literature nor any of the arts can be understood in the heart as well as the mind, without a spiritual philosophy," he said. "Unless we have spiritual insights and well-developed spiritual emotions, we had better say as little as possible about what Michelangelo put on the ceiling of the Sistine Chapel."[15] Coss agreed. During World War I, he drafted the "Religious Organizations" section of the federal government's *National Service Handbook,* which contained advice for a wide range of American groups who wanted to aid the war effort. Coss wrote that the best defense from German degradation was that "America is, by and large, a religious country." He urged American religious bodies to take seriously the task of preserving democracy through promoting the relationship between faith and civic duty.[16]

The civic orientation of white liberal Protestantism's form of Christian republicanism was made manifest in the ways those Protestants thought about the notion of civilization in the second decade of the twentieth century. Such ideas had been percolating for many years. In 1898, the United States went to war with Spain over the Philippines and Spanish possessions in the Caribbean. Theodore Roosevelt, soon to be president, resigned his post in the Department of the Navy to fight the Spanish. Roosevelt believed that ideas of "democracy, of liberty under the law, of social progress through peaceful industry, education and commerce" depended on what he called "uncorrupted Christianity."[17] He and many other Americans were convinced that the presence of Catholic Spain in the Americas would lead to degeneracy in American culture and society. But "uncorrupted Christianity" was linked to a variety of desirable features a civilization might have, from liberty to education to a free economic system. For Protestants like Roosevelt, triumph over Spain was a sign of progress, the spread of Protestant Christianity, and hence the inevitable growth of democracy.

These links revealed the way that many white Americans had begun thinking about civilization in the late nineteenth and early twentieth centuries. They thought of their civilization as the result of cultural evolution. It had, like the animals described in Darwin, overcome challenges and earned strengths conducive to human flourishing. Anthropologist Lewis Morgan's scale of civilization—from savage on one end of the spectrum to civilized on the other—was only one of a number of works of popular and academic scholarship that offered white Protestant Americans a ladder of progress on which they perched, unquestionably, at the top. Joseph McCabe, author of *The Evolution of Civilization,* praised the "slow and gradual development of the higher and more complex institutions—the higher standards of art and knowledge and commerce and politics—which do raise us . . . high above that of early man."[18] Such acclaim helpfully contrasted white Protestant Americans with the presumably less developed Catholic Spanish in ways that linked religion and race. As one Methodist minister put it in 1899, "Our civilization is Anglo Saxon and Anglo Saxon civilization is Protestant civilization. Latin civilization is Roman Catholic civilization." He assailed "Catholic civilization" for any number of ills, from the severe ("In countries of Latin civilization an accused man is considered guilty until proven innocent") to the trivial, accusing Catholics of "pretensions and dogmas" that stultified art and culture.[19]

For many white Americans, civilization was to some degree a question of racial inheritance. Many believed that they were "Anglo-Saxon," a confluence of Germanic and Celtic ancestry particularly given to vigor, individualism, and hence Protestantism and democracy. Theodore Roosevelt began his triumphalist series *The Winning of the West* with an account of the "Germanic peoples'" defeat of the "all-conquering Roman power," which ensured their own liberty, a story he claimed was paralleled on the American continent. In the 1880s the minister Josiah Strong prophesied a "final confrontation of races for which the Anglo-Saxon is being schooled. If I do not read amiss, this powerful race will move down upon Mexico, down upon Central and South America, out upon the islands of the sea, over upon Africa and beyond."[20]

Often these writers linked ethnicity and religion. Herbert Baxter Adams, who received his PhD in Germany before accepting a post in history at Johns Hopkins University in 1876, was a leading proponent of this idea. Adams rooted British egalitarianism in the rough self-government of the German tribes that had brought down the Roman Empire. American democracy derived from the Puritan town meeting, he argued, but those "town institutions were propagated in New England by old English and Germanic ideas."[21] Adams worked within a broader tradition of nineteenth-century American Anglo-Saxonism, an ideology that persistently linked three elements: democracy, Protestant Christianity, and the vaguely defined "Anglo-Saxon" people. Woodrow Wilson, who studied under Adams at Johns Hopkins University, believed that for centuries in the ancient world, "private rights had no standing as against the State," until two influences brought freedom: "Christianity and the institutions of the German conquerors of the fifth century. Christianity gave each man a magistracy over himself. . . . There must be for the Christian an individuality which no claim of his state upon him could rightfully be suffered to infringe."[22]

But for white liberal Protestants at the turn of the twentieth century who like Erskine believed at least theoretically in human equality and divine potential, education in Protestant Christianity could offer some measure of the benefits of Anglo-Saxon civilization to those who lacked it, provided they received guidance from the West.[23] This hardly preserved liberal Protestants from cultural chauvinism, of course; it meant simply that they came to believe that the superior qualities of the civilization they called "Western" should be taught to those civilizations that lacked it themselves. John Erskine's encounter with Torao Taketomo is a case in point. One evening just before the United States entered World War I, Erskine attended a lecture on Japanese and American cultural exchange. He was interested in the topic, and the lecturer—a Professor Kuryagawa—was a friend. After the lecture Kuryagawa introduced Erskine to Taketomo, a Japanese student who came to mean a great deal to Erskine. The young man spoke English well. He was the son of parents educated by Christian missionaries in Japan, and, inspired by them, had come to America to attend Yale Divinity School, seeking in Christianity "the source of Western knowledge." Erskine took the young man into his poetry classes at Columbia and became a mentor of sorts. They had long conversations about human nature in Erskine's office. Once Taketomo wrote to Erskine that though he had been taught not to "imitate western civilization," he had to admit Japanese civilization had produced nothing like Homer or Bunyan or Milton. The two corresponded for the rest of Erskine's life, and only a few years before Erskine died, he received a letter from Taketomo telling him that Taketomo had just finished translating the *Divine Comedy* into Japanese. "Could I have a pupil of whom I might be prouder?" Erskine wondered.[24]

In Taketomo Erskine found an ideal potential American. Taketomo was Japanese, it was true, but the democracy which Erskine was beginning to imagine in the early twentieth century derived from the moral discipline that grew out of European Christian civilization, and other peoples could be trained to at least some degree in its benefits. The young man was proof to Erskine that the Christian republicanism given fullest flower in the United States would be naturally appealing to all humanity. In 1918 Erskine wrote the introduction to a selection of Japanese stories that Taketomo had translated into English. Given the virtues celebrated in the tales, Erskine speculated that "perhaps Mr. Taketomo has chosen from authors under the influence of Western literature," because their "power comes from a way of living, rather than from a way of writing." He praised their ability to represent the moral "seeds of friendship and justice."[25] In Taketomo Erskine saw a young man becoming civilized under the influence of the Christianity Erskine believed in.

The sentiment, of course, sits in tension with the condescending language in which Erskine described his memories of Taketomo, whose native culture seemed mostly of interest to Erskine insofar as it reflected evolution toward the values the professor saw in his own. Indeed, though Erskine rejected inevitable racial determinism, he was convinced that some civilizations did more to foster Western values than others, and that his own Anglo-Saxon civilization stood at the apex of those. His famous 1915 essay "The Moral Obligation to Be Intelligent" declared that "our conscience . . . began in the German forest" and went on not to celebrate that inheritance but to condemn it for its neglect of rationality, autonomy, and the capacity for moral exploration. American democracy derived not from racial inheritance, Erskine insisted, but from the pursuit of intelligence, which Erskine deemed a Protestant virtue. "Intelligence," Erskine wrote, "is the will of God. . . . It is only virtue's other and more precise name." Intelligence led to the "long liberation of the human spirit"; intelligence during the Reformation worked to "rob the altar of its sacrifices and the priest of his mysteries"; intelligence led to the Protestant triumph that was the United States.[26]

Erskine's faith that Taketomo's encounter with Western civilization would lead to his uplift reflected an emerging white liberal Protestant belief that religion could drive the evolutionary development of a society. Students of religion like Edwin Starbuck and William James were beginning in the late nineteenth century to describe "religion" as a category of human experience—normally using Protestant interest in ideas and ethical behavior as a yardstick for measuring its value. The emerging notion of "comparative religions," which sought to categorize belief systems, allowed Americans to visualize religion as a staircase. Its steps were discrete religions, the most "primitive"—by which was generally meant the least like Protestantism—at the bottom and, of course, liberal Protestant Christianity at the top. Liberal Protestants, then, imagined human societies ascending, as did Torao Taketomo, toward their own civilized values. As James Freeman Clarke described the aim of his landmark 1871 book *Ten Great Religions*, he sought to show "the relation of each partial religion to human civilization, and . . . how each religion of the world is a step in the progress of humanity."[27]

The conviction that liberal Protestantism and democracy stood hand in hand at the peak of human civilizations was evident in Erskine and many other intellectuals who believed that art sustained the spiritual foundations necessary to preserve a democratic society. As Erskine instructed his students in Beaune, one "must assume in every human being a soul. . . . It is impossible to . . . define man as a biological or chemical accident, or as the byproduct of economic forces."[28] His revulsion was not to the theory of evolution but to biological determinism, and he affirmed that the liberty of American democracy was premised upon the metaphysics of liberal Protestantism. But democracy was a fragile creature, and they had to look no further than across the Atlantic for a cautionary tale about the dissolution not only of democracy but of the Protestant Christianity they believed its very foundation.

Germany and the Crisis of Materialism

This white liberal Protestant notion of civilization explains why Germany was so troubling to people like John Erskine. The apparent failure of Germany belied their expectations of how civilizations functioned. When the United States entered World War I, the War Department hired an educator named Frank Aydelotte to take charge of teaching American soldiers why their country was fighting and what it was fighting for. Aydelotte took a survey of the men in the ranks and observed that they asked the same question again and again: "Why does the world look upon Luther as so great a reformer if Germany has no sound Christianity now?"[29]

The question came not only from soldiers. Robert Hutcheon, a Pennsylvania pastor, spent his evenings throughout early 1918 in his study, emerging later that year with a lecture series that explored a similar question: "How did a country with so rich a spiritual heritage come to get into the state of mind which has revealed itself so completely both in the national interests and ambitions before the war and in the excesses of the war itself?" Aydelotte determined that American soldiers needed to understand the nature of Western civilization in order to answer the question; Hutcheon found "wide public interest" around Pittsburgh in his study of the differences between "the Germany which has given such mortal offence [sic] to the world over against the older and more idealistic Germany."[30] The comparison implied declension. As Hutcheon and the bewildered soldiers saw it, Germany was previously something admirable but had since lost its way in a forest of "no sound Christianity," excess, and authoritarian government. This was not supposed to happen to a Protestant civilization.

The lesson many Americans took from the story was that the decay of Christianity inexorably led to immorality and tyranny. The *Literary Digest* blamed a cadre of powerful atheists in Germany who had convinced the nation it would be to their benefit if they "gave up Christianity for materialism." That ideology encouraged the German leadership toward overconfidence, strict regulation of its people, and finally violence and militarism.[31] Germans were indeed heirs to the great heritage of the Reformation and the freedom-loving Germanic tribes, which meant the nation had tremendous potential and progress. But their success carried with it immense temptation to set aside the human soul, democratic government, and Protestantism itself in favor of the industrial strength and political power which a rigidly organized society promised.

Materialism was not simply greed or an interest in luxury. Rather, it was a philosophical infection. American Protestants feared that Germans had placed their faith in the impersonal forces of science, empiricism, bureaucracy, and institution rather than in what they took to be the central Christian teaching of individual liberty. Many evangelical Protestants associated materialism with German scholarship that suggested that what they took to be the arrogant assertion that the Bible was of human rather than divine composition would lead to the devaluation of humanity. "The new theology has led Germany into barbarism, and it will lead any nation into the same demoralization," said Arno Gaebelein, the editor of the theologically conservative Protestant journal *Our Hope*.[32] Liberal Protestants understood such fears, but came to them for different reasons. On the second day of his voyage to France, Erskine attended a reception for passengers bound for the university at Beaune. After some hearty singing, a YMCA official stood to welcome them. "No doubt his merits were numerous, but on this occasion he was tragically miscast," Erskine remembered. The man exhorted the crowd "that as Christian men we should seize the opportunity" to re-Christianize Europe. "The evil habit of cigarette smoking, he asserted, had come to us from France," Erskine recalled the man declaring. "What greater kindness could we do than to help them give up the bad habit?"[33] Despite Erskine's own faith he remembered trading distressed glances with others in the room while the YMCA man spoke. This sort of thing hardly comported with Erskine's goals in France.

Erskine and other liberal Protestants worried about a wider set of materialist sins. Rather than the source of individual immoral behavior, they viewed materialism as a structural problem. The *Methodist Review* said that Germans had embraced "material prosperity, the destructive effect of historical criticism, and the universal spread of materialistic interpretations of the sciences among the cultured classes, resulting in their renunciation of the spiritual principles of the gospel for a coarse materialism." Materialism in all its guises, the *Review* editorialized, had "done more to change the German people than all other causes combined."[34] Joseph Crooker, a Unitarian minister, complained that the German industrial and economic success bred "contempt of the church" and "indifference to religion," because it drew on technical skill and ignored issues of ethics, morality, and the human soul.[35] Hutcheon, the Pennsylvania pastor, pointed to the amorality of science. "Just one hundred years ago," he wrote, "Mary Wollstonecraft Shelley gave to the world her powerful but ghastly story Frankenstein." He compared the creature of the novel to modern Germany, a "man endowed with the power of thought, but lacking soul, who entering the world thus under unnatural conditions becomes the terror of his species, a half involuntary criminal and finally an outcast whose sole resource is self-immolation."[36] Germany revealed that modernity could corrupt the normal inclinations of humanity into a mechanical stimulus-and-response system devoid of any moral consciousness.

Such theoretical flaws manifested themselves in practical social failure. The experience of the British teacher and journalist Thomas Smith was a case in point. One day shortly before World War I broke out, Smith's son came home from a German *Oberreichschule,* a secondary school that provided educational and religious instruction. He brought with him a statement from the German Minister for Church and School Affairs instructing the boy and his parents that dissent at school was forbidden and boys were encouraged to report deviance in all matters to the headmaster. Smith was appalled. He observed, sadly, that such was the state of affairs in a country where the state ran the church. Smith remembered that a short time before, the Salvation Army had petitioned the town for the right to hold services there. But a German divine of Smith's acquaintance named Theodor von Kolde, a man "without either wit, humour, or piety," advised the minister that the Salvation Army was a "dangerous heretical army" that would rile up "the Bavarian faithful." Accordingly the Army's petition was denied. The affair "defines very exactly the meaning of liberty of conscience as understood among Germans," wrote Smith.[37]

Smith conceded that the Germans had "succeeded in building up a wonderfully well-ordered State Church." But the national mania for regulation had choked off the mercy of Jesus Christ and the power of the Holy Spirit, offering the German church a new trinity: "God, who is the virtual head, the Kaiser, its nominal chief, aided by the Minister of Worship and Education." Under such rigorous organization the average German learned only obedience to the state, conformity to social expectations, and interest in the material rather than spiritual world.[38] It was not so great a leap to the assumption that state-controlled religion went hand in hand with dictatorship, and even enabled it. The English professor Alexander Crawford mourned that "the Germans have seemed as a people to be devoted to material ends and have had no interest in the spiritual advantages of free self-government."[39] The failure of Protestantism led directly to the failure of democracy.

The Rise of "Western Civilization" in the Classroom

The ruination of Germany was a warning: if religious and intellectual leaders did not carefully safeguard the tender shoot of democracy, it would wither on the vine. The solution the Columbia academics offered was education in liberal Protestantism. The president of Columbia, Nicholas Murray Butler, insisted that Germany had failed to understand the human soul. "The most precious thing in the world is the individual human mind and soul with its capacity for growth and service," he said. "To bind it fast to a formula, to hold it in check to serve the selfish ends of mediocrity, to deny it utterance and expression political, economic, and moral, is to make democracy impossible."[40] Many of his faculty had distaste for his leadership; Butler was perceived as autocratic and harsh, particularly after several professors were forced out of the university for demurring on Butler's insistence at mobilization in support of the war. Nonetheless, Butler's analysis of Germany's metaphysical blundering found wide support among the intellectuals at the university.

Germany had already been the subject of much discussion in the American classroom. In the late nineteenth century, American colleges and universities had begun jettisoning the strictly regulated classical curriculums of earlier years, slowly dropping traditional focus on ancient languages and incorporating more electives. Many added "modern history" courses for first-year students, which often began with the rise of the German tribes and taught students that American democracy derived from the confluence of Anglo-Saxon ethnicity and Christianity.[41] One textbook, Roscoe Lewis Ashley's widely used *Early European Civilization,* claimed, "The unity of western Europe was preserved, chiefly by the Christian Church. . . . It preached industry as well as brotherly love." For Ashley, Christianity found its perfect complement in the early Germans, who "loved personal freedom as none of the Mediterranean peoples had done." This joining of order and liberty, "the fusion of German and Christian," brought about contemporary European civilization.[42] During World War I, Columbia's educators concluded that this narrative had to be revised.

During the war, Columbia was one of many universities that at the request of the Wilson Administration offered a special "War Issues" course designed to inculcate Americans involved in the war effort with an essentially liberal Protestant justification for American involvement in the war. Soon, Columbia educators decided that the concept was worthy, and in 1919 Columbia spun "War Issues" into a new course, "Contemporary Civilization," required for all Columbia students.[43] It sought to systematize a historical narrative that linked the rise of Protestant religion to the rise of American democracy. The presence of the word *civilization* in the title revealed the sort of thinking which made the course possible. Harry Carman, who served on the faculty and later spent two decades as the director of the Contemporary Civilization program, explained that the course was "in a broad sense genetic," which was to say it sought to depict American civilization as the evolutionary product of Christian Europe and German civilization as America's dark doppelganger, an evolutionary failure.[44] Along the way, the Columbia academics reified liberal Protestantism, showing that it was the highest form of Christianity. In so doing, they defined what Christian civilization was: a liberal Protestant society, a religious community in which religion meant individual moral commitment which fostered democracy. By default, it was therefore also white, whether European or American.

The course emerged partly from the immediate pressures of the war and partly from older trends already present at Columbia. For one thing, professors like Erskine worried that the emergence of a modern industrial society in New York portended the sort of materialism that had been Germany's doom. By the time of the war, a quarter of Columbia's students were Jewish and another quarter Catholic, many the children of working-class immigrants.[45] Bestowing the values necessary for American democracy upon these students—cultivating in them the premises of liberal Protestantism through their new notion of Western civilization—became an imperative for Columbia's professors.

Similarly, much of the research engaged in by members of Columbia's faculty supported liberal Protestant premises, and hence was drawn into the composition of the Contemporary Civilization course. Columbia theorists argued the German state was based on dark premises. When the war began, the sociologist Franklin Giddings dashed off a polemic explaining that Germany was a "metaphysical monstrosity." He explained that any state was a "religious phenomenon," an expression of social cohesion that welded diverse human souls together into a transcendent whole greater than the sum of its parts. Germany was a false amalgamation that achieved unity through the threat of force rather than through the empathetic interactions Giddings prized.[46] The philosopher John Dewey argued that the United States and Britain shared a common moral sense, which he described as "Protestant, evangelical, and individualistic. . . . Their moral defense instinctively takes a personal, a moralistic form." The Germans, on the other hand, were afflicted with what Dewey called a "gospel of a Duty devoid of a content." He argued that they had come to worship power, authority, and efficiency, "a police conception of government."[47]

The historian James Harvey Robinson made a historical argument for German perversion, arguing that German material success had led to pride. He claimed, "Germans have been taught, during the past hundred years, by their philosophers, teachers, and clergymen . . . to regard themselves as the leading nation of the world," subject only to "a German God."[48] To Robinson it seemed evident that Americans were also in danger of such materialist temptations, and he offered a pedagogical solution. Instead of teaching "irrelevant and unedifying details" Robinson proposed history teachers should embrace what he called the "New History." History should be "educational, religious, aesthetic, moral, and intellectual," he insisted.[49] Students in his classroom and readers of his books should not simply acquire facts but internalize a moral narrative that would impel them to improve their present society. "Civilization—language, religion, beliefs, morals, arts and manifestation of the human mind and reason—none of these can be shown to be handed down as biological traits," he declared. "They can only be transmitted to a new generation by imitation and instruction."[50] Other faculty concurred: the anthropologist Franz Boas rejected Robinson's enthusiastic teleology but agreed that academic study could promote virtue. "It is our duty to enlarge that freedom of mind that will develop an enlightened

democracy," he wrote. He called such freedom "spiritual freedom," arguing
that it derived from coming to understand that human equality transcended
social particularity.[51] Robinson and Boaz both emphasized that civilization
emerged from the winnowing of the moral formation of one's soul.

All of these ways of thinking framed the Contemporary Civilization
curriculum. The course took solid form between 1919 and 1921. In the former
year a group of Columbia faculty guided by John Coss produced a two-
part syllabus; in 1921 these parts were consolidated into a single syllabus,
which largely stood until the course was revised in 1928. The 1921 course was
divided into three sections: The first drew on humanistic disciplines—
philosophy, theology, sociology—as well as the harder sciences to explore
the formation of human nature. The second surveyed what it called "Western
history" since the Reformation. The third considered "the insistent problems
of to-day," like "imperialism and 'backward peoples,'" economic issues, and
education.[52] It relied heavily on the work of Columbia faculty members, as-
signing writings by Dewey, Edman, Robinson, Giddings, and Erskine, among
others.

The Formation of Human Nature

The first section of the course was built around Edman's textbook *Human
Traits and Their Social Significance* as well as a number of other readings from
authors like William James and George Santayana. Edman's book described human civilization as a steady march of upward progress, refined
through trial toward moral perfection. Edman defined "the four great activities of the human mind and imagination—religion, art, science, and
morals," and proposed to show how each "developed, through the process of
reflection, in the fulfillment of man's inborn impulses and needs."[53] He argued that these activities developed on parallel tracks: ancient religions that
accepted human sacrifice and worshiped totems facilitated the brutal tyran-
nies of Egypt and Babylon, while liberal Protestantism, which focused on
ethics, sponsored democracy. Following William James and other liberal
Protestant students of religion, Edman argued that "religion" as a category
was "a total attitude toward the universe . . . the sense of the reality of the
divine." Religion was not theology; religion was concerned with one's relationship to social order and commitment to values. Edman thus connected
a healthy religion with healthy social behavior, a rejection of materialism,
and an embrace of individual autonomy and moral discipline.[54]

The first section of the syllabus sketched out human evolution away from "primitive emphasis on the power of the objects of veneration" toward a "developed emphasis on divine goodness." The course tied the former to "ritual and ceremony" and the latter to "social duty and participation in social betterment."[55] Like many Protestants, Edman associated ritual with self-abnegation and supplication; he judged it ethically inferior and degrading. Although Boas warned his Columbia fellows of the danger of assuming the natural inferiority of other cultures, that did not stop the developers of the syllabus or Edman, in *Human Traits and Their Social Significance*, from using the word *primitive*. "Primitive" religious beliefs fostered what Edman called "customary" morality, "the rigidly custom bound life of primitive societies." In a society premised on customary morality, Edman claimed, humanity behaved in moral ways only because of pressure, punishment, and discipline. Such beliefs led to autocracy. "The imperial character of the Japanese government to-day," Edman wrote, "is said to be greatly enhanced in prestige by the widespread popular belief that the Emperor is literally descended from deity."[56] Thus, Edman concluded, human society in all its aspects was best served by the philosophy of liberal Protestantism.

The Creation of the West

The second unit of the course, which dealt with history, argued that Christianity enabled the escape of the people of France, Britain, and the United States—which the syllabus generally referred to as "the West"—from imprisonment in Edman's customary morality toward democracy. The textbooks it assigned made the case clearly—for example, Carlton J. H. Hayes's two-volume *Political and Social History of Modern Europe*, and his later *A Brief History of the Great War*. Hayes, a Columbia professor of history, was a Catholic comfortable with liberal Protestant assumptions, and his work reflected that confidence. In his introduction to his history of Europe, Hayes maintained that progress toward Protestantism went hand in hand with progress in social and political life. He declared that the "most distinguishing achievements of modern time" were the "establishment of religion as an essentially private, not public[,] affair" and the "successful compromise between the modern exaltation of the state and the modern exaltation of the individual." All of this, Hayes claimed, showed that religious and political progress were linked and that progress inevitably tended toward human autonomy. "Back of political democracy there is a certain faith in human nature," he wrote. "We must acknowledge its debt to Christianity. . . . Christianity gave Europe a great and lasting lesson—a lesson however slowly learned—in true democracy."[57] For Hayes, Christianity's insistence on essential human equality gave Westerners the grounds to insist on democratic government in a modernizing world.

In 1926 John Herman Randall's newly published *The Making of the Modern Mind* became the primary textbook of Contemporary Civilization. It remained central to the curriculum for decades. Randall was not a churchgoer but was son of a Baptist minister, and shared basically liberal Protestant assumptions about the relationship between morality, Christianity, and democracy. While Hayes credited Christianity's emphasis on human equality with inspiring democracy, Randall selected a different virtue to celebrate. For him, Protestantism fostered a capacity for self-reflection, self-examination, and, hence, moral development. This argument reflected his own genealogical Puritanism as well as his dependence upon the work of Max Weber and other scholars of Protestant Christianity. Thus, for him, the "West" was essentially the home of Protestantism, which made the nations constituting it dynamic and creative, productive both of democracy and of capitalism. "The fact that the west has never crystallized into the stable societies of India or China, however great their achievements in themselves, must be in large part attributed to the essential nature of its moral tradition," Randall wrote. "From its conflicting elements have come flexibility, adaptation, and what we like to call moral progress."[58] This capacity for change was what Edman called "reflective" morality, premised not upon adherence to authority, but upon individual judgment, attention to conscience, and the capacity for course correction—or, one might say, repentance.[59] For Randall these ideas lay at the heart of democracy.

For these writers, what liberal Protestant civilization achieved was to blend the moral imperative of Christianity with the Enlightenment's confidence in individual capacity. Indeed, distancing the true achievement of democratic Christianity from Germany, Randall had only moderate praise for the Reformation. The Reformers were "thoroughly medieval in belief," Randall wrote, with a weak estimation of human nature and persistent reliance on supernaturalism. The Reformation broke Catholicism's political power but did not alone elevate individual human freedom. The Contemporary Civilization syllabus concurred. Even though the Reformation was not "in sympathy with the new science nor inspired by a faith in man's ability," it did "weaken the authority of the mediaeval tradition over the mind." Science had not progressed before the Protestant Reformation because medieval Christians were afflicted with "reliance upon authority and upon deductive reasoning—scholasticism," the syllabus lectured.[60] The Industrial Revolution, said Hayes, invigorated democracy by mobilizing the masses of the population, but also contained within it the seeds of danger by introducing mechanical rather than spiritual ways of thinking about social organization.[61]

Indeed, according to the syllabus, mature liberal Protestant Christianity, the "reasoned interpretation of religious experience," emphasized "duty" and "experience." "The worship of God is a bond between men of different nations," it observed. For Randall, the great accomplishment that defined Western civilization as essentially Protestant was its willingness to discard "whatever seemed irrational or unnatural in the Christian ethic" and to emphasize "those elements that seemed sound and useful for the ordering of the good life. The main principles of Christian morality, however they were founded, were retained." Even in the modern age, he said, when "skepticism and indifference" become "respectable," nonetheless "Deists and atheists and orthodox alike accepted without question all of the gospel ethic."[62] Randall thus illustrated the extent to which liberal Protestant ideals had become—at least for liberal Protestants—the unquestioned bedrock of American democratic government.

The "Insistent Problems of Today"

The Contemporary Civilization course was concerned not only with how democracy might be birthed; it was concerned with how it might fail. Both Hayes and Randall saw in Germany the failure of their ideals. For Hayes, German materialism wrecked German respect for individual liberty. He linked "materialism and determinism," arguing that both "flourished and flowered mightily and poisonously in Germany." German democracy had failed because leaders were committed to the nation's "huge military machine," to power, and to industrial strength.[63] Germany similarly weighted on Randall's mind. "Today we tremble lest the measures we must take to meet the insistent call of our industrial machine for a more efficient integration destroy our whole legacy of painfully acquired intellectual and moral values," he warned his students, drawing the same tension between industrial mass society and human nature that so many other Americans had.[64] Though Germany had lost the war, Americans were left with the worry that

Protestantism's faith in progress and its commitment to spiritual liberty were perhaps not compatible. The debate over Woodrow Wilson's proposal that the United States enter the League of Nations exemplified these concerns: Wilson urged Americans to promote Protestant civilization across the globe, but his opponents worried that a new international organization would smother American democracy in foreign bureaucracy, and if Germany had taught them anything, it was that foreign bureaucracy could be morally bankrupt. As Randall put it, the question was "Is the democratic ideal compatible with efficient industrial organization?"[65] Was liberal Protestant civilization doomed to enable its own undoing?

The third section of Contemporary Civilization's syllabus worried over that question in various iterations. Many assigned readings were skeptical. Homer Folks's despairing *The Human Costs of the War* declared that the war was "the most serious strain which western civilization has ever undergone, and it inevitably raises the question whether that civilization could stand another." Folks suggested that the war promoted "skepticism, both in man and in God," and that this lack of faith meant the world might become "less democratic than before."[66] Nor did James Bryce, a British theorist whose two-volume survey *Modern Democracy* was also assigned, offer a great deal of hope for democracy's progress. He linked the decay of religion to the fading of democratic government. Due to the war, the question of the future of religion "will be answered less hopefully now than it would have been at any time in the hundred years preceding," Bryce observed. Additionally, "Democracy shows signs of decay," he wrote, "for the reputation and moral authority of elected legislatures . . . have been declining in almost every country."[67]

Contemporary Civilization thus presented simultaneous narratives of optimism and anxiety. On the one hand, it clearly articulated the conviction that liberal Protestantism and American democracy were the endpoint of European civilization's progress. Insofar as liberal Protestants believed—and many did—that progress was inevitable, American Protestants were thus given reason to believe in the inevitable triumph of their civilization. But yet, at the same time, the specter of Germany lingered. Writers like Bryce and Folks warned that materialism ran more freely than ever before. Liberal Protestantism may have been triumphant, but it looked into the twentieth century with unease.

On the one hand, the Contemporary Civilization course helped promote an essentially liberal Protestant public religion. In addition to his duties administering the Contemporary Civilization program, John Coss spent much of the 1920s directing a committee seeking ways to improve student life at Columbia. The committee declined to endorse any particular church, but resolved that students "should be encouraged to maintain a connection with the church of his previous or present choice," because "the spiritual life should be the particular care of the College."[68] The next month the committee resolved to invite "representatives of various denominations agreeable to the University" to hold "office hours at stated periods on and [sic] University Campus, making various connections [and] inviting students to their church."[69] In a handwritten note Coss added that since Columbia hosted "Jews, Orientals, as well as Christians . . . the churches of New York offer ample opportunity for religious work and affiliation."[70] Coss worried that students distracted by "pre-professional" programs of study, "the general rush of appointments, the formal ordering of life" would lose the "personal, and idealistic" aspects of their education. He hence believed that such training should be supplemented with the "solid virtues of their own faith," whatever that faith might be.[71] Meanwhile, his course became the ancestor of the "Western Civilization" courses that were introduced at hundreds of American educational institutions in the mid-twentieth century, and the archives of Columbia University contain dozens of letters requesting copies of the syllabus from institutions as far-flung as Reed College in Portland, Oregon, to Barber Scotia College in North Carolina to an educator in the Panama Canal Zone. And all those in one year alone.[72]

In politics, Coss's version of Christianity proved popular. Through the 1920s and 1930s, American politicians invoked a generalized Christian language short on dogmatics or theology but long on the notion that Christianity offered Americans a sense of moral individualism that sustained electoral government. It drew on Contemporary Civilization's premises as well as the historical narrative that rooted American democracy in the heritage of the Reformation. On the Fourth of July, 1926, the dour president of the United States, Calvin Coolidge, stepped before a crowd of thirty thousand people in Philadelphia and warned them that their democracy was imperiled by their lack of faith in Christianity. "No other theory is adequate to explain or comprehend the Declaration of Independence," Coolidge instructed. "It is the product of spiritual insight of the people. . . . Democracy is Christ's government." For Coolidge, American democracy emerged from the spiritual heritage of the Puritans, whose rigorous focus on individual moral discipline bequeathed the Revolutionary generation with a respect for individual liberty. Extolling the austerity and discipline of his own New England ancestors, Coolidge then warned his hearers that they were threatened by a "pagan materialism," which he defined as the child of "material prosperity."[73]

Such accusations reverberated from both parties throughout the 1920s, a decade in which Democrats watched three Republican presidents preside over an exploding stock market and an avalanche of consumer goods. The 1924 Democratic race for the presidential nomination roiled with juxtapositions of materialism and Christian virtue. Candidate William McAdoo, who had served Wilson as secretary of the treasury denounced "the growing influence of money and materialism" in American politics and called for a restoration of the "Christian democracy under Woodrow Wilson."[74] Four years later, at the 1928 Democratic convention, the vice-chair of the Democratic National Committee, Nellie Ross Smith, declared that "the great masses of the people who have not surrendered utterly to materialism but who are still jealous for the spiritual welfare of the nation" would support Al Smith for president. Smith, said the Mormon senator William King, understood the "sordid and cynical materialism which seeks to destroy that fine idealism indispensable to true human progress and to moral and spiritual growth and development."[75] That a Mormon could laud a Catholic for such virtues illustrates the ecumenism of the language of liberal Protestantism. Its confidence in the spiritual nature of human progress and its emphasis on ethical behavior stripped of overtly theological content allowed its penetration into the broader political discourse of the United States.

At the same time, the fear of materialism spread among American Christians of many types. Theologically and culturally conservative Protestants saw materialism where John Coss saw strength. The resurgent Ku Klux Klan of the 1920s, for instance, illustrated how fears about materialism, democracy, and Euro-American civilization could be combined in ways counter to the ideals of liberal Protestants. Like the Contemporary Civilization course, Klan rooted American freedom in the Protestant Reformation. "The Reformation has taken residence in the Klan," declared a Klan paper, the *Union Leader*.[76] But while white liberal Protestants spoke of uplift and education, the Klan used the argument to insist that non-Protestants and non-Caucasians could not be heirs to Protestant democracy. Catholics, Jews, and African Americans, Klan leaders warned, were not inheritors of Protestantism's legacy and were thus by their very nature materialistic. These groups responded to "the modern and monstrous cheap labor idea," complained Hiram Wesley Evans, leader of the Klan, which meant "humanity has become a commodity." Evans blamed American industrialists for taking advantage of these immigrants, but he also believed that African Americans and Catholic and Jewish immigrants were materialistic by nature and thus enabled the system. Jews held to a "materialistic motto" of selfishness and individual gain, Catholics' freedom was stifled by their church's hierarchy, and African Americans could not grasp the higher principles of Protestantism.[77]

Similarly, Protestant fundamentalists spent much of the 1920s warning Americans that the progress and education liberal Protestants so treasured was itself a materialist trap. The politician William Jennings Bryan, the best known fundamentalist in America, warned that the theory of evolution taught in public schools would lead Americans into bondage. Bryan cited a British writer to warn that Darwin's "purely mechanical and materialistic process . . . had become the Bible of the doctrine of the omnipotence of force."[78] It was from there a short step toward a Germany that "denounced Christianity as 'the doctrine of the degenerate' and democracy as 'the refuge of weaklings.'" On the other hand, Bryan had great faith that democracy in America could be successful because of the goodwill of Christian citizens. "I fear the plutocracy of wealth; I respect the aristocracy of learning; but I thank God for the democracy of the heart," he said. Thus, he argued, "the real credit for leadership belongs not to any party or to any section but to those whose consciences were quickened by the teachings of the Bible."[79] A moral country rested upon a moral citizenry, and to Bryan, materialism threatened to destroy the individual capacity for belief and hence wreck democracy itself.

These insurgent imperatives against liberal Protestant ideals of assimilation and education left white liberal Protestants in a state of tension. They believed they possessed the solution to the world's ills, but that solution was itself vulnerable; it was both the inexorable end of human progress and poised at the brink of failure. Thus, they felt increasingly bound to protect their Christian civilization. In October 1919, Secretary of State Robert Lansing gave a speech to the regents and faculty of the State University of New York in Albany. He said the war had taught Americans that they "possess nationality in the spiritual sense," identifying American democracy as the natural extension of American faith. Further, the world had learned from Germany that democracy was a spiritually and morally superior form of government. "Democratic nations are not aggressive and domineering,"

Lansing believed. "They are not influenced by cupidity or improper ambitions. They are just to the powerful and powerless." Finally, though, Lansing warned that democracy was in danger and required preservation. Materialism had risen in Germany to "to stay the wheels of progress and imperil Christian civilization."[80] Lansing worried that the threat would continue. Contemporary Civilization deeply entrenched the links between Protestantism and civilization, liberal theology and individual liberty, and European ethnicity and American democracy that the war had threatened. But the same war which inspired the course also inspired fears that these links were weaker than many Protestants had assumed. Lansing's speech warned that their survival demanded constant maintenance.

CHAPTER THREE

Challenging Western Civilization at Howard University

IN 1938, the philosophy professor Alain Locke sat down in his office at Howard University to draw up a syllabus. He called it "History of Civilization, or Thought and Culture." Locke's notes indicate that he intended to trace the "humanizing of mankind" along an arc stretching from "animism, magic, totemism" and other such "survivals of primitive belief" toward "the emancipation of man," a word he chose with full knowledge of its meaning.[1] In the surveys of religion and philosophy he frequently taught, Locke outlined a similar narrative: humanity, he argued, rose from "primitive thought" toward the "higher development of religion" manifest in the "emergence of the ethical as supreme." He believed that ancient religious systems were based on "totem obligation," ritual, and unquestioning obedience to social superiors. Progress toward "higher development of religion" facilitated evolution away from blind obedience and toward individual liberty of conscience.[2] It was essential to Locke that his students recognize that religious progress was intimately connected to political progress: individual freedom, as exemplified in democratic government, emerged hand in hand with liberal Protestantism.

The course echoed the Contemporary Civilization class offered by Columbia University in more than this narrative arc. Locke's primary textbook was Randall's *The Making of the Modern Mind*. In addition, he based his syllabus on the "Introductory General Course in the Humanities" then being taught at the University of Chicago, itself derived from the Columbia curriculum.[3] The Chicago course argued that Christianity infused "the common consciousness" of the West with certain ideas: "high standards of conduct," "the fatherhood of God and brotherhood of man," and "the higher significance of the spiritual and the heavenly over the material." American democracy, the Chicago course maintained, depended upon these essentially liberal Protestant ideas.[4]

Locke's dependence on the ideas behind the Contemporary Civilization curriculum illustrates not only his immersion in liberal Protestantism, but also a degree of sympathy with the ideology of "civilizationism," which he shared with many educated African Americans of his time. These African American leaders were often liberal Protestants themselves. They agreed with white liberal Protestants' assumptions that liberal democracy reflected the moral values of Protestant Christianity and hence the highest achievement of human civilization. Thus, black leaders like Locke believed African Americans might, through education and moral commitment, "uplift" their race and lay claim to political and social equality with white Americans through the embrace of principles of liberal Protestantism.[5]

But Locke's civilizationism, and that of other black intellectuals at Howard University, was not simply identical to the liberal Protestant democracy heralded by the white faculty at Columbia University. Rather, Howard's academics perceived a great disjuncture in Contemporary Civilization's narrative. While white Protestant Americans took for granted that American democracy was the highest consummation of Christian values, African American leaders argued that the blight of racism indicated that this narrative of progress was a lie. Liberal Protestant ideals might be true, but this was not the same thing as saying that American democracy was their perfect consummation. African American liberal Protestants like Locke argued that the degradation into materialism feared by white liberal Protestants had already occurred. Jim Crow laws and legal segregation revealed that white Americans were ready, and even eager, to allow dehumanization and oppression to flourish in their society.

Black leaders formulated their objection to white liberal Protestant narratives of progress in a number of ways. Some rejected European Christianity entirely. Black nationalists like Timothy Drew and pan-Africanists like Edward Blyden argued that Islam was better for black people than Christianity; they offered narratives of human history that de-centered Christianity completely, depicting it as a confused ideology that caused only tyranny and racism.[6] But Howard academics like Locke were committed enough to liberal Protestant ideals that they preferred instead to argue that while it was true that Protestantism fostered democratic values, Americans had yet to truly attain those values. Some sought to use liberal Protestant language against white liberal Protestants. They insisted that if Christianity really promoted human freedom then it demanded an end to racism, and they insisted that America's failure to realize that ideal indicated that Christian values had yet to be achieved there. Other faculty members clung to liberal Protestant ideas about human equality but jettisoned the West. Instead they said that Christian values were fully articulated not in the Euro-American civilization that Columbia academics celebrated, but in Africa.

The intellectual environment at Howard University in the 1920s was fertile ground for a wide range of such ideas. The Howard faculty reread the white Protestant story of Christian civilization in creative ways, accepting some of its premises, rejecting others, and reframing still more. They argued that racism was a religious problem, a manifestation of materialism that made it impossible to believe that American society fully embodied Christian ideals. By inserting the experiences of Africans and African Americans into the narrative generated by white liberal Protestants, Howard's faculty forced white Americans to grapple with its blind spots, and they prepared the way for the eventual collapse of a white Protestant Christian consensus.

Liberal Protestantism and the African American University

James Stanley Durkee, the white Methodist minister inaugurated as Howard University's president on the drizzly morning of November 12, 1919, had a rocky tenure in office. He was often confused about why; he considered himself enlightened and, as a member of the National Association for the Advancement of Colored People (NAACP), had a reputation as a staunch supporter of civil rights. In his inaugural address Durkee blasted the "naïve feeling on the part of white America that colored people should be trained only for better servants in industry" and argued for more educational opportunities for African Americans.[7] But he was also an advocate of the Christian republicanism articulated in the Contemporary Civilization course at Columbia and—as with many other white Americans—did not recognize why African Americans found it inadequate. Durkee believed that the defeat of racism would be accomplished through the link between

Christianity and democracy that emerged from the Reformation and flourished in the United States. He had difficulty mustering sympathy for attacks upon racism that did not draw upon that narrative.

"The foundation on which American democracy rests is Christian education," Durkee's inaugural address abruptly began. Such an education, he claimed, would make it possible for "the colored race of America . . . to contribute its part to the advancement of the world," and would also teach white Americans to "discover in every person the divine right to all the best things God can give . . . all that is best and noblest in all the outreachings of humanity."[8] Like many progressive-era white liberal Protestants, Durkee believed that an education in liberal Christianity could overcome ethnic and cultural distinctions, teach human beings of their fundamental equality, and hence stoke the fires of American democracy. For Durkee, if the ideals of liberal Protestantism were taught in schools nationwide, "how many of our ills, our sins, our national crimes would be blotted out. . . . [We] would see clearly the contribution which each class of people and each race has really to offer for the larger glory." These peoples would become "Americans all, voting for noblest American ideals." For Durkee, the progress of American democracy would be manifest in the assimilation of minorities as partners in the cultural norms of white liberal Protestantism.[9]

But events outside Howard's Washington, DC, gates showed how difficult it would be to actually implement these solutions. Washington may have been the national capital, but Jim Crow was as powerful there as anywhere in the South. Six years before, the Cabinet of the new president Woodrow Wilson began to segregate the federal workforce, hardening an economic and social divide evident in the crowded, poverty-stricken neighborhoods into which zoning laws and landlords crowded African Americans. Only a few months before Durkee's 1919 inauguration, on the sweltering night of July 19, a mob of restless white men gathered near Howard's campus. They had heard rumors that a black man had been arrested for sexually assaulting a white woman. In reprisal they punished two African American men, Charles Ralls and George Montgomery, who were guilty of nothing more than crossing the mob's path. They beat Ralls senseless with pipes and sticks and fractured Montgomery's head with a brick. A band of angry African Americans retaliated, and for the next four days, street fighting erupted, dwindled, and erupted again up and down the streets of the city, until Wilson used the army to enforce order. Among the dead at the mob's hands was William Stuart Nelson, a Howard professor killed while wearing his cousin's World War I uniform, which he had donned in an attempt to shame the mobs into peace.[10]

Durkee deplored the riot, but it quickly became apparent that his confidence that liberal Protestantism would foster equality foreclosed his willingness to engage with the lived experience of African Americans or consider alternative notions of what Christianity demanded. He embraced the traditional role of many African American institutions, including colleges and universities like Fisk, Morehouse, Hampton, and others. Such schools were founded during Reconstruction to provide opportunities for African American students in the South, and as Jim Crow laws slowly constricted access to state schools, they became even more important to the African American community. Durkee's whiteness was not an exception. These colleges were usually founded by white missionaries and run by white educators, and they provided largely technical training. By the early twentieth century most embraced civilizationist ideology that linked African American progress to the cultivation of moral virtue.[11] John Hope, who served as the first African American president of Morehouse, from 1906 to his death thirty years later, captured this sentiment on his school's fiftieth anniversary in 1917. "If asked what best constitutes a college for Christian leadership, I would say the moral and spiritual element in the teacher," he said. "Rightly protected and promoted, our colleges will cease to be centers of learning that serve only negroes, be lifted out of mere racial service and made indispensable to the entire country."[12]

Perhaps the most famous African American educator in the era concurred: Booker T. Washington, who joined the Howard Board of Trustees in 1907. Washington, founder of the Tuskegee Institute, an industrial educational college, had spent three decades before his death in 1915 asserting that classical education like that offered in most American universities put the cart before the horse for African Americans. As Washington saw it, classical education at schools like Howard and Morehouse gave the freed slave "moral and intellectual freedom; but it did not actually equip him to live in the new world which emancipation had brought him."[13] Washington grew up in the rural South and spent a great deal of time there as an adult, coming to know the region's African American residents and determining what he believed they required. In his mind, hard work led to Christian morality, which in turn led to success. In 1909 he told the American Academy of Political and Social Sciences that he was proud that Tuskegee Institute faced relatively few disciplinary problems. This was a feat, for the school had a moral code which could be described as military: expulsion for tobacco or alcohol, regulation of personal grooming and clothing, required uniforms and chapel attendance, and so on. There were many rules to break. Washington, though, had a theory. "In considering the relation of industrial education to the nation," he said, "we should not leave out a consideration of its importance as a method of moral training. The boys and the girls who are studying to fit themselves for some definite vocation are gradually forming in their minds an ideal of life which is to direct and govern their conduct in after life."[14] Washington saw a distinct relationship between a person's commitment to labor, their religious life, and their capacity for participation in democracy.

"The Revolt of the Negro Intellectuals"

But to many other black intellectual leaders, even those who shared his hope for uplift, Washington's vision was misguided. Just as white liberal Protestants linked materialism to authoritarianism and moral decay, so did black liberal Protestants identify materialism with racism. To them Washington's fixation on economic and ethical advancement overlooked the real meaning of Christianity: that human beings were fundamentally equal. "The tendency here is . . . to regard human beings as among the material resources of a land to be trained with an eye single to future dividends," warned W. E. B. Du Bois of industrial-education movements like Washington's.[15] Howard University dean Kelly Miller agreed. Early in his career, in an 1899 address at the Hampton Institute, an industrial school, he acknowledged that it was fair to call "industrial knowledge the basis of all progress." But he also expressed worry about Washington's focus, claiming, "We reprobate this material spirit only when it begins and ends in itself, leading to no higher aim." Miller fretted over the focus of industrial education because he believed that "the Negro has now reached a critical stage. . . . It thus becomes all the more imperative that the race should gain for itself the primary principles of knowledge and culture." He urged black people to reject "the aggressive, materialistic, and domineering qualities of the 'haughty Caucasian'" and cultivate instead "the black man's . . . aptitude for Christianity."[16] Miller's belief that black people had a natural capacity for Christianity was a controversial idea among black leaders, but it laid the groundwork for Miller's own later conviction that white Europeans and Americans fundamentally misunderstood the faith.

As Miller did, for a long time Howard University's professors vacillated between commitment to civilizationism and worry that its implementation enabled racism. The founders of Howard had intended the university to serve the training of ministers and teachers, and the curriculum had long paid attention to the liberal arts alongside more conventional courses in sewing, typing, bookkeeping, stenography, and the like, offered through a department variously called the Industrial Department and the Commercial Department. In the two decades before Durkee took office, the school several times considered eliminating the latter. Then several new deans who were in favor of an increased emphasis on the liberal arts gained power, and by the time Durkee gave his address, the mood at Howard was changing. What Howard University historian Rayford Logan called "the revolt of the Negro intellectuals"—a mounting opposition among African American scholars to the work of Booker T. Washington, and a growing sense that achieving equal rights required a confrontation with racism rather than the cultivation of conventional American ethical standards—was emerging at Howard.[17]

One of the earliest of these voices at Howard was Miller, who became dean of arts and sciences in 1907. His administration hired new professors in sociology and English, and began pushing the school to adopt courses in African American history and culture. These reforms seemed to gain the approval of students. Each year through the 1910s the school granted several dozen AB and BS degrees through the College of Arts and Sciences but only a handful of diplomas through the Commercial Department.[18] That drift reflected the faculty's growing certainty that Washington's emphasis on material success could not end racism. Rather, after World War I inspired many liberal Protestants to renew the link between Christianity and democracy, Kelly Miller, Alain Locke, and other faculty began pushing Durkee toward what seemed to them the logical conclusion of his own professed beliefs. To their eyes there was a central paradox in Durkee's assertions of Christianity: the narrative of Christian history he cited as the source of democracy described a civilization that embraced slavery and allowed racism to flourish. The Howard academics argued that this narrative had to be revised to decenter the West as Columbia's Contemporary Civilization course defined it, and instead to incorporate the full story of people of color. While Durkee perceived himself to be an advocate for civil rights, he balked at revision of what he believed to be the story of American democracy. It was here that Howard's faculty reached the limits of J. Stanley Durkee's white Protestant liberalism.

This disillusionment signaled a growing gap between Howard's administration and its faculty. Due to its location in Washington, DC, and a charter that provided that a good deal of the university's income would be derived from federal allotment, Howard's leaders were eager to cooperate with the Wilson administration during the war. Its faculty, though, were less enthusiastic. On March 1, 1917, President Wilson spent the day preparing for his second inauguration a few days thence. The morning's papers publicized what Wilson already knew: the British had intercepted a telegram from Arthur Zimmerman, the German foreign minister, to the German ambassador to Mexico and passed it to Wilson's government, who were horrified to learn that the Germans were asking Mexico for an alliance against the United States.[19]

On the same day, despite the national uproar, Howard University began a celebration of its semicentennial. The centerpiece of the celebration was a series of speeches by scholars and community leaders, culminating in a conference dedicated to Howard University's role in the previous fifty years of African American history. Franklin Lane, the secretary of the interior, gave the opening address. He declared that racial progress was the product of "the Divine . . . which lifts man out of the slime and makes him like unto God."[20] Racial equality, Lane said, would proceed as quickly as African Americans embraced moral discipline and education. This was in line both with what Durkee asserted and black educators like Washington and Hope believed. It also echoed a genre of African American writing popular toward the end of the nineteenth century, the "vindication" or "contributionist" histories of writers like George Washington Williams and Anna Julia Cooper. These writers sought to justify African Americans' claim to dignity and equal citizenship by arguing that black people's character, hard work, and Christian commitments made them equal heirs with whites to the benefits of a civilization defined by those values. Williams's description of the slave rebels who had seized control of the ship *Amistad* and won their freedom encapsulated the point. They were "poor, naked, savage pagans, unable to speak English, in less than three years able to speak the English language and appreciate the blessings of a Christian civilization," he declared.[21]

But Wilbur Thirkield, who had served as president of Howard from 1906 until he became a Methodist bishop in 1912, pushed even further when it was his turn at the podium. He called attention to the fact that while more and more African Americans were seeking education, uplift did not necessarily follow. Thirkield blasted the rise of Jim Crow in America, declaring that Christianity required not merely African Americans to cultivate character but white Americans to recognize their own failures as well. Overcoming racism, Thirkield maintained, was indeed dependent upon the Christian notion that human beings were persons rather than objects. But he also argued that recognition of that fact required full integration of African Americans into the power structures of American life and the story of American history. "The ballot in the hand of the Negro for the first time awakened the consciousness of manhood," he said, connecting the project of true Christianity to that of African American political liberation. He stated that Howard's mandate was to build the kingdom of God, but he also clarified that the kingdom was a tangible place, which required political equality. "The Kingdom stands for the principle that every man is a child of God, not a thing," he said. "A genuine Christian democracy may be the outcome of the realization of this ideal."[22] This did not necessarily reject civilizationism, but Thirkield did call attention to its internal tensions."

Thirkield's address illustrated Howard's rising interest in the African American experience and the racial activism of W. E. B. Du Bois and the NAACP. In many ways Du Bois was an advocate for civilizationism, calling for a "talented tenth" to uplift and instruct their fellow African Americans, guiding them away from the tedious manual labor of sharecropping. But at the same time, Thirkield and Du Bois gave voice to a sense that African Americans could not define a Christian civilization in the same way that white Americans did. Du Bois himself spoke at Howard's commencement on June 5, three months after Thirkield, and was by that point advocating for a more Afrocentric civilizationism. He associated liberal Protestant values of equality and suspicion of materialism with African, rather than European, history. In his essay "What Is Civilization? Africa's Answer," Du Bois argued that African civilization focused on the value of the person and thus produced moral individuals. Africa, he said, "socialized the individual completely, and yet because the village was small this socialization did not submerge and kill individuality." Quite the opposite was true in Western civilization, where "when the city socializes modern man he becomes mechanical, and cities tend to be all alike."[23] Howard's faculty was increasingly sympathetic to Du Bois's critique of Western materialism and consequently became aggressive in offering revision of earlier definitions of Christian civilization. The tension slowly became evident on Howard's campus, and the war exacerbated it.

On May 23, 1917, Howard's board of trustees reviewed the proceedings of the semicentennial and announced that they "deemed it unwise at this time to make further investigation of such subjects."[24] The United States had entered the war six weeks earlier, and Howard found itself in a delicate position. The mostly white board of trustees was less eager than the faculty to place Howard at the forefront of African American activism. They were comfortable with Howard's traditional balance of Booker T. Washington's stern moral uplift and a classical curriculum: the latter might be proof that African Americans possessed capacities equal to those of white Americans, but the former had long been the backbone of the university. Furthermore, they worried that discontent would seem disloyal in a critical time. Almost immediately upon the outbreak of the war, the board approved the creation of a school of radio in the fall of 1917 and a Student Army Training Camp (the forerunner to the Reserve Officer's Training Corps) in early 1918.[25]

This evident eager cooperation, however, masked deeper uneasiness on campus. In lieu of Howard students and alumni joining a regular Officer's Training Camp, the U.S. Army announced that it would offer only a segregated Colored Officer's Training Camp. Many members of the black press, including some Howard students, were outraged, though many black leaders understood the conundrum as a question of swallowing an insult in the interest of, as Du Bois put it, placing "black men in positions of authority. Our choice is as clear as noonday. Give us the camp," he wrote.[26] Several hundred Howard students and a few professors flocked to serve. But the episode left a bad taste in the mouths of some Howard faculty, a sense compounded in a series of confrontations in Durkee's early administration over the nature of Howard's curriculum.

The Battle of the Curriculum

During the war, Howard's board continued a long pattern of seeking to limit the integration of African American history and culture into the curriculum. Early twentieth century Washington, DC, was a hub for African American intellectual life and the home of many efforts to revise how Americans thought about African American history. In 1897, the Episcopal minister Alexander Crummell organized the American Negro Academy in Washington's Lincoln Memorial Church. The ANA periodically organized public conferences designed to elevate intellectual conversation in Washington's African American community. In 1901, the Howard dean Kelly Miller tried to secure the academy an official university affiliation and a budget line with Howard. The trustees turned down the opportunity.

At a 1913 ANA meeting the independent scholar Arthur Schomburg read a paper called "Racial Integrity: A Plea for the Establishment of a Chair of Negro History in Our Schools and Colleges." It was important to teach black history, Schomburg said, "not merely that we may not wrongfully be deprived of the spiritual nourishment of our cultural past, but also that the full story of human collaboration and interdependence may be realized."[27] Schomburg enunciated two themes popular in nineteenth- and early twentieth-century writings about African American history, the first being that African American history carried meaning that could not be understood apart from Christianity. "Race histories," another genre of African American writing popular in the nineteenth century, often began the story of African Americans with the primeval history of the Bible and rooted the meanings of their history in theological claims. Schomburg's second theme was that African American history was intertwined with the history of humanity generally, and neither the story of African Americans in particular nor humanity generally could be understood in isolation.[28] Both of these ideas challenged the Contemporary Civilization curriculum's narrative of European Protestant ascendency. By the time of World War I, Howard scholars began insisting that these ideas could be demonstrated with the methods of modern critical scholarship.

But they continued to meet resistance from a Howard administration more convinced than ever that such ideas were dangerous, precisely because they challenged the white narrative. In 1915 Alain Locke proposed a course in "inter-racial history," and the board of trustees rejected it. The next year, Kelly Miller's proposal for a course dealing with African American social history was also rejected with the explanation, "The Committee thinks it inexpedient to establish a course in Negro problems at this time." Later, Miller recalled that these proposals failed because of "the squeamishness of certain members who at that time did not wish to perpetuate any racial terminology in the archives of the University." The looming war made the board nervous about any suggestion that Howard University might express displeasure with American democracy. Locke ended up delivering his course as a series of lectures titled "Race Contacts and Inter-Racial Relations: A Study in the Theory and Practice of Race."[29]

The most catastrophic curricular dispute came several years later, when Durkee clashed with Carter Woodson, a leading African American historian who had been hired the same year Durkee joined the university. The conflict signaled the beginning of the faculty's loss of confidence in Durkee, which several years later would be his undoing. This collision was particularly dramatic because of the personalities involved. Neither Durkee nor Woodson was easy to deal with. Woodson had been raised in rural West Virginia by fiercely religious parents, and throughout his life his single-minded dedication to his work recalled the habits of the long hours on his parents' farm. His austerity was legendary, marked by regular worship in a Washington Baptist church. Although his work was admired by other academics, his harsh personality made him few friends. Durkee, for his part, was known for a touch of self-righteousness and a love of pomp.[30] Such foundations did not promise a strong working relationship.

Woodson quickly found Durkee's administration intolerable. Later he complained that most black colleges in America were bound into white narratives of human history. "Upon examining the recent catalogues of the leading Negro colleges, one finds that invariably they give courses in ancient, medieval, and modern Europe but they do not give such courses in ancient, medieval, and modern Africa," he fumed. "Yet Africa . . . has contributed about as much to the progress of mankind as Europe."[31] He came to Howard in part because he expected that the strongest African American university in the nation would offer alternative readings of human history. There was some reason for him to hope so. Another history professor, Victor Tunnell, taught a course on Reconstruction with particular focus on emancipated African Americans, and only a few years earlier Miller had orchestrated Howard's acquisition of the vast collection of Jesse Moorland, a trustee and collector of African American books, art, and manuscripts.[32] But soon Woodson—whose tenure at Howard would last only one academic year—came to believe that the Durkee administration viewed these concessions simply as tokens rather than as central to the mission of the university.

Durkee believed the rhetoric of his inaugural; he saw himself as a defender of African American rights. Woodson was not so sanguine. He came to perceive Durkee's moral confidence as the product of a blind adherence to Eurocentric notions of Christian civilization which was, despite Durkee's good intentions, premised upon white domination; his repeated mantras of uplift and progress were simply a palliative for the stain of racism. Woodson instead offered a narrative of oppression and resistance designed to puncture the hollow version of Christianity that Durkee and so many other liberal white Protestants embraced. The richer, bloodier version he advanced took into account the suffering, achievements, and progress of African Americans and their ancestors.

Woodson found Durkee unsympathetic and complained vociferously about it to Jesse Moorland in late April 1920. "The same white leader of the negro race which you have forced on us here is doing you some harm and I want to tell you about it," Woodson began.[33] Moorland was himself African American, and his race and gregariousness made him a confidant for many Howard faculty. Woodson was about to test that relationship. Moorland was a mediator, inclined to bridge-building and compromise, and he urged Woodson to moderate his moods, warning, "I fear you have driven yourself into a position which is not doing yourself justice."[34] But Woodson was having none of it. He repeated the phrase "white leader of the negro race" over and over in their correspondence, attacking Durkee's position as well as his views.

The phrase was designed to undermine Durkee's vision of what a Christian civilization would look like. The historical narratives that Woodson used to describe Durkee were revealing. He classified Durkee as simply another in a line of "northern teachers of the missionary spirit . . . less qualified in their fields than the average Negro teacher." Repeatedly, he called Durkee and his methods "medieval," and asked Moorland, "Will you permit such inefficient white leadership to bludgeon well educated Negro instructors among them into submission to their medieval methods thrown aside centuries ago?"[35] Woodson insisted on placing Durkee in the past rather than in the present. Rather than a forward-thinking liberal Protestant, Durkee was in Woodson's eyes a throwback to the tyranny many Protestants associated with the Roman Catholicism of the Middle Ages. In the spring of 1920, fed up, Woodson resigned his post.

The policy complaints that Woodson and other faculty mounted against Durkee were twofold, and the complainants used both to label him a retrograde primitive according to the definitions promulgated by the Contemporary Civilization curriculum from Columbia. First, a major sore point for Durkee's opponents was the emphasis the new president put on chapel attendance. Kelly Miller reported to Moorland that "for years chapel attendance has been required by the Faculty along with Sunday morning Bible class, afternoon vespers, and prescribed Bible study." It was, however, a rule without teeth; students routinely neglected to attend, and the faculty routinely neglected to punish them. Rather than enforcement, Miller said, the faculty believed in "moral suasion," which he believed treated the students as free moral agents. He interpreted enforced religious behavior as a throwback to slavery, the ultimate expression of materialism.[36] Durkee, though, seemed to believe that African Americans required force, not persuasion. To the Howard faculty, this hardly reflected his professed liberal Protestant ideals.

According to Miller, soon into his presidency Durkee found a group of students meeting unofficially and without his leave in the chapel for purposes other than worship; he attempted to dismiss them, and when they refused he announced his intention to charge "the president of the student council with insubordination." In 1920, at Durkee's request, the university implemented a rule that any student would be "penalized by one third of a unit if he missed eight engagements, including chapel attendance, during any quarter." The students revolted. In Miller's words, they "became very much aroused[,] and petitioned" for the rule to be revoked. It was.[37] Durkee, however, was not done. Woodson reported indignantly that "Dr. Durkee is a fanatic on religion and wants me to take a part in checking up on teachers' attendance at chapel." Woodson had a joint appointment as professor and dean, so faculty supervision was part of his job. He was also a religious man who attended church regularly. Durkee's request, though, seemed completely out of bounds to him and thus was the impetus behind the accusation that Durkee's methods were "medieval."[38] They seemed to Woodson to violate the principle of conscience that liberal Protestants prized so much, and revealed that Durkee believed that African Americans were not capable of self-government.

Woodson's other complaint echoed the same point: he believed that Durkee was attempting to control Howard's curriculum by punishing members of the Howard community who did not always subscribe to his ideologies. Again, the underlying complaint was that the president believed that African Americans could not govern themselves. In 1920 Durkee acceded to a congressional request to remove material on communism from the university library, and Woodson charged him with paternalism. The faculty's feelings were illustrated most dramatically in an incident in May 1925, when a group of students announced their intention to strike. They sent a letter to Durkee listing their demands; they wanted more student control of student organizations, greater options to take electives, and an end to mandatory attendance at ROTC training, which had been instituted during

World War I.[39] They carried signs that declared, "Don't Be an Uncle Tom," and "An Army or a University?" They were mounting not simply a policy revolt but a deeper protest against their reading of Durkee's beliefs about the nature of civilization. The faculty regarded Durkee's adamant opposition to the strikers as essentially racist. In support of the students, they pointed out that during World War I the military had been segregated. They also consistently framed Durkee's opposition to the strike as a failure of his Christianity. When Durkee ordered students and faculty to cease their protests, they protested his lack of respect for their moral freedom. "Though a minister of the gospel with the religious fervor of a camp meeting preacher, he entered upon his administration with a bitter and indescribably hostile feeling toward Professors Cook, Miller, and Tunnell," reported Howard English professor G. David Houston, writing under the pseudonym "Alumnus" in the Baltimore *Afro-American*. (Cook, Miller, and Tunnell were three professors sympathetic to the strikers.) Houston captured the paradox Durkee presented to Howard's faculty: the president simultaneously professed Christian virtue and failed to enact it. A minister like Durkee, Houston noted bitterly, should be "least likely to be suspected of conduct unbecoming of a Christian."[40]

A month after the strike, in June 1925, Durkee fired Alain Locke and three other professors, citing a salary dispute. The move, however, was received as evidence that Durkee's professions of civilization and racial progress were in fact embedded in an infrastructure of white supremacy, and that he feared the alternative vision of Christian civilization the faculty advocated. "Dr. Locke was dismissed because he was suspected of being sympathetic with the students," said Houston. "To drive a man like Dr. Locke from Howard University is to announce to thoroughly trained Negro scholars that their type . . . is not wanted at Howard University."[41] The second reason, a confirmation of Woodson's suspicions that Durkee did not really want Howard University to sponsor or teach scholarship that undermined Durkee's own ideas, quickly became the preferred explanation for Houston and other faculty. Alain Locke and the sociologist Franklin Frazier worried that Durkee's preferred educational philosophy emphasized the "materialistic individualism of middle-class American life" and that his vision of civil rights involved primarily preparing black students for "the professions as a means to wealth."[42] These professors believed that Durkee's materialism undergirded his resistance to their claims—that his views lay closer to the accomodationist philosophy of Booker T. Washington than to what they saw as a truly equal Christian society.

Houston's explanation was simple: racism. "An incompetent Durkee becomes the superior officer over brilliant Negros, and in his bitter hostility to their superior training begins immediately to humiliate them until he is satisfied that servility has displaced scholarship and manhood," he wrote. In invoking manhood he connected masculinity to true Christianity and linked both ideas to the question of materialism, accusing Durkee of treating black men as something less than human beings. Later that year he and other journalists reported in an outrage that Durkee and Kelly Miller had clashed over Miller's more incendiary writings, with the college president calling Miller a "contemptible puppy." Durkee reportedly asserted lamely that he had only used the word "pup."[43]

By the end of Durkee's tenure, Houston was bristling at any echo of Durkee's high-flown inaugural rhetoric. In November 1925 Durkee hosted the NAACP official Neval Thomas at Howard to participate in a symposium on the progress of American racial relations. Thomas and other speakers invoked well-worn liberal Protestant language about the brotherhood of God and the fatherhood of man, and Houston was apoplectic. "To hold a religious convocation and to discuss among other topics fellowship and brotherhood is palpable hypocrisy," he wrote. "The administration of Howard University, with its president a minister and its board president the dean of a theological school should first make the religion of Christ fashionable in their acts and actions and then talk about it and hold convocations."[44]

By the middle 1920s, Houston's accusations of religious hypocrisy and Woodson's allegations of medievalism had come to characterize the way Howard's faculty thought about their president. The professors were not simply attacking the man's leadership. Rather, they critiqued the version of "Western" civilization that white liberal Protestants embraced. In linking Durkee to medieval Catholicism, liberal Protestantism's crowing image of spiritual and political tyranny, they illustrated how incomplete the project of spiritual democracy as proclaimed by white liberal Protestants still was. In labeling Durkee a fanatic, they made him unacceptable according to the mores of his own religion. In 1926, Durkee resigned himself to the state of affairs and left his post. But the faculty continued on. More than simply protesting the malign influence of Durkee and Wilson's war, they were opening the path to an alternative narrative of what it meant to be a Christian civilization. These new stories placed the experience of people of color at the center of Christianity, offering reframed notions of what Christian politics should be.

Reclaiming Christianity

As Arthur Schomburg's 1913 talk at the American Negro Academy illustrated, African American narratives of history often focused on Africa and the black experience. From the early years of the republic, African American "race histories" rooted their own experience in the United States in the ancient worlds of early Christianity and African civilizations, blending the Bible with stories of racial uplift. They often invoked a Protestant evangelical form of Christianity to link their lives to a sacred past.[45] "The children of Africa have been called, in the divine providence, to meet the demands of civilization, of commerce, and of nationality," American Negro Academy founder Alexander Crummell wrote during the Civil War. He and others believed that God had ordained a special place for Africa in human history.[46] Other black nationalist African American Protestants agreed with Crummell's Afrocentrism and his moralism. Leila Pendleton, who taught with Woodson in the public schools of Washington, DC, explored the Christian ramifications of the African past in her book *The Narrative of the Negro*. After reviewing Africa's ancient past, she emphasized that Protestant missionaries linked Africans to Europe and America, and in her narratives righteous missionaries and virtuous Africans tended to find each other more similar than not. Mtesa, king of Uganda, for instance, was a "cultured, civilized" Muslim, who after his encounter with the explorer Henry Stanley "agreed to observe the Christian as well as the Moslem Sabbath. . . . Under his government Uganda was a healthy, prosperous country."[47] Meanwhile, many evangelical African American Baptists and Methodists maintained that strict evangelical Biblicism demanded an end to racism, interpreting the New Testament to denounce division by skin color.[48]

But as Alain Locke's syllabus for "History of Civilization, or Thought and Culture" indicates, by the early twentieth century most of the Howard faculty had abandoned an evangelical form of Christianity in favor of a liberal Protestant ethic. They were hesitant about the staunch confidence in divine providence and biblical orthodoxy held by evangelicals like Crummell. This did not mean, though, that they had ceased to read their history in religious ways; rather, the religious values that guided their reading of the past had shifted. Many educated Americans—mostly white, but also much of the Howard faculty—associated the charismatic foot-stomping, singing, weeping, and emotion of black churches with the undiluted primitive impulse of the African heritage. They vacillated between seeing such religious enthusiasm either as the sign of a naturally spiritual and generous people, or, alternatively, as an alarming exhibition of precisely how far African Americans were from the moral self-discipline required of democratic citizens.[49] Many Howard faculty found themselves in the latter camp, in part because they either embraced or sprang from a northern urban culture. Alain Locke, for instance, was born in Philadelphia and raised by a mother with deep involvement in the Society for Ethical Culture. As an adult he was drawn to the ethical and tranquil faith of the Bahá'í. Kelly Miller and Carter Woodson left the South to study in the urban North, and joined churches more inclined to social justice than evangelical conversion. Their general beliefs about the function of religion, then, followed closely those of other liberal Protestants. Locke's syllabus depicted contemporary American religion as a struggle between humanity's primitive and positive impulses. On the one hand many believers held to the "reactional tendency," as expressed in "intolerance [and] suppression of individual initiative." But the "future of the church" lay in ethics, not theology, in the "substitution of practical and empirical for theological and theoretical." Liberal Protestantism's emphasis on ethics and individualism led to human emancipation and what Locke called "voluntarism," the right to choose foundational to a democratic society. Rather than dogmatics, Locke embraced the ethical progressivism of many of Columbia's faculty.[50]

These ideas framed how many Howard faculty interpreted American history, just as they did for many white Americans. The bitter critique they leveled at Durkee should not then obscure how much they shared with him. Indeed, their sense of betrayal stemmed from their conviction that he should have known better. Locke himself, due to his liberal religious sympathies, believed that democracy was a spiritual achievement. "We must manage to disentangle the main values and objectives of democracy from the particular institutional forms by which we practice it," he wrote. "The great prerequisite for this is a spiritual virtue . . . a sense of basic commonality in spite of difference." He saw in Christianity the potential for that vision but also a distressing tendency toward social division. "The idea that there is one true way of salvation . . . is a tragic limitation to the Christianity which professes the fatherhood of God and brotherhood of man," he wrote. Christianity rightly understood would "vindicate its claims to universality, and so bring about moral and spiritual brotherhood."[51] The key distinction that drove a wedge between Locke's faith and Durkee's was the relationship of that faith to history. Locke insisted that the racism that infected European nations and the United States blinded those countries to their own failures to achieve the ideals all of them shared. He warned that cultures tended to construct racial hierarchies consonant with their values, and that these "race creeds" can "control social and even political policies."[52]

The counternarrative Locke and his colleagues erected shared more values with those of liberal Protestants than it did with the earnest providential Protestantism of Crummell or the race histories, but it was no less invested with religious meaning. In 1924, Miller and Locke convened the Sanhedrin, a gathering of major African American thinkers, politicians, and organization leaders in Chicago. Miller took the opportunity to deliver an address arguing that Europeans had perverted Christianity and explaining what its true meaning was. "The negro's religion must not be derived from the white man but from its original source," he said. "The function of the church is to unite men into one solid phalanx of Christian brotherhood."[53] He visited the theme regularly. "The Hebrew-Christian religion has much of the fundamental requirements of universality," he said two years later at the same gathering, but "from the beginning there has been constant apostasy from this universal ideal." This problem hampered further social progress in America. "Race prejudice is the greatest vice of our generation and stands squarely athwart the kingdom of heaven," he declared. "Christian inconsistency is bringing Christianity into disrepute. To the non-Christian all of this must be amusing to a high degree."[54]

For much of the 1910s and 1920s, the Howard faculty devoted themselves to proving that a true Christian civilization should overcome the human tendency toward racism. As with the Columbia scholars, their argument would be based on history. Woodson believed that history could accomplish two tasks: first, it could demonstrate that humanity was far more interconnected and interdependent than the Columbia narrative assumed; second, it would invest all people with the moral imperative needed to correct racial injustice. "If a race has no history, if it has no worth while tradition, it becomes a negligible factor in the thought of the world," he warned. On the other hand, "If from the record we can show how far we missed the mark of justice in the past," Woodson wrote, "we may be constrained to do more than ever to attain a level of equality and brotherhood in the future."[55]

The historical narrative the Howard faculty constructed reclaimed Christianity for a world beyond Europe. It reversed Columbia's narrative. Rather than the culmination of the expansion of egalitarian Protestantism, the rise of Western civilization to them represented a contraction of

Christianity, the smothering of its democratic possibility under a thick blanket of racism and inequality. While to the Columbia faculty the German destruction of Rome propelled democracy forward, to Kelly Miller the real lesson was quite the opposite. "The race question was never so sharp and determined in the history of mankind until the Nordic became dominant," he said. Miller also reversed the conventional narrative of the rise of Protestantism, finding in the Reformation another loss. "Catholic states are superior to Protestant countries in controlling the virulence and rancor of race prejudice," he said, observing that the Latin American nations experienced far less segregation and fear of interracial marriage than did the United States.[56] After leaving Howard Woodson devoted his full attention to the Association for the Study of Negro Life and History, which he had founded in 1915. He steered its work toward public education and advocacy, trying to promote a version of American history that countered that of Columbia by rooting Christian values in the history of Africa. He stowed in his papers a clip from the *St. Louis Herald* that reported on a school pageant put on by black children using ASNLH materials. The pageant showed the "historical development of the Negro beginning with the splendors and lavish display of the Egyptian court," and ending with a final display of contemporary life in which "the shackles of ignorance, Old Religion, and other shackles which bound the Negro were gradually broken."[57]

Howard faculty argued that the rise of the West actually inhibited Christian ideals. In a number of articles Woodson sent to the members of the ASNLH, he constructed a meticulous argument documenting that before the rise of Germans, the Greeks, Romans, and Africans had interacted as equals. The Greeks, he showed, "considered the Ethiopians a remarkably beautiful people who held their feasts among the Gods." The Romans may have enslaved Africans, but they also allowed those slaves great influence and freedom. From this, Woodson argued that the modern West had roots in Africa, particularly Egypt and Ethiopia.[58] "Both the Greek and the Roman are Egyptian because the entire Mediterranean was civilized from Egypt. Egypt in turn borrowed from Ethiopia and the Hither Orient," he pointed out. From this perspective, Woodson argued, to say that the United States rose because it inherited democracy from the Germanic tribes and Protestant Christianity from the Reformation was incoherent. Rather, he wrote, "There is no way to eliminate the Negro. . . . The history of the United States is mainly the history of the negro."[59]

Other Howard faculty did not merely argue that ancient racial equality was choked off by the rise of the German tribes and Protestant Christianity. The most creative, William Hansberry, maintained that in fact the fullest and best expression of Christianity was found in Africa, not Europe. Many African American writers had advocated for what was sometimes called "Ethiopianism," after the ancient African civilization they celebrated most. Schomburg believed that a close study of ancient Africa would demonstrate that Ethiopian civilization embodied all the virtues liberal Christians valued.[60] The journalist Drusilla Dunjee Houston's book *Wonderful Ethiopians of the Ancient Cushite Empire* reflected the interest many lay African Americans took in this past, and argued that Ethiopians of old had been tolerant monotheists before their encounter with Christianity. "The primitive worship of the Ethiopians was pure," she argued, which meant that their descendants, the Nubians, eventually defended the relics of Egypt from destruction at the hands of Islam. Pauline Hopkins, another African American writer, claimed that early Ethiopians were aware of the Trinity and pioneered human rights.[61] For a long time, such arguments were ignored by academics, in large part because they were written by women who lacked academic training, even though they gained great support within the African American community. Hansberry, then, was determined to back up these ideas with his own research. While he followed many of Houston's interpretations, he also wanted to prove that such viewpoints should be included in the American political and social conversation about race and racism, and to bridge the gap between African American writers and the American political and academic public sphere.

Hansberry came to Howard in 1922 with wide support from the faculty and trustees, including Durkee, who viewed his work as a demonstration that commitment to liberal Protestant ideas could uplift African Americans. At Howard's commencement in October 1922, Durkee introduced Hansberry to the student body. "The ignorant have ever declared," Durkee said, "that the racial group which we at Howard represent, has no past history save that of ignorance and servitude." Despite the fact that Hansberry shared many convictions with other faculty members with whom Durkee was butting heads, Durkee found Hansberry's research into ancient Africa both far enough from the United States and yet close enough to liberal Protestant ideals to be safe. That winter, Charles Wesley, a professor of history, told Woodson, "I believe Hansberry is prepared to lay a foundation for our American Negro History by bringing to the surface most that is now known regarding Ancient African History."[62] By 1926, Hansberry reported that he had taught twelve hundred Howard students.[63]

One of Hansberry's primary aims was to contest the narrative offered in Columbia's Contemporary Civilization course, in which the ancient Near East served as an incubator for the raw materials of Western civilization—democracy, Christianity, and so on—which then flowered across the oceans in Europe and America, their true home. That story, Hansberry argued, was an act of intentional distortion. Hansberry stubbornly argued that Ethiopia—by which he meant northeastern Africa south of Egypt—was the true home of human civilization. He argued that "Africa . . . was in all probability the birthplace of the human race. It was they who first learned and then taught the rest of mankind how to make and use tools, to develop a religion . . . and to create and maintain a deliberately constructed and tradition-bound state." As to religion, Hansberry argued that the notion of a personal deity derived from Africa as well, for "the Ethiopian forms of these gods were probably the oldest and very likely furnished the prototypes for those of Egypt, and ultimately by way of Egypt . . . Greece." He found in Homer's depiction of the Ethiopian king Memnon the earliest account of an ideal ruler, the highest of "paragons of virtue and valor."[64] For Hansberry, the traditions of religious faith and moral virtue that Contemporary Civilization traced to the conflation of Christian theology and German vigor actually had their origins in Africa. Furthermore, Hansberry alleged that white American narratives deliberately hid that fact.

When Hansberry looked at ancient sources, he saw allusions, homages, and acknowledgments of the greatness of Ethiopian civilization scattered everywhere. And yet these references never seemed to appear in the history taught in most American schools. Over the centuries, Hansberry argued, Americans and Europeans had grown increasingly determined to purge the Ethiopian influence from their own histories. "It became customary in the modern world to associate Ethiopia and Europe in much the same general way as dominant contemporary thought associates the expressions Negro and Nordic," he wrote. "The one was thought of mainly in the terms of savagery and slavery. . . . The other was generally pictured . . . as an immortal fount of culture."[65] Thus, Hansberry saw white historian after white historian discounting Homer's and Herodotus's praise of Africans as "entirely outside serious historical interest."[66] Hansberry saw his work at Howard as critical to undermining that narrative. "In the revision of history which is now underway, this travesty on truth will be corrected and the Negro will be restored. . . . It is not reasonable for the Negro to expect European or American scholars to take the proper lead," he told an audience at Howard in 1923.[67]

Hansberry was at his finest when he offered a counternarrative to the history of Christianity in the West as promulgated by courses like Contemporary Civilization. In 1922–1923, he taught "Introduction to Ancient and Mediaeval African Civilization" at Howard, covering "Ancient Ethiopia," among other civilizations. He taught the material with an eye, as his course description said, to elucidating "the Downfall of African Civilizations and the explanation for their omission from World history."[68] According to Hansberry, Ethiopia offered an alternative vision of what a Christian civilization might look like, which was, perhaps, why it was so often omitted. According to Hansberry, Ethiopian Christianity was nearly as old as the religion itself. "Ethiopia, like Nubia," he wrote, "had served for many generations as a refuge for the Egyptian, Syrian, and other Levantine Christians who had been forced to flee from various parts of the Roman Empire." Ethiopian Christianity, in Hansberry's telling, succeeded, and Ethiopia itself flourished, due to its broad-mindedness, its tolerance, and its capacity for inclusion. Under the guidance of the humble bishop Frumentius, the fourth-century Ethiopian kings Ezana and Ashbeha accepted Christianity and made their kingdom a haven of care for the poor and the welcoming of strangers. "Ezana was a man of deep humanitarian impulses. . . . There is every reason to suppose that these benign elements in his character were broadened and intensified after he had publically committed himself to ordering his life in accordance with the teachings of Christ," Hansberry wrote. Hansberry approvingly quoted a historian who described Christianity in Ethiopia succeeding because "there was no war to introduce it, no fanatic priesthood to oppose it, no bloodshed to disgrace it; its only argument was truth."[69]

Hansberry repeatedly contrasted the peaceful spread of Ethiopian Christianity with the chaos simmering in European religion at the same time, and showed how the former led to Ethiopian strength while the latter tore Europe apart. "The strife between Christian and Christian," he claimed, "was one of the primary causes, if not the primary cause, of the debilitated condition in which the Roman Empire found itself." In contrast, at the same time, "the newly established Christian kingdom of Ethiopia was passing through a period of great peace and prosperity."[70] Soon after the 325 Council of Nicea, the Roman emperor Constantius (son of Constantine) embraced the Arian heresy, which taught that Jesus was a created being rather than eternally existing as part of the Trinity. Hansberry recounted with disapproval Constantius's persecution of Christians who disagreed, and noted

that Constantius sent to Ethiopia a delegation of priests and soldiers to demand the allegiance of the Ethiopian church. According to Hansberry, the
delegation was "kindly received," and though he found no records to document an official response, Hansberry claimed that "it is safe to assume that
the two Ethiopian kings were truly astonished at the impertinence of the
Roman potentate."[71]

According to Hansberry, Ethiopian Christians were continually befud-
dled at the doctrinal schisms and bloody persecutions of heretics that
plagued the European Christian church. At the same time, their own commitment to doctrinal tolerance and a focus on the pastoral aspects of Christianity helped Ethiopia to flourish. When Constantius began persecuting
his opponents, many fled to Ethiopia. A hundred years later the Roman
state prosecuted the followers of another Christian leader deemed heretic,
Nestorius, and again many fled to Ethiopia. Hansberry stated that "there
are good reasons for believing that many of the outlawed partisans of the
deposed patriarch were granted religious asylum," and that these groups
"contributed substantially to the growth of Christianity in their adopted
land."[72] They brought their learning and often their property to Ethiopia,
thus enriching that kingdom at the expense of Rome, and Hansberry documented the great architectural and literary achievements to which such
refugees contributed. Eventually, when the collapsing Roman Empire tore
itself apart through battles over orthodoxy, Ethiopia mobilized its armies to
defend "those unjustly attacked" and to "aid their brothers in the faith, and
on more than one occasion put an end to their distress."[73] Ethiopian inter-
ventionism, Hansberry argued, lacked imperial designs and instead exemplified Christian selflessness.

Hansberry devoutly hoped the Ethiopia of his research would provide
African Americans of his day with a model for a Christian black society.
Indeed, many of his ideas were echoed among black nationalists of his time.
George Alexander McGuire, a follower of black nationalist Marcus Garvey,
gained some support and publicity from Garvey for his "African Orthodox
Church," an Episcopal schism centered in Africa that sought to affiliate
with the Orthodox churches of the Middle East rather than with any European denomination. Garvey argued that Jesus was African in his ancestry,
and McGuire urged his followers to "go back to the native Church, to our
own true God."[74] While agreeing that historic African Christianity was
superior to contemporary Euro-American Christianity, Hansberry was not
a separatist like Garvey. He believed that Ethiopia should serve as a model

for any state that aspired to Christianity. The Christianity of Hansberry's Ethiopia possessed the virtues which Christians in his contemporary United States sorely needed: tolerance, generosity, and the willingness to sacrifice for ideals like egalitarianism and equality. Hansberry was determined to provide a model for that standard.

Indeed, Hansberry and the other Howard faculty grew the most scathing when they assailed the pretentions of the United States to be the pinnacle of Christian civilization. Like Miller, Woodson saw the moment which white historians credited as the blossoming of Protestantism and equality as instead its moment of greatest failure. "Christianity had its greatest test in the Western hemisphere where such a large number of European Christians immigrating to America came into contact with Africans who had been brought to America. Very soon the Christians in America forgot the religion of brotherhood," he wrote.[75] Indeed, in the United States Woodson saw not the triumph of Protestant democracy, but the basest betrayal of what Christianity stood for and the subsequent collapse of the West into bigotry.

That collapse was rooted in slavery, which the Howard historians saw as a crime because it was philosophically materialist; it reduced humanity to property. No wonder, then, that they believed slavery retarded the moral progress of its victims; it was to them what the Columbia faculty believed the modern German state had become to German Christians. Miller, Locke, and Woodson placed the pathologies of the black church at the feet of slavery, and thus neatly illustrated again how destructive the white West was. Kelly Miller claimed in 1908 that "slavery made requisition upon the Negro's physical faculties alone, and therefore the higher susceptibilities of his nature were ingeniously denied and prudently suppressed." This, then, all but "ordained intellectual and moral inferiority" among African Americans.[76]

In the highly charged context of the First World War, Kelly Miller indicted the American government as another Germany. The snub of the Colored Officer's Training Camp was compounded with race riots in East St. Louis, Illinois, in May and July 1917, when mobs attacked the homes and persons of African American workers who had replaced striking white workers. The National Guard offered aid in May, but in July Wilson declined to intervene.[77] That pause convinced Kelly Miller that Wilson was willing to compromise the war effort and sacrifice black lives in order to maintain segregation. In an open letter to Wilson he took on one of the nation's most repeated slogans: Wilson's optimistic proclamation that America fought to "make the world safe for democracy." In so doing, Miller also enunciated a critique of the close connections between Christianity, democracy, and the West so many white Americans assumed.

"As the nation could not exist half slave and half free under Abraham Lincoln, so it cannot continue half law abiding and half lawless under Woodrow Wilson," Miller began. The racism he saw in America in 1917 was as searing as slavery was in Lincoln's time. Therefore, unlike white Americans, Miller did not see the war against Germany as a struggle between Christian democracy and godless authoritarianism. When he heard of the East St. Louis riots, Miller wrote, "I could not but think of the godless war which is now convulsing the world—a war in which Christian hands are dyed with Christian blood." The violence in Europe had its counterpart in the segregated officer camp and the blood on the streets of East St. Louis. From that vantage point, America suddenly seemed little better than Germany. "In the United States alone, of all the civilized lands, these atrocious outrages are heaped upon the helpless negro," he wrote. But Miller did see a solution. He pled with Wilson to embrace what Miller deemed true Christianity. "Ten million of your fellow citizens are looking to you and to the God whom you serve to grant them relief," he wrote. "The negro's helpless position may yet bring America to a realizing sense that righteousness exalteth a nation, but sin is a reproach to any people."[78] The Christianity Miller urged on the president was the Christianity of Locke, Woodson, and Hansberry: inclusive, peaceful, and destructive of rather than sustaining of racial distinction.

This was, of course, the Christianity that white Americans like Durkee fully believed they subscribed to, and when the Howard scholars confronted them with its gaps they vehemently reasserted their faith. It was true that Durkee and many others fully conceded that the state of African Americans in the United States called into question the present execution of their ideals, but they also were convinced that the problem was transient, offering little challenge to the grand procession of the true West's spiritual democracy. Americans educated at Columbia could believe this because the story of the West which Contemporary Civilization synthesized exalted the United States, emphasized its role as the culmination of centuries of progress, and wove together liberal Protestantism and democracy in such a way that made their national achievement seem not merely grand but inevitable, not merely functional but Christian.

The West that was represented by Contemporary Civilization as taught at Columbia made many things possible. It formulated a connection between the United States and Europe that both gave Americans a new sense of their own origins and drew their nation into a grand narrative of Christian progress. It also, however, rendered counternarratives like those produced at Howard University increasingly threatening. In the alternate pasts they offered, Kelly Miller and William Hansberry did not merely seek to revise what Americans believed about their history; they also told Americans that what they believed about themselves, about their Christian identity, and about their faith in the righteousness of their civilization was insufficient. Over the next decades, Howard faculty like Howard Thurman and Benjamin Mays continued to question the identification between Christianity and Western civilization. When the black-freedom movement gained momentum in the 1950s and 1960s, the debates seen in microcosm at Howard University offered multiple, and sometimes competing, precedents for understanding the relationships between race, Christianity, and civilization in America.

CHAPTER FOUR

Catholic Community in the Great Depression

D URING A CAMPAIGN stop in Detroit, Michigan, on the first Sunday in October 1932, New York governor Franklin D. Roosevelt, the Democratic candidate for president, greeted the crowd with an apology for campaigning on the Sabbath. He explained that because of the day he would not stoop to "talking politics," but he would venture into the territory of religion. "Back in the days of Noah, there was the theory that if we make the average of mankind comfortable and secure, their prosperity will rise upward," he claimed, in a somewhat confused Bible reference. He then turned to an unlikely authority for a candidate from America's old and respectable Protestant establishment: Pope Pius XI. Roosevelt wanted to discuss *Quadragesimo Anno*, an encyclical the pope had issued the year before. Therein, Pius called for a reorganized and regulated economy, stressing that "the right ordering of economic life cannot be left to a free competition of forces." Roosevelt read the pope's words: "Immense power and despotic economic domination . . . [are] a natural result of limitless free competition which permits the survival of only those who are strongest." He lifted his head from the paper and observed that the document was "just as radical as I am." As his speech wound down, he confessed somewhat sheepishly, "I feel a little as if I had been preaching a sermon."[1]

Some Catholics were delighted. The sermon Roosevelt preached was exactly what they had been waiting to hear from an American politician. John Ryan—a widely respected Catholic priest, a professor at the Catholic

University of America, and an activist who had for forty years been fighting for economic reform—had been rather dispirited during the campaign. Roosevelt had given little indication of a coherent political philosophy, and the priest deemed the incumbent, Herbert Hoover, whose response to the Depression had been lethargic, outright unacceptable. But soon after the speech, Ryan's friend, the reporter John McHugh Stewart, wrote happily to the priest that in Roosevelt, Catholics would "have in the White House . . . a knowledgeable friend and intelligent champion of the social and economic doctrines recommended to us by Authority and experience."[2] Roosevelt was not so educated in Catholic doctrine as Stewart might have imagined, but the language of his speech reflected the long-standing Catholic conviction that God endowed the universe with natural law, and that human freedom was best enjoyed through adherence to that law. Ryan believed that this concept was the solution to the Great Depression. "The most fundamental obstacle in the way of the economic reforms which our society needs is disregard of the moral law," Ryan told an audience in Hartford, Connecticut, in 1937.[3]

Ryan believed that this disregard stemmed from ignorance, so through the 1930s he and other Roman Catholics sought to educate Americans about the Catholic vision of human freedom, and the ideas about democracy and civilization that grew from it. Like Protestant Americans, they used the term *materialism* to describe principles that opposed their ideas about freedom. But for many Catholics, materialism might mean unfettered capitalism as much as the tyranny liberal Protestants had focused on since World War I. Furthermore, Catholic concepts of democracy and freedom did not imply the degree of individual autonomy that Protestants took for granted. As Ryan and other Catholics sought to reform the nation, these differences proved stumbling blocks difficult for some of them to surmount.

By the third and fourth decades of the twentieth century, Catholics like Ryan were worried that American civilization was starting to come apart. In the midst of the Depression, Ryan ironically suggested to the Columbia historian Carlton Hayes that Hayes write a book called "A Generation of Disillusion" mourning the collapse of the economy.[4] But the Depression also offered new possibilities. "All Catholics who desire to give practical effect to the principles of social justice laid down by Pope Pius XI will see that Governor Roosevelt's opportunity . . . is likewise the Catholic opportunity to make the teachings of Christ apply to the benefit of all," claimed the lay-operated, liberal Catholic journal *Commonweal*.[5] To his audience in

Hartford Ryan laid out proposals he thought the Depression might make possible. He proposed to them a series of laws to advance unemployment insurance, higher wages, and stronger regulation of monopoly, and he told his audience that these things were "demanded by the moral law of nature and of reason. They would be adopted by an intelligent society of pagans." It was not that Americans were moral idiots, necessarily; it was rather that they misunderstood Christianity and trusted the notion of individual rights too much. Catholics looked askance at Protestant notions of civilization, which equated the rise of Protestantism with the rise of democracy but, to Ryan's eyes, lost Protestants the guidance of the Church that was essential to understand natural law. "In addition to the guidance provided by the natural law we Catholics possess the authoritative teaching of the church," he said in Hartford.[6]

Ryan's Hartford speech reflected many of the impulses felt by American Catholics who were interested in social and economic reform during the Great Depression: a conviction that unfettered capitalism ignored the essentially communal aspects of human nature, a desire to restructure the American society and economy to better organize them along Catholic models, and the need to grapple with the capacious power of Protestant Christian republicanism. The efforts Ryan and other Catholic leaders exerted to bring Catholic ideas to bear upon these problems differed, and frequently Catholics found themselves in conflict with each other. While all accepted the notion that democracy should promote social order rather than unfettered liberty, different Catholics tried with varying levels of effort to reconcile their ideas with establishment Protestant Christian republicanism. Some, like Ryan and the Catholic convert Dorothy Day, refused to compromise much at all, and hence found Protestant Americans wary of their work and hesitant to believe that they represented either Christianity or democracy. But other Catholics proved more capable of finding reconciliation. Some, like the demagogue Charles Coughlin, were talented at translating their ideas for Protestant ears, but they still distressed the liberal Protestants of the American establishment. By the end of World War II, however, leaders at the Catholic University of America had discovered a way of translating Catholic language about democracy in such a way true to Roman Catholicism and which allowed them participation in an American Christian consensus.

John A. Ryan and a Catholic Democracy

Several times during his first term of office, Roosevelt asked John Ryan to deliver a radio speech on the president's behalf. Ryan was a natural choice; for years he had been a nationally known advocate for the sort of policies the New Deal promoted. In 1919 Ryan had sent America's Roman Catholic bishops a twelve-point recommendation on what to do to aid in the labor unrest and collapsing economy that plagued the country after World War I. When the bishops built the National Catholic Welfare Council from his ideas, Ryan became the director of its Social Action Program, and he became well known in the 1920s for his frequent speaking, writing, and lobbying on behalf of social reform. He wanted minimum wage laws, protection for labor unions, and a constitutional amendment to end child labor, and he butted heads with everyone from Supreme Court justices to William Cardinal O'Connell, archbishop of Boston, when they opposed his proposals.[7]

Ryan was usually glad to defend Roosevelt. He relished politics and believed that his faith gave him special insight into its principles. "The Catholic citizen is in a better position and is charged with a greater responsibility than the majority of his non-Catholic fellow citizens," he declared. "Obviously, the common good will be furthered in proportion as the laws of the state are in agreement with the principles of morality."[8] But Ryan's vision of democracy was not so wed to notions of individual autonomy as many Protestants assumed it should be. Nor did he find that it derived from the heritage of the German tribes or the Reformation. Instead, in his oft-reprinted book *A Living Wage*, Ryan offered a different model for an ideal society, one drawn from *Rerum Novarum*, an encyclical on the economy issued by Pope Leo XIII in 1891. "The accepted principle of medieval society," Ryan wrote, "was that some kind of social organization was necessary in order to protect the standard of life of the workers." He praised medieval Europe for its "sense of solidarity, mutual dependence, and mutual responsibility," and claimed that "this attitude . . . was the result of Christian conceptions of fair dealing, and of the widespread influence of the Christian church."[9] Ryan dwelt unashamed in the world of the Middle Ages, frequently praising it for the economic strictures imposed by the church and the guild systems, which, he claimed, ensured a fairer economy than existed in Depression-era America. "In the middle ages the doctrine of just price prevented unlimited profits," Ryan claimed. "Since the industrial revolution the doctrine that a free exchange is always a fair exchange has taken the place of the doctrine of just price."[10]

Ryan's steady gaze to the Middle Ages is significant for three reasons. First, it showed Catholic rejection of white liberal Protestants' theory of civilization, which linked democracy and progress to the rise of Protestantism. Ryan blamed the Reformation for the "grasping" force of contemporary individualism and saw in medieval Europe a more stable society. Second, Ryan looked to the Middle Ages because he saw there proof that the social principles taught by Roman Catholicism were equally applicable in all times and all places, and just as relevant in the years of the Depression as it had been six hundred years before. Following his description of the Middle Ages in *A Living Wage,* he claimed that from that era down to the year 1891 (the year Pope Leo XIII issued the encyclical *Rerum Novarum,* which presaged many of the ideas in *Quadragesimo Anno*), the "doctrine on the ethics of wages seems to have undergone no important development."[11] In this passage Ryan simultaneously rejected a progressive notion of civilization, which held that events like the Reformation propelled forward individual liberty, and advocated for the universal applicability of the principles he saw in the Middle Ages.

Catholics like Ryan believed that American democracy was an outstanding example of the universal applicability of Catholic principles. In the nineteenth and early twentieth centuries, many Catholics showed a renewed interest in medieval Catholic thought, particularly that of St. Thomas Aquinas, whom Leo XIII had admired. Ryan and other Catholics drew on Thomas's ideas to argue that all humans possessed natural rights. Many, including Ryan, accepted a theory that the framers of the American Constitution had drawn on the ideas of Robert Bellarmine, a sixteenth-century expert on Aquinas who argued Aquinas's thought impelled governments to preserve those rights. For American Catholics, the link to American constitutional government was obvious. As Peter Guilday, a prominent Catholic historian, put it in 1926, "The heart of the Middle Ages was the Catholic church; and it was from the heart of the Middle Ages that America was born." Ryan himself declared that Bellarmine's influence on democracy was "accepted and defended by the great majority" of Catholics, and he edited a volume that asserted, "There is every reason to believe that Madison and Wilson, at least, were acquainted" with Bellarmine's writings.[12]

Finally, Ryan's fondness for the Middle Ages meant that he emphasized that democracy's worth derived not from its exaltation of individual liberty, but from its ability to promote the values of order and justice. According to John Rager, who received a PhD from Catholic University in 1926 for a dissertation on Bellarmine's influence on democracy, Bellarmine believed that "the best type of government is that which best serves the greatest number of men; which distributes the opportunities and goods of this earth as justly and equitably as the varying needs and capacities of men dictate."[13] For Ryan as for Bellarmine, democracy was the best form of government because it promoted order, the common good, and shared values, virtues he ascribed to medieval Europe and prized as the product of Catholic teaching. "The only important limitation is that the polity must be conducive to the general welfare," Ryan said, and in that requirement rested multitudes.[14] Democracy for Ryan was achieved when "the individual develops his faculties, gives glory to God and reaches his true dignity and nobility."[15] But these goals might be accomplished in a number of ways.

For instance, Ryan did not believe that voting rights were essential to a democratic society. As a practical matter, he held that "the welfare of the weaker and poorer classes . . . requires that all adults should have the power to vote," but he did not think that voting was inherently a moral right in the same way that a living wage was.[16] Instead Ryan argued for a society organized according to what he called "organic" principles. "The Catholic conception of society is organic, implying a hierarchical order of social functions, subordination of the whole to God and public authority derived from and representing the authority of God," he said. "Any society which does not hold to this conception mistakes its nature and function and cannot adequately promote Christian welfare."[17] A democratic society for Ryan was devoted to the well-being of the individual, achieved through the healthy interaction of a variety of groups.

These convictions made him an advocate for a stronger regulatory state but also sometimes an awkward interlocutor with Protestants who believed quite differently. In 1943, Ryan was invited to speak at Howard University. There he offered a Catholic interpretation of what racial equality in democracy would look like. "Of all the discriminations against the Negro those in the economic field are the most important and fundamental," he insisted, because they violated the natural rights all humans possessed.[18] Ryan also made a measured case against Jim Crow. By the time of the speech Ryan had been a member of the NAACP for years, and he consistently denounced segregation.[19] At Howard he said the "fundamental principle" of democracy should be that "the human being . . . has intrinsic worth." Given that axiom, in Jim Crow laws "the human dignity of the Negro is outraged." Ryan listed examples case by case: "The exclusion of Negroes from restaurants and other eating places" was "unreasonable." The "exclusion of Negroes from institutions of higher education has no rational justification." And on and on, from segregation in the military to hiring practices. Ryan's holistic understanding of the nature of democracy led him to insist that human equality extended across a wide range of social activity. But, after all this, he stated he did not believe it imperative that African Americans have access to the ballot, because he understood democracy to be achieved in the protection of the general welfare, not in the protection of equal access to the ballot. "The only moral right possessed by the citizen in the political field is the right to have a government that promotes the common good," he said. "This end can be attained without moral suffrage."[20]

The Protestant academics at Howard, accustomed to associating true Christianity and repudiation of racism with those individual rights Ryan seemed to neglect, were somewhat puzzled by Ryan's position. It seemed to them insufficient and incomplete, misunderstanding what they took Christian teaching to be. The *Baltimore Afro-American* noted, "Ryan provoked a controversy among his hearers, some of whom thought he did not go far enough in urging an all-out attack on intolerance."[21] One member of the audience later wrote a letter to Ryan addressing the definition of "interracial democracy," arguing that a truly democratic society required equal access to the ballot.[22] But Ryan did not see it that way.

The tepid response Ryan drew at Howard illustrated one aspect of the difficulty in persuading Protestants of any sort to subscribe to his vision of democracy. Another was evident in his critique of capitalism. "Individualism has destroyed the organic character of society by abolishing the great variety of institutions and associations which once stood between the state and the individual," he complained.[23] The austere product of a working-class Minnesota Irish family, Ryan was generally hostile to the American consumer economy, blasting the "individualistic, irresponsible conception of private property" in the United States and the "artifice and vulgarity" fostered by too much luxury and leisure.[24] He believed that capitalism warped humanity's character by separating individuals from human relationships that fostered morality. Francis Haas, Ryan's colleague at the Catholic University of America, offered an anecdote to demonstrate how. A businessman "will visit an old employee who is ill in a hospital," Haas said. "But he will not scruple to order the speeding up of his machines in a distant city, though the result may be a score of accidents."[25] For Catholic leaders, materialism fostered both industrial capitalism and communism, both of which neglected human rights in favor of mechanical efficiency. "In the socialist conception society is atomistic, individualistic, mechanistic, and organized merely for the abundant production of material goods," Ryan explained. "Communist doctrines . . . uphold materialistic evolution, which deny natural right to human personality."[26]

Ryan refused to compromise his vision of the purpose of a democratic society. He held to language which many Americans would have found jarring. For instance, Pope Leo XIII's encyclical *Rerum Novarum* attacked the abuses that industrial capitalism inflicted upon the laboring classes, but it also argued that states should accept the pope's moral leadership as they organized their economy. Ryan was too much the intellectual and loyal Catholic to soft pedal the nuances of the encyclical's doctrine. He maintained that even in a democratic government, "The people have not the moral right to do what they please with their governing authority. They have only the right to do that which is morally lawful."[27] This was further than most American Protestants were willing to go, and it is unsurprising that Ryan's interlocutors tended to accuse him of hostility toward democracy according to definitions that privileged Protestant ideas about individual autonomy. As one correspondent of Ryan's complained, "You prefer communism in preference to Christianity."[28]

Ryan was not completely happy with the New Deal. At times he confessed that he wished for it to go further, worrying that its half measures would cost more than a thoroughgoing social transformation. "The main difference," he explained, between the New Deal and his interpretation of Catholic economic teaching was that "the Pope's program was the more radical and realistic of the two."[29] Ryan was known more for his moral confidence than for his soft-spoken or gentle personality, and he bristled when the president was attacked. He was particularly horrified when the antagonist in question turned out to be one of his own. Roosevelt, as an advocate for the urban working class of immigrants and their children, enjoyed great popularity among America's Catholics. But some of his most vocal opponents were also of the faith. Moreover, they invoked the same ideas Ryan drew upon to assail him. The arguments that American Catholics had about the Roosevelt administration demonstrated the diverse ways those ideas could be applied.

Charles A. Coughlin and Catholicism as "Christianity"

One reason Roosevelt often asked Ryan to speak on his behalf was the growing threat he perceived from the fame and hostility of Charles A. Coughlin. Coughlin was also a Catholic priest, and he was far more famous than even the prominent Ryan. A radio program he started in the late 1920s propelled him to the front ranks of American celebrity, and his popularity only grew as the show transitioned from its original focus on homily and devotion to politics as the Depression worsened. Coughlin quickly became known for histrionics and lack of nuance, but in 1932 Ryan stood shoulder to shoulder with him in support of Roosevelt's campaign. After Roosevelt's victory Ryan said, "As between those who are fighting for social justice and those who are fighting against it Father Coughlin is on the side of the angels."[30]

Before long, Coughlin was claiming thirty million listeners and reportedly receiving more mail than Roosevelt himself. He constantly forwarded advice to the White House and asked the president to give his blessing to his pet political causes, like abolishing the Federal Reserve. Roosevelt normally declined. Frustrated, Coughlin invited his hearers to join his National Union for Social Justice, an organization which served mostly as a mailing list and donation mill, but which also avowed Catholic ideas about the common good. It preferred "the sanctity of human rights to the sanctity of property rights" and insisted that every citizen should "receive a just and living wage." The group proved to be a powerful lobbying tool.[31]

On January 27, 1935, Coughlin's Sunday night broadcast lacerated the World Court, an international organization Roosevelt had proposed joining. Roosevelt was blindsided. The January broadcast came only two days before the Senate voted on the World Court treaty, and the radio priest insisted that the treaty would de-Christianize, and hence de-democratize, the United States. It would place power "in the hands of the international bankers," Coughlin warned, reeling off a list of Jewish names. "The Rothchilds [sic] and Lazerre Freres [sic] . . . the Warbergs and Morgans and Kuhn Loebs."[32] "We were and are ardent believers in democracy, in Christianity," he said, "but now we are asked to entrust our religious and political destinies with the communistic atheism of Moscow, with the dictatorships of Germany and Italy."[33] Ryan appeared on air the next night and insisted that to the contrary the court promoted Christian politics. "The person who says 'I am not my brother's keeper' is no worse than the person who says, 'We have nothing to do with the good or evil fortunes of the rest of the world,'" Ryan declared. "That is not Christianity, that is not the law of love."[34]

By any measure of the national response, Ryan lost the debate decisively. The Senate was flooded with letters and telegrams denouncing the treaty, and the measure failed by seven votes. Emboldened, Coughlin began further contrasting the New Deal and what he called Christianity. By 1936, he had turned entirely on the president, and he could be crass about it. In July of that year, he stood before a screaming crowd of thousands in a Cleveland, Ohio, stadium and stripped his clerical collar from his sweaty neck as he castigated "the great betrayer and liar, Franklin D. Roosevelt, he who promised to drive the moneychangers from the temple and succeeded in driving the farmers from their homesteads."[35] He announced that the National Union for Social Justice would form its own political party, the Union Party, which would endorse William Lemke, a congressman from North Dakota, for president. With typical theatricality, Coughlin promised he would leave the air if Lemke garnered fewer than nine million votes.

Even at their most demagogic, Coughlin's jeremiads had ideas behind them. He claimed inspiration from the same papal encyclicals as did Ryan. His denunciations of the World Court showed that he believed democracy dependent upon Christianity. He claimed that the New Deal was materialist, because it "lacked that divine spark known to human children of the Lord," as he told his audience in Cleveland.[36] The communist dictatorships and Jewish bankers he lambasted had neglected Christianity and to his mind were thus given to autocracy. It is common to dismiss Coughlin as an ignorant demagogue and his critique of Roosevelt as the product of personal pique against a president who seemed to want little to do with him. But however shallow his grasp of economics and theology—and Ryan made sure its tenuousness was well publicized—Coughlin shared with his fellow priest the conviction that economic inequity was the product of an inhumane materialism, and thus violated particularly Catholic ideas about democracy.

A month before the presidential election of 1936, at the request of the president, Ryan gamely renewed the priestly feud and denounced Coughlin on the air. He defended the policies of the New Deal as "no stronger than the demands of Pope Pius for a more just distribution of wealth and a comprehensive organization of all the economic classes."[37] To drive the point home, Ryan then rather stuffily listed his credentials. "It is more than thirty years since I published my first book," he observed. "At that time, Father

Coughlin had not yet entered college." It seemed to the professor that the very reason why Coughlin's Catholicism was so popular was that it over-simplified Catholic ideas to the point of incoherence. Ryan could not help engaging in pedantry, noting that he had "written at least half a dozen other books on economics, labor and the ethical aspects of our industrial system," while "Father Coughlin's monetary theories and proposals find no support in the encyclicals of either Pope Leo XIII or Pope Pius XI. I think I know something of those encyclicals myself."[38]

The laboriousness of Ryan's footnotes and tendentious invocation of his education played right into Coughlin's hands. The rhetorical battle between the two was, in essence, an argument over which man's version of Catholic social teaching Americans could legitimately embrace. Despite Ryan's at-tempts to draw a stark distinction between their respective ideologies, they shared in the broad strokes a diagnosis of the problem with American life. The two had a common disdain for the social order capitalism fostered. Coughlin followed the liberal Protestant tendency to downplay particulari-ties of doctrine, and instead worked to form a Catholicism compatible with a broad Christian rhetoric that emphasized virtues Catholics might partic-ularly embrace but Protestants also found appealing, like morality, justice, and equality. Like Columbia University's Contemporary Civilization course, he told a story about the origins of democracy, and like Ryan he re-jected a narrative that equated Protestantism with progress.

However, his story was not the same as Ryan's. Coughlin understood that the Middle Ages seemed esoteric and inaccessible to his American au-dience. Instead he invoked for his listeners an ideal society that he said was described in the pages of the New Testament, a primitive Christian world that existed according to God's perfect design and stood in stark dichotomy to a contemporary world destroyed by capitalism. Like other primitivists, he called to his listeners to return with him to that idealized ancient age of the New Testament, escaping the broken present. "What has gone wrong with this world of ours?" he wondered aloud on his radio broadcast.[39] More, Coughlin's primitivism allowed him to avoid the challenge of sectarianism, sidestepping theology to appeal to the social structures of the primitive church.

This rhetorical strategy had multiple benefits. Though Coughlin's inter-pretation of the Bible reflected the Catholic prism through which he read it, he rarely invoked the popes (though when he did so, he did it with pride). Rather, it was far more common for him to assert that his reading of the

Bible was simply "Christian," which in turn he equated with "American," claiming community with both Protestant and Catholic listeners, even when his assertions reflected the clear influence of papal encyclicals. "That a man must starve because no one will hire him," he fumed, "that is not American and that is not Christian." Instead, he called for an "America for Americans living under the standard of Christ's principles, where a fair, a just and an equitable wage shall be extended to every man."[40] Though this was no more than Ryan's own argument about the natural right to the living wage, Coughlin spoke as though these principles were self-evident in the New Testament, shearing the ideas from their Thomistic and papal roots and clothing Catholic critiques of modern economic problems in a simple language of scripture that Protestants as well as Catholics could embrace. In one 1932 speech he claimed that poverty was "a condition which is opposed to the tenets of the Christian religion," and that "there can be no other prosperity except that based upon Christian principles which are traceable to the first law of life."[41] He discarded Ryan's nuanced theologizing in favor of the simple authority of the word *Christian*.

Coughlin's followers responded. Many saw him as being more of a Christian than a Catholic. Susie Kaufman invoked as proof of Coughlin's claims that Coughlin appealed to "protestant, catholic, jew, black, or white." Coughlin's listeners like Kaufman saw Ryan as too Catholic, too committed to esoteric dogmatism, too loyal to institution. Elizabeth Seymour informed Ryan that she had tried to read Ryan's books, but "they are cumbersome and not easily understood." This, unfortunately, was true. Many of Ryan's correspondents assumed that the dogmatic opacity of his writing reflected a cold and arrogant soul, which they equated with institutional Catholicism. "We have always wanted to take a squint at one of these proud, original thinkers," Ambrose Tenure wrote to Ryan, his pen dripping with sarcasm. "You have little regard for the truth," Tenure continued, marveling at the "over-inflated Ego of your dimensions."[42] To many of Ryan's correspondents— Catholic or not—the Church was as much a symbol of the power of wealth and institutionalism as any business, and Ryan's loyalty hence reflected hypocrisy rather than democracy. "You no doubt have accumulated a small fortune of your own and you are afraid you will have to part with a few nickles [*sic*]," Mrs. Frank Lamphear wrote to Ryan.[43] For Coughlin's followers, the Christian democracy invoked by the radio priest was by its nature free from large and threatening institutions and instead committed to individual liberty.

Neither Coughlin nor his followers defined the presumably pure Christianity Coughlin preached as a variety of Roman Catholicism, despite its links to papal encyclicals. Sometimes Coughlin's listeners barely saw Coughlin as Catholic at all. They credited him with Christianity because they associated Christianity with a practical concern for the suffering and the poor. A man who identified himself only as "Jim" informed Ryan that Coughlin was like Jesus because he was a "rabble-rouser" on behalf of the people against the powerful, and mused, "I would like to see Coughlin leave the priesthood." Marguerite Frost told Ryan that Coughlin alone "knows the pulse of the poor people, 'God's people.' He has gone down in the mines and out in the factories, worked with the people in overalls and been one of them."[44] To his listeners, Coughlin's Christianity derived from their belief that he grasped their lived economic experiences.

Ryan believed that democracy required that all receive sufficient support—a living wage—which would occur naturally when the economy was sufficiently organized. But to Coughlin, Catholic teaching instructed that democracy required a wide distribution of wealth and financial independence for all. These two aims were not necessarily incompatible, but the difference led Coughlin to a very different vision of the problems with American democracy than Ryan believed was logical. Coughlin issued a warning. "Either the industrialists will reform themselves immediately or the aroused democracy of our people will accomplish this reform in no uncertain manner," he declared in the cold February of 1934. The vague threat was no mistake. If Ryan's call for democracy was abstract and philosophical, Coughlin's was conspiratorial and populist. A pure Catholic democracy had not been achieved because of the connivance of selfish capitalists and financiers who did not want it to be achieved. Coughlin believed that the poor around the world suffered at the hands of a shadowy, powerful, un-Christian class not so different from the atheists Americans had presumed dominated Germany during World War I. Industrialists cared for "first, mass-productionism and secondly, gold controlled capitalism," he said. None "cared directly for the social, the spiritual, or the intellectual developments of democracy." Both Coughlin and Ryan associated capitalism with materialism, but while Ryan condemned the system, Coughlin's conspiratorialism led him to condemn particular individuals—chief among them, Franklin Roosevelt.[45]

Coughlin's decline in popularity in the late 1930s is usually credited at least partially to an anti-Semitic bent in his rhetoric that emerged in those years. While it is true that his language became particularly heated after

1936, his suspicion that Jews had orchestrated the rise of capitalism and the destruction of democracy was present in his thought from the beginning. To Coughlin, Jews served the same function as did the Catholic church for many of Ryan's correspondents: a distant un-Christian power unconcerned with natural rights and committed instead to materialism. Indeed, in a peculiar way anti-Semitism derived from the same impulses that made Coughlin far more popular among average Americans than Ryan, and extended his popularity to Protestants. It spoke to their fear of authoritarian control and their association of economic and political autonomy with Christianity. "The Rothschilds re-established in modern capitalist times the pagan principle of charging interest on non-productive, or destructive debt," Coughlin announced in 1933. In the act the great Jewish banking family was "clinging to the Egyptian heresy," and "mocking the doctrines of the Talmud and the precepts of the Old Testament."[46] The equation of the banking industry with paganism and tyranny balanced Coughlin's equation of economic justice with Christianity and democracy, and made the links he hoped to construct all the more real for his followers.

The struggle between the two priests bore mixed results. Ryan spent the decade rising in eminence within Roman Catholicism. On December 8, 1933, the feast day of the Immaculate Conception, he was invested as a monsignor at the Shrine of the Immaculate Conception in Washington, DC. "Monsignor" was an honorific title held alternately by high-ranking Catholic clergy or by those who had earned the special favor of the Vatican. In Ryan's case, it was the latter. At the event, Frances Perkins, the secretary of labor, praised Ryan for his service to the administration. Seven years later, at Ryan's seventieth birthday party, the accolades were repeated.[47] Coughlin, on the other hand, clearly earned the enmity of Catholic leadership. His own bishop, Michael Gallagher, had supported and defended him, but after his Cleveland speech there were reports that the Vatican had rebuked him for his harsh language about Roosevelt. On July 23, 1936, a week after the speech, he issued a public letter apologizing for his intemperate language, which he said was used "in the heat of civic interest and in righteous anger."[48] In keeping with a promise, when his chosen presidential candidate William Lemke won fewer than a million votes, Coughlin departed the airwaves for several months. Though he would return, his audience slowly faded.

But the story was not so simple as a Ryan triumph. During the heated years of 1935 and 1936, the Catholic press split between the two. The *Baltimore*

Catholic Review shook its head at the "two political priests" who, the paper advised, would both do well to "retire for some time to the Carthusian order where perpetual silence is observed." The *Review* spurned the sort of political agitation that both Ryan and Coughlin believed was dictated by their faith. Rather, the paper pointed out, "There are 30,000 Catholic priests in the United States. Of that number 29,998 are attending to their business, which is that of their heavenly Father." Finally the paper sniffed, "Sensible Americans never had any use for political parsons."[49] Though the complaint came from a Catholic paper, it reflected a sentiment that consistently dogged both priests as they sought to actualize their visions of a more robust American democracy. Just as Coughlin's followers consistently accused Ryan of more loyalty to the wealth and power of the Catholic church than to American democracy, so did Coughlin's critics blast him for stepping out of the place of a priest. The Catholic J. S. Nelson sighed that "Father Coughlin has been most unfair to the president," but Nelson sought to press Ryan out of politics as well. "One of the things that appealed to me in the Catholic Church was its strict adherence to its Divine Mission to preach the Gospel and teach that our Kingdom was not of this world. I fear now that I have been wrong or else you have departed from your Divine Mission."[50]

Nelson's fears about Roman Catholicism illustrate why Ryan would always remain half-satisfied with the New Deal, and partly why Coughlin's movement proved ephemeral. For many Americans, ideas about the relation between Christianity and democracy that emphasized autonomy and freedom from institutions outweighed Catholic calls for a more substantial democratic system. This did not mean, though, that Catholics ceased making their case. Other Catholics continued to promote ideas similar to those of Ryan and Coughlin while avoiding the bumptious world of partisan politics. Ryan and Coughlin had tried to change government in America. Other Catholic movements that outlasted both men presented two alternatives. Dorothy Day's Catholic Worker movement simply bypassed electioneering and the administration of American democracy entirely. On the other hand, the Catholic Citizenship movement offered a form of Catholic democracy less radical than that of either Coughlin or Ryan, one that sought not to change the deeply Protestant notions about the centrality of individualism and capitalism to democracy, but to find ways that Catholicism might nestle within them.

Dorothy Day and the Mandate of Personalism

One year to the day before John Ryan entered the Shrine of the Immaculate Conception for his investiture as a monsignor, Dorothy Day knelt there in prayer. She felt the same schism within herself that Ryan and Coughlin had identified in the nation at large. On the face of it, Dorothy Day stood as far from Coughlin as it was possible for an American Catholic to stand. The priest was grandiloquent and dramatic, glorying in the waves of applause and adoration that followed his public appearances. Day shared with Ryan an intense austerity, a preternatural single-mindedness and a disdain for fame beyond what she believed would communicate her message. In counterpoint to Coughlin's National Union for Social Justice, devoted to propagating the priest's fame and influence, she and a friend named Peter Maurin founded the Catholic Workers, a near-monastic organization whose members devoted their time and energy to caring for the poor. Day seems on the face of it eminently more respectable than the bombastic Coughlin, and yet in many ways her fears mirrored his. She shared with Ryan a distrust of materialism and a certainty that capitalism was destroying American democracy. And yet, like Coughlin, she dissented from Ryan's conviction that the New Deal was the right path toward a just society.

In December 1932 she was in Washington, DC, to cover the Hunger March, yet another Depression-era rally of hundreds of homeless and jobless Americans demanding action on their behalf. Day sympathized with them; for much of her life as a journalist, she had worked for the rights of the poor. But the Hunger March was organized by Communists, and five years earlier she had been baptized a Catholic. "I stood on the curb and watched them, joy and pride in the courage of this band of men and women mounting in my heart," Day wrote, "and with a bitterness too that since I was now a Catholic with fundamental philosophical differences I could not be out there with them."[51]

Charles Coughlin's hunger for the spotlight drove him toward electoral politics, while John Ryan's reading of the papal encyclicals convinced him that the state was an essential tool for the reordering of society. But Day felt instinctively that this was not the case; the Catholic democracy she wanted would not be gained through administrative reform. After the march she went to the shrine to pray. When she returned to New York City from Washington, she found Maurin, a wandering French philosopher in a rumpled suit, waiting at her door. He confirmed to her that her suspicions were right. He recited a poem to her:

> People go to Washington
> asking the Federal Government
> to solve their economic problems,
> while the Federal Government
> was never intended
> to solve men's economic problems[52]

Maurin could recite by heart portions of the papal encyclicals Ryan so treasured, but he insisted to Day that the path to that society was not political reform. Rather it was what he called "personalism." Personalism was distinct from individualism. It had become popular among European Catholics in the 1930s and 1940s because it enunciated a middle way between communism and the corporatism that Pius XI believed lay behind fascism. For Catholics, personalism was a tool to denounce "stateolatry" and protect the sanctity of the individual in the organic community of the church. Personalism thus taught that the ultimate worth of the human personality derived through humanity's relationship to the divine, positing that the starting point for any conversation about society, politics, or knowledge generally should be the experience and dignity of actual people.[53] It affirmed liberty but rooted it in communities like the Church rather than in individual autonomy; it was usually invoked in Europe to denounce overweening government and defend other communities. Maurin's interpretation of personalism centered upon the notion that large-scale social change came through the embrace of personalist ideals, not law or legislation.[54]

Day articulated this idea later, when she wrote about Maurin that before meeting him she "had emphasized wages and hours while he was trying to talk about a philosophy of work."[55] Together they founded the *Catholic Worker* newspaper, first published in 1933, and the Catholic Worker organization. In the October 1933 issue of the *Catholic Worker*, Maurin published another poem:

> Although you may be called
> bums and panhandlers
> you are in fact
> the ambassadors of God.
> As God's ambassadors

you should be given
food, clothing and shelter
by those who are able to give it.[56]

The poem encapsulated the differences between the Catholic Worker movement and what Ryan and Coughlin were trying to accomplish. Both men cared deeply about wages and hours, sweatshops and strikes, and both focused on achieving reform through regulation and legislation. Indeed, it was to such an end that Ryan endorsed democracy; it was the mode of social organization that bestallowed individuals to register their needs and resolve complaints, and it did so through politics. The Catholic Worker movement shared Ryan's indictment of oppressive systems. "We oppose the 'finance capitalism' of the American industrial system because it is truly materialistic and hence atheistic," Day wrote, restating the aims of the Catholic Worker organization on its third birthday.[57] But Day also drew a distinction between her personalism and reform politics. "We do not believe that legislation is going to bring us out of the morass we are floundering in," she observed.[58] It was less that Day distrusted Roosevelt's programs in particular than it was that she distrusted state action in general. To be sure, she consistently called for more efforts to aid the poor, including government benefits. "We do not deny that the State is bound for the sake of the common good, to take care of the unemployed and the unemployable," she wrote.[59] And yet she was fundamentally wary of the New Deal.

In December 1933, Maurin and Day had begun talking about "Houses of Hospitality," places to sleep for the indigent and needy. That month, Day recalled, a young woman knocked on Day's door and asked for a place to sleep. Day had no place, but paused, took the girl in, and later she and Maurin rented "an apartment which will house ten homeless women." It was to be called "the Teresa-Joseph Co-operative," for "St. Teresa because she was forced to find shelter for her nuns," and St. Joseph because he "had to provide both house and food for the blessed Virgin and Child." They moved the young woman in that night and began taking in others.[60] The experience taught Day an important point. "It is no use turning people away to an agency," she insisted. "It is you yourself who must perform the works of mercy. Often you can only give the price of a meal, or a bed . . . but we must act *personally*, at a *personal* sacrifice." Only, that, Day insisted, could "combat the growing tendency to let the State take the job which Our Lord Himself gave us to do."[61]

Her insistence on personal contact, personal sacrifice, and personal change illustrates how she believed democracy should work. From her study of Maurin's personalism, Day came to emphasize with spiritual zeal the concept of the Body of Christ, a mystical union of all humanity in Jesus through his atonement for the sins of the world. "We cannot live alone. We cannot go to heaven alone," she wrote. "This teaching, the doctrine of the Mystical Body of Christ," touched everything she did. It framed how she understood "the racial question; it involves cooperatives, credit unions, crafts; it involves Houses of Hospitality and Farming Communes." That was why personality was so important to her; she believed that it was critical every time a Catholic Worker gave aid to another that they did so "to see Christ in him. If we lose faith, if we stop the work of indoctrinating, we are in a way denying Christ again."[62]

This vision of humanity as the Body of Christ drew Day away from calls for secular reform. Growing demands to turn over care for the poor to an institution led her to fear that the state itself inevitably tended toward materialism, drowning individual personality in regulation and institution. In the *Catholic Worker* Day offered a grim warning that the New Deal might lead to eugenics. Since the Public Works Administration "has failed to make any appreciable dent in the number on government doles, the next step seems to be that such 'social undesirables' at least don't reproduce their kind."[63] Ten years later she mourned the existence of the Social Security Act. "We believe that social security legislation, now hailed as a great victory for the poor and for the worker, is a great defeat for Christianity," she wrote, because of what it revealed about American society. "Since the employer can never be trusted to give a family wage, nor take care of the worker as he takes care of his machine when it is idle, the state must enter in and compel help."[64]

Like Ryan's, Day's notion of democracy expanded beyond the administration of the state; unlike Ryan's, her notion of democracy, if ideally implemented, had little to do with government but rather with a way of living. In July 1940, she was called before Congress to testify on her opposition to the Selective Service Act, then being debated. "Democracy, in American parlance, does not signify a form of government," she said. "It means a conception or philosophy of government founded in respect for the free will of the human individual. This God Himself respects, and it is not for any government to trample upon it."[65] Democracy meant an activist people, not an activist government.

Such a position led the Catholic Workers to reject association with the American state. During World War II, Day wrote, "In the present war we stand unalterably opposed to war as a means of saving 'Christianity,' 'civilization,' 'democracy.' We do not believe that they can be saved by these means."[66] Rather, she claimed, the existence of war itself was the product of a failure of true democracy. "People have come to accept the idea that we are a nation of industrial slaves, creatures of the State which doles out relief and jobs, and which is now going to seize the young and the strong for defense. We have lost our democracy because we have lost our faith in men," she claimed.[67] The American nation, dominated by an industrial economy and a powerful bureaucratic state, was collectively incapable of moral change; only individual contact could promote the sort of humanistic values personalism taught. The increasingly nationalized American state was, to Day, a threat to a Christian democracy.

The Commission on American Citizenship and the Task of Reconciliation

As the Depression gave way to a world war, however, many other Catholics began to rally around the American state. Day's mystical personalism was part of a 1930s Catholic cultural revival which saw an explosion of Catholic movements, philosophy, and art, everything from the Friendship House movement, which promoted racial justice, to the Catholic Educational Association.[68] All these undertakings sought to create a stronger sense of Catholic identity in the United States. Some like Day concluded that their faith and America's liberal Protestant public piety were incompatible. Many others, however, were coming to see that the things they found threatening—materialism, atomism, atheism—were manifest in the dictatorships of Europe, and by comparison American democracy came to seem increasingly appealing.

In 1931, in the depths of the Depression, Pope Pius XI had issued *Quadragesimo Anno,* but the intervening years changed the cause of his worry. In 1938 he sent an official greeting to Catholic University commemorating the school's fiftieth anniversary and sounding a warning about the rise of totalitarianism. "From the watch tower of the Vatican the Holy Father during his Pontificate had seen the spread of powerful forces trampling down private morality and civil well-being," reported a Catholic University committee, explaining their directive. In consequence, Pius asked the university to generate "a constructive program of social action" that "must, because of the exigencies of the present age, give special attention to the sciences of civics, sociology, and economics."[69]

The leaders of Catholic University seized upon the opportunity, seeing in it a way to reconcile American democracy and Roman Catholicism once and for all. Dennis Dougherty, the archbishop of Philadelphia, writing on behalf of the American bishops in council, declared that the pope's message was a mandate directing Catholics to be "ever better instructed in the true nature of Christian democracy. A precise definition must be given both of democracy in the light of Catholic truth and teaching and of the rights and duties of citizens." While Ryan, Coughlin, and particularly Day believed that Catholic visions of democracy impelled a critique of the American system, Dougherty left no doubt that he disagreed. "They must be held to the conviction that love of country is a virtue and that disloyalty is a sin," he wrote.[70]

Under such inspiration, Joseph Corrigan, rector of the Catholic University of America, created a Commission on American Citizenship. Corrigan and many of his fellows at CUA were part of a long-standing "Americanist" movement in American Catholicism that believed that democracy as practiced in the United States and Catholic teaching could ultimately be reconciled. Motivated by Pius's warning, the commission sought a way to reconcile the nagging disjunctures between the powerful Protestant narrative of individualist democracy and the vision of collective society Catholics spent so much energy describing. As Corrigan put it, the mandate of the commission was twofold. First, "to reaffirm the traditional allegiance of the Catholic Church in the United States to free American institutions," and second, to train Catholics to "become citizens who will exercise the responsibilities as well as the rights of their freedoms."[71] The program executed by the commission sought to blend American individualist democracy with the Catholic worldview John Ryan and Dorothy Day struggled to actualize.

A number of other Catholics were engaged in a similar project at the same time. Jacques Maritain, a French academic and Catholic convert who reached North America in 1933, delivered a series of lectures and taught courses at the Pontifical Institute of Medieval Studies, in Toronto. Throughout the 1930s and 1940s, he toured Columbia, Princeton, and the University of Chicago, cultivating the ideas behind two important books, *Christianity and Democracy* (1944) and *The Rights of Man and Natural Law* (1943). As early as

1934, *Commonweal* pointed out wryly, "Maritain, Maritain—We are beginning to be beset by his name."[72] John Ryan attended some of Maritain's talks and carefully preserved his copy of a Boston address titled "The Reconciliation of the Gospel and Democracy." Therein, Maritain claimed, "Democracy is grounded on the idea of the rights of man and the pursuit of happiness," which he called "the human values of which the gospel has made us aware." For Maritain, most modern democracies were "trapped by commitment to economic liberalism," which led them to neglect human values in favor of a market economy. Thus, "the tragedy of the modern democracies is that they have not yet succeeded in bringing about democracy" in the fullest sense of the word.[73] For Ryan, this meant that American society would have to change the way it thought about democracy. For other Catholics, it offered a path to reconciliation.

Two members of the Catholic University faculty—the education professor George Johnson, who served as director of the Commission on American Citizenship, and Ryan's friend Francis Haas, who chaired the organization—recruited Mary Synon and Mary Joan Smith to produce an educational program designed to teach Catholic children about American citizenship. Synon was a lay doctoral student (who soon earned a PhD in education), and Smith was a Dominican sister.[74] Between them the pair wrote several textbooks and directed the publication of many more, including the Faith and Freedom series of basal readers, which mixed fiction and instruction in narratives set in Catholic communities throughout the world. Books for younger children bore titles like *This Is Our Family* and *This Is Our Town;* more advanced children read *This Is Our Heritage,* which provided a sweeping account of Catholic history, and *These Are Our Freedoms,* a survey of American political history. All the books featured stories of fictional Catholic children approximately the same age as the presumed readers, mixed with hymnody, discussion questions, and texts from scripture and other Catholic authorities.[75]

The books drew on the same theory of education that John Dewey had promoted and that was evident in the New History of James Harvey Robinson and in the Contemporary Civilization course at Columbia. Rather than abstract theory or doctrinal principle, lessons were grounded in practical application and situations readers would find relatable. In the words of two of their authors, the purpose of the teachings was to present "a body of truth which tends to create in the mind of the child certain fundamental understandings, which lead to an attitude of determined desire to bring his conduct into conformity with Christian ideals."[76] The textbooks were premised on the notion that right Christianity was fundamentally pointed toward good behavior—a principle strikingly similar to that of liberal Protestant theories of citizenship. As George Albert Coe, the leading Protestant theorist of religious education in the early twentieth century, claimed, "The interest of socialized religious education in the public schools is not that they should teach religion in addition to reading, writing, and arithmetic, but that they should teach democracy."[77]

Many Catholics sympathetic to the Americanist position agreed with Coe. *Americans All: A Student Handbook of the Catholic Civics Clubs,* issued under the auspices of the Commission on American Citizenship, put the issue succinctly, instructing students, "You wish to be a good citizen. How can you do this? . . . Christian social living means knowing that all human beings are children of God and putting this knowledge into practice."[78] Many associated with the commission agreed, emphasizing the personalist ideal of the value of the individual in relation to community. Soon before American entry into World War II, George Johnson warned that the effort required to defeat Nazi Germany would also change education in America. "There will be much emphasis on training, military training, industrial training, clerical training," he cautioned, which might dull the human moral impulse. Democracy, on the other hand, was "an ideal of government and association that will best serve the development of the noblest and finest in human beings."[79] A teacher's manual put out by the commission instructed educators that "fascism, Nazism and atheistic communism" endorsed "worship of the state and the correlative denial of the rights of the individual." The Catholic church bore therefore a great responsibility, for "only through Christian teaching can the sacredness of human personality be safeguarded [and] true democracy . . . maintained."[80]

The readers of the Faith and Freedom series soon numbered in the hundreds of thousands. The commission reported that between six and eight thousand Catholic schools all over the country adopted the texts.[81] Students who opened them discovered Johnson's blend of Catholic politics, religious education, and American electoral democracy. The subtlety of presentation varied, but the foundational ideas did not. Unlike the ideas put forth by Ryan or Day, the texts did not call for drastic transformation in American society. They warned against the abuses of capitalism but promised that these could be mended when individuals embraced moral behavior. They did not condemn individualism but urged Catholics to seek commitments to community within an individualist society. The books were designed to encourage students to consider the ways in which their Catholic faith supported a particular vision of American citizenship, which blended liberal Protestantism's emphasis on the sanctity of the individual with a Catholic insistence upon active participation in the life of the community. The books sought to illustrate this principle by describing the nature and history of Western civilization. Rather than disputing the triumphal Protestant narrative fostered by the Contemporary Civilization course, the volumes cunningly wove Roman Catholicism into the rise of the West, arguing that Catholicism was essential to the rise of democracy as Protestants understood it.[82]

The texts accomplished this feat in three ways. First, they emphasized that recognition of human equality Protestants celebrated actually derived from Catholic teachings. In *This Is Our Heritage,* Catholic children are present at significant events in the rise of Western democracy. A thirteenth-century English girl named Alice Garland witnessed Stephen Langton, the archbishop of Canterbury, inspire English leaders to adopt the Magna Charta. One day when the English countryside was afire with hostility to King John's taxes, Langton mounted the pulpit and preached that "God has given all of us dignity. He has given all of us rights. . . . No one, king or anyone else, can, in justice, take them from us."[83] In response to the archbishop's call, the nobles of England rose up to defend their rights. The king, bowing to the moral authority of the Church, acceded.

Second, the books emphasized that Roman Catholicism taught a sense of mutual obligation, which they placed at the center of the functioning of American democracy. *This Is Our Town,* intended for grade-school children, recounts the story of "Timber Town," a small community on a river. Most of the narrative is given over to Rose and Peter, two of Timber Town's children. When a flood swamps a nearby community, Peter aids Timber Town's priest as he ventures downriver to help. When Rose is taken to the nearby Twin City after Timber Town is flooded, she is lost and lonely until a group of Catholic girls recognize her as a student at St. Agnes's School. "Some of our friends go there to school," they say, welcoming her. When the flood is finally cleared, the local Catholic bishop praises the citizens. "You the people of Timber Town, have lived and worked together as true Christian citizens. . . . You have shown that you are all children of one same heavenly father," he tells them.[84]

American society as presented in these readers bears little resemblance to the oppressive economic system Ryan, Coughlin, and Day condemned.

Instead, the solution to capitalist abuses are respect for human worth and a commitment to mutual obligation. Indeed, when the flood devastates Timber Town, its merchants willingly pitch in supplies to aid the poor, and in a central narrative of *This Is Our Heritage,* a medieval merchant's young son, Angelo Ricci, praises his father for willingly setting his prices at levels the poor can afford.[85] The books demand no structural reform of the economy; rather, they call for individuals to practice moral business. They link economic suffering to the lack of the moral authority of Christianity. "Without the guidance of the Church," *This Is Our Heritage* warns, "in time the business of the great industrial nations of the world came to be run on an evil system. This system treated men like machines instead of like human beings." But again, Catholicism offered social reform. The church "took up the cause of the workingman," and organized unions. Popes issued encyclicals. Just Christian employers aided their poor, and, as the volume had it, the problem was solved.[86]

Finally, the texts credit the emergence of American democracy to these Catholic ideas. *This Is Our Land* focuses its study of colonial America on the colonists of Maryland, English Catholics who possessed "the fine Catholic spirit of culture and refinement," arguing that they "had practiced the social amenities of their faith so long that their use of virtue in their social relationships was second nature." The influence of Catholic education in America spread the notion that "inasmuch as every person possesses human dignity, everyone has a right to freedom consistent with the freedom of all others." The book also urges teachers to emphasize the influence of Catholic education on the spread of American democracy.[87] Similarly, another textbook condemns the French Revolution, during which the French government sought to eliminate the Catholic presence in national life, as "one of the most awful times of history," when "great numbers of men no longer measured their thoughts and words and deeds by the Rule of Jesus Christ."[88]

The books' willingness to emphasize that the communal ideas of Catholic theology provided a system of ethics for good citizenship in the United States allowed them to encourage students to recognize the importance of religious pluralism and to teach that a common commitment to virtue can lead to accommodation of doctrinal difference. Far from Ryan's insistence that only Catholic ideas could save the nation from the Depression, the "Faith and Freedom" series taught that Catholics and Protestants should seek mutual accommodation. "The city or town or village in which we live is not all Catholic. Only those people who are Catholic would wish to celebrate the feasts of the Church," instructs one. "Think of some of the guests you have in your home. Are you always polite to them?"[89] In a neat inversion, acceptance of non-Catholics marked the true awareness of Catholic teachings. In the textbooks, John Ryan's Catholic medievalism blend with the Christian republicanism of the American Protestant establishment, seeking to unite Catholic community with Protestant faith in individualism and democracy.

Some Catholic leaders during the Depression called for drastic transformations in American democracy, urging an abandonment of traditionally Protestant ideas about individual autonomy, laissez-faire capitalism, and the relationship between the individual and the state. But the Catholic University of America sought rather moderation, to find a form of Catholicism still true to basic Catholic ideas but which could also wholeheartedly embrace American democracy as it functioned. The success of the Commission on American Citizenship was that rapprochement, which in the postwar world allowed Catholics to participate in a broader American consensus that American democracy as it presently operated was true to the essence of the Christian faith.

CHAPTER FIVE

The Anxiety of Christian Anticommunism

BY 1948, when the journalist Whittaker Chambers testified before Congress that he had been part of a communist spy ring in the 1930s, he and his family had lived on a Maryland farm for seven years. Chambers eventually became famous for his testimony, telling Congress that during the Depression the state department official Alger Hiss had been part of a spy ring that had passed Chambers classified documents and microfilm. Chambers sent some of this material on to the Soviet Union, but he also hid some in the pumpkin patch on his farm, thinking he might someday abandon espionage and need proof of his activities. Meanwhile Chambers did very well as a correspondent at *Time,* becoming one of the magazine's most celebrated writers, but he insisted on teaching his children to bale the hay and weed the crops and milk the cows, rising with them early every morning to care for the farm animals. "Sometimes we fell asleep at the supper table from fatigue," he remembered. His reasons were partially religious. According to Chambers, he wanted his children to see "the wild geese flying overhead in fall, and to stand with him in the now celebrated pumpkin patch and watch the northern lights flicker." He wanted them to learn "reverence and awe," qualities he feared had "died out of the modern world and been replaced by man's monkeylike amazement at the cleverness of his own inventive brain."[1]

Soon after leaving communism, Chambers was baptized Episcopalian and began worshiping with Quakers. He was not alone. He was only the most celebrated of a group of ex-communists turned fervent religious believers who became prominent in the American public eye in the late 1940s and early 1950s. Chambers's Protestant leanings made him an exception among them, as many became Roman Catholics, but that Chambers was entirely representative of their type indicates that during the Cold War many American Protestants and Catholics came to a broader consensus about the role of Christianity in American politics. This consensus faith opposed materialism and emphasized virtue and autonomy. They were traditional ideas, but Chambers's worries indicate important particularities about Cold War Christianity. He believed that the important aspects of Christianity for his purposes had to do with its use in preserving the "West"—which to he and millions of other Americans was increasingly defined as democratic Europe and America locked in combat with an irreligious, tyrannical "East."

Furthermore, Chambers's distaste for New York City's world of bureaucracy, subways, and industry indicated what the West suffered from, and hence how it could be saved. He associated Christianity with freedom, and both with human flourishing, mentally and physically. He claimed that the story of his own descent into communism was terrible "because of what it tells us about men."[2] His anxiety and gloom about human nature in a world of bureaucracy and commercial capitalism matched both the atmosphere of the time and the introspective and deeply personal memoirs of other ex-communists, whose "literature of witness" offered Cold War Americans a new reason to fear materialism. While earlier Christians had fixated on the political threat of materialism, the, ex-communists drew on the burgeoning language of psychology to describe how materialism degraded the individual as well as the state, corrupting the mind as well as the body politic.[3]

This psychological interpretation of the Christian struggle with materialism inspired any number of acts of public piety in the United States as efforts to ward off social decay. The numerical and financial strength of American Christian denominations in the era outmatched anything that had come before and fueled such symbolic gestures as the addition of the phrases "In God We Trust" and "under God" to the nation's currency and Pledge of Allegiance. For a largely white American elite, Protestant and Catholic alike, the notion of a common Christian consensus that could bring together Americans in a devotion to both God and the nation seemed powerful, a bar against the officially atheist Soviet Union and a sign of moral and mental fitness.[4] Dwight Eisenhower's famous extemporaneous declaration that "our form of government has no sense unless it is founded in a deeply felt religious faith" seemed to drive home the connection American elites sought to generate between their faith and their democracy.[5] Paradoxically, though, this rising public piety was matched by a receding commitment to doctrine. Christianity became associated with health in mind and in society.

These developments had two ramifications for American Christianity in the Cold War era. First, while the 1940s and 1950s were banner years for public devotion, the nature of that commitment was matched with renewed anxiety about materialism.[6] People in the Cold War feared two ways materialism might degrade the American mind. On the one hand, materialism in politics was best exemplified by the authoritarian philosophy of communism, which American Christians worried would reduce once independent citizens into mindless automatons. While earlier generations saw a similar threat in Germany's military might, Americans who joined the Cold War Christian consensus worried about communism's ability to inflict mental subversion. On the other hand, these Americans also worried that the economic materialism of consumer capitalism was undermining national moral rigor, fostering a corrupt hedonism that created morally vacuous consumers who lacked the virtue to resist the Soviet Union. Both threats were essentially psychological. Americans thus sought a middle way between the Scylla and Charybdis of communist and capitalist materialism.

Second, Catholic University's citizenship commission indicated that American Catholics had already begun to find ways to accommodate their faith to allegiance to American democracy, and the Cold War's emphasis on the public-minded and psychological aspects of the faith made that accommodation easier. The Catholic bishop Fulton Sheen, who personally won some of the most prominent converts to Catholicism in the era, declared, "Christians will have to unite in real Christianity to preserve it against the anti-Christian forces which would destroy it."[7] And yet, Sheen's particular commitments to Catholicism were often not mirrored by public figures (including some he had converted), who tended to be less concerned with particularities of doctrine and denomination than with whether any particular brand of Christianity fostered those virtues that could resist materialism: a commitment to human dignity and liberty on the one hand and a concern for moral rigor on the other. Americans often praised "Judeo-Christianity" or "biblical" religion, emphasizing that the critical distinction Americans faced was between monotheism and materialism, the key distinction between the free West and the enslaved East. The West that Columbia's Contemporary Civilization course imagined had thus expanded and taken on a new identity. It was Western, to be sure, but no longer necessarily Protestant; simply Christian.

Psychology and Ecumenism in an Age of Anxiety

For many Americans in the public arena during the Cold War, the 1940s and 1950s were an age of religious anxiety. A renewed interest in religion erupted in the American media in the late 1940s, and theologians and pastors achieved unlikely fame warning that the state of the nation's faith made America vulnerable to conquest. Evangelicals like Billy Graham traveled the nation calling for national repentance and revival; theologians like Reinhold Niebuhr and Will Herberg became public intellectuals for preaching that Americans' faith was being suborned by materialism. *Time* magazine ran cover stories on multiple American religious leaders under headlines like "Man's Story Is Not a Success Story" or "No Easter without Good Friday." As the journalist and academic William Lee Miller observed, the media seemed to "especially like original sin."[8] Americans enjoyed the fruits of their victory in the war, but were also haunted with guilt over how they earned it. The atomic bomb was powerful, but it was also a dangerous symbol of technology's destructive potential; prosperity was rewarding but also a moral corrosive. Given such anxiety, such rapid change, and such worry, perhaps it is not surprising that the field of psychology seemed to be booming in the years after the war. Membership in the psychological and psychiatric professional organizations quadrupled during World War II, to roughly 4,000 in each. By 1970, membership in the American Psychological Association was 30,839; membership in the American Psychiatric Association was 18,407.[9]

Some religious leaders in America saw this movement toward psychology as a natural response to the rising materialism of modern life. The intense, dark-eyed Sheen explained that engagement with psychology was unavoidable for those who wanted to promote a more Christian society. "Not the order in the cosmos, but the disorder in themselves; not the visible things of the world, but the invisible frustration, complexes, and anxieties of their own personality—these are modern humanity's starting point when people turn questioningly toward religion," he wrote early in his book *Peace of Soul*.[10] He believed that the modern person was uniquely afflicted with psychological conflicts, because the modern world was dominated by materialism.

"The complexes, anxieties, and fears of the modern soul did not exist for previous generations because they were shaken off and integrated in a great social-spiritual organizing of Christian civilization," he told his radio audience, echoing earlier Catholics' praise of the Middle Ages. But unfortunately, Sheen claimed, the solutions modernity offered for these problems were themselves only more materialism. The "Freudian" explanation rooted human anxiety solely in childhood trauma and sexual urges that Sheen found distasteful; the "biological" explanation sought to medicate them away; the "intellectual" explanation insisted that with more study and expertise all such problems could be solved. Finally, the "economic" explanation promised that with increased wealth and financial security, anxiety would pass. Sheen scoffed at them all.[11] Instead he offered Catholic Christianity as the salve for the soul.

The experience of Clare Boothe Luce was a case in point. When she heard of the dropping of the atomic bomb on Hiroshima, Japan, on August 6, 1945, Luce, a member of Congress, was preparing to go onstage. On a lark she had taken the title role in a small New York City production of George Bernard Shaw's *Candida,* and despite the news and protestors outside the theater—who called out, "Stop playing, Clare! These are serious times," as the audience filed in—the show went on. Luce later worried that she should have listened to them. In the months after the surrender of Japan she found herself often brooding alone in her apartment. Her daughter Ann, a student at Stanford, had recently died in a car wreck, and Luce's grief mushroomed into a grim fixation on the ease of death in the modern age. She traveled widely during the war, and later remembered dead babies "bobbing like apples" in the harbors of China, the devastation of concentration camps in Europe, and now, the destruction the bomb wrought on Japan. She told Congress that she worried Americans were fixed on "the building of a modern, aggressive, war machine." The war had prompted Americans to look to technology for their salvation; it had turned them willingly into cogs in that machine.[12]

She eventually turned to Fulton Sheen. Over the winter of 1945–1946, Sheen and Luce sat often in his Washington, DC, study sparring about heaven and hell and good and evil. After weeks of debate, on the second anniversary of her daughter's death, Luce had an ecstatic epiphany. "It finally took two world wars, the overthrow of several dozen thrones and governments, the Russian revolution, the swift collapse, in our own time, of hundreds of thought-systems, a small number of which collapsed on me, the death of millions as well as the death of my daughter, before I was willing to take a look at this extraordinary institution, the Catholic church," she said. Sheen baptized her on February 16, 1946. She came to understand her suffering as a microcosm of the materialism of the age, and Roman Catholicism as its cure.[13]

Sheen was relatively careful with his use of psychology. Other Christian leaders were assailed for being less so. There is no better demonstration of the fascination psychology held for American Christians in this period than the resounding fame of Norman Vincent Peale, the pastor of New York's Marble Collegiate Church and author of the monumental best seller *The Power of Positive Thinking*. He swore that modern psychology had actually unlocked the true promise of Christianity. "We are at last awakening to the close relationship between religion and health," he wrote. "The laws are so precise and have been so often demonstrated when proper conditions of understanding, belief and practice are applied that religion may be said to form an exact science."[14] Peale followed earlier advocates for the New Thought movement, which tied religion to health, and he argued that divine power should be applied like any other medicine.

To other Christians, though, such appeals to psychology threatened to reduce the particularities of the religious experience to a mechanical process. In 1953 Pope Pius XII warned that while psychotherapy could indeed be useful, it too often failed to consider that "no purely psychological treatment will cure a genuine sense of guilt. . . . As every Christian knows, it consists in contrition and sacramental absolution by the priest."[15] Many others followed. Peale's adversaries routinely ignored the minister's protests that his techniques were religious. Instead they insisted that his embrace of psychological language was secular, because it adopted materialist understandings of what it meant to be human. James Pike, an Episcopal bishop, warned that Peale offered "hidden secularist presuppositions . . . wrapped up in the same package with psychological truth." In *The Atlantic*, the writer Curtis Cate compared Peale to a "Madison Avenue advertiser plugging a new barbiturate."[16]

That Sheen routinely used psychological language while Peale was routinely attacked for doing the same reveals the complicated relationship American Christians had with psychology. As the attacks on Peale demonstrate, many Americans were wary that materialism threatened to suborn American religion. And yet, psychology's popularity and its usefulness for forging a pan-Christian alliance were undeniable. Books written by Sheen,

Peale, and a dozen other authors who followed the lead of one or the other were routinely promoted by bookstores and book clubs across the country. Furthermore, as American cultural and political leaders increasingly invoked mental health, peace of mind, and strength of personality to describe the benefits and appeal of Christianity, psychology became a vernacular many Christians were comfortable with. Increasingly, the language of psychology proved a valuable tool for uniting American Christians behind a version of the faith that promoted individual well-being and personal autonomy, downplaying the importance of doctrine in favor of peace of mind.[17]

The Psychological Faith of the Ex-Communists

After the war ended, the ranks of ex-communists who published memoirs and exposés of their departure from the ideology swelled, and routinely they argued that communism preyed on mental angst and that Christianity was its only cure. They seemed to have some proof. William Z. Foster, who led the American Communist Party off and on in the 1930s and 1940s, confirmed that communists actively sought individuals who were in economic turmoil, writing in his book *The Twilight of World Capitalism* that "the tensions of their barbarous capitalist society are undermining the mental health" of Americans.[18] In his famous 1948 book *Communism and the Conscience of the West,* Sheen explained why so many were deceived. Communism, Sheen argued, was the product of the Industrial Revolution, capitalism's accidental Mordred, a child raised to destroy its parent. "Communism begins with the liberal and capitalistic error that man is economic and instead of correcting it merely intensifies it until man becomes a robot in a vast economic machine," he instructed.[19] It was no surprise to the priest that so many of his penitents had once seen good in communism: it offered them a false solution to a real problem, the rampant materialism of American capitalism.

The ex-communist writers agreed. Over and over they depicted their embrace of communism as the tragic conclusion of an anxious mind ignorant of Christianity and yet striving to resolve the strains of materialism. For some, materialism was a shallow, status-obsessed, hedonism. Whittaker Chambers, the spy turned journalist, painted the gloomiest image. In his autobiography he depicted his youth as a hell of shallow idiocy, obsessed with status and devoid of meaning. His parents, Chambers said, were "arty" but not artistic, obsessed with collecting obviously valuable decorations, throwing parties, and generally, he thought in retrospect, being vulgar. They embraced science. His mother insisted to him that "the world was formed by gases cooling in space," but only because that was the interpretation most accepted among her friends. To Chambers, such a belief, and furthermore the reasons to seize upon it, indicated a moral superficiality that left him a vulnerable intellectual vagabond in his youth.[20]

Other ex-communists linked their embrace of communism to the mental strain of capitalist struggle. Bella Dodd, an attorney and educator who left the Communist Party in the 1940s, claimed that during the Depression "millions of people formerly regarded as middle class found themselves on relief or on WPA and had been merged into the comradeship of the dispossessed. To people of this group the Communist Party brought psychological support."[21] Louis Budenz, a journalist who served various communist publications, said that while he was young he was a "Catholic syndicalist" who believed in the solutions offered by leaders like John Ryan: "the restoration of the worker to the tools which had been his in medieval times." And yet, at the peak of Budenz's highest hopes, in the months immediately following World War I, he found his confidence in Catholicism dashed. He had spent the war in St. Louis organizing labor unions, so at war's end he hoped for the League of Nations, for more international cooperation, and for aid from government and business to a working class that had largely supported the war. Instead, Budenz found that the "comfortable, well-fed men" running the government and the American economy happily destroyed the League of Nations and "refuse[d] even to talk with the unions." The shock drove him toward a different philosophy. He called himself an "an incipient Marxist at the end of the St. Louis period." He found that after these series of betrayals, "the materialist conception of history," which insisted that those well-fed liberal elites were by virtue of their class inexorably opposed to Budenz's unions, "was to captivate my mind and imagination."[22]

The black writers Richard Wright and Claude McKay, for their parts, remembered how they found in communism a place where, as Wright put it, the "Negro experience could find a home, a functioning value and role." To that point in his life, he said, he had grown "cynical," convinced that no white person could "possibly have a sincere interest in Negroes." He made an informal study of other black men who turned to communism, men who were "distrustful but aggressive," one of whom had a "bundle of the weaknesses and virtues . . . of a man living on the margins of a culture."[23] McKay believed similarly; a native of Jamaica, he wrote that before he migrated to the United States, "I had heard of prejudice in America but never dreamed of it being so intensely bitter."[24] On the other hand, when he was welcomed to the Soviet Union a few years after the Russian Revolution, he observed that "Russia is prepared and waiting to receive couriers and heralds of good will and interracial understanding from the Negro race."[25] The dehumanizing impact of racism matched Budenz's and Dodd's senses of economic alienation.

All these writers' emphasis on the trauma of their conversion to communism evidenced the internal angst to which many ex-communists attributed their embrace of the ideology and their rejection of Christianity. When he finally drew near to joining the Communist Party in 1935, Budenz said that he had been overcome with a "spiritual numbness. . . . I thought almost exclusively in terms of production—which eventually destroys all moral values." He was growing distant from his parents and had lost his taste for the literature that had once inspired him, the spiritual writings of Willa Cather and Sigrid Undset.[26] Other converts offered similar experiences. Wright remembered feeling shame when his mother, a "gentle woman," discovered him studying communist materials. "Her ideal was Christ upon the cross," he observed.[27] Elizabeth Bentley, who worked with Chambers's spy ring and later gave his name to Congress, wrote in her autobiography that her experiences at college were jarring, both politically and personally. An upper-middle-class child raised in pastoral New England, she traveled in her youth and saw fascism rising in Europe and poverty in New York City. She blamed these social problems for communism's appeal to her. "There was no going back to the old fashioned small town world in which I had been brought up," she claimed. "All this had been replaced by a vast impersonal industrial civilization which somehow, if life was to have any meaning, must be reconciled with the basic Christian ideals that my parents had taught me."[28] For these prisoners of mental trauma, communism seemed to promise the only possible achievement of their religious ideals.

Americans who read of Wright's, Bentley's, and Budenz's small apostasies saw worrying parallels in the international news. In December 1948, a Catholic prelate, Cardinal Jozsef Mindszenty, was arrested in Hungary for resisting the communist regime. The next year he was given a show trial and imprisoned.[29] Before his arrest, Mindszenty had dashed off a note repudiating any confession he might make during his trial. And indeed, at the trial the priest appeared—wild-eyed, exhausted, occasionally drooling—and offered an outlandish confession that he had fomented a plan to seize control of Hungary himself. Western Christians were appalled but also terrified. The Catholic writer Nicholas Boer warned that Mindszenty had been drugged and wrote indignantly that communists had inflicted upon the prelate a "broken, tortured mind, the unhinging of his mental balance and loss of his self-control."[30] *Life* magazine hyperventilated, "Incredible as it may seem, the Communists have in fact discovered a process by which a man's soul can be tore [*sic*] apart and put together again. . . . Man's spiritual personality can be made to disintegrate."[31] In horrible confirmation, the United States sent troops to Korea only months later, and Americans watched in fear as their own captured soldiers began delivering denunciations of American imperialism and accusations of germ warfare into film cameras.[32]

The emergence of brainwashing illustrates the logical conclusion of the traumatic conversions Budenz and the rest described: Christian Americans' fear that materialism reduced the self to mindless apathetic conformity, producing a sense of nihilism and alienation and a loss of personal identity to authoritarian control. Americans concluded that communists' combination of technical acumen and lack of morality went hand in hand, leaving them capable of and willing to subvert the individual soul. While Sheen attacked Freud, to many Americans the most frightening form of psychology was the ascendant model of behaviorism, which seemed to deny the existence of a fundamental human identity. In 1948, the noted psychologist B. F. Skinner published the utopian novel *Walden Two,* which introduced behaviorist theories of psychology to a mass audience. Skinner's book horrified many Christian anticommunists, who read it as a blueprint for the cultivation of a communist society by reducing human beings to machines. Skinner famously defined the "self" as "a functionally unified system of responses"— a series of verbs, not nouns.[33] People were, simply, what they did. In *Walden Two,* the characters who run the utopian community consistently deny that the "self" is a reality independent of its conditioning. Augustine Castle, a horrified visitor to the community, objects to the communal raising of children, protesting on behalf of "mother-love" and claiming that the children look like fish in an "aquarium."[34] To the shocked Castle, Walden Two's child-rearing wrecks the humanity of the children.

Popularizing and simplifying these ideas, Christian anticommunists made much of communism's supposed reliance upon Skinner's theory. Cleon Skousen, author of *The Naked Communist,* claimed that Marx "visualized a regimented breed of Pavlovian men whose minds could be triggered into immediate action by signals from their masters."[35] The journalist Edward Hunter made a career of popularizing the notion of "brainwashing," warning in books like *Brainwashing in Red China* (1951) and *Brainwashing: The Story of the Men Who Defied It* (1956) that communist command of science posed a profound threat to the spiritual autonomy of the human race. "The intent is to change a mind radically so its owner becomes a living puppet—a human robot—without the atrocity being visible," Hunter wrote. He insisted that brainwashing need not be on the personal, intimate scale of the abuse suffered by Mindszenty; rather, the techniques worked on a mass scale to reduce the citizens of a communist society to "bees in a hive," functioning only "in a way determined by a central authority."[36] But Hunter promised that one sure way to resist brainwashing was through Christian faith. The three strategies at the top of his list were "faith, convictions, [and] clarity of mind." He recounted the stories of a number of captives who "survived" brainwashing and who told him their religious convictions were key to their resistance.[37]

Reduction of personal identity by a mechanical society was a common fear in the 1950s, and often writers linked it to the loss of meaning religion might provide. Even seemingly secular authors like C. Wright Mills or William Whyte, who wrote, respectively, *White Collar: The American Middle Classes* (1951) and *The Organization Man* (1956), could produce in their books warnings that modern commercial society would drain the spiritual and moral vigor of American individuals, severing them from their vital connection to their values and reducing them to mere cogs in the capitalist machine. As Whyte described those who worked for American corporations, "They are the ones of our middle class who have left home, spiritually as well as physically, to take the vows of organization life." Mills warned, "Men are estranged from one another as each secretly tries to make an instrument of the other, and in time a full circle is made: one makes an instrument of himself and is estranged from it also."[38]

Certainly, Bella Dodd learned this lesson. Dodd spent the Christmas holidays of 1949 alone in her room. She had grown estranged from the American Communist Party earlier that year, nominally for representing a landlord in a legal dispute with a tenant, but, as she recounted the episode later, in fact it was because she had grown weary of the absolute conformity demanded by Communist leadership. That Christmas she sat, miserable, in her small apartment, listening "with utter despair to the gaiety and noise from Times Square and the ringing bells of the churches. More than once

I thought of leaving New York and losing myself in the anonymity of a strange town. But I did not go. Something in me struggled with the wave of nihilism engulfing me." She realized her departure from communism had cost her all human companionship. As she observed, "Affection in that strange communist world is never a personal emotion. You were loved or hated on the basis of group acceptance," simple membership in the right movement.[39] Wright had a similar experience. When a Communist official criticized his writing and teaching for failing to match the aims of the party, the official did so in a way "more patronizing than that of a Southern white man," and Wright soon found there was little room for black freedom within American communism.[40]

Another way in which Christians expressed their fear of materialism and its corruptions appeared paradoxically to be the opposite: materialism could produce hedonism and licentiousness. If the first form of materialism led to a psychological predisposition to accept authoritarianism, the second led to a loss of virtue, which similarly sapped one's will to resist tyranny. While Americans on the political left, like Mills and Wright, worried particularly about the first, many American conservatives were suspicious of the second. Joseph McCarthy, the senator from Wisconsin who waged a flamboyant assault on supposed communist infiltration in the United States in the early 1950s, was perhaps the most obvious of these. According to McCarthy, communism's infiltration of the United States could be seen, unexpectedly, in American elites' status and wealth. McCarthy frequently contrasted the masculine rigor and asceticism of true faith with the hypocritical luxuries enjoyed by communist sympathizers. His 1952 book, *McCarthyism: The Fight for America,* opened with McCarthy recalling the two circumstances under which he learned how urgent the fight against communism was: in service as a tail-gunner in the Pacific theater of World War II, and over "two saddle-sore days which I spent on [a] desolate but friendly cattle ranch" in Arizona. In these places, he claimed, deprived of material comfort, he "began to fully appreciate the great wisdom" of America's struggle with totalitarianism; he also contrasted his experiences with the "starry-eyed planners," the "dupes" who stayed behind in Washington.[41] Famously, McCarthy lambasted the "lace handkerchief crowd" who "have never had to fight in the cold"—those in the American government he believed were too venal and effeminate to fight communist materialism properly. At the 1952 Republican Party national convention, McCarthy denounced the secretary of state, Dean Acheson, for believing that communists could be stopped by "hitting them with a perfumed silk handkerchief." He mourned, "Within our own boundaries we battle crass materialism," and he linked the problem to the power of New Deal liberals, whose "spending, taxing, and debt programs have minimalized our chances of security."[42]

Elizabeth Bentley offered support for the same narrative. She recalled watching in astonishment as her Soviet handler judged her Christmas presents to him before plowing into an expensive restaurant meal. "'The scarf is all right,' he said precisely, 'but the gloves are not well made.' With difficulty I suppressed a hysterical laugh as I watched him charge into his food." Watching the man's "well-fed flabbiness, his well-tailored and expensive looking clothes," Bentley discovered that indeed, the Soviets were equally prisoners to materialism as were Americans, and soon after the meal she stared hopelessly into a mirror, finding her very identity gone. "I once started out with high idealistic hopes and now I look like someone who is not even human," she wrote. "We had been corrupted and smashed by a machine more merciless than anything the world had ever seen . . . had become, in the hands of the communist movement, no longer individuals but robots."[43] The language of corruption and the language of destruction are here linked; her loss of humanity mirrored her realization that, all along, she had been serving not humanity and moral progress, but the economic enrichment of those in power.

The Materialist Destruction of Gender Roles

Perhaps the most obvious place in American life where materialism wreaked havoc was the arena of traditional gender norms. Each materialist method levied its own form of destruction. When Bella Dodd met with Fulton Sheen and began the process of reconversion to the Roman Catholicism of her youth, she "meditated on the mockery I had made of my marriage; how I had squandered my birthright as a woman." She wept as she described to Sheen how communism had strangled her femininity in a materialist vise. She opened her memoir with a long sequence relating how her mother had worked hard to protect her from the machine of materialism, first leaving her in the idyllic farm country of Italy while the rest of the family moved to Harlem, and then, in New York, teaching her traditionally feminine tasks like sewing and cooking, "for she would not let me spend time in the city streets." Nonetheless, Dodd was drawn ever further into urban industrial life, and her self-presentation allowed her to draw intentional contrasts between her own dissolute life in communism and her idealized attentive, traditional mother. She pursued an education rather than marriage, admitting that she had "given little thought to marriage" when her husband proposed to her, because "I was thinking about a career. . . . The Party did all it could to induce women to go into industry." Further, marriage for communists was a hothouse both literally and ideologically, "the process of living with a man or a woman in quarters so small that release and satisfaction had to be found outside the home." Married communists were not to place their highest priority on personal intimacy, but on the cause.[44] Whittaker Chambers claimed that the Communist Party wanted his wife to abort their first child, a confrontation he read as symbolic: he remembered marveling at the "miraculous" perfection of his daughter's ear and realized that communism sought not only to stomp out her life, but to deny the divinity of her creation.[45]

The other way communism might ruin traditional gender roles was through the same sort of dissolution and hedonism that McCarthy scorned in Acheson. Bella Dodd sneered at what she called the "attractive communist 'cheesecake' in the Party"—young women who did not receive much training in Marxist ideology but rather spent their time "calling on men and women of wealth, in an effort to get them to open their pocketbooks." These "girls" were mostly from the countryside, Dodd observed, again drawing a distinction between the idealized family farm of her youth and the perversions of industrial society, and thus they "still had a fresh-faced look and an innocent charm."[46] A Senate committee explained that "deviates" had a "tendency to gather other perverts about [them]," and thus could be vulnerable to destructive movements like communism.[47] Elizabeth Bentley was well aware of this fear. When she testified before the House Un-American Activities Committee, she claimed that she had been seduced by Jacob Golos, a Ukrainian-born leader in the American Communist Party. In fact, Golos and Bentley were longtime lovers, but it served Bentley's narrative to claim that her wits had been dulled by "this emotional process." When a congressman asked her, "Who spurred this emotionalism on you? Was it this man Golos?" she said yes, and affirmed that she was "devoted to him so much that [she] followed him blindly."[48]

These ex-communists constructed a common narrative. Invariably, they presented communism as a false solution to the anxiety materialism produced. Though they sought mental relief in the American Communist Party, they all eventually came to see that its promises only exacerbated their pain and could only ever exacerbate it because communism was itself materialism. The true source of relief was Christianity, but the fact that they spoke of the problem and solution in psychological language meant that which particular brand of Christianity was on the face of it not terribly important. What was important was that the Christianity they embraced had to promote anticommunist ideals, exalt individual autonomy, and offer a psychological language they could embrace.

Building an Antimaterialist Ecumenism

The forms of Christianity that Americans had invoked during World War I and the Depression decades earlier seemed to promise a new solution to the twin threats of materialism. The use of psychological explanations for the appeal of communism highlighted for many Christians that the conflict was less about how best to organize a society than how to rightly understand human nature. The way to solve materialism, then, was not to reorganize American government but to fix the American psyche. The ways in which Catholic converts like Budenz or Bentley presented their experiences, binding together mechanical tyranny and immoral materialism in the person of Bentley's jowly Soviet handler, reflected Catholic ideas that had been present in the cultural catastrophes of the previous decades, but that moved to prominence in American religious rhetoric during the Cold War.

For much of the three decades since the rise of the Soviet Union, Catholics had been the loudest critics of communism, invoking personalist ideas to attack its core tenets. In 1937, Pius XI condemned Russian communism in much the same language he had used to critique Nazism in *Mit brennender Sorge* and unrestrained capitalism in *Quadragesimo Anno:* "because it ignores the true origin and purpose of the State; because it denies the rights, dignity and liberty of human personality."[49] After the war, personalist ideas infused the United Nations' 1948 Universal Declaration of Human Rights, which claimed that "recognition of the inherent dignity and of the equal and inalienable rights of all members of the human family is the foundation of freedom, justice and peace in the world."[50]

Similarly, in the United States Christians of all denominations came to use personalist language to argue that "Judeo-Christianity" as a whole supported the human personality against unrestrained capital on the one hand and communism on the other, arguing that both ideas harmed humanity. Fulton Sheen argued that too many Americans subscribed to "false liberty . . . the right to do, say, or think whatever you please." This liberty tended toward communism because it encouraged people to pursue materialist rather than spiritual ends. "Dictators gave man a purpose," he observed, "but instead of making this purpose the development of the human personality, they imposed a purpose, as the race in Nazism, the state in Fascism and the class in communism."[51] The Protestant theologian Reinhold Niebuhr made similar arguments. He warned that the nation was becoming overly secular, by which he meant that Americans ignored "ultimate questions about the meaning of existence," because they were told "that science has answered these questions." This meant that the nation ended up in a state of uneasy complacency, in a "gadget filled paradise suspended in a hell of international insecurity." American Christian leaders like Niebuhr and Sheen united in agreement that what Niebuhr called "Biblical faith (from which Judaism and Christianity are derived) . . . justifies the institutions of democracy."[52] In short, American Christians of all sorts came to believe that because human beings were specially created by God, governments and societies should be simultaneously politically free and virtuous in the face of material capitalism. As leaders of the National Conference of Christians and Jews, an organization promoting antimaterialist ecumenism, put it in the script for their national presentations, "Biblical religions" had "common elements in our original heritage." Robert Ashworth, a NCCJ official, declared, "Those who differ deeply in religious beliefs may, nevertheless, work together in the American way toward mutual goals."[53]

This sort of antimaterialist ecumenism quickly spread across American culture and became an organizing principle as Christian Americans sought to refine their notions of civilization. As American Christians embraced the notion that "biblical" religion more generally led to healthy-mindedness and a healthy personality, which in turn led to virtue, and in turn to the sustenance of democracy, they also increasingly began to define Western civilization along the same lines. Bella Dodd, for instance, juxtaposed the terrible and lonely Christmas she had spent in 1949, when she had just become estranged from the Communist Party, with her next. That year found her in a church, the Catholic St. Francis of Assisi, which was crowded with believers. Dodd looked around and realized, "Here was what I had sought so vainly in the Communist Party, the true brotherhood of all men. Here were men and women of all races and ages and social conditions cemented by the love of God."[54] The comparison between the two holidays was telling. In the first, she experienced the destructive isolation and anomie which materialism induced in individuals; in the second, she learned that Christianity united people of all types in a warm brotherhood that repudiated communism.

Similarly, soon after her crisis before her mirror, Bentley wrote about wandering in the small town of Old Lyme, Connecticut, near where she was raised. She stood for a time gazing at the town's old white Congregational church. The worshipers there were "sturdy and independent and solid, I thought. They have an innate sense of the worth of the individual. . . . We had needed a new faith that reaffirmed the brotherhood of man and the worth of the individual."[55] Soon after her experience in that church, she was baptized a Roman Catholic. In the story she told the lines between Roman Catholicism and the old stock Congregationalism of her youth faded to imperceptibility next to the line between Christian faith and communist materialism. The West the Cold War created, then, was Christian but not of any particular type. By the 1950s, many white Americans both Catholic and Protestant had thoroughly assimilated the notion that Christianity depended not on denomination but on freedom of the individual premised on human dignity and moral behavior.

Redefining Western Civilization

This antimaterialist ecumenism shaped how Americans in the Cold War thought about the meaning of Western civilization. Three writers in particular adapted the story of Western history to the age, incorporating the ecumenical, antimaterialist, psychological interpretation of Christianity produced by the Cold War into the story of the rise of the West.

Arnold Toynbee's *A Study of History* was in its original form a dense and theoretical multivolume work of interest mostly to academics. He visited the United States in February 1947 to deliver a series of lectures at universities, and suddenly found himself a national phenomenon. In March of that year Oxford University Press published a single-volume abridgment of Toynbee's first six volumes. With the help of Henry Luce, publisher of *Time* magazine and a decided Toynbee fan, Oxford's publicists mounted a national campaign to turn a very British, very solitary, very private writer into a national mentor for the United States. As the *New York Times* observed, "The interest in Toynbee is presumably the reflection of a vast uneasiness." The historian warned that civilizations all tended to fail, but also offered a potential escape, an answer to a pressing question: "What must we do, here and now, to be saved?"[56] Toynbee willingly gave himself over to the capable machinations of Oxford and Luce, who farmed him out for interviews, columns, and articles in dozens of American media outlets over the next few years. More than two hundred thousand copies of the abridged version of *A Study of History* sold in the first year it was on the market. By the late 1940s Toynbee was appearing in the columns of society reporters, who breathlessly noted, "Indeed, there is a Mrs. Toynbee."[57] In March 1947, he appeared on the cover of *Time*, the subject of a story by Whittaker Chambers. The cover image captured the peculiar nature of Cold War celebrity: next to Toynbee's dark suit and baggy features appeared the encomium "Our civilization is not inexorably doomed."[58]

The resolutely American Will Durant's appeal matched Toynbee's. While the professor was starchy and formal, Durant was twinkly, cheerful, and short. In old age he grew a neatly clipped white mustache. While a young man during World War I, he had dropped out of a Catholic seminary in favor of teaching at a working-class school, and by the 1920s he was lecturing at the Labor Temple, a Christian socialist chapel in New York City. That decade he began work on what would become his long-running best-selling series, *The Story of Civilization*. In 1950 Durant published *The Age of Faith*, the fortuitously timed fourth volume. Over the next decade he produced additional installments on the Renaissance and Reformation. Beginning in 1961, his wife Ariel joined him as co-author and the two produced four more volumes covering Western history until the fall of Napoleon in 1815. While Toynbee's book sought to unearth and describe the deep patterns that formed human history, the Durants' books were rousing narratives of the steady progress of European and American civilization.

Like the liberal Protestants at Columbia, none of these authors was conventionally religious, but that stopped none from holding the conviction that an ecumenical, moral Judeo-Christianity was essential to stave off both tyranny and decadence. Will Durant had abandoned training in a Catholic seminary to embrace what he called "a sentimental pantheism." Ariel Durant was a Jewish immigrant from the Ukraine who called her faith "not one of fear or celestial promises"; she renounced "doctrine of heaven or hell" but clung to religion as a "rich heritage in consoling myth, prophetic fervor, and noble poetry."[59] Reflecting a lack of interest in theology or the afterlife characteristic of liberal believers, the Durants insisted that religion served a vital public function. "There is no significant example in history, before our time, of a society successfully maintaining moral life without the aid of religion," they claimed.[60] Similarly, throughout the 1930s and 1940s, when he began work on *A Study of History,* Toynbee was resolutely unpersuaded by the placations of his devoutly Catholic wife. But as he worked through the 1940s and into the 1950s (and, ironically, after a divorce), he came to embrace a middle-class liberal Protestantism. In 1956, having completed *Study,* he echoed the spiritual moralism of the Columbia academics: "The true purpose of a higher religion is to radiate the spiritual counsels and truths that are its essence into as many souls as it can reach."[61]

For Toynbee and the Durants, religion was a public rather than a private good, and Americans hoped their work offered a map to political and religious salvation. Luce's *Life* magazine summarized Toynbee's arguments and concluded that the West's commitment to religion might save it, much as Toynbee had concluded that "the purpose of civilizations may be to spread opportunities among men for a fuller knowledge of God."[62] Similarly, in March 1945, as World War II wound to an end, Will Durant headed a group of American notables who issued a "Declaration of Interdependence," largely drafted by Durant himself, which declared that all humans were "children of the same Divine Father," and thus all nations should have "respect for the dignity and liberty of man."[63]

These authors believed that materialism was an ever-present threat to civilization as they defined it, and following the middle way of the Cold War Christian consensus, condemning both excessive capitalism, which led to hedonism, and tyrannical communism, which led to slavery. In New York in 1955 Toynbee explained that what he called "the conditions for freedom found in the Judeo-Christian tradition" included a necessary acknowledgment that the American obsession with technology could not fill its spiritual needs. "Western man is in a position of practicing a technological way of life and still believing in freedom without its religious foundations," he said. "History teaches that this paradox cannot long continue."[64] The volumes in *The Story of Civilization* were far easier to read than Toynbee's books, but they contained similar messages, presenting "Judeo-Christian" religion as the alternative to materialism of any sort. "Heaven and utopia are buckets in a well; when one goes down the other goes up; when religion declines communism grows," the pair wrote. The Durants asked skeptically whether Americans had "developed a natural ethic—a moral code independent of religion—strong enough to keep our instincts of acquisition, pugnacity, and sex from debasing our civilization into a mire of greed, crime, and promiscuity?"[65]

For all three "Western civilization" was premised on these virtues, which they deemed "Judeo-Christian" without bothering much with further distinction. They offered a definition of the West updated for the Cold War. Western civilization for them included the Catholic and Protestant regions of Europe and North America. While the Columbia academics had targeted Germany, these writers instead took care to separate "the East" from the West, and for the first time began presenting the two in contrast of a sort that made sense given the nature of their world. In Durant's first volume he argued that "the theme of the twentieth century seems destined to be an all-encompassing conflict between the East and the West," dividing "Occident" from "Orient." He claimed it was the West that would "conceive man as a citizen rather than a subject; it would give him political liberty, civil rights, and an unparalleled measure of mental and moral freedom."[66] For Durant the "East" remained stagnant and tyrannical, while the West was dynamic and free. So it was for Toynbee as well, who defined his civilization as "Western Christendom," separate from the "Orthodox Christian Society" of Eastern Europe and Russia, which he believed was more given to collectivism and political passivity, as well as from civilizations he dubbed "Islamic," "Hindu," and "Far-Eastern."[67]

American politicians seized upon the ideas these writers popularized. They stressed that an American Cold War religious consensus should seek a middle way between the twin materialisms of communism and capitalism, and should defend the free, Christian West against the atheist, totalitarian East. The defenders of the New Deal liberalism built by Franklin Roosevelt and Harry Truman argued that its combination of a strong national defense and managed capitalism embodied the ideals of this Cold War Christian consensus. Arthur Schlesinger, an academic who advised Franklin Roosevelt and other leaders, produced a widely read tome called *The Vital Center*, which was shot through with diagnoses of the American psyche. As with Sheen or his converts, Schlesinger diagnosed communism as a mental disorder derived from a failure to engage with the challenges of American materialism; communists were "lonely and frustrated people" who were "craving social, intellectual, and even sexual fulfillment they cannot obtain in existing society." Thus, to prevent the spread of communism in the United States, the government should eliminate "conditions of want and insecurity, which invite the spread of Communism." Schlesinger acknowledged that his strategy derived in large part from his reading of contemporary Christian theology, which taught him that humans were "capable of reason and purpose, of great loyalty and great virtue, yet also . . . vulnerable to material power."[68] New Deal liberalism, then, was not simply a sound political strategy; it was more metaphysically valid than the alternatives.

Schlesinger's diagnosis and cure for America's ills profoundly affected two significant public advocates for the Cold War Christian consensus: the Kennedy brothers John and Robert. Raised Catholics, the two possessed varying levels of private devotion to the faith, though they vigorously defended their allegiance in public. In so doing, they modeled the integration of Catholic and Protestant believers into a broader Christian, antimaterialist consensus which downplayed doctrinal specifics and instead emphasized the relevance of Christian ideals that resembled liberal Protestantism. Most famously, John F. Kennedy in 1960 ventured into the lion's den of the Greater Houston Ministerial Association to reassure nervous Protestants that he conceived of Christianity the same way they did. He promised to govern "in accordance with what my conscience tells me to be the national interest, and without regard to outside religious pressures or dictates." In the question-and-answer session which followed, he repeatedly refused to engage in debate on Catholic doctrine, denying that he had read the *Catholic Encyclopedia* and insisting that his conscience served as his primary guide.[69] In so doing Kennedy was echoing the arguments of a number of other American Catholics, most particularly those of the Jesuit John Courtnay Murray. Murray's book *We Hold These Truths: Catholic Reflections on the American Proposition*, published that same year, maintained that Catholics could be part of what Murray called "the American consensus," because American democracy was premised upon the sovereignty of God and sought to preserve the dignity of the human person. In Murray's accounting, this religious consensus enhanced the United States' ability to protect those suppositions. Murray's ideas had influence at the Second Vatican Council (1962–1965), and many American Catholics took the Council's declaration on religious liberty as endorsement of his work.[70]

After he assumed the presidency Kennedy became a powerful advocate for an ecumenical Christianity which downplayed sectarianism but exalted freedom conditioned with ethical behavior. He told one ecumenical Christian gathering that Americans were in danger of confusing "a system of freedom with one of disinterest, uninterest, cynicism, materialism." This disillusionment with American democracy could be cured with "religious conviction. Religious freedom has no significance unless it is accompanied by conviction." Kennedy claimed he was not concerned with which particular religious faith this conviction stood in service of, but he made clear three things. First, he assumed that it was a biblical faith, crediting "the prophets and the saints" for their examples; second he believed that conviction could alleviate the anxiety he saw in American society, replacing restlessness and "despair" with "hope"; and, finally, he understood "conviction" to be not belief but action. Christian commitment required not subscription to particular doctrine, but rather a willingness to "under the most difficult of circumstances, in great hardship" choose to live well.[71]

His brother Robert, always a more fervent Catholic, was also more vehement and aggressive as he assaulted threats to the nation's Christian consensus. As he was contemplating a presidential run of his own in 1967, Robert published a book titled *To Seek a Newer World*, in which he warned Americans that communism laid siege to the "battered framework of nineteenth century liberalism, of Enlightenment humanism, of traditional Christianity." He drew, as had liberal Protestants for a hundred years and Catholics for far less time, parallels among Christianity, individual autonomy, and moral values. Based on that presumption he worked hard to unite a wide range of Americans beneath the canopy of an antimaterialist Christian consensus. He urged Christian Americans to see themselves in the student protestors against the Vietnam War. "Distasteful to the young, as it has been to moralists for thousands of years, is the ethic that judges all things by their profit," he wrote. "It is more than the abuses of the profit motive they reject; often it is the very nature of materialism in our society. . . . Sameness is the denial of individuality and the denial that human beings matter."[72]

The Emergence of Dissent

At the same time as this consensus was forming, however, signs of dissent from it emerged. Unlike the Kennedys, some Catholics were uncomfortable with accommodation of their faith to the Cold War Christian consensus. A young Catholic named William F. Buckley offered a mixed review of John Courtnay Murray's book in his journal, *National Review,* applauding the Jesuit for recognizing that "the Founders established a republic on the pre-sumption of a natural law," but worrying that Murray was "never so spe-cific as to identify himself with any current movement, except of course the Christian movement."[73] Buckley found the ecumenism of the Cold War consensus stifling. In his *God and Man at Yale,* he blasted the university's teachers of religion for preaching "ethics" instead of real religion. "I make no apology for defining 'religion' in the Christian sense, and eschewing the nebulous, personalized definitions given to that term by so many latter-day psychologists, sociologists, et al.," Buckley wrote. He insisted that the sort of ecumenism the Christian consensus preached wore down the strength of the faith. Genuine Christianity indeed supported individual liberty, Buckley believed. "The duel between Christianity and atheism is the most important in the world," he wrote, and the "struggle between individualism and collectivism is the same struggle reproduced on another level." But the bland "tolerance and relativism" embraced by leaders like the Kennedys led, in Buckley's opinion, to psychological dissonance, because it rejected the true Christianity that alone could foster a free society.[74] Just as communists suffered mental strain, so was ecumenists' "continuing blindness" to their own inevitable dissonance a sign of a "deep psychological problem."[75]

Like Buckley, some evangelicals condemned the Christian consensus for its mushy ecumenism. In 1942, several fundamentalist Protestant leaders organized the National Association of Evangelicals and insisted that it was evangelical Christianity in particular that preserved democracy. Indeed, declared NAE leader Harold Ockenga, Americans could choose two paths: "One is the road of the rescue of Western civilization by a re-emphasis and revival of evangelical Christianity. The other is a return to the Dark Ages of heathendom."[76]

Other Americans also found the consensus Christianity of Cold War liberalism insufficiently attentive to their particular needs. In 1965, the United Farm Workers union, led by Cesar Chavez, began a strike against grape planters in Delano, California. It would last for five years. When he was young Chavez had learned of the Catholic social teachings of John Ryan from a parish priest, including "social justice and the Church's stand on farm issues and reading from the encyclicals of Pope Leo XIII, in which he upheld labor unions."[77] But in addition to this older vision of a just society, Chavez was steeped in the tradition of Latin American Catholicism, which did not have a place in the story of civilization that Americans heard from writers like Toynbee and the Durants. Chavez was quite aware of this. In March 1966, he led the strikers on a march from Delano to the state capitol of California. He declared the march distinctively Latin American and derived from traditions of the "Spanish-speaking world," as distinguished from the United States. Chavez invoked pilgrimage for "some sincerely sought benefit of body or soul" and "the Lenten penitential processions, where the penitents would march through the streets, often in sack cloth and ashes, some even carrying crosses, as a sign of penance for their sins." The hope of the march, Chavez claimed, was to entwine the aims of each tradition. Marchers sought to demonstrate humility and penitence for their sins, but also to call the nation's attention to the sins committed against them and to gain divine aid in their mitigation. After all, Chavez observed, the penitents of Catholic Mexico who went to the shrine of the Virgin were "the poor, the downtrodden, the rejected, the discriminated-against." The pilgrimage to Sacramento likewise would be undertaken by a "cultural minority who have suffered from a hostile environment."[78] Thus, the march would be named "Peregrinacion, Penitencia, Revolucion." Pilgrimage, penitence, revolution. Chavez was as good as his word: the marchers carried images of the Virgin, and Chavez himself limped along on bare, blistered feet, mirroring Catholic penitents and enacting in the United States a version of Christianity far from the Protestant consensus that white Americans were comfortable with.

The rise of William F. Buckley, Harold Ockenga, and Cesar Chavez foreshadowed the coming fragmentation of the Cold War Christian consensus. Opposition to communism combined with the Great War's legacy of "Western civilization" had allowed Americans to create a "Judeo-Christian" tradition and to wed it closely to European and North American civilization. Still, the universal claims of this synthesis concealed the essentially contestable nature of Christianity as well as the artificial ethnic and geopolitical borders drawn around it. Consensus Christianity militated against both tyrannical communism and rapacious capitalism, carefully arguing that New Deal liberalism's middle way unlocked Christianity's true potential. But other groups within and without the United States disagreed. Many Americans like Chavez felt shut out of the hard-won prosperity that consensus promised, or like Buckley rejected its political assumptions. They were less content with a consensus Christianity that assumed a white European origin for human freedom, or which rendered Christianity simply a form of ethics shorn of particular metaphysical claims. While they drew on some of its tactics, like the appeal to psychology, they also resisted its presumptions. Soon, it would become evident that the seeming Christian consensus of the Cold War would itself come apart.

CHAPTER SIX

Global Christianity and Black Freedom

⊹

B Y THE EVENING of April 3, 1968, Martin Luther King Jr. had a sore throat. He had spent a good part of the day traveling to Memphis, Tennessee, a city that had drawn much of his attention over the previous months. In February a malfunctioning garbage truck had killed two of the city's sanitation workers. A week later, the thirteen hundred employees of the City's Department of Public Works, mostly African Americans, had gone on strike. In March King arrived, delivering a speech and leading a rally of thousands of citizens in support of the strikers before returning home. But as the strikes persisted, riots broke out and the mayor called in the National Guard. The morning of the day his throat began to ache, a weary King returned to the city. He had developed a fever as well but made his way through cold rain to the Bishop Charles Mason Temple, a Pentecostal sanctuary. The crowd was calling for him.

His appearance there spoke to what King believed God wanted human civilization to look like. He told the union workers and their supporters that their movement was evidence of "God working in this period of the twentieth century." God was working, King knew, because "the masses of people are rising up. And wherever they are assembled today, whether they are in Johannesburg, South Africa; Nairobi, Kenya; Accra, Ghana; New York City; Atlanta, Georgia; Jackson, Mississippi; or Memphis, Tennessee, the cry is always the same: 'We want to be free.'"[1] He was assassinated the next day.

For a long time, King had linked the struggle of his Southern Christian Leadership Conference (SCLC) and other African American organizations that fought against Jim Crow and white supremacy in the United States to the liberation movements of black people in Ghana and Kenya and South Africa. As early as 1957 he joined the American Committee on Africa (ACOA), an interracial group that protested apartheid in South Africa and colonial injustice in other nations on the continent. The ACOA called that year for Americans to "concentrate their mental and spiritual forces in a universal effort—through prayer, public meetings, and all other peaceful means" toward the end of apartheid.[2] In connecting the American movement to the broader processes of decolonization, King was part of a tradition that included Howard University intellectuals Howard Thurman, Carter Woodson, and William Hansberry, who argued that white supremacy in the United States rendered white Americans' desire to identify their nation as a Christian civilization impossible. Like them, King argued that a true Christian society would embrace the imperative toward equality and justice that emerged from the lived experience of the world's peoples of color, not from Euro-American civilization. These ideas upended white Protestant belief that American democracy was the fruit of the uninterrupted march of European Christianity from the Reformation forward, and they contributed to the fracture of the Cold War Christian consensus.

But King also grounded the mission of the movement he led in the liberal Protestant tradition that described American democracy as the product of Euro-American Protestantism and that identified white supremacy as a blight upon rather than a feature of Western civilization. Indeed, his most famous speech, delivered at the Lincoln Memorial in Washington, DC, in August 1963, claimed that his own aims of racial justice were "deeply rooted in the American dream." He invoked the liberal Protestant slogan the "brotherhood of man" and presented the work of equality as the work of white and black Americans together. "There are some white people in this country who are as determined to see the Negro free as we are to be free," he insisted.[3] In his book on the SCLC's work in Birmingham and the 1963 March on Washington, King argued, "For too long the depth of racism in American life has been underestimated. . . . The strands of prejudice toward Negroes are tightly wound around the American character." The language describing racism as something entangling the American character rather than something inherent in that character was politic, and King constantly returned to it. "The surgery to extract [racism] is necessarily complex and detailed," he wrote. But the work was both possible and essential, because "this long-standing racist ideology has corrupted and diminished our democratic ideals."[4]

King's confidence in the Christian republican tradition's ability to produce an egalitarian society could sometimes stand at odds with his sense that the struggle with racism had to reach beyond that tradition, and the disjuncture reflected both a larger dispute within the black-freedom movement and a growing tension among American Christians more generally. Although he and other black Christian leaders dearly hoped to show the desegregation of the United States could emerge from the Christian republicanism valued by white Americans, as the wearying conflicts of the movement dragged onward King more and more often was willing to insist that Western democracies fell short of his oft-invoked ideal of an egalitarian "beloved community." He began to unravel the threads of Christianity and the Euro-American West that many white Americans took for granted were intertwined.[5] He insisted that American Christians should embrace the robust democratic activism of the South African Defiance movement, the nonviolent movement that gained Ghana independence, and, indeed, the massive resistance of King's own Southern Christian Leadership Conference. He moved toward a broader conception of what Christian civilization might be.

It is common for modern historians to emphasize the importance of the black Baptist and Methodist churches in the South to King's movement. The SCLC was committed to integration and to the notion that white American Christians could be brought to see that segregation violated those very Christian republican values they believed underlay their democracy. But historians have not always linked Christianity to other factions in the black-freedom movement. The Black Power movement, for instance, emerged in the middle 1960s as it became clear that despite the passage of federal laws like the Civil Rights Act and Voting Rights Act, violence and racism targeting African Americans had not ceased. Its advocates questioned whether King's dream of peaceful racial integration was possible and called instead for self-determination and sometimes racial separatism. Black nationalists, for their part, saw the black-freedom movement less as a story of integration in the United States than that of the struggle of a common international black community against white power. Many of these people rejected Christianity outright. The Nation of Islam held to the belief that, as Malcolm X put it, "The black masses that are waking up don't believe in Christianity anymore. All it's done for black men is help to keep them slaves."[6] The scholar Gayraud Wilmore argued that the rise of Black Power and black nationalism marked a "de-Christianization" of the movement, and some historians have agreed.[7]

But it is also possible to understand the relationship between the integrationist Christianity of the SCLC and the black nationalism of King's last speech not as a dispute between Christian and non-Christian movements, but as an argument over what exactly Christianity should mean to African Americans, and what sort of Christianity might advance the cause of human equality.[8] It was a debate present in Martin Luther King's mind, but hardly in his alone.

Christian Integration

Many of the educated, male leaders of the civil rights movement were trained in seminaries steeped in liberal Protestant ideas about the relationship between Christianity and democracy. True Christianity, they were taught, was ethical, egalitarian, and concerned with social progress—values they saw in core American documents like the Declaration of Independence. The language King and other African American Christians sometimes used to call for civil rights, therefore, echoed the confidence white American Christians had in the basic consonance between Christianity and the functioning of American democracy in the Cold War. When they criticized American racism they did so in the language of materialism used by white liberal Protestants, presenting racism as an act of dehumanization and violation of individual liberty. In 1956, at the Dexter Avenue Baptist Church, King declared that the economic abundance and ease of life in the United States "can cause one to live a life of gross materialism. . . . If you are to be a truly Christian nation you must solve this problem." But King in the same sermon declared that economic injustice and racism were simply two manifestations of the deeper evil of materialism, because "the segregator relegates the segregated to the status of a thing rather than elevate him to the status of a person." In total, King warned, Americans who embraced materialism of any sort "have lost the true meaning of democracy and Christianity." King could echo the Cold War Christian consensus's criticism of European totalitarianism and American greed alike, warning that racism was equally one of materialism's sins. He called this "prophetic Christianity"—a warning to the nation that materialism wrecked its own ideals. Prophetic Christianity did not share liberal Protestant confidence in progress, warning instead that sins like materialism demanded uncomfortable disruption and repentance.[9]

This sermon encapsulated many of the ideas that African American Christian leaders used as they advocated for racial equality. "Redeem the soul of America here in Alabama," declared one handbook for SCLC demonstrators.[10] The duty of black Christians in the United States was to remind Americans that the Christian republican ideal of human equality, derived from divine creation and underlaying American democracy, could be corrupted. SCLC leaders believed the values they preached were those of the nation's Christian republicanism, born of its legacy and espoused at its founding, and if the United States were to achieve these ideals Americans had abandon the sins of racism and segregation. As King told John F. Kennedy upon hearing the president's call for a law protecting African American civil rights in the fall of 1963, "The legislature [sic] which you will propose if implemented will move our nation considerably closer to the American Dream."[11] This sort of language was particularly useful when speaking to white leaders like Kennedy who believed in the Cold War Christian consensus at a time when patriotic language was politic.

Other African American leaders similarly framed the struggle for racial equality in terms of Christian republicanism and American ideals in twinned confrontation with materialist power, greed, and authoritarianism. Thurgood Marshall, a leading attorney for the National Association for the Advancement of Colored People (NAACP), spent the late 1940s and early 1950s stumping the country raising money for the NAACP's Legal Defense Fund. He frequently spoke at black churches and before black audiences at universities, clubs, and other gathering places, and he often drew upon the language of the Cold War Christian consensus to link the work of the Legal Defense Fund to American democracy. "The Fourteenth Amendment was no more or less than a codification of the Judeo-Christian ethic," he once said.[12] But he also pushed back against racial separatism or black nationalism. "Let's stop drawing the line [between] colored and white," he told a restive black audience upset about white Southern resistance to the *Brown v. Board of Education* decision and the murder of Emmett Till in Mississippi. Instead, Marshall urged patience and promised that democracy was coming. "Let's draw the line on who wants democracy for all Americans," he said.[13]

As a gay black man, Bayard Rustin, a veteran organizer who worked with King to assemble the Southern Christian Leadership Conference, found himself marginalized in both American society generally and in the heavily Baptist and Methodist SCLC, forced to resign from the SCLC's board after having helped to found the organization. But he also believed that the American democratic system was built upon a basically Christian impulse toward egalitarianism, and that civil rights workers should appeal to that impulse.[14] Like Marshall, Rustin argued that "the Judeo-Christian tradition and ethic" taught that human beings could instinctively tell right from wrong, and that "the moral, political, and social foundation of the Negro's position is so overwhelmingly just" that Americans could not help but be sympathetic to it. "America, the first nation to electrify the world with a new concept of man's capability of self-rule without Monarchs or Regents, must fulfill the promises of its Constitution and Declaration of Independence," he declared.[15] Rustin had faith that a prophetic reminder of the country's Christian heritage could inspire Americans to embrace racial equality.

In 1947, inspired in part by Gandhian nonviolent protest in India, Rustin organized what he dubbed the Journey of Reconciliation with fifteen other men, white and black, who intentionally rode segregated bus lines together throughout the south. Just outside Petersburg, Virginia, a white police officer stopped the riders and arrested one of them. Rustin's colleague George Houser confronted the officer and asked if he would sit next to a black man on a bus. The officer said no and confessed rather sheepishly, "I'm just not Christian enough, I guess." Rustin took this statement to be enormously important, enough that he referred to it twice in his summary report of the Journey of Reconciliation. Rustin believed the officer's resigned angst signaled a broader "psychological struggle" in the American conscience. Historian David Chappell has argued that by and large most white southern Christians had little solid theological rationale for preserving segregation, and based on his own experiences Rustin came to the same conclusion. But "in the South, where the caste system is rigidly defined, this confusion is extremely dangerous, and leads to frustration." Most of the people sitting on the buses who watched Rustin and his companions board, sit, break Jim Crow laws, and get arrested were "apathetic," even "where it was apparent from facial expressions that certain of them actually were for or against the action." For Rustin, their simultaneous confusion and unwillingness to act demonstrated that Americans struggled with "despair and cynicism." These passengers were reluctant to defend the system, could sense that it was wrong, but feared placing themselves in a confrontation.[16] Rustin seized upon this sentiment to urge black activists to make manifest the "spark of

God in each of us" and reject the false safety of "the material"—the weapons, laws, and bureaucracies that protected injustice.[17] In doing so, Rustin joined the ranks of King, Marshall, and other leaders who used the language of Christian republicanism to confront America with a conception of Christian democracy that included African Americans. At the same time, however, black leaders were looking to another source of inspiration as they sought to understand the relationship between Christianity and democracy: Africa.

Africa and the Challenge to the Christian West

In 1964, Andrew Young, a Baptist minister who was also the executive director of the SCLC, served on a committee of the World Council of Churches (WCC) that was studying the relationship between Christian evangelism and racism. He helped produce a report called "The Freedom Movement," which sought to frame the struggle for African American equal rights as a contest between Christian principles and the "cultural captivity" of racist American social institutions. The report claimed, as Rustin had believed, that Americans preferred the cultural captivity of racism simply because it was familiar, and if they were properly inspired by Christian teaching they would abandon it. That was the role of the movement. The report claimed that black Americans had "a sense of destiny . . . that God is calling them to be a reductive suffering group for all the people of America."[18]

As had Bayard Rustin, Young used the language of Christian republicanism: materialist forces in America were strangling its democratic Christian virtues, and only their restoration might allow democracy to thrive. But the WCC commissioned Young's report in the context of a broader debate over the role of Christianity in the decolonization movements of the postwar era. Young's report was intended to frame the black-freedom movement as one example of the relevance of Christianity to a wider range of issues of freedom and democracy across the globe. One Russian Orthodox WCC official observed that churches in the decolonizing world must "completely submerge themselves in the spirit of the country," but also that "in all this they must be true Christian witnesses."[19]

By the 1960s Martin Luther King Jr. was making the same argument. At a rally in December 1960 he said, "Within less than three years more than eighteen countries have received their independence in Africa. They are looking over here. . . . They want to know what we are doing about democracy." With the eyes of those nations on America, King pleaded with Americans to recognize that democracy "affirms there are certain basic rights. . . . They are God's gifts."[20] But more and more, King and his fellows also wanted to know what those nations were doing about democracy. African American leaders like Howard Thurman and Benjamin Mays had begun building connections with activists of color worldwide, drawing on what they learned to formulate an African American critique of colonialism. Particularly in India and Africa, these leaders learned lessons from non-Christian activists like Gandhi, and had begun to consider whether African American Christians might have more in common with non-Americans than with white American Christians who supported white supremacy.[21] But even so many African Americans did not perceive Africa to be relevant to their struggles. Joel A. Rogers, a prominent black author and newspaper columnist, observed that stories of Egypt and Ethiopia were widespread in the black community, but they were so ancient as to seem irrelevant to black people in the modern day. "The Negro, for centuries, has had drilled into him that all Africa had were huts," Rogers argued. He wanted to see this idea revised, and believed that better engagement with African history would do so. "Jim Crow's survival is going to depend largely on what Negroes, themselves, do about it. They must first know their history."[22] He urged reengagement with Africa.

Soon enough, events in Africa began encouraging African Americans to reconsider what that continent might offer their ideas about Christianity. In 1948 Daniel Malan, leader of the National Party, became the prime minister of South Africa. Malan and his party had run on a platform of strict segregation between the races, appealing to the anxieties of white Afrikaners who had seen migration of black Africans into the nation's cities during the industrial boom of World War II. Upon gaining power the National Party began to disenfranchise black citizens and discourage black migration to the city to satisfy white Afrikaner racism and to ensure that black South Africans remained a cheap source of labor. Whereas the South African government already provided for some degree of segregation, most notably in schools, the National Party promised to extend the rule. They called it *apartheid*, an Afrikaans word for "separation."

Malan was a Dutch Reformed clergyman, and he insisted that apartheid was a Christian principle. As one South African clergyman put it, some human beings, "having fallen into sin by the sin of their parents [Adam and Eve] have the mercy and justice of God revealed to them." Because God was merciful he saved some. But at the same time, "God is just in leaving others in the sin and ruin in which they have involved themselves."[23] Reformed Christians had long believed that God had predetermined some for salvation and some for damnation. Malan turned the idea into political theory for a Christian civilization: racial segregation, he believed, derived from the spiritual distinctions God had embedded in humanity. As Malan explained, apartheid was "based on what the Afrikaner regards as his godly calling and privilege—to convert the heathens to Christianity without wiping out their national identity. . . . The conversion of the heathen [is] a primary step in his march to civilization."[24] For its backers, then, white supremacy simply reflected the reality that white people were favored of God and black people required subordination.

The notion that Christianity taught democracy's dependence upon white supremacy had some backing in the United States as well. Some were overt. The American Nazi Party denounced Rustin's March on Washington for undermining a "White Christian Republic!!!" As had earlier advocates of Anglo-Saxonism, American Nazis believed that since Christianity was by its nature the property of white people, democracy based upon Christianity could only be implemented by white people.[25] Thus Sam Bowers, a Ku Klux Klan leader, believed that the civil rights movement sought to "destroy Christian Civilization and all Christians," because, he insisted, only "the Anglo-Saxon system of Government by responsible, FREE, Individual Citizens" could ensure that Christianity would persist.[26] For Bowers, "Christian" was a synonym for "Anglo-Saxon."

Other white American Christians were less overt but equally insistent that the black-freedom movement violated the social norms they associated with Christianity and democracy. The evangelical pastor J. W. Long argued that American Christianity was predicated on correct doctrine and obedience to the political order. He informed King in a letter, "You are in a position to help your own race, Americanism, and Christianity more than any other colored leader in America." But Long attacked King as a "false prophet" for studying at a liberal Protestant seminary and warned that King was not actually a Christian due to his activism but rather "a Communist, or a tool of the Communist Party."[27] Others were just as insistent on defining what a Christian politics looked like in ways that excluded King and the black freedom movement. The Mormon Levi Reynolds told King, "I do not countenance any man's being treated other than as a man," and voiced support for equal rights. But, he warned King, "Unless your people are willing to exemplify dignity and courtesy"—what Reynolds called "the rules of fair play in respecting the rights of others in the spirit of The Golden Rule"—they would never gain integration. The demonstrations the SCLC persisted in holding, and the riots that had recently swept the Watts neighborhood of Los Angeles, demonstrated for Reynolds that African Americans did not fit his conception of Christianity as respect for established institutional authority.[28] All these critics, like Malan, linked Christianity to the preservation of the social order they valued in the United States and therefore to the maintenance of white supremacy.

Some African American leaders sought to separate the notion of apartheid from the notion of Christian civilization, reading it as King was capable of reading American racism: as an aberration from and rejection of Christian values. Benjamin Mays, president of Morehouse College and a mentor to King and many other civil rights leaders, was a committed believer in liberal Protestant ideals and had spent time with Gandhi in India. He served as a delegate to the World Council of Churches. He pushed for a denunciation of apartheid at the First and Second Assemblies of the WCC, held in Toronto in 1950 and in Evanston, Illinois, in 1954. The latter year Mays chaired a commission that issued a report called "The Church Amid Racial and Ethnic Tension." Delivering the report before the council, Mays declared that "the early church and the church of the Middle Ages did not segregate on the basis of race. . . . Yet segregation remains the great scandal of the church, especially in the United States and South Africa."[29] For Mays, as for other critics of white liberal Protestants' notion of Christian civilization, to find a truly Christian society, Americans would have to look outside their own borders and national history.

Mays fused a liberal Protestant confidence that Christianity was the foundation of human equality with an unshakable certainty that racism demonstrated a sickness at the core of white Western society. Christianity and Western civilization could thus not be identical. As the years went on, a number of black leaders followed him. To many, the rise of apartheid called into question not only whether segregation was Christian, but whether white Euro-American civilization was capable of defining what Christian civilization was. The educator and activist Mary McLeod Bethune, who served as a delegate to the 1945 San Francisco organizing convention of the United Nations, argued that Christianity required repudiation of "civilization" in favor of the notion of "humanity." Bethune described the delegates to the convention as seeking an international "common good": "A spiritual something began to weld them together and to undergird their efforts as they worked on the development of a program for the common good. The leaven of democracy was at work." She called the event a "modern Pentecost," the moment in the New Testament when the Holy Spirit made Christianity available to every person in his or her own language.[30]

Bethune's vision of a Christianity that transcended conventional definitions of nation and civilization to promote an international democracy became particularly vivid to other African Americans in the 1950s and 1960s, as the struggle against apartheid intensified and as other African nations were gaining independence. More and more, black leaders began to describe visions of a Christian society that resembled American democracy less and the grassroots activism they saw in Africa more. One vocal leader seeking to direct black Christians away from the idea of Western civilization was A. Philip Randolph, the labor leader and activist who had led the fight to integrate the U.S. military in the 1940s. By the 1960s Randolph saw apartheid as a signal of the essential religious emptiness of Western electoral democracy, and the activist antiapartheid movement of black South Africans as the true representative of the democratic, egalitarian embodiment of Christianity.

Randolph's speeches from this era demonstrate his conviction that the problem of apartheid was a sign of Western civilization's lack of true Christianity. Repeatedly Randolph revised the myth of Western progress, decoupling racially segregated societies from their claim to Christianity and progress and instead linking them pagan Europe and medieval tyranny. In 1960 he called South Africa "a so-called Christian, democratic nation" and predicted that the antiapartheid protests taking place there were the "beginning of the decline and downfall of this modern Rome."[31] Indeed, Randolph declared, the true Christians—and hence the true democrats—were people of color who resisted dehumanization. "Verily, the test of Christianity is the test of the color line, as the test of democracy is the test of the color line," he insisted. Randolph believed that a true narrative of Christian history should link ancient Christians who resisted Rome to contemporary freedom movements. "The blood of martyrs has been the seed of the Church," he said. "By the same token, the blood of the martyrs of Africa [is] the seed of African freedom."[32] It was not the West but what he called "the Coalition of Conscience" that lay at the point of greatest

Christian progress toward the "very truth, all men, white and black, Jew and Protestant, African, Asian, European and American[,] are members of one common human family of which God is Father and Creator."[33]

That white Westerners could deny this truth and yet still continue to profess that they had a Christian civilization seemed to him a demonstration of "the illogic in modern thought." In June 1967, before the American Negro Leadership Conference on Africa, Randolph quoted Jan Smuts, former prime minister of South Africa. Smuts was often celebrated by Americans for being less extreme than his replacement, Malan. Indeed, Smuts had pressed for a human rights charter in the United Nations. American leaders viewed him as someone who shared their commitment to democracy, and because of him they understood South Africa and the United States to be, in the words of James Meriwether, "English speaking, Christian, capitalist, anti-communist western allies."[34] But Randolph pointed out that Smuts had also called for the "suppression of the Negro" in South Africa. This double-mindedness was telling; indeed, Randolph said, it illustrated "the twisted contradiction of thought in the minds of white Western man." He placed alongside apartheid the paradoxical American founding, in which the Declaration of Independence and slavery went hand in hand.[35]

On April 6, 1952, leaders of the African National Congress in South Africa held a "National Day of Pledge and Prayer," beginning the Defiance Campaign of nonviolent resistance to apartheid laws. Over the next few months thousands were arrested, and demonstrations, protests, and resistance escalated. In March 1961, South African police opened fire into a crowd of demonstrators in the city of Sharpeville, killing sixty-nine. Between these events, American civil rights leaders began pointing to the African National Congress and other protest organizations as exemplars of Christian protest. In 1953 Rustin, Randolph, and several other leaders organized Americans for South African Resistance. In January 1953, the organization declared that Africans who resisted apartheid were "putting Christianity into practice. They are refusing to consent to oppression; but they in their turn are refusing to injure their opponents. Such methods point to a future South Africa which will award equal value to persons of all colours."[36] Nearly three years before the Montgomery bus boycott, African American leaders saw a confrontation between a racist regime that claimed a Christian mandate and an alternative Christian society in the grassroots insurgency of those who defied it. It signaled the solidification of a perceived common identity between the two movements.

Over the next few years, African American leaders began to denounce what the newspaper the *Washington Afro-American* called "the great myth" of "friction between colored Americans and Africans." The "enormous impact Africa's successful freedom drive has had on the colored American's efforts" had, according to the newspaper, created an "emotional interrelationship" between black Americans and Africans. Declining tensions with the Soviet Union made Americans more willing to engage with international revolutionary movements, and African Americans in particular had resources directing them toward a common international black experience given the power of cultural trends like Negritude, a Francophone literary movement that spread throughout the African diaspora.[37] Influenced by these ideas, various civil rights leaders affirmed the newspaper's description of the relationship as "emotional," which implied a sense of spiritual identification beyond the bureaucratic formalities of citizenship. Martin Luther King, endorsing the South African resistance group Christian Action, said their commitment to "dignified nonviolent resistance" drew his support. As King said later, "Negroes were dispersed over thousands of miles and over many continents yet to-day they have found each other again."[38] Like Randolph, he was building an alternative narrative of Christian history.

African American leaders' cultivation of a sense of solidarity with African protests inspired frustration with the American government's unwillingness to forthrightly confront the apartheid regime. They took it as a sign that the white establishment of the United States was emotionally attached to the apartheid regime in the same way that they as African Americans were emotionally bound to its protestors. Speaking to black audiences, King was willing to argue that their common cause was generated in part because their enemies were in fact the same: "Colonialism and segregation are nearly synonymous; they are legitimate first cousins because their common end is economic exploitation, political domination and the debasing of human personality," he told the American Negro Leadership Conference (ANLC) on Africa in 1962. Segregation in the United States and the racial domination Malan defended were in fact both materialist, anti-Christian social orders. Thus, King told the ANLC, the problem could not be solved through "political or economic stratagems," but only through the "moral influence" of a righteous people mobilized to fight it.[39]

He did not see many righteous white Christians ready to take up the cause, and he blamed most white Americans' fascination with their nation's power, a symptom of the disease of materialism. In 1964, King reported, discouraged, "The shame of our nation is that it is objectively an ally of this monstrous government [of South Africa] in its grim war with its own black people." As had Randolph, King refused to subscribe to a narrative of Western progress, instead reversing ideas about who was civilized and who was not: "Africa has been depicted for more than a century as the home of black cannibals and ignorant primitives. . . . Africa does have spectacular savages and brutes today, but they are not black. They are the sophisticated white rulers of South Africa who profess to be cultured, religious and civilized, but whose conduct and philosophy stamp them unmistakably as modern-day barbarians."[40] Americans' commitment to profit and military strength made moral civilization impossible for them.

But as apartheid seemed to be tightening its grip in South Africa in the late 1950s, another African state gave the leaders of the black-freedom movement hope and a new sense of what a Christian civilization might look like. On March 6, 1957, Kwame Nkrumah, the leader of the Convention People's Party and the prime minister of the Gold Coast, a British colony on the west coast of Africa, led the nation in celebration of its independence as Ghana. Nkrumah had spent years in the United States studying theology and politics, and years in Africa agitating for independence. Ghanaians took immense pride in this achievement, and Americans found themselves on the wrong side of a comparison. In April 1957, a Ghanaian musician known as Ucano interrupted a performance in Los Angeles with a ten-minute impromptu sermon. A reporter speculated that he was "moved, no doubt, by the surge of pride in the newly won independence of his native Ghana." Regardless of his motives, after his calypso band finished a song in their set, Ucano delivered an oration comparing Ghana to the United States and denouncing the latter as "neither civilized nor Christian." For Ucano, neither term applied to a nation that accepted racial segregation.[41]

King and Randolph and a number of other civil rights leaders were present when Nkrumah announced Ghanaian independence, and they emphasized that, like the Defiance movement, the new nation illustrated the emergence of Christian values in a decidedly non-Western environment. Ghanaian independence, Randolph declared, was the child of nonviolent resistance and Christian equality: "the genius to achieve freedom and independence without recourse to violence and bloodshed," and the "universal passion of men for self-rule."[42] When King returned home, he told his congregation at the Dexter Avenue Baptist Church that a few days earlier he had seen Cecil B. DeMille's movie *The Ten Commandments*. DeMille explicitly framed the biblical story of Moses and the Exodus from Egypt as a metaphor for the role he believed Christianity should play in the Cold War, inquiring of the audience in a preface to the film, "Are men property of the state? Or are men free souls under God?" De Mille also presented the Exodus as the story of the United States, posing Moses descending Mount Sinai like the Statue of Liberty, with the eponymous commandments in one arm and his staff upheld in the other, and closing the film with Moses's recitation of the verses in Leviticus that are also inscribed on the Liberty Bell.[43]

King, however, read the story of Moses against DeMille's wishes. He saw in it the story of Ghanaian independence and by extension a story of Christianity manifest in the struggle of the world's peoples of color. Egypt in the film was much like the European and American civilizations that had colonized Africa for centuries. King put in the mouth of the British the evil Pharaoh's words: "The British said that we will not let you go."[44] In the Israelite slaves, he saw the people of Ghana, who intuitively grasped the that true Christianity demanded human liberty. "There seems to be an internal desire for freedom within the soul of every man," King observed. "The masses of people never profit by Egypt, and they are never content with it. And eventually they rise up and begin to cry out for Canaan's land." King bound racism and economic exploitation together, arguing that true Christianity called not simply for the freedom that white liberal Protestants cherished, but struggle, activism, and solidarity. "Like any breaking loose from Egypt, there is a wilderness ahead," King said. The wilderness was economic exploitation by the West. "In order to make the economic system more stable, it will be necessary to industrialize," King observed, and then he urged, as a solution, African Americans to migrate. "Right now is the time that American Negroes can lend their technical assistance to a growing new nation. . . . It's going now through the wilderness. But the Promised Land is ahead."[45]

Other African Americans found in the liberation of Ghana a similar story. Jane Bond, research and information secretary of the Southern Christian Leadership Conference, recalled in a letter that the inspiration of Nkrumah had changed her vision of what the black-freedom movement was. While originally she had the "desire to end specific instances of segregation," now, she wrote, "I have enlarged this view and now I see myself as part of a struggle for freedom." Quoting Nkrumah, she declared her aims to be the cultivation of "a genuine respect and appreciation for each other" and the "eradication of the evils of oppression, exploitation of man by man, racialism and intolerance." Seeing the American civil rights movement through the lens of the African freedom movement led Bond to expand her desires from mere political policy to a reformulation of what civilization was.[46]

In the protests against South African apartheid and the Ghanaian independence movement, African American Christians saw vivid examples of non-Western Christian civilization. Both of these developments inspired civil rights leaders in the United States to broaden the scope of their thinking past America's boundaries, sharpening their religious critique of American racism. They also made some African American Christians less confident that the Christian consensus of Cold War white America, with its roots in European Christianity and its essentially liberal Protestant optimism, could solve the problem of racism itself. Instead, many of them began looking for other options and found in particular two: a reformulation of what democracy was and a wholesale rejection of Westernized narratives of Christianity.

The Freedom Schools and a Grassroots Christianity

This identification of Christian civilization with the African oppressed who recognized their subjugation and defied it shaped in practical terms how many of the movement's leaders understood what it meant to be Christian in the United States. On March 21 and 22, 1964, a number of educators and other civil rights leaders attended a National Council of Churches workshop in New York City. Their goal was to construct a curriculum for the Freedom Schools, summer-long institutes for black teenagers to be held in Mississippi that year in conjunction with the massive voter-registration drive called Freedom Summer. "The only thing our kids knew about Negro history was Booker T. Washington and George Washington Carver and his peanuts," said Ralph Featherstone, a Freedom School coordinator. The Freedom Schools aimed not just to educate African American children about their own history but to reframe what it meant to be a Christian civilization by privileging the world's people of color.[47] Likewise, they sought to identify the Christian roots of democracy not with liberal Protestant ideas about individual liberty and virtue but with the imperative toward collective activism.

One of the earliest lesson plans the curriculum committee reviewed was on the revolt of enslaved Africans on the slave ship *Amistad* in 1839 and the 1841 U.S. Supreme Court decision ordering them freed. The committee recommended the lesson to begin instruction in the Freedom Schools because it laid out their intended approach to American history. "Within this story can be found most of the major issues to be included in the subsequent curriculum," the syllabus stated. The themes the lesson drew from the incident included the pivotal idea that "protest is nothing new for Negroes," as the syllabus instructed. Educators were instructed to link the *Amistad* revolt to slave rebellions and to the abolitionism of Frederick Douglass. But beyond that tradition, the committee chose the *Amistad* story because "the primary assumption of this course outline is that America is the result of the fusion of African[,] European, Indian and other peoples and their cultures," as the syllabus stated. The episode illustrated that the tradition of communal action—of protest and democratic involvement—lay near the heart of the society African Americans sought to build in the United States and that this tradition derived from their African heritage, not from Western history.[48]

In the spring of 1961, the SCLC began sponsoring the Citizenship Education Program (CEP), a group that encouraged black participation in politics through education and mobilization of the poor farming and working classes. Septima Clark, a teacher in South Carolina's Sea Islands who had been directing the CEP for four years when the SCLC got involved, claimed in 1965 that more than fourteen hundred black people, mostly in South Carolina and Georgia, had received the standard week of "intensified training" in "adult literacy" and a "basic understanding of politics."[49] But the aim went beyond teaching simple skills. Highlander, the program's parent organization, was invested in a vision of a grassroots Christian democracy bound into the international Christian movement that was emerging in part from Africa. One of Highlander's defenders, the college professor Eugene Kayden, called Christians to the "'work of reconciliation.' . . . These words reveal the purpose of the Christian way of life, the task of Church and Society. Highlander is part of a world-wide movement . . . for responsible citizenship in a democracy."[50] Highlander thus emphasized less the Christian republican tradition that stressed individual virtue than to an understanding of Christian politics that stressed collective solidarity and democratic action.

To Clark and many others involved in the movement, Christianity brought to politics not only liberal Protestant ideas about virtue and equality. Instead, they looked to Africa and declared that Christianity also required a sense of collective belonging and mass consciousness. Clark claimed to have been raised with ideals close to those of Christian republicanism. She remembered the "strict code under which I had been reared," as she called it.[51] She credited this upbringing with a sense of dignity, remembering that her mother had insisted on being addressed as "Mrs." and her father as "Mr. Poinsette." Her mother's emphasis on self-respect derived from her role as the custodian of the family's morality. "I have thanked a kind Providence for my parents, for the fact that they were persons of strong character, of great personal integrity, for the pride they had," Clark wrote in her autobiography.[52] Her upbringing thus reflected the sense of racial uplift popular among early twentieth-century African Americans.

But on the other hand, by the time she became involved with the Highlander programs, Clark had concluded that her parents' Christianity was too passive and docile, and she blamed white supremacy. "They had Christianized him," she said of her father, who had been born in slavery. "He was one of the house servants."[53] After she married she found what she called "a more advanced idea of what being a Christian really means," derived from a growing consciousness of her African American identity.[54] She took classes from W. E. B. Du Bois and at Columbia University; she got involved in community service and social activism, joining the NAACP and the branch of the Young Women's Christian Association for African Americans. To the sense of moral worth and rigorous self-discipline she had gained from her parents, she added an impulse toward social activism and community involvement. While King and Rustin drew on liberal Protestant notions of civilization to demand racial integration, Clark's work pointed toward a vision of a black Christian democracy as a mobilized, participatory community. A 1959 citizenship-education workbook Clark used defined democracy as both "a goal that will bring dignity and freedom to all" and a process. "We hold that democracy is inactive unless workers are given a full voice in industry through unions; or farmers are given a voice in the market place through cooperatives; or when freedom of thought and discussion is limited; that democracy is outlawed by legally entrenched discrimination and segregation."[55]

The CEP's work in Georgia is a good case study. On February 25, 1963, Clark and Andrew Young were in Jacksonville, Georgia, making the traditional visit marking the opening of a Citizenship School and the beginning of an accompanying voter-registration drive. Clark had been running training sessions for teachers for several weeks before Young arrived. That night, roughly two hundred people gathered for the formal announcement of the opening of the school. Over hot cocoa, Young preached a sermon called "The Bible and the Ballot," and Clark declared, "We have now within our grasp a new kind of society. A learning society made up of educative communities" among a mobilized people.[56] That mobilization was best achieved through the church, because the church was to be understood as a vehicle for the creation of a Christian society. The CEP's manual for civic organizing and voter registration stated, "We should understand that there is a difference between Church Work, and The Work of the Church. The 'Work of the Church' is to bring the world into relationship to God. This can not be done by preaching and teaching alone. The Church must be out in the world actively working and witnessing."[57]

The Citizenship Education Program came to Albany, Georgia, in August 1962, and offered a similar vision. For nine months, starting in November of the previous year, the SCLC, NAACP, and Student Non-Violent Coordinating Committee (SNCC) had organized demonstrations, boycotts, and protests. The city's chief of police, however, offered careful and measured responses, avoiding violent incidents and confrontation. When in July African American protestors began throwing objects at police, King urged an end to the demonstrations and left town. Annell Ponder, who worked under Clark in the Citizenship Education Program, arrived soon after to try a different tactic. She urged not demonstration but organization to overcome the city's segregation; an appeal not to King's Christian republicanism but to the solidarity and community of Septima Clark. In a report to Clark, Ponder particularly lambasted the black churches of the city for the movement's failure. "The majority of the ministers in Albany seemed unaware of the relatedness of the church to the everyday life of their members. Many of them were openly against the actions of the Albany Movement," she wrote. She announced a "Religion and Community Life" course, directed at local ministers and designed to promote "consideration of the individual churches' conception of the community and the role of their church in it."[58]

Ponder's distinction between demonstration and organization was important to Septima Clark. Whereas some civil rights leaders argued that the purpose of demonstration was to prick the consciences of white Americans and remind them of their Christian duties, Clark believed just as strongly that the aim of the movement was to organize an African American society following what she called "a Christian Philosophy of Life." As she reported in 1964, having run a series of trainings in South Carolina, "The Citizenship School Teachers reported that the ministers, both white and Negro, had become committed to a Christian Philosophy of Life." She described what she meant by the phrase in two ways. The first example she gave was "a city-wide mass meeting, [where] citizens were asked to give $2.90" each to support young African Americans ready to test the recently passed Civil Rights Act by seeking to integrate schools, motels, movie theaters, and other facilities. A Christian philosophy of life supported integration, but also demonstration, activism, and protest. Second, Clark warned that this shift could cause dissonance. Many black people, she said, "cling to methods and instruments, schedules and curricula, that belong to past conditions." Those conditions were "stable" and "predictable," but they also discouraged action. At the mass meetings, Clark said, "church members were converted and had learned to feel truly comfortable with change."[59]

There was persistent worry among citizenship activists like Clark that the professional ministers at the head of the SCLC did not fully understand the CEP's vision of what democracy should mean. Many such activists were women, less educated in the liberal Protestantism of the north and instead shaped by the black churches of the South. Dorothy Cotton, who ran the Citizenship Education Program from SCLC headquarters in Atlanta, wrote to one minister in Albany, Georgia, after the CEP's sessions there had concluded: "Too many of our leaders move away from the people physically and spiritually—away from those who need our help the most."[60] Clark recalled urging Martin Luther King to spend less time organizing demonstrations and more time training others who could also organize demonstrations, and remembered that King found her exhortations amusing. Despite King's commitment to an active, democratic Christian community, he grounded himself in the traditional moral and social authority of the male minister in the black Baptist churches. His churchly authority as a minister derived from his education in liberal Protestantism, so his faith in white America's capacity to redeem itself was intimately linked to the authority that led him to dismiss Septima Clark.[61]

Toward a Christian Black Nationalism

In 1961, the *Evening News,* a Ghanaian newspaper founded by Kwame Nkrumah, aroused some distress in the American Christian community. "Nkrumah is our Messiah," it declared, "the Christ of our day, whose great love for mankind wrought changes in Ghana, in Africa and in the world at large." To Americans the declaration cast some of Nkrumah's earlier actions in an ominous light. In 1958 his government had asserted the authority to imprison anyone it deemed a threat to the regime, and the World Council of Churches heard protests when Nkrumah began expelling white clergy a few years later. Christian Baeta, a Ghanaian Presbyterian minister, told the WCC that "many things have happened in Ghana in which the Church can rejoice, but there are things we do not like so well." Nkrumah's paper, for its part, warned the West, "God does not like imperialist chicanery." Nkrumah asserted independence from Cold War polarization and the Cold War Christian consensus alike.[62]

Nkrumah identified as a "non-denominational Christian and Marxist socialist" and stated, "I have not found any contradiction between the two."[63] To Americans accustomed to the Cold War Christian consensus that emphasized individual virtue and feared communism, this was gibberish. But Nkrumah asserted that, in fact, both philosophies contributed to what he called the African personality. He believed atheism incompatible with the African personality, and that socialism helped colonized people understand their situations. Thus, while to American Christians his religious ideas seemed dangerous, Nkrumah maintained they simply reflected Christianity as seen through the eyes of people of color. He saw in the African personality a set of "humanist principles" that echoed W. E. B. Du Bois's praise for the supposedly egalitarian nature of traditional African society, and he blasted Western Christianity for surrendering its own notion of "the accountability of the individual conscience" and embracing slavery and racism.[64]

By the late 1960s, black Christians in South Africa were echoing similar themes. Groups like the Pan-African Congress and the South African Students' Organization (SASO) rejected integration as long as, as SASO leader Steve Biko put it, "integration, whose virtues are often extolled in white liberal circles, is full of unquestioned assumptions that embrace white values." Those assumptions, Biko said, had similarly polluted the form of Christianity that upheld Western democracy. European missionaries who came to Africa insisted that "people had to discard their clothes and their customs in order to be accepted in this new religion." The Christianity the missionaries brought taught white supremacy, and thus, "with the ultimate acceptance of the western religion down went our cultural values." For Biko, white Christianity was a "cold and cruel religion." It had created a society that enforced racial hierarchy, ruled through fear, and promoted cultural imperialism.[65]

To Biko, this sort of Christianity had very little in common with true Christianity, which far more closely resembled what he described as traditional African religion. "There was no hell in our religion. We believed in the inherent goodness of man—hence we took it for granted that all people at death joined the community of saints and therefore merited our respect," he wrote. Both African indigenous religion and Christianity as Biko understood it promoted values of communal solidarity and inherent human worth. Biko called for a "Black Consciousness" movement, which like Nkrumah's African personality necessitated self-respect and a rejection of the racist assumptions he believed undergirded too much talk about integration with white society. He hungered for a black version of Christianity. In 1974 he preached a sermon from Ezekiel 37, a chapter in which God instructs the prophet to resurrect dry bones by preaching to them. "I likened the Black people in this country to the bones that Ezekiel talks about," he remembered. He interpreted the story to mean that "we, the people, would come and lead the people of God . . . Ezekiels in the Black community." Beginning in the 1960s and 1970s, a number of African Christians shared these ideas, building a corpus of African Christian theology which emphasized solidarity, reliance on African tradition and culture, and suspicion of white culture.[66]

In the early 1970s, a number of African American theologians held a series of conferences in Africa, meeting with African theologians in Tanzania in 1971 and Ghana in 1974. Important differences between the African Americans and the Africans emerged—particularly, as Union Theological Seminary's James Cone observed, in conversation about "the relationship between liberation and selfhood." Cone's own paper at the Ghana meeting argued that because of the experience of African Americans in a racist society, "Black theology emphasizes liberation as the central message of the Christian gospel." Cone stressed Jesus's suffering and the promise of salvation as political liberation illustrated in the Exodus. However, a number of African theologians, particularly Kwesi Dickson of the University of Ghana, disagreed. Dickson argued that "Africans must approach God in

Christ and not in Westernism." Instead, he said, "African theology, as it is developing, might be considered as a theology of selfhood." Rather than emphasizing liberation, Christianity to Dickson meant the recovery of identity, "indiginisation," against the power of colonialism. Like Cone, he emphasized the Old Testament, but while Cone read it as a text of liberation Dickson understood it as the story of a people who discovered themselves in the creation of ritual, culture, and community. Dickson praised the book of Leviticus rather than following Cone's emphasis on Exodus, finding in the rituals of the ancient Israelites forerunners to contemporary African practices.[67] Cone, though, believed that "both terms represent two ways of talking about the same reality" and identified the central problem both Africans and African Americans confronted as "colonization," which "dehumanized" both peoples.[68]

Cone's attempt at reconciliation used the language of materialism, arguing that both Africans and African Americans could find in Christianity a vitalizing language to preserve the sacredness of their humanity against forces that denied it. That theme, which characterized much of Cone's theological work in the late 1960s and early 1970s, drew together the varying themes that had characterized African American activism in the previous decades. Inspired by the notion that Christianity taught racial solidarity and thus was less than supportive of American democratic government, many Christian African Americans began to feel more kinship with African leaders like Biko and Nkrumah than with white Christians in their own country. These ideas came closer to Septima Clark's vision of Christianity as a vital community than to the Christian republicanism of white Americans.

Cone, though, confronted some disagreement. In 1966, the SNCC leader Stokely Carmichael began to popularize the term *Black Power*, emphasizing black self-reliance rather than integration. He warned that the Christian religion white Americans had adopted "was not originally intended to include [black people and it does not include the black masses today." If black people needed a Christianity, Carmichael said, it should be the religion of the Exodus—the Old Testament, not the New. "A God of justice and of ultimate and righteous retribution. A god who absolutely forbade oppression and was not mocked."[69] While Carmichael rejected Cone's insistence on rooting himself in Christianity, some African American women, like the activist and Episcopal priest Pauli Murray found Cone's emphasis on black liberation paradoxically limiting. She criticized Cone for "little understanding of the problems of Black women as women" and argued that theologians like Cone made the category of blackness too sweeping. Murray urged instead "a universal perspective within the context of particulariza-tion," arguing that Cone limited Christianity's liberating message by reading it only through the lens of racial oppression.[70] However, she also blasted the presumption that white Euro-American civilization had special claim to Christianity. In a sermon Murray preached "Christ, in whom there is no East or West, no North or South, no Black or White, no Red or Yellow, no Jew or Gentile, no Islam or Buddhist, no Baptist, Methodist, Episcopa-lian, or Roman Catholic, no Male or Female."[71] Murray's expansive vision of oppression led her to a Christ completely divorced from human constructs of civilization, a Christ who brought reconciliation across many identities.

Albert Cleage, a minister in Detroit and friend of Cone and Malcolm X alike, on the other hand, attempted to articulate what a black nationalist Christianity might look like. As had William Hansberry, Cleage tried to escape Christianity's Western influences and looked instead to Afrocentric inspiration. In the early 1960s Cleage had gotten involved in Detroit poli-tics, engaging in a school-board battle over textbooks and faculty that he felt supported white supremacy and denigrated African history. By the middle 1960s Cleage was arguing that Christianity as understood by white Ameri-cans was corrupt. Both white and black Americans, he said, believed in a false "slave Christianity," by which he meant ethically rigorous Christian republicanism. "But the whiteness of Jesus and Israel was basic to slave Christianity. Old master taught Black people that God was primarily con-cerned with petty sins (you don't fornicate, you don't smoke, you don't play cards, you don't drink)." Both white and black Christians, he said, were still prodigiously committed to slave Christianity, and this fixation ren-dered America itself a nation of "escapism and individualism." For Cleage, Christian republicanism's concern for individual morality was simply a veneer over a true obsession with materialism, profit, and the maintenance of power.[72]

Like some African theologians like Steve Biko, Cleage identified true Christianity with the African community in total; he also spurned the no-tion that Christianity was the foundation for American democracy. Rather, Christianity was intended to be coterminous with an independent black nation. Like Carmichael, Cleage preferred the Old Testament to the New. "Only if we can rediscover the historic roots of Christianity and strip from them the mystical distortions that are not basic to the concept of nation as revealed in the Old Testament and in the revolutionary teachings of Jesus, will we be able to bring the Black Christian Church into the Liberation Struggle and make it relevant to the lives of Black people," he declared. For Cleage, the mission of Jesus was to call the black nation of Israel to unify against its oppression. By "mystical distortions," he meant an excessive focus on individual spirituality, which was the fault of the apostle Paul, who altered the revolutionary message of Jesus to make it acceptable to the white rulers of Rome. As William Hansberry had, Cleage identified ancient African civilizations as the true source of Christianity, though Cleage was blunter than Hansberry. He declared that Jesus Christ was a black African, a "Black Messiah who came to a Black Nation," and he taught that the ancient nation of Israel was black as well.[73]

But unlike Hansberry, who had little to say about Africa as it stood in his time and who, like other African American believers in civilizationism, basically sympathized with liberal Protestant ideas, Cleage held a view of Christianity that was defiantly non-Western. It encompassed both African Americans and black Africans, who were common heirs of a cultural tradition distinct from the Christian West of the Cold War Christian consensus. "Black children must be taught that the communal life of Africa is essential for the survival of Black people," Cleage exhorted, encouraging African Americans to perceive Africans as their true family. "The white man is controlling Black people everywhere in the world. . . . We must send representatives to Africa. We must join with our African brothers in redefining the revolutionary religion of the Black Messiah."[74]

Cleage's passionate fusion of the American black-freedom movement with African theology brought together a number of ways of thinking about the relationship between Christianity and civilization in the United States. He repeated the call for a Christian church focused less on the rigorous morality of the Christian republican tradition and more upon community solidarity. African decolonization movements proved to Americans like Cleage that Christianity could inspire black people to perceive themselves as such a community. At the same time, this vision increasingly drove Cleage and other black leaders to separate that Christian community from American democracy, denying the Christian republican synthesis and severing the instinctive connection between Christianity and American democracy that many white Americans took for granted. Particularly in the context of the Cold War Christian consensus, to many white Americans this act seemed a betrayal both of the nation and of the faith. Indeed, as the 1960s went on, the Cold War Christian consensus seemed to many

Americans who had always supported it to be coming unraveled, facing challenges from other versions of Christianity, straining to embody its own ideas, and increasingly failing to protect American democracy. In fact, the nation was facing a debate over what precisely it meant to be a Christian nation after all.

CHAPTER SEVEN

Cult and Countercult

TOWARD DUSK ON DECEMBER 14, 1973, Richard Nixon left the White House, prepared to light the National Christmas Tree on the Ellipse a few hundred feet south. When he arrived, he was greeted by hundreds of young people cheering him wildly and carrying signs that read, "God Loves America. God Loves Nixon. Support the President." Nixon, apparently a bit abashed, shook the hand of their leader, Neil Salonen, after the ceremony, but later the White House issued a statement that the lighting of the tree "was not the place for a political rally."[1]

The president's ambivalence continued. After the Christmas tree dedication, Salonen and his followers organized the National Prayer and Fast for the Watergate Crisis Committee which appeared at the White House fences several times to pray for Nixon. Six weeks later, after the January 31 National Prayer Breakfast, Salonen's group held another rally at Lafayette Park, behind the White House, and the next day Nixon agreed to meet with Salonen's superior, the Reverend Sun Myung Moon. Salonen was a member of Moon's Holy Spirit Association for the Unification of World Christianity, commonly called the Unification Church, or, more derisively, the Moonies. On February 1, 1974, Nixon and Moon sat down in the White House for twenty minutes, and Moon told the president, "Don't knuckle under to pressure. Stand up for your convictions." He bowed his head and prayed fervently, and he urged Nixon to declare a day of fasting and national repentance. After the meeting, the White House issued a statement, explaining that the visit was impromptu, and that "the President wanted to take the opportunity to personally thank Rev. Moon for his support."[2]

Nixon welcomed Moon into the White House because that winter the president needed friends. He had recently won reelection by a historic margin, but in 1973 and 1974 a decade's worth of strain upon the nation, some of which Nixon himself had inflicted, was unraveling the Cold War Christian consensus. According to the Gallup Poll, over the course of 1973 Nixon's popularity plummeted from a high of near 70 percent to barely 30 percent.[3] By late that year oil prices had skyrocketed due to war between Egypt and Israel, and Nixon was bogged down in a mushrooming corruption scandal the media labeled Watergate, which would end his presidency by the fall of the following year. By then American soldiers had been fighting in Vietnam for nearly ten years.

One way Nixon tried to combat these problems was through embrace of the Cold War Christian consensus. Nixon invited the evangelist Billy Graham to pray at his inauguration, and Graham denounced the country's "materialistic and permissive" sins, pleading for a "moral and spiritual restoration." A few weeks later Graham visited the president at the White House to talk about faith, and a reporter observed that Nixon spoke about religion "in personal and ethical terms," emphasizing the importance to democracy of a nation of moral citizens. Graham visited the White House throughout Nixon's presidency, lending the president the weight of his spiritual authority.[4] But such attempts were failing, because by the 1970s the Christian consensus seemed to be weakening both inside and out. On the one hand, leaders like Nixon failed to offer the nation moral leadership, and increasing numbers of American Christians (Moon's followers among them) worried that the public-minded Christianity of the Cold War had become morally flaccid. On the other hand, Moon also represented the challenge posed by the nation's burgeoning religious pluralism to the ecumenical Christian consensus.

Graham's support for Nixon meant that it was particularly devastating to both men when Graham, shaken by Watergate, stated publicly that Nixon's scandals "will cause Americans to realize how fragile our democracy is, how fragile our security is. And I think this was demonstrated in the case of Viet Nam, and the energy crisis as well. . . . It should bring us to a point of national repentance." For Graham, all these things were signs of national drunkenness on power, wealth, and other material fixations. "When six per cent of the world's population controls so much of the world's wealth, we have a terrible responsibility," he said. "We're not almighty, as we thought for a while."[5] Graham's criticism of the Nixon administration echoed an increasingly vocal cadre of Christian critics of the Vietnam War and American capitalism, who by the 1970s were willing to call for a thorough-going revision of the meaning of Christianity in the American public sphere.

While Nixon's corruption weakened the Christian consensus from within the American establishment, there seemed to be pressure from the outside as well. In 1965 President Lyndon Johnson signed the Hart-Celler Act, which loosened border laws that had long held immigration from non-European countries to a trickle. By the late 1970s, 40 percent of new migrants to the United States were Asian.[6] The law paralleled, and in part drove, a growing sense of diversity in American culture. For instance, throughout the 1950s a mere two thousand immigrants from the Indian subcontinent came to the United States. By the 1980s, the number was more than a quarter million, and there were nearly a million practicing Indian Hindus in the United States.[7]

Those numbers were far outstripped by Americans who embraced some form of what has been called "American Hinduism"—a loose cluster of practices and beliefs drawing on the traditions of the Indian subcontinent, but also reflective of American culture and American ideas.[8] Prominent figures like Swami Vivekananda had popularized Hindu philosophies in the United States in the nineteenth century, but in the 1960s a host of new popularizers emerged, from the Beatles (who made heavily publicized trips to India and took up Transcendental Meditation) to the author and ex-Anglican priest Alan Watts to the ex-Harvard professor Richard Alpert, who took the name Ram Dass on a trip to India in 1967. Maharishi Maresh Yogi, the founder of the Transcendental Meditation movement, appeared on the cover of *Time* magazine and on the popular *Merv Griffin Show* in 1975, attracting wide attention and thousands of followers. One journalist visiting a Jewish gathering in 1979 noted, watching the crowd, "One man, a dentist in the orange shirt and trousers of a Swami, is on his way to Muktananda's ashram in India; a schoolteacher has done Transcendental Meditation; several people wear Hindu meditation beads; two men have come from a Gurdjieff community in West Virginia."[9] In the 1960s and 1970s dozens of groups like these appeared on the American cultural scene. Many called themselves Christian, but offered practices other self-identified Christians found foreign and disturbing. They reached out to Americans discontented with the Cold War consensus, argued that Americans had already succumbed to the pressures of materialism, and offered different visions of what a Christian society might look like.

Nixon's lukewarm embrace of Moon thus reflected the conundrum many American Christians faced in the 1960s and 1970s. Moon's version of Christianity seemed to these Americans to be their own in a funhouse mirror: recognizable but at the same time strangely skewed by Moon's race and rhetoric. Though Moon professed himself to be a Christian and an American patriot, these people were suspicious of the Unification Church for two key reasons.

First, they consistently labeled such movements, even those that had little contact with Asian religious traditions, "Eastern" rather than "Western." The label echoed Will Durant and indicated the extent to which many Americans believed Christianity to be necessarily white, derived from Europe, and present in Asia only in derivative or counterfeit form. They worried, then, that non-Western Christianities would undermine the political norms that they believed derived from the faith. Moon, depicted as a sort of authoritarian stereotype, seemed to them a particular example of the sort of government an illegitimate Christianity might enable. After Nixon's resignation in August 1974, reporters discovered documents revealing that Moon referred to Nixon as an "archangel" (by which, to be fair, Moon meant a defender from the evil of communism, but a title that the *Washington Post* considered deeply strange for an elected official). The same year, a Unification newspaper reported that Moon "knew that in a world where evil already prevails, the President must have that kind of right, even the right to dissolve the House and Senate, if necessary." Reacting to such reports, the evangelical senator Mark Hatfield said he believed that Moon was "dangerous, particularly . . . the cultic adoration of his followers." A few months after Nixon's resignation, the *Washington Post* called Moon's church "something other than just another brand of Christianity."[10]

Second, Americans critical of these movements associated them with immoral behavior that stood in opposition to the virtues which they believed derived from the Christian consensus. While liberal Protestant virtues called for self-discipline, individual liberty, and public spiritedness, new Christian movements were attacked for being decadent, collectivist, and separatist—also traits long associated with stereotypes about Asians. "Eastern" Christianity seemed to Americans an oxymoron for all these reasons, and the back and forth between these movements and their critics reveals the extent to which Americans linked race, democracy, and religion.

Perhaps Sun Myung Moon's chief interlocutor was the evangelical countercult movement. Evangelical Protestants had long combatted what they called "cults," and by the late 1960s they were beginning to link cults to the social and political transformations they saw in American society. Facing the rise of the cults on the one hand and an increasingly ecumenical Cold War Christian consensus on the other, conservative evangelicals feared the emergence of a materialist society that threatened the morality and liberty they believed undergirded American democracy. The rise of the political movement termed the "Religious Right" in the late 1970s and 1980s was a reaction to that fear but was also presaged by the countercult movement. The Religious Right's arguments against political liberalism and the countercult movement's arguments against new religious movements mirrored each other closely, because to conservative evangelicals they were two manifestations of the same materialist problem.

The Children of God Opt Out

The most publicized and perhaps infamous new religious movement of the 1970s, other than the Unification Church, was David Berg's Children of God. The two groups shared some characteristics. Both flourished on the West Coast. Before Moon arrived in the United States in 1972, Unification missionaries from Korea had built communities in Moon's name around Washington, DC, and in the San Francisco Bay Area. By the early 1960s, the movement was slowly growing in both areas, attracting Asian immigrants and lower-middle-class white Protestant families. By the later 1960s, though, the makeup of Moon's converts had shifted. Particularly in California they were younger, less educated, and less attached to institutions or family networks; they were also more interested in activism and social change.[11] Likewise, David Berg settled in southern California in 1967 to work at a coffeehouse run by an evangelical Christian ministry. He was the son of two Pentecostal missionaries with histories of visionary experiences and a suspicion of established American denominations; in her autobiography his mother denounced churches in which "everything was done in perfect decency and order" but without the "warmth or power of God." In 1961 Berg received a revelation affirming his mother's wisdom, and he moved to the disorganized and fragmented world of hippie California in search of the social change he believed Christianity mandated.[12]

Berg despised what he called "Churchianity," the bland religion of the Cold War Christian consensus, which he believed affirmed the American status quo and posed few real demands upon its followers.[13] He was in this sense typical of a radical fringe of evangelical Christians in the late 1960s and early 1970s. Discontented with the war in Vietnam and the strength of American consumerism and inspired by the protests of the black-freedom movement and the New Left, young evangelical leaders like John Alexander, Sharon Gallagher, and Jim Wallis tried to revise what it meant to have a Christian politics in the United States. "Jesus was being crucified again by our American Christianity," Wallis remembered, because it had "become captive to its culture and trapped by a narrow vision of economic self-interest and American nationalism." Wallis founded a magazine called *The Post-American,* and Gallagher and some associates formed a group called the Christian World Liberation Front—titles which revealed their alienation from the Cold War Christian consensus. In 1970 Wallis and some allies issued a manifesto denouncing American capitalism, racism, and the militarism of the Cold War and condemning the Cold War Christian consensus for supporting these things. "Because Christians are not living the gospel they are proclaiming, the church has become tragically irrelevant to our times and problems," the manifesto warned. Underlying these positions was a conviction that American Christians had misunderstood their faith's politics. These evangelicals argued that American capitalism had seduced citizens into a radical individualism, centered entirely on personal gain and progress. Rather, they contended, echoing older Catholic opinions, that Christianity required a sense of communal responsibility and that individual liberty was best expressed through membership in the community.[14]

The Christian World Liberation Front and Wallis's Sojourners community sought to enact these ethics through experiments in communal living, civil actions in imitation of the black-freedom movement, and efforts to politically mobilize the evangelical community. But David Berg, who emerged from the same radical evangelical Californian community as the Christian World Liberation Front, and who shared a similar distaste for the American status quo, was to attract more media attention than either. Beginning in 1967 Berg organized the young people who gathered at his coffeehouse into a movement he called "Teens for Christ" and eventually the "Children of

God" or "the Family." He gave up suits and ties and embraced the disillusioned youth of the 1960s, whom he called "the last generation . . . crusading for a return to primitive faith and the simple lives of the patriarchs."[15] He decided to dress like his converts, remembering "that's when I began to come down and teach in my dark glasses, beret, baggy pants, old torn jacket, and tennis shoes."[16] By the early 1970s, Berg was grabbing headlines with his practice of crashing church services in mainline denominations, marching into sermons at the head of dozens of followers with bare feet and ragged robes and shouting "Praise the Lord!" In New York City in September 1969, every day for more than a week some fifty of Berg's followers dressed in burlap and carried seven-foot staves and Bibles through the streets of midtown Manhattan, quoting scripture at puzzled passersby and identifying themselves as "Revolutionaries for Christ."[17]

The staves and rags Berg's followers displayed marked an essential idea behind many new Christian movements of the 1960s and 1970s: a rejection of American capitalism and democracy for their materialist corruption rooted in a conviction that original, pure Christianity demanded separatism. By the early 1970s Berg had adopted the biblical name "Moses" and retreated into reclusiveness, communicating with his followers largely through "Moses letters" or "Mo letters." His family and early associates performed most of the administrative work of the movement and wielded a great deal of power in the series of "colonies" or "homes" scattered across the United States.[18] In the Mo letters, Berg explained that American society had descended into a plague of corruption, that the "sins of the system from Whitehouse [sic] to Capitol, UN to Cathedral, and coast to coast" were provoking God. For Berg, American individualism encouraged selfishness. He presented himself as the savior of "tomorrow's youth" from "a fiendish, anti-God, social, economic, educational and religious system" which produced an "impersonal educational system, their routine job slavery, their cold and unsympathetic churches, and their unfeeling Government!"[19]

The Children of God, Berg's young converts, embraced the challenge, systematically substituting their own patterns of living for those of the society around them. As the membership grew, Berg led the group to a ranch in Texas for a few years, followed by a return to California, and then separation into various communes across the country, and by the early 1970s around the world. Whereas the Cold War Christian consensus balanced a fear of corrupting consumerism with a deathly fear of communism, Berg urged his followers to opt out of both options and to instead found a communalist society. "We believe Jesus wants us to win the lost and warn the nations at the cost of our secular jobs," explained an informational letter sent to those who requested information about the organization. Over and over the letter listed those things the Children of God would sacrifice—not merely objects and money, but participation in capitalism. "We believe Jesus wants us to win the lost and warn the nations at the cost of our formal education . . . our possessions . . . our reputation," it explained. If the recipients of the letter felt moved to join the Children, they were encouraged to "bring only one piece of luggage and a sleeping bag or bedroll, as you may have to sleep on the floor." In their colonies, each member would "give 100 percent, or our total income . . . and such a contribution goes immediately into fulltime service and 100 percent of it used for this mission work." The Children lived together in communal homes and dormitories, supporting themselves through "litnessing"—that is, raising money through donations and the sale of Children publications. This common commitment, Berg said, was reminiscent of the "simple communism of the Early Church," a word he chose with full knowledge of its provocation.[20]

Berg also rejected the principles he believed lay behind American democracy—chief among them the rational faith in science which drove both government policy making and the medical and psychological establishment whose language had colonized so much of the Christian consensus's rhetoric. Instead, the Children of God insisted that true human freedom could emerge only from obedience to divine authority. Berg's daughter, Faith David, illustrated the movement's rejection of these principles in her autobiography, in which she in quick succession dismissed any number of outside institutions in favor of the spiritual direction that her father provided. "Doctors are only technical men and really can't heal the body if there is something wrong. . . . The Lord has to make it run right. . . . The army was a drag, with the most terrible anti-Christ spirit. . . . I entered school at fourteen & graduated at fifteen. . . . They accepted me in the middle of the year on the condition that I would write all the mid-year exams. . . . God's spirit anointed me and I got the best grade in the class!" She exhorted her readers to seek "a new way of life, free of the System and its cares!"[21] Indeed, consistent with Berg's Pentecostal background, the Children frequently reported faith healings, miracles, and visions that trumped the authorities of American society with direct divine experience; one member, "Sara," declared that after experiencing nausea and fainting spells, a doctor diagnosed her with a liver infection but could not cure it.

After prayer, "I stood up praising the Lord and I was miraculously healed!"[22] Other members reported being healed of brain damage, angels appearing in photographs, and even, memorably, a child being raised from the dead. Nearly always, the stories presented the faith of the Children against a medical professional unable to account for miraculous cures.

Central to Berg's alternative systems of authority were sexual and relationship patterns that set the Children apart from the moral order of the Christian republican consensus. In 1974, David Berg issued a Mo letter titled "The Law of Love," in which he explained that for the Children of God, sexuality was not bound to the prescriptions of the Western tradition. "When Jesus came, He abolished all other laws but Love!" Berg later wrote. "He gave only one law which fulfills all the laws of the Bible, both old and new, and that is Love!—For God and fellow man!"[23] Berg rejected the moral expectations that had congealed around sexuality in the United States and argued instead that God had intended sex as an expression of his love for humanity and humans' love for each other. Berg left his wife Jane for a woman named Karen Zerby in 1970, explaining in a Mo Letter that his divorce and remarriage was an act of renewal that would symbolize the coming forth of a new church. "Therefore shall the old vestures be removed," Berg's revelation said. "I will have a new bride who will love Me and obey Me and do My will and bear Me children." By the late 1970s many committed members of the Children had begun wide sexual experimentation across their ranks. Berg also began a practice called "Flirty Fishing," in which female members offered romantic and sexual attention to men in order to draw them into the movement. Berg insisted that this was not immoral; rather, it was an expression of God's love. "If they fall in love with you first before they find it's the Lord, it's just God's bait to hook them!" he insisted.[24]

During this period, Berg began calling his movement "the Family," explaining that real freedom derived not through individual liberty but through patriarchal familial relationships. In 1978 Berg wrote in a Mo letter, "MARRIAGE IN THE FAMILY is to Jesus . . . and we are all married to each other in His love."[25] His own title shifted. Earlier he had been known as "Uncle Dave"; by the late 1970s he was referred to as "Dad," and Karen Zerby, became "Maria," after the biblical Mary. Berg said to the outside world that, as he put it in a Mo letter, "our women play a much more equal and active role than your women do." But he also insisted that men were "the stronger vessel . . . in the home relationship of husband and wife."[26] Women in the Children of God worked and witnessed alongside men, but

Berg's commitment to biblical patriarchy and the sexual order of the Law of Love pressed back against the moral expectations of Christian republicanism and second wave feminism alike.

Given their expectation that their lives would defy American social norms, many parents in the Children of God embraced homeschooling. Berg's son, Hosea David, wrote a tract explaining that his father believed that teaching was "one of the gifts or offices of the Spirit." He offered parents detailed advice on everything from classroom techniques to homework, using his father's Bible studies as a model.[27] Newsletters and magazines that circulated within the movement contained frequent discussion of teaching techniques and aims. Recommended lessons discarded classroom instruction in favor of participation in the religious life of the commune; as a Children of God newspaper reported, students at one Children commune were so "busy either in the studio, with video, with the mail or witnessing that they don't have so much time for the normal school curriculum. But our oldest children . . . are learning things far more vital for the salvation of man." On Christmas Day, these children performed a skit in which a young boy rejected "gifts and toys" in favor of a nativity scene, whereupon he was greeted by an angel who introduced him to Jesus. The show concluded with a round of Christmas carols and hymns. The Children traveled to area rest homes and orphanages performing the piece.[28]

The instructor who helped the children write and produce their show told her readers of its success and urged them to adopt a similar program. "We must do all we can right now to produce the musical tools for the Family before the war breaks out in its final atomic fury," she placidly observed.[29] One of the reasons for the Children's separatism was its conviction that postwar American society—with its capitalism, electoral democracy, and "Churchianity"—was what Berg called "modern Nineveh, modern Babylon and its king, King Richard—the Last! King Richard the Lyin-Hearted!"[30] Its dysfunctions would lead to its own destruction. Despite hostility from conservative evangelicals, Berg accepted much of the dispensational prophecy that emerged from the Protestant fundamentalist movement, much of which he had learned from his mother. He was convinced that the biblical books of Daniel and Ezekiel foretold a rapidly approaching cataclysmic global war, as many conservative evangelicals believed, and received throughout his career revelations that affixed particular dates to prophesied biblical events.[31]

And yet, Berg's apocalypticism diverged in important ways from that of Protestant evangelicals. He condemned both the United States and the Soviet

Union for being corrupt and anti-Christian. Americans, he said, were "as foolish as the Russian Communists, who [tried] to stamp out the true Church of God." The United States possessed a "corrupt and Godless government, more anti-God than Russia could ever hope to be." He predicted that as a consequence of American wickedness, God would allow the Soviet Union to eventually rise up and destroy the United States. "The vast majority are nearly always wrong and wicked," insisted Berg. As a result, American history would splinter into "revolution upon revolution, war after war, rich and poor, pollution and disease, the vain babblings of science so called, and political religion."[32] Only the Children of God would survive, because they had God's favor, but in the meantime they expected persecution. "I will see Jesus come, if I'm not killed first," Berg's daughter Faith told a reporter.[33]

The Children of God's alternative structures of authority led Berg to construct his own definition of democracy. As he explained in another Mo letter, "The so-called democratic rule of the majority will never voluntarily bring about perfect government and perfect peace on earth, a fair economy, a Godly education, or a righteous religion."[34] Human frailty, for Berg, made democracy, science, and capitalism all unreliable and unrighteous. The sort of society Berg encouraged in the stead of rationalistic, postwar capitalism was instead intensely communal and centered on the charismatic authority channeled by Berg himself. As Berg claimed, God intended to build "His own kingdom of totally righteous and authoritarian rule here on earth."[35] For Berg, human weakness made his own authoritarian rule more Christian than democracy could possibly be and hence more productive of true human righteousness.

Sun Myung Moon and the New Pilgrim Movement

Berg rejected the notions of majoritarian rule and individual liberty that most other American Christians associated with democracy because of his mistrust of human capacity. Sun Myung Moon did as well, but for different reasons. While Berg's critique emerged from radical evangelical discontent with the seemingly bloated and corrupt Cold War Christian consensus, Moon represented a different challenge: the surging diversity of postwar American religion. In his book *The Divine Principle*, Moon offered a form of Christianity deeply informed by Confucian and Taoist emphasis on hierarchy and social order to produce a form of Christianity unfamiliar to most white American Protestants.[36] While Berg believed that the entire world was corrupt, Moon emphasized dualism, teaching that the righteous world guided by God and the wicked world guided by Satan would remain locked in permanent conflict until the eschaton, when a messianic figure would usher in God's final judgment. Moon readily identified those two worlds as the democratic world, led by the United States, and the communist bloc, which he said was led by the Soviet Union.[37] That notion made him as fiercely anticommunist as any American Christian, but Moon's solution seemed to many premised on unfamiliar ideas: the importance of social hierarchy, of communal rather than individual achievement, and the rejection of individualist capitalism.

For Moon, reality was built upon binary relationships, which began with the positive and negative ions formed by atoms, proceeded to the physical and spiritual aspects of each person, and culminated in the male-female dyad of the ideal heterosexual marriage that Moon saw as the foundation of the Kingdom of God. Moon taught that God had intended to construct a series of perfect reciprocal relationships between God, men, women, and children, each giving and taking from the other in hierarchy and exchange. But by illicitly inserting himself into that ideal "Four Position Foundation," Satan had disrupted these relationships. Moon taught that Jesus Christ's crucifixion was not God's original intention but a catastrophe born of Satan's opposition; moreover, the fall of Adam and Eve resulted from an act of illicit sex between Eve and Satan, followed by another between Eve and Adam. Mending the rifts these tragedies tore in history was the task of the Unification Church.[38]

For Moon, the power of materialism in the United States was evident in the crumbling of relationships, particularly relationships that enforced moral restraint. He deeply disapproved of the pursuit of profit, which he believed degraded American morality. "Is this your money? Is it American money? No, it is God's money," Moon told a rally in Washington, DC. "Does God dwell in these buildings?" he asked of the financial centers of Wall Street. Furthermore, members of Unification worried that materialism led to social decay and dysfunction. James Edgerly, a journalist for the Unification Church's newspaper, wrote that American "spiritual life has been replaced by numerous expressions of materialism" and denounced the pursuit of material pleasure, sexual gratification, and profit. These fixations upon wealth were for members of Unification invariably related to the destruction of relationships and the breakdown of American society. "Problems within society—such as drug abuse, sexual license, discrimination, collapse of the family unit," claimed the Unification newspaper *Sunrise,* derived from "lack of communication between individuals, generations, [and] groups." The paper stated that these "problems . . . have been overcome through application of the Divine Principle."[39]

Moon endorsed the calls of many other Christians for more rigorous morality to curb this excess materialism. But he also advanced a particular interpretation of what it meant to be Christian in America that reflected the distinctive principles of the Unification Church. Throughout the bicentennial year of 1976, Moon delivered a series of speeches laying out his understanding of the relationship between Christianity and American democracy. He emphasized not individual liberty but individual sacrifice for the common good. Over and over he returned to the Pilgrims, who "felt a strong desire to create community of their own." But in so doing, they had to give up all they had to embrace "total reliance on God." They were, he said, "the Abrahams of modern history," specifically invoking the patriarch's abandonment of his original home to build a holy family in a new land. Moon believed that the pursuit of wealth would destroy a Christian society and hence wreck democracy, and through a historically questionable comparison of the United States to South America, he drove the point home. The Pilgrims, Moon said, "came for God, [and] they not only found God, but they also found freedom and wealth." The Spanish colonists, Moon believed, came for "gold," but "could find neither gold, nor God nor freedom, and the South American countries remain underdeveloped." Moon denounced American individualism as the antithesis of the sort of relationship-oriented community he believed Christianity to mandate. He warned that Americans, like the Spanish conquistadors, had embraced "an extremely individualistic outlook of life and are moving further toward selfishness"; he also declared that "a revolution of the heart must come. Individualism must be tied into God-centered ideology."[40]

Moon and his followers frequently compared members of the Unification Church to the Pilgrims, celebrating members' willingness to give up individual profit, careers, and privacy for the aim of a collective Kingdom of God on Earth. Unificationist James Edgerly claimed that the "American Ethic" the Pilgrims had taught depended upon "harmonious and successful human relations" that were premised on "vertical" and "horizontal" deference to God and to others. Moon himself told members of Congress, "I have instituted a youth movement which is probably the only one of its kind in United States history. This is a new Pilgrim movement." Frequently

Moon and other Unificationists invoked the word *sacrifice* to illustrate what should be expected of a righteous society; as one Unification training session put it, new members must be taught to "live individually and collectively" and to regard "the suffering of all mankind as our own suffering. . . . By dedicating ourselves completely in the spirit of sacrifice, we must now become the servants of love."[41] Members of the church were encouraged to sacrifice their relationships with the sinful world and to enter into new, purified associations through the vehicle of Unification.

Over the church's early decades in the United States, Moon and his lieutenants implemented a number of practices that carried out these principles. New Unification Church members were encouraged to surrender their property to the church and to live communally in Unification centers, where they were given "austere" allotments of food and clothing. As one member recalled, "We ate an awful lot of peanut butter sandwiches."[42] Perhaps most famous was the practice of the Blessing, in which Moon solemnized arranged marriages en masse. Members spent their days in worship peddling copies of the *Divine Principle* and various trinkets on the street. In response to scorn for this lifestyle, an official Unification report declared, "We are serious about applying the vision taught by Reverend Moon" and about living what it called a "sacrificial and heroic life." Dismissing a reporter who criticized Unification for demanding so much from its members, the report stated, "In contrast to her very limited, materialistic view of freedom, we see our ability to live and teach our ideals as the ultimate freedom."[43] For members of the Unification Church, the communal society Moon organized was the fullest expression of human nature and thus was more truly free than the materialist, brutally individualist capitalism that prevailed outside their community.

Other Americans, though, rejected Moon's claim to have secured the American Christian heritage. Instead, they believed that Moon's form of Christianity was un-American and thus not really religious. For them Moon's heresy was intimately connected to his ethnicity and origins. Throughout the 1970s and 1980s Unification was labeled, variously, a fifth column in service to the South Korean government, a profit machine for the Moon family, or a decadent Orientalist court directed to Moon's own pleasure. In the late 1970s Congressman Donald Fraser began an investigation into the relationship between the Unification Church and the South Korean government, unearthing evidence that Salonen's pro-Nixon demonstrations received foreign encouragement and financing. An uproar ensued in the press, followed by public investigations into the wide array of businesses Moon had founded. This process would eventually result in Moon's imprisonment from 1982 to 1984 on charges of income tax evasion.[44]

The accusations revealed implicit assumptions long-standing in the United States that a true Christian church would be European or American in genealogy and hence would necessarily support rather than critique American society. "Rarely has a non-Western Christian cult brought a message to lands whose missionaries first brought them the Bible—which the cult leaders now interpret in a new way," wrote a wary Russell Chandler of the *Los Angeles Times*, drawing a clear distinction between "Western" and "non-Western" Christianity.[45] In 1976, as investigations of the Unification Church intensified, the American Jewish Committee, the National Council of Churches, and the Catholic Archdiocese of New York held a joint press conference in which a spokesman for the three organizations repeatedly denied that Moon was actually Christian in order to delegitimize his political influence. "This is an ominous political ideology clothed in religious garb," stated Rabbi A. James Rudin of the AJC. The unified faith leaders cited Moon's ties to the Korean government, his increasing wealth, and his "antidemocratic beliefs," including his sole control of his sect, as reasons for doubting the sincerity of his faith. The columnist Ira Pearlstein called Moon an "Elmer Gantry of the East," a "weapon entrepreneur" who founded a church to make himself rich and his home country powerful.[46]

The Unification Church defended both its ties to Korea and its economic investments by invoking its theology of relationship. Unification's business holdings in the media, financial, and other industries were understood as a means of transforming the world's economic relationships from a state of sin to one of holiness. Part of Unification's mission was to bring the world's institutions into the same set of blessed relationships as its individuals. "Does it seem strange that a man from Korea is initiating an American youth movement?" Moon asked members of Congress. "A doctor comes from outside your house." Moon argued that the Unification movement demonstrated that the United States was neither unique nor alone; rather, it was part of a larger democratic family that fought on God's side against communism and Satan. In fact, the presence of Moon and other Koreans in the United States indicated that God's plan of redemption was proceeding apace. "God originally planned one world of unification," he said, "between mind and body, between families, tribes, and nations, between the Orient and the Occident." While early in his career Unification theology was decidedly Korea-centered, by the 1970s Moon had adapted his theology to elevate the role of the United States—though he expected the United States to function as a facilitator of relationships among nations. "Korea . . . is now serving as a link to bring harmony between the civilizations of the East and the West," Moon declared. Therefore he argued that the United States had a responsibility to defend Korea. "God expected America to further strengthen her leadership of the Allies and to safeguard and manage" the free world, he explained.[47] Other Unification members developed these ideas further, calling for the United States to "seek positive relations with those nations who share similar ideals" and make "promises and grants of benefits" to nations threatened by communism, particularly South Korea.[48] Subtly, Moon undermined the traditional Protestant narrative of Western Christian civilization while seeming still to uphold it.

Moon and other members of the Unification Church all vehemently maintained that their version of Christianity was compatible with democracy—indeed, it was by definition democracy. Their economic practices were congruent with this notion. San Ik Choi, one of the original Unification missionaries to the United States and the progenitor of many of the church's more controversial practices like communal living, called the group's practices "divine democracy": freedom structured around "the truth which is constructive and instructive for all."[49] David Berg's similar rejection of individual liberty likewise derived from a vision of democracy that emphasized internal loyalty and separation from the rest of the world. To Americans steeped in the notion that Christianity privileged the individual and safeguarded personal autonomy, this idea seemed bizarre. But given the predicates of Moon's or Berg's vision of reality as seen through the lens of the two men's vision of Christianity—which emphasized on the one hand common dependency and the importance of relationship, and on the other the paramount importance of loyalty to their rescued remnant of believers—this conditioning of liberty seemed perfectly understandable to their followers. Real freedom, after all, sprang from possession of the truth.

The Evangelical Struggle with Secular Humanism

For decades, American evangelicals had been sparring with movements like these, which they called "cults."[50] Until the rise of mid-twentieth-century groups like the Unification Church and the Children of God, evangelicals seemed mainly concerned with cults' theological failures. *The Fundamentals*, an important collection of essays on various Christian topics published from 1909 to 1917, included entries on a variety of small movements and carefully documented their doctrinal heresies. Soon, fundamentalist and evangelical leaders began using the term *cult* to describe, as one minister put it, "any group that claims to be Christian but falls short of an evangelical definition of Christianity."[51] The word *cult* thus served as a boundary marker, a tool to diminish the claim of non-Protestant forms of Christianity to full participation in the American Christian tradition.[52]

For many years conservative Protestants cared mainly about the theological threat posed by cults. Anticult tomes counseled evangelicals on useful interrogatories: "Does the doctrine of the Trinity imply that God is a 'three headed freak'? . . . Is it a small matter to misrepresent and reject the doctrine of the Trinity?" were among the questions Edward Tanis advised Christians to ask Jehovah's Witnesses in *What the Sects Teach*. This useful compendium of dagger-sharp questions ("Is Christian Science Christian? Is it scientific?") aimed to help evangelicals trip up their cultist interlocutors.[53] In the early twentieth century a minister in Boston observed, "Some ministers are studying Christian Science and preaching sermons against it." Though he worried that disputation was destructive, he also gratefully noted, "We have in four years dismissed four who have entered their fellowship, while at the same time winning thirty-seven."[54] The crowning work of these theological efforts was Anthony Hoekema's massive 1963 tome, *The Four Major Cults*. Hoekema, a professor of systematic theology at the Reformed school Calvin College, insisted that whatever lurid garb they might dress in, all cults were the same. "We need to understand the teachings of cults in their totality, so that various doctrines can be seen to fit into a certain theological pattern," he claimed. A "cult" was a religion that persisted in materialism. For Hoekema and other evangelicals, "materialism" meant overreliance on humanity rather than on God.[55]

Evangelical fear that cults were all essentially one, a single manifestation of materialist temptation, meant that when the preservation of true Christianity became increasingly connected to national survival during the Cold War, evangelicals began worrying more and more about the political impact of orthodoxy or heterodoxy. In the 1960s that dry theological debate of the older evangelical crusade against cults developed into the "countercult movement." In 1960, the Baptist minister Walter Martin founded the Christian Research Institute (CRI), an organization devoted to training speakers, producing tracts and pamphlets, and gathering information to debunk cults.[56] Other organizations, such as the Spiritual Counterfeits Project (SCP), a branch of the Christian World Liberation Front, followed in the late 1960s. Cults, the SCP insisted, were counterfeits because they were not truly religions. Rather, using the language of psychological materialism familiar to American Protestants during the Cold War, SCP leaders declared that cult followers were trapped in "psychological and spiritual bondage" to forces that used mental manipulation rather than promoting faith.[57]

The language the countercult movement used to describe cults was significant because it revealed developments taking place in conservative evangelicals' understanding of the relationship between Christianity and democracy. The struggle with the cults indicated the extent to which they were becoming convinced that democracy depended upon evangelical Christianity in particular, not the generalized liberal Protestant and Catholic "biblical" religion of the Cold War consensus. This was clear in their ready associations of cults with the same materialist failures and techniques they abhorred in the Soviet Union and in the political liberalism of the New Deal order. Thus, as conservative evangelicals began to organize entry into electoral politics in the late 1970s, the language they would use to assail political adversaries would mirror their attacks on the cults. In a rhetorical sense, then, the Religious Right used the tactics of the countercult movement, and its arguments about American public policy were another front in the war for a Christian nation.

By the 1970s many American evangelicals had come to believe that American democracy depended on the preservation of what they called a "Christian worldview." The concept of worldview was newly popular, but the basic idea was not. It had been developed in the nineteenth century by Reformed Protestant intellectuals like James Orr, Abraham Kuyper, and Cornelius Van Til. The concept proposed that human beings interacted with all aspects of the world through a basic set of "presuppositions," which shaped their perception and behavior in ways both conscious and unconscious. Thus, Christians do their banking, garden, and raise their children in particularly Christian ways, inflected and colored by Christian beliefs about the nature of reality. This was not so different from older notions about "civilization" which proposed that a society's order would follow its values, the same idea underlying the way American Christians had denounced German materialism a half century before. Just as American Christians at that time feared that German ideology would ruin American democracy, so did evangelicals in the 1970s see un-Christian worldviews as threats to the nation's order. The evangelical theologian Carl Henry warned, "The modern mind will come to maturity only when its contemporary reversals are transmuted into a return to that Christian theism which makes intelligible the scene of human activity." Henry worried that "the secular philosophy of humanism or naturalism" had come to foster an incoherent vision of human life.[58]

Many evangelicals believed that the rise of cults was but one symptom of the deeper decay of the American Christian worldview, and more than anybody else, Francis Schaeffer, an iconoclastic Presbyterian, linked the idea of worldview to unease about the state of American culture and politics. Oddly enough Schaeffer seemed to share a great deal with the counterculture. He wore eccentric, old-fashioned clothing, favoring nineteenth-century European styles, grew his hair and beard long, and gave up on American society in favor of living in monastic retreat in Europe. But in a series of books, speeches, and documentaries that he generated between the late 1960s and early 1980s, Schaeffer showed American evangelicals that their nation's social and cultural stability depended upon evangelical Christianity. In a documentary series and accompanying book, both titled *How Should We Then Live?*, Schaeffer argued that what he called people's "thought world" or "presuppositions" or "basic world view" would "flow through their fingers or from their tongues into the external world. This is true of Michelangelo's chisel and it is true of a dictator's sword."[59] He then set about debunking the Christian consensus which had emerged over the previous sixty years, attacking its confidence and emphasizing instead the relevance of its anxieties. Schaeffer claimed that the Christian worldview was under siege and that the Cold War Christian consensus, in its politics and ecumenism, actually enabled its decay.

Though Schaeffer shared much with the Protestant assumptions behind Columbia's Contemporary Civilization course, his commitment to a particularly evangelical form of Protestant Christianity and science tinged his understanding of history. The optimism of Columbia's liberal Protestants celebrated history as essentially progressive and cheered the rise of the Enlightenment and its exaltation of human reason. Like many other Christians who did not share the assumptions of the white liberal Protestant establishment, Schaeffer's vision of history was darker. Though unlike many African Americans he accepted the notion of a Western Christian heritage, like those groups he rejected the idea that the course of Western history revealed the progress of Christian civilization. Schaeffer boiled all of

Western history down into two competing forces—the "scientific" or "humanistic," and the "religious." Instead of steady progress for the one, Schaeffer viewed history as an ongoing war between the two—a war in which religion was slowly but steadily losing ground. The Renaissance was humanistic; the Reformation, religious. Michelangelo was humanistic; Rembrandt, religious. The French Revolution was humanistic; the American Revolution, religious.[60]

Liberal Protestants believed many of the things Schaeffer labeled humanistic contributed to the progress of Christian values. Schaeffer and other evangelicals maintained that humanists could not but help construct a materialist world, relying "on their own human wisdom," ignoring the "absolute, universal values" of religion, and consequently neglecting the "basic dignity and value of the individual as unique in being made in the image of God." Humanism was, essentially, the materialism American Christians had been lambasting for decades: the elevation of the human and the tangible over divine authority. "On every side people are taught that people are only machines," Schaeffer mourned. "The Christian consensus gave a basis for people being unique, as made in the image of God, but this has largely been thrown away." Schaeffer particularly emphasized that humanism fostered not only religious but also cultural and political decay. Americans were anxious because they could sense that something was not right, but they remained unsure what was skewed.[61] It was that anxiety, evangelicals believed, that had given rise to cults that threatened both orthodox Christian belief and democratic government alike.

Just as Schaeffer translated worldview theology into a refutation of traditional progressive narratives about American civilization, his reference to anxiety illustrated how evangelicals had begun using the language of psychology in new ways. Evangelicals shared in the pervasive Cold War belief that materialist forces like communism would harm American minds, and they saw the threat in cults. By the 1950s, evangelicals trained in psychology and counseling, like Hildreth Cross (author of the "first textbook in general psychology screened through the Word of God," 1952's *Introduction to Psychology*) and Clyde Narramore, began suggesting, as Narramore put it, that "the basic psychological needs of man" might be "met most fundamentally through knowing Christ and living the dynamic Christian life."[62] Throughout the decade, Narramore broadcasted a radio show called *Psychology for Living*, which dispensed a mixture of psychological and theological advice. By the 1960s and 1970s works on psychology from an evangelical perspective were multiplying.[63]

These parallel developments in evangelical psychology and worldview theory helped evangelicals tie the survival of their particular version of Christianity to social stability. While Christian republicanism's emphasis on moral behavior fostered the ecumenism of the Cold War consensus, evangelicals' emphasis on worldview linked evangelical orthodoxy to mental stability. If worldview influenced behavior, a correct worldview became imperative for the preservation of a good society. "God wants people to be born anew spiritually," Narramore claimed. "The secular world has found its imagination and vocabulary bankrupt as to the description of things to come."[64] Evangelicals believed that a faulty worldview could cause mental turmoil. New religious movements were therefore the logical end of a society dominated by materialist, humanist values. They were a symptom, not a cause, of a non-Christian society. As another manifestation of materialism, they promoted pride, enabled hedonism, and exalted wealth and secular power. If that vision were given free rein in American society, evangelicals believed it would wreck democracy and lead to a totalitarian state. They had proof: that calamity had happened to groups like the Children of God and the Unification Church already.

The Countercult Vision of Western Civilization

From June 4 to 6, 1975, a Chinese Christian who called himself "Witness Lee," leader of a group called "the Local Church," visited the campus of the University of California, Berkeley, with several hundred followers. Most of them seemed to be affluent, white, young college students who followed Lee in a practice of "pray-reading." Lee described pray-reading as reading the Bible out loud "in a quick way, with short phrases, praying something new and fresh." It was intended to be a meditative rather than cognitive engagement with scripture. Pray-reading, he said, "exercises our spirit and does not give us time to use our minds," thwarting worry and overthought. At their meetings Lee and his followers chanted the text of scripture and offered impromptu testimony. At one point Lee led more than a hundred followers in a chorus, chanting "O Lord Jesus" again and again, drowning out any sound around them. The leaders of the Spiritual Counterfeits Project were horrified. They formed circles surrounding Lee's followers when they encountered them and waited until late at night outside the buildings where Lee held his meetings so they could press leaflets and literature upon the attendees as they emerged.[65]

SCP confrontations with Witness Lee revealed many of the fears harbored by its members, and by evangelicals more generally, about such new religions. In 1982 the SCP offered three points to describe their purpose. First, to "examine the culture's shift from it's [*sic*] Judeo-Christian heritage to a society of conflicting world views"; second, to "biblically critique today's spiritual trends and movements based on Eastern philosophies"; and third, to "equip the church with information and tools for further response."[66] These stated aims revealed what evangelicals had taken from the Christian consensus and what they brought to it. Since they vocally associated Christianity with "the West" and American democracy, evangelicals feared that the religious pluralism and ecumenism that the Christian consensus had inadvertently fostered was simply a Trojan horse for humanist materialism. The success of the Unification Church and leaders like Witness Lee seemed evidence that the Cold War consensus would allow the Christian, democratic West to succumb to a non-Christian, materialist East.

Contrary to their feelings about leaders like Witness Lee, countercult leaders tended to be sympathetic to Americans who joined cults because they concluded that cultists genuinely, if subconsciously, desired Christianity. They believed that Americans sensed the drift of their world from a Christian worldview toward a materialistic, humanistic ideology and were looking to fill that void, even if they did not know precisely what they were missing. Indeed, Schaeffer wrote that young people who joined protests in the 1960s and cults in the 1970s were "right in their analysis of the problem, but they were mistaken in their solutions." The SCP's Brooks Alexander claimed that until the 1950s "most people in this country had somewhat the same concept of the meaning of life and personal values, one based primarily on Judeo-Christian concepts." Now, though, the SCP declared, Americans were "living in a world that increasingly espouses the explicit premises of anti-Christ. These presuppositions are subtly conditioning people at all levels of culture to accept a definition of reality which denies the personal god of the Bible, asserts the autonomy, power and inherent divinity of Man, and condemns as obsolete any absolute statement of moral values." Cults were therefore "the natural consequence of the spiritual decadence of western civilization, which has left this generation starving for Reality, and therefore vulnerable."[67]

That hunger, evangelicals said, both caused and resulted from the socioeconomic changes they saw in 1960s American society. The evangelical sociologist Ronald Enroth observed that "today's youth" confronted problems far exceeding those of previous generations. In particular, he cited the "boom in entertainment and the pervasive impact of the mass media," the "alienation of youth from the larger society," and the "a rejection of many traditional virtues" as paradigmatic of the age. Enroth warned that materialism was sapping American spiritual vigor, and that "a crisis of identity" was common among "children of affluence." Most youth who joined cults were "white, middle or upper middle class, with at least some college education." But, Enroth cautioned, this did not mean they were psychologically healthy. Many, he mourned, were possessed of only a "nominally religious upbringing" because American society now glorified the pursuit of pleasure rather than God. Drowning in affluence, young people had "dropped out of school, have been involved in the drug scene, come from broken homes, or have a history of emotional problems."[68]

Walter Martin's 1965 book *The Kingdom of the Cults* remains perhaps the most prominent countercult work ever published, in part because it enunciated many of these ideas so clearly. Martin used the work of psychologist Milton Rokeach to diagnose what he called the "psychological substructure of cultism." He was the most prominent evangelical theorist to argue that cults, like communism, appealed to those Americans suffering psychologically because they lacked true Christianity. He claimed that cults were "heady stuff for the lonely, the weak, the confused, the ineffectual, and the mentally or emotionally ill." But also like communism, cults created a dysfunctional "cult personality," characterized by submission to authority, consumed with destructive habits, and trained through "psychological conditioning which elicits a definite pattern of religious reflexes in response to a given stimuli." Martin painted a picture of a cultist who "will spiritually and emotionally salivate" whenever directed, as did Pavlov's dog. This is what the members of the SCP thought about as they watched the followers of Witness Lee chant their "vain repetition of, 'O Lord Jesus!'" and recite "fervent testimonies about how good it is to be out of dead Christianity and in the Local Church."[69] Much as earlier Christians had accused communism of psychologically destroying free individuals, so did countercultists worry that the cults employed the same methods—because, of course, cults grew from the same warped materialism as did communism.

In February 1979, in the wake of the mass suicide of the members of the Peoples Temple in Jonestown, Guyana, the previous November, Congress began holding hearings on "the cult phenomenon" in the United States. A panel of senators and representatives, chaired by Senator Bob Dole of Kansas, expressed worry about cults' "brainwashing" techniques and heard from countercultist luminaries. John Clark, a psychologist at Harvard Medical School, informed the panel that in his opinion those who joined cults "are often deluded, hallucinating, and confused in a new highly manipulative environment, in their altered states of consciousness." Clark carefully avoided the term *brainwashing*, but he was comfortable suggesting that cult followers' "highly manipulated minds are effective only under total control and are less able to manage the unexpected." In short, Clark warned, cult members had become unsuitable citizens for a democracy, for that manipulation "injures the normal capacity of an individual to cope with an always uncertain future in a free society." Testimony like this gained wide coverage in the media and reflected a common consensus emerging in the 1970s: cults gained their membership through the mental manipulation of the vulnerable.[70]

It was common for evangelical members of the countercult to seize upon statements like Clark's to argue that cult leaders exploited people whose moral capacities had been crippled by a materialist lifestyle. Thus, converts did not find a cult's doctrine appealing; rather, cults preyed upon the damage materialism had already inflicted on their minds. They did not convert but were "brainwashed," language used intentionally to deny cults the status of religious movements and instead associate them with fears of communism and other materialist philosophies. Walter Martin's newsletter warned that the Jehovah's Witnesses offered potential converts "seven steps to slavery," beginning with accepting a Witness tract and ending with being sent out, penniless and severed from their former friends and family, to distribute tracts themselves. This was, warned the newsletter, reminiscent of the "brainwashing tactics of totalitarians." Ronald Enroth warned that the handwriting of cult members would "usually become smaller and more childish," because he was convinced that cults' techniques reduced capability for independent thought and moral agency.[71]

Language linking "brainwashing" with both communism and the "East" became common. In 1967 *Time* magazine speculated that the confessions recorded by several American pilots captured by the North Vietnamese "raised fears that the Communists were once again resorting to the inhuman brainwashing techniques whose widespread use during the Korean War horrified the world." However, *Time* asserted, such efforts "only accentuate Viet Nam's endemic ignorance of Western idiom, intellect, and ideology," because the confessions were obviously manufactured, and some American pilots refused to give them. In a single article the magazine expressed Americans' simultaneous confidence that the "Western" mind was too strong for such techniques as well as the fear that it could nonetheless be corrupted.[72]

Drawing on these ideas, countercultists employed racially coded language contrasting the "West" and the "East" to link "brainwashing" and other stereotyped fears to cults' beliefs and practices. As SCP leader Brooks Alexander put it, cults were the product of "the infiltration of Eastern ideas into Western Judeo-Christian culture."[73] When countercultists used terms like *Eastern,* they meant everything they feared about materialism: it promoted decadence, collectivism, the exotic, the irreligious. Hunger for wealth was a common trope countercultists used to denounce cult leaders, because they associated it with both materialism and the East. Hence avarice was doubly un-American. Reuben Baerwald, a Lutheran countercultist, dismissed the Unification Church and Sun Myung Moon in a characteristic fashion: "The primary reason for the cult's existence is to make money. . . . Moon, for example, lives in oriental splendor."[74] As the Baptist deprogrammer Ted Patrick said contemptuously of Sun Myung Moon, "Moon's got nothing to do with religion. . . . They're all crooks. You name 'em. Hare Krishna. The Divine Light Mission. Guru Maharaj Ji. The New Testament Missionary Fellowship. Brother Julius. Love Israel. The Children of God."[75] Patrick's off-the-cuff critique (delivered, so his coauthor noted, while eating an old ham sandwich in a small kitchen) was echoed by many other countercultists, who concluded that the pursuit of wealth generally was inimical to sincere faith.

But the "East" did not only mean decadence and wealth to countercultists; it also meant an inappropriate glorification of humanity, which led to totalitarianism. Cults in the United States, SCP writer David Fechto claimed, were "moving this generation toward adopting the classic occult / mystical presuppositions about Reality," which derived from Eastern faiths. In a manifesto, Fechto, a former member of a vaguely Hindu movement who became an evangelical Christian, argued that Eastern ideas were destructive in two ways. On the one hand, Eastern religion pressed its followers into meditation, equating "absolute truth with [one's] radically subjective experience." But countercultists also found in Hindu and Buddhist theology a sort of pantheism that collapsed this subjective experience into a universal divinity that absorbed individual consciousness. "All is one, Man is God," Fechto scornfully rehearsed the cults' promises. This eliminated the special divine status of humanity. Combined, these two principles encouraged human beings to embrace "hedonistic, humanistic, and nihilistic philosophies," both indulging their own desires and avoiding personal moral responsibility for them.[76]

That lack of individual accountability led countercultists, steeped in their version of Protestant Christian republicanism, to conclude that cults were simply not true religions. Sometimes countercultists credited them with being pagan, false religions, a label which had the double benefit of denying both Christian orthodoxy and a place in modern Western civilization to these groups. Hal Lindsay, a contributor to the SCP who became a famous inter- preter of biblical prophecy, argued for a distinction between "religion" and "Christianity." "Christianity is not a religion. Religion is the process of man trying to achieve goodness, perfection, and acceptance with God by his own efforts," he said. Christians, on the other hand, depended on God. "Reli- gions," Lindsay declared, were all part of a "one world religious system," which emerged, in his telling, ultimately from the decadent ancient capital of Babylon.[77] Other times, they simply denied that cults were religions at all. In 1980, for instance, Steve Scott of the SCP claimed, "Mormonism is a variant form of agnosticism."[78] But whether pagan religions or false ones, cults, their critics consistently insisted, focused more on the material than on the spiritual, more on the world than on God.

Whatever way they phrased their complaints, all such efforts boiled down to evangelicals attempting to deny legitimacy to cults. That legitimacy was both theological and historical; they placed cults simultaneously outside Christianity and outside the story of Western civilization which led to the United States. This tactic accomplished two things. First, it allowed evangeli- cals to define genuine religion as, essentially, Christianity. Second, separating the cults from the genealogy of the United States bolstered evangelicals' faith that the survival of democracy in the United States depended upon Chris- tianity. The tactic allowed them to challenge the alternative social, familial, and political practices the cults engaged in not as the product of legitimate religious faith, but rather as dangerous to Western civilization. The evan- gelical writer John Charles Cooper warned that young people involved in new religious movements "spoke of the death of democracy" and instead followed "sorcerers and seers." Enroth warned that cults promoted "alien- ation from Western society," which led to the destruction of democracy, as the practices of cults posed "a direct violation of [members'] rights to freedom of speech and freedom of association." Seemingly sputtering, Enroth de- clared that cults rejected loyalty to the American system while true Chris- tians supported it. "Pseudo-Christian cults like the Alamo Foundation and the Children of God proclaim that Jesus demands all—anything less is not enough," Enroth observed, denouncing the groups' demands that converts surrender all property. "Evangelist Billy Graham frequently uses similar phraseology in his preaching but he means something entirely different."[79]

In Enroth's estimation, then, Billy Graham's gospel demonstrated that the demands of true Christianity fit nicely with the values of contemporary American life and would push Americans no further than they were accustomed. Indeed, Graham claimed that his was an "individualistic gospel," and the National Association of Evangelicals, of which Graham was a member, produced a tract titled *Scriptural Proof of the Free Enterprise System*, which argued that American capitalism was the economic system Christ intended.[80] For Enroth, Graham, and many Americans accustomed to the Christianity that emerged from the Cold War, Christianity focused on the self, the individual's mind and heart. It concerned itself with individual well-being rather than social structures—and therefore found the democratic, capitalist moral order of the United States congenial. The threat of the cults was the threat of a Christianity bound to a differing social order. Thus, as evangelicals came to perceive the threat of a new social order emerging not simply from the false Christianities of Moon or Berg, they had ready a language to combat the menace of American political liberalism.

CHAPTER EIGHT

Civil Religion, the Religious Right, and the Fracturing of Christian Republicanism

IN SWIFT BACK-TO-BACK rulings in 1962 and 1963, the Supreme Court issued two decisions that reshaped the public expression of American Christianity. In 1962's *Engel v. Vitale,* the court ruled that a brief prayer composed by the New York State Board of Regents for recitation in the classroom violated the First Amendment's stricture against a government establishment of religion. The next year, in *Abingdon v. Schempp* and a sister case, *Murray v. Curlett,* the court ruled that formal reading of the Bible in the classroom violated the same clause.[1]

Supporters of the laws argued that such public expressions of piety were essential to the maintenance of the national Christian consensus they believed enervated American democracy. These supporters ranged across the spectrum of American Christianity, demonstrating how broad the Cold War Christian consensus was. Billy Graham and Reinhold Niebuhr, who had little love for each other, each defended the New York Regents' prayer as meaningful to what Niebuhr called the "tradition of the nation." Graham warned that the *Engel* decision was "another step toward secularism in the United States." The dean of Harvard Law School, Erwin Griswold, worried that the loss of such laws would lead to a rise in religious pluralism and subsequently the loss of Western civilization and ultimately American democracy. "The Moslem who comes here may worship as he pleases," Griswold observed. "But why should it follow that he can require others to give up their

Christian traditions?" After all, he noted, American constitutional traditions emerged "out of Christian doctrine and ethics."[2]

And yet some Christian leaders found ways to accommodate the rulings, for reasons similar to those given by the people who opposed them: concern for the preservation of the Cold War Christian consensus. Most commonly, they followed the conservative evangelical magazine *Christianity Today*'s observation: the Regents' prayer was so void of Christian specifics—even avoiding mention of Christ—that it was better called a "corporate" prayer than a Christian one.[3] It was so bland it did little to strengthen the national faith. Indeed, during and after their deliberations, the Supreme Court justices who approved and wrote the rulings made clear that they feared that such laws would backfire and undermine the Judeo-Christian nature of the Cold War consensus. Justice William O. Douglas noted during the court's deliberations in *Murray* and *Abingdon* that his colleagues worried that if the court upheld local governments' laws promoting Bible reading, the door would be open to other groups. "Schools can't be opened to every sect. How about Black Muslims? How about screwball groups?" Justice Arthur Goldberg asked his fellow justices during deliberations.[4] During oral arguments in *Murray*, Chief Justice Earl Warren asked the defendants whether a hypothetical school district made up of 51 percent Buddhists would have the right to impose reading of their sacred texts. Later in the case the Maryland attorney general agreed that, hypothetically, students could be forced to read the Book of Mormon. As Douglas observed, the question would come down to "which church could get control of the school board."[5] In an America marked by increasingly obvious religious diversity, that was a disturbingly open question.

In the 1970s and 1980s, two Christian groups sought ways by which the Cold War Christian consensus might be saved. Each wanted to reinvigorate the notion that American democracy depended upon a particular sort of Christian republicanism. Each also was forced to draw only selectively on the Cold War Christian consensus, because by the 1970s the illusion of national unity that had sustained that consensus had fragmented. Dwight Eisenhower's presumption that American society depended upon "the Judeo-Christian tradition" could no longer be taken for granted. While these Christian groups hoped to strengthen the Protestant roots of American democracy but each also had to grapple with growing national awareness of America's religious diversity.

One group was made up of left-leaning American academics, intellectuals, and politicians like President Jimmy Carter and the sociologist Robert Bellah who believed that the American public needed a revival of what they often called "civil religion." As Bellah defined it, the phrase meant "an institutionalized collection of sacred beliefs about the American nation," which linked American democracy to the transcendent through national rituals like presidential inaugurations and meaningful language like the allusions to divinity on American currency. The concept was not new, but Bellah made the term "civil religion" famous in the 1960s and 1970s in a series of publications extolling his particular version of the concept. Civil religion as Bellah described it was in part the Christian republicanism of the old liberal Protestant establishment, shorn of overtly Christian language, devoted to good citizenship, and stretched to meet the demands of the turbulent 1960s and 1970s. Proponents of Bellah's version of civil religion sought ways to incorporate groups they found congenial—like Martin Luther King's Southern Christian Leadership Conference—while excommunicating those they did not—like many new religious movements. The uneasy balance they felt between their inherited Christian republicanism and their awareness of modern religious diversity made them reluctant to label their values "Protestant" or even "Christian." Rather, they spoke of "civil religion," moving from the ecumenism of the Cold War "Judeo-Christian" or "biblical" consensus toward even more generalized words like "religion." Advocates of civil religion were attempting to thread a tight needle. They insisted that "civil religion" as they described it was not indebted to any particular religion, but its implicit liberal Protestant commitments despite its rejection of a "Christian" heritage led to uneasy relationships with other groups that claimed Christianity.[6]

Conservative evangelicals on the other hand, raged against the sort of lukewarm religious politics they saw the civil-religion movement endorsing and mounted an effort to claim the word *Christian* at the same moment as Bellah left it behind. Just as evangelicals believed that cults promoted theologically false and socially destructive modes of being religious, so did they come to see the civil-religion movement as a counterfeit Christianity that similarly wreaked havoc on American society and government. They observed unacceptable changes in the state of the American family and witnessed what they believed to be the growing power of the false faith of secular humanism in the American government. Under the formal title of the Moral Majority and the informal label "the Religious Right," some began to promote a usable notion of Christian civilization, drawing on and

altering older stories of what it meant to be a Christian democracy to preserve the sort of society they believed only the true faith could sustain.

Civil Religion: Resurrecting Christian Republicanism

Early in the morning on July 9, 1979, the sociologist Robert Bellah, a student of Asian and American political culture at the University of California,
Berkeley, got a phone call from Anne Wexler, assistant to President Jimmy
Carter. She asked if Bellah could be in Washington the next day for a meeting
with the president. When he arrived, Bellah found himself in the company of
an Eastern Orthodox archbishop, a past president of the Southern Baptist
Convention, the president of the University of Notre Dame, and administra-
tors from the National Council of Churches and the American Jewish
Committee. At Camp David, the president's private retreat, Carter told the
assembled religious leaders he was worried for the nation's mood. He was
convinced that behind Americans' unhappiness with the skyrocketing price
of energy, their ongoing funk about the Vietnam War and Watergate, and
their fears about the disintegrating politics of the Middle East lay what he
called a "spiritual crisis." He wanted help in addressing it.[7]

Bellah was there because for the previous twelve years, ever since the
publication of his famous essay "Civil Religion in America," he had become
one of the nation's leading moralists. He and a group of intellectual allies
had developed a particular interpretation of the term "civil religion" and offered it as an antidote to the tribulations of the 1960s and 1970s. The concept
was not new. Bellah drew the term from European philosophy and the
roots of his particular theory from the long tradition of American Christian
republicanism, altered to fit the times. He called his version of "civil religion" a twining of the "traditions of Protestant covenant theology and republican liberty." And yet Bellah was wedded less to Christianity's orthodoxy
than to its ethics, a believer more in education than in miracle. Like most of
his allies he was a white intellectual who stood in the cultural genealogy of
liberal Protestantism, among a group of mid-century Protestants sympathetic to religious diversity and primarily concerned with social ethics
whom David Hollinger has called "Protestant ecumenists."[8]

Bellah presented his version of civil religion as a middle way between the
"militantly secular" on the one hand and the "church and synagogue" on the
other. Like earlier liberal Protestants, Bellah rejected particular theological

content while maintaining the presence of the "transcendent" in American public life. Therefore, he disclaimed earlier theories of "civil religion" which, as he said, "argued that Christianity is the national faith." And yet, Bellah's civil religion was still an attempt to marshal religious ideas into a political project he believed the nation needed. Bellah worried that the United States had once had "just the right amount of autonomy and guilt, decency and efficiency to run a vast industrial economy," he wrote. He and his allies struggled with how to promote these values in a nation where the Cold War Christian consensus seemed increasingly fragmented. Bellah's "civil religion" was an attempt to rehabilitate Christian republicanism for an age of religious diversity. A decade after his first essay describing civil religion Bellah argued its distance from any particular religious tradition reflected a society with mature religious pluralism. To republican values like moral rectitude and public-spiritedness, its advocates joined an emphasis on democratic deliberation and inclusivity. Influenced by the French sociologist Emile Durkheim, Bellah believed such public rites of democracy linked the nation to transcendent values. But those values revealed liberal Protestant assumptions and limited the possibility of a new Christian consensus to replace the battered rhetoric of the Cold War.[9]

Bellah claimed that his version of civil religion was not related to "any religion in particular," specifically repudiating indebtedness "to Jesus Christ, or to Moses, or to the Christian church."[10] This language reflected how ecumenical and ethically oriented liberal Protestants like Bellah had become. But at the same time Bellah said the civil religion he observed was based on "biblical" values, a word he drew from Cold War writers he admired, like Reinhold Niebuhr and Will Herberg, who emphasized religion's function rather than theology. Bellah had briefly fled the United States for Canada in 1955, dogged in the McCarthy era by his history of sympathy toward socialist politics. In his exile he embraced Herberg and Niebuhr's sense of religious humility, finding that it gave him a sort of "chastened liberalism"— which emphasized the importance of human equality and liberty—tempered with worry that Americans were subject to pride and selfishness.[11]

Bellah and other advocates for his version of civil religion argued that the resemblance to Protestantism was a strictly historical phenomenon. Phillip Hammond, Bellah's ally and sometime coauthor, insisted upon the distinction. He claimed that civil religion was "not a naïve belief that America can return to a colonial past, let alone a belief that such a past is preferable because it was Protestant." Nonetheless he insisted that the Protestant nature of American politics derived from historical inevitability. "The American civil religion *is*, whether or not we recognize it," he said, revealing his assumption that American history was Protestant history. Likewise, despite his lack of personal commitment to Calvinist theology, Bellah believed that the assumptions of American political life were ultimately rooted in Puritanism. But despite such protests that they were simply being descriptive, much of these scholars' work was written in the imperative. It reflected moral prescription as much as academic description. Bellah and his allies believed that Christian republican ways of thinking about the relationship between the individual and society should be normative. As Hammond claimed, civil religion was the process of making "individuals with self-interests become responsible citizens." These scholars did not merely observe civil religion but advocated for it. Hammond warned that religious pluralism might make a society bound together by explicit Judeo-Christianity "cease to be a society," and argued that pluralism demanded a "new, more generalized common meaning system." This was what he and Bellah saw in their civil religion.[12]

Bellah's primary protest was against the same devil American Christians often invoked: materialism. But in the years since the formation of Columbia's Contemporary Civilization course and driven by the reconciliation with Roman Catholicism that had underlay the Christian Cold War consensus, liberal Protestants had become increasingly enamored of the importance of engagement with pluralism and diversity and increasingly self-critical about what the Baptist minister Harvey Cox called "an enforced Protestant cultural religion." Cox argued instead for a "secular city," in which Christians' focus lay on what they took to be God's purposes of equality and liberation rather than on the success of any particular brand of Christian practice.[13] Cox's controversial work reflected liberal Protestants' trend away from orthodoxy and toward a conception of Christianity that emphasized the pursuit of justice in the world, which particularly meant an embrace of diversity in the religious, political, and racial sense. Earlier liberal Protestants had been securely confident that democracy, whiteness, and Protestantism went hand in hand, but by the late 1960s their descendants were not so sure. For them as for the Liberal Republicans of the Reconstruction period, materialism came to mean the dangerous power of American institutions.

Bellah and his supporters, influenced by this turn, resurrected the language of materialism to lacerate the Vietnam War and the corruptions of the Nixon presidency. They argued that American industrial and financial power damaged civic virtue, a crime that by the 1960s seemed to enable imperialism and racial injustice as well as fostering domestic illiberalism.

Bellah denounced American commitment to the Vietnam War as "religious nationalism . . . our very intoxication with our own power."[14] In Congress, a network of Protestant legislators began using similar language to assail the Vietnam War. Though in 1964 the Arkansas senator J. William Fulbright had sponsored and voted for the Gulf of Tonkin Resolution, which granted President Lyndon Johnson broad powers to wage war in Vietnam, by April 1966 he had changed his mind. "A great nation is particularly susceptible to the idea that its power is a sign of God's favor," he warned, and pointed out that German soldiers during World War I were issued belt buckles imprinted with *Gott mit uns* (God with us). The association was clear: Fulbright feared that American commitment to military dominance was "pernicious and undemocratic." Instead, he urged Americans to recognize that Christianity might demand the nation to stand down, which he knew would be an unpopular solution. After all, he drily said, "People are equally horrified at hearing the Christian religion doubted, and at seeing it practiced."[15]

The most visible critic of the Vietnam War from a Christian perspective was Oregon senator Mark Hatfield. At the 1973 National Prayer Breakfast, Nixon said that American policy in Vietnam should be trusted because America was historically a moral nation. "Let there be peace on earth, and let it began with me," Nixon intoned, reciting a popular Christmas carol, written in 1955 as a Christian commentary on the Cold War.[16] Hatfield followed Nixon and offered a starkly different assessment of American foreign policy. "Let us beware of the real danger of misplaced allegiance if not outright idolatry," he declared, should Americans worship at a shrine of religious nationalism. For a long time Hatfield had believed that American military adventurism was essentially materialistic rather than virtuous. While a young man serving in China during World War II, he had written to his parents, "It is a crime the way we occidentals have enslaved these people in our mad desire for money." Thirty years later, the same essential thinking framed his approached to Vietnam. In his book *Conflict and Conscience*, whose publication shortly preceded the prayer breakfast, Hatfield declared flatly that American soldiers remained in Vietnam only "on the basis of national pride or to avoid national humiliation." As an antidote to such fear he called Americans back to their "largely religious . . . heritage." He defined the American heritage in the "Puritan ethic," which embraced humility, industriousness, and moral virtue. Hatfield argued that a vast swath of what was good about American life was due to the Puritans, from "the early success of the nation's economic life" to "the institutions of limited government with divided powers." Bellah saw in both Hatfield and

Fulbright allies for his own cause, and his cooperation with these overtly Protestant congressmen illustrates how closely civil religion was connected to tradition Protestant Christian republicanism.[17]

Hatfield's link between the war in Vietnam and the growing power of American capitalism gestured to the other target of Bellah's civil religion: the growth of what he called the "technical-regulative state," which he was convinced degraded democratic deliberation and hence, like Vietnam, stunted the moral growth of American citizens. The institutions that governed American society, Bellah said, had "come unhinged from a larger religious and moral context," and hence promoted the enhancement of material and economic power rather than democratic virtues. This sin lay at the root of various scandals of the Nixon presidency, which Bellah lambasted for asserting "American goodness without any sense of a need for judgment at all."[18] In early 1972, Charles Henderson, associate dean of the chapel at Princeton, published the best-selling *The Nixon Theology*, attacking the president's stubborn confidence in "perfect harmony between faith in God and in the nation and . . . the will of God with the good of the state." Henderson insisted to the contrary that what he believed to be real Christianity would offer a "recognition of the tragic and the demonic [and] the human propensity" toward sin manifest in the imperialism of the Vietnam War, in the oppression of African Americans, and in the growing gap between rich and poor. Henderson believed that Nixon, "lacking a transcendent God . . . seems to make patriotism his religion."[19]

Bellah's followers argued that these problems led to national anomie, loss of interest in moral virtue, and the collapse of democratic deliberation into passive consumerism. In 1974 Paul Starr, an academic who wrote for the *New York Times*, visited a number of young people who in the previous decade had been part of what he called "the movement"—the protests against Vietnam, the civil rights movement, the counterculture—and were now settling unhappily into careers as teachers, lawyers, and scientists, having failed to transform the nation. Starr invoked Bellah's ideas to describe their dilemma. They were living, he said, "with contradictions," embracing the order they had once sought to reform. They balanced on a painful knife's edge, watching the United States slip into chaos but also agonizingly unable to escape it. "They know, for example, that America consumes more than her share of the world's resources—and they help consume it," Starr wrote. He portrayed them as prophets slowly being subsumed by the sin against which they prophesied, painting a grim picture of anxiety and self-loathing.[20]

Christopher Lasch, an iconoclastic historian whose critique of American capitalism lacerated the culture of materialism, also echoed Bellah's assessments in his scathing portrait of the former radical Jerry Rubin, who in the 1960s had famously warned of the dangers of trusting anyone over age thirty. By 1979 he was a successful financier who claimed that his old "revolutionary politics concealed a 'puritan conditioning'" which had made him anxious and unhappy. Lasch, a fan of the Puritans, could not restrain his sarcasm at Rubin's newfound wealth and spending on personal luxuries. "No strenuous psychic exertions," he wrote in his blistering 1979 book, *The Culture of Narcissism,* "seem to have been required" for Rubin to embrace "his celebrity and material rewards." In total, said Lasch, in the success of postwar American capitalism had a reached a "dead end of a narcissistic preoccupation with the self" that strangled any possibility of cultural change.[21] Material success brought a deeper failure.

Producing a History of Civil Religion

Though Bellah and his supporters were willing to make allies of iconoclastic academics like Lasch and Christians like Fulbright and Hatfield, their commitment to Christian republican values meant that their movement's boundaries were only semiporous, and the story of American history they produced reflected those boundaries. The way they treated the black-freedom movement and the Puritans illustrated the ways their version of American history differed from that of earlier Christian groups.

Bellah and Hammond celebrated the work of Martin Luther King Jr.'s Southern Christian Leadership Conference as the most important event in recent American history. For Bellah, one of the great hallmarks of Christianity was its commitment to human equality; indeed, he said his own allegiance to Christianity derived from the moment when he realized that "identification with the body of Christ meant identification with all men without exception."[22] Thus, Bellah and his fellows found in Martin Luther King a hero—in fact, Bellah called him one of the "greatest heroes"—of American civil religion, along with stalwarts like Abraham Lincoln and Thomas Jefferson, and Bellah considered the SCLC's movement to be one of the great crusades "to make America more fully realize its professed values"—which they took to be coterminous with their own.[23]

Yet Bellah and his allies also interpreted the black-freedom movement selectively. Associating their civil religion with the SCLC was a useful way to fuse the moralism they drew from Christian republicanism to the present fact of American diversity. Bellah and Hammond were strongly sympathetic with the cause of African American equality, but praised most highly King's integrationism, which they read as part of the Christian republican tradition, locating King as the only black representative in a stream of otherwise white figureheads of a univocal Protestant civil religion, rather as a representative of black Christianity. "The Protestant clergyman remains a central spokesman for American culture," Bellah claimed. "Up to the present day, through men such as Reinhold Niebuhr and Martin Luther King, the tradition continues." Thus, Bellah and his allies tended to identify the entire black-freedom movement with Martin Luther King and to select only certain of King's values to celebrate, emphasizing his commitment to the procedures of American democracy and to integration while ignoring his more radical views and his claimed inspiration from non-Western figures like Kwame Nkrumah. In so doing they integrated King's accomplishments into the ideology of civil religion, presenting them as part of a broader national embrace of the virtues of Christian republicanism. In January 1979, speaking in Atlanta, Jimmy Carter declared, "We can speak out now as a nation with one voice on the sensitive issue of human rights all around the world, because Martin Luther King, Jr., and the civil rights movement helped to liberate all Americans from the chains of official racism here at home."[24]

Reading King this way separated him from the complex and often fractious world of the black-freedom movement and promoted the sort of triumphal faith in progress long characteristic of liberal Protestantism. It also allowed them to dismiss the rest of the black-freedom movement. Indeed, quite explicitly, Bellah was willing to claim that Martin Luther King aside from the civil rights movement lacked much religious depth. Writing of the civil rights and antiwar movements, he said, "In spite of the leadership of Martin Luther King . . . those movements as a whole remained indifferent if not hostile to religion." Thus did Bellah delegitimize the black-freedom movement outside the genteel Martin Luther King of his imagination.[25] Bellah's frequent collaborator, Phillip Hammond, declared King "a true interpreter and prophet of the American civil religion." In so doing, he made King congruent to the concerns of Bellah and Hammond themselves. Not only did King call down moral judgment upon the racism of the American state—a judgment that Bellah and Hammond thought was richly deserved—he also exemplified the sort of deliberative virtues the two valued in civil discourse. "The nonviolent character of King's protests, his readiness to accept penalties imposed by the very system he was challenging, reflect precisely civility elevated to civil religion," Hammond declared.[26]

While Bellah's civil religion movement sought to celebrate the growing diversity of American life, its promoters continually imagined an ideal national community as one also bound to their version of Christian republicanism. Rejecting proposals from other Christian groups to abandon the notion of the "West," they instead proposed that Americans look to a particular version of Western history that depicted their own values. Bellah, for instance, commended to his readers the Puritans, who offered "a heritage of moral and religious experience from which we have much to learn." Linking the founding of the United States to the God-drenched language, mission, and government of the Puritans seemed a savvy move in the Cold War, and through the 1950s the Puritans achieved greater and greater prominence in popular retellings of the American founding. But scholars like Lasch and Bellah also began praising the Puritans as the true progenitors of American civil religion. Lasch lauded the Puritans for their evident lack of fixation on the self and observed that they saw "personal aggrandizement as incidental to social labor."[27] Lasch's understanding of the Puritan movement depended on the midcentury rehabilitation of the New England colonies, one that revised the dour Puritans depicted in Columbia's Contemporary Civilization course. There were naysayers, of course; John Herman Randall warned that the Puritans "sought . . . to regulate all men's lives by [their] own light" and that moral concentration led "to a prying interference with others." He was skeptical of the Puritans' contribution to democracy.[28] But to Bellah and Lasch, each of whom used the groundbreaking work of Harvard historian Perry Miller as their primary source for understanding the New England community, Puritanism applied the notion of covenant to cultivate an ethical public-spiritedness that laid the moral foundation of American democracy.

This fondness for the Puritans, as well as their sense that American culture had departed from the liberal Protestant principles they valued, led Bellah and other philosophers of civil religion to embrace the term *prophetic* to describe their philosophy. Martin Marty distinguished between the "prophetic" and "priestly" styles of American civil religion, arguing that Americans were more accustomed to the latter: invocations of religious language or ritual that conferred approval or celebration upon American government.[29] In 1970 the historian Sacvan Bercovitch published the first version of what would become his 1978 book, *The American Jeremiad,* in which he observed that "we have begun to see the impact of Puritan rhetoric on our culture." Bercovitch argued that the Puritans had used their "rhetoric of promise, doomsday, and millennium entwined" to promote social change and summon Americans to fulfill their political, religious, and social ideals. Bercovitch later observed that his book was born as "a product of the radical sixties and seventies . . . students' rights in the universities, women's rights in the workplace, gay rights in society at large, the embrace of ethnic and racial diversity."[30] For him the legacy of Puritan prophecy was a language that could call America to moral account and promote its egalitarian ideals. Similarly, the Jewish theologian Abraham Joshua Heschel observed that Hebrew prophecy was social and political as much as it was religious. "Prophecy," then, as advocates of civil religion defined it, was the application of moral, religious language to those political ideals they were committed to: selfless public service, faith in democratic government, inclusive and egalitarian participation in politics.[31]

The civil religion model put forth by Bellah, Lasch, and others was profoundly influential, swaying many national leaders, including President Carter. Carter finally delivered the speech Bellah had consulted on July 15, 1979, from the Oval Office. He invoked Reinhold Niebuhr and echoed the language of Bellah and Lasch to warn Americans that the greatest challenge to national morale they faced was a lack of faith in the spiritual meaning of American democracy. The Vietnam War, the Watergate scandal, and the assassinations of the Kennedy brothers and Martin Luther King, Carter said, had led to a nation with "disrespect for government and for churches and for schools." While Americans had once "believed that we were part of a great movement of humanity itself called democracy, involved in the search for freedom," now "too many of us . . . tend to worship self-indulgence and consumption." Carter declared that he would use the challenge of rising energy prices to reform American morality. He called upon Americans to accept rationing of gasoline, to lower their thermostats, to abjure consumption. Renouncing materialism in favor of public sacrifice would, he said, "conquer the crisis of spirit in our country."[32]

Carter's version of civil religion drew on the principles of Christian republicanism, but the response to it showed how fragile the American Christian consensus had become. He faced critics who blasted his earnest moralism for its naivete and overt religiosity. The columnist Art Buchwald taunted the president who promised a solution to the energy crisis then vanished into the wilderness for days. When Carter finally, like Moses, "came down the mountain," he offered no real solutions, Buchwald wrote. But he did on his next foreign trip to South Korea "try to make President Park a Christian." Buchwald recalled a friend who, upon hearing this news, told the columnist that he must be joking. "I wish I were," he drily wrote.[33] Buchwald, like many Americans in the 1970s and 1980s, was increasingly uncomfortable with overt Christian language in American politics. At the same time, disgruntled radical evangelicals like Jim Wallis excoriated the president for his timidity and unwillingness to assail the exhausted Cold War consensus. Wallis raged that Carter was unwilling to question the capitalist-inspired greed that underlay the energy crisis. "It is these standards of social righteousness that our evangelical president has set aside during his first year in office," he proclaimed.[34] "Prophetic" civil religion in the hands of a Bellah or a Carter was Christian republicanism under siege: it was exhortative rather than celebratory, moralistic rather than theological, and anxious about its narrowing place in American life.

Defining the Boundaries of Civil Religion

Though they were able to assimilate the black-freedom movement through reenvisioning Martin Luther King, Bellah and his allies set the boundary of civil religion at what they were not afraid to call the "cults": new religious movements. To them these groups illustrated the fragmentation of American life because they strained the Cold War Christian consensus. The "cults," said Phillip Hammond, were "uncivil"; that is, they "offered an opportunity to commit oneself and to do so in ways that were neither middle class nor even particularly American." Cults, he said, offered an alternative civil religion, one designed to "alienate" rather than "envelope [sic] people into mainline America."[35] Unlike the SCLC, cults seemed to these observers completely distinct from what they understood "civil religion" to be.

As the 1970s progressed Bellah was growing increasingly uneasy about the notion of "civil religion." He believed his work was misunderstood and oversimplified, and gradually backed from the term. But he remained committed to the set of civic values he believed it described. In middle of the decade he and a colleague supervised a team of graduate students in intensive study of new religious movements in and around Berkeley, California. Bellah came away uneasy. His worries illustrated his commitment to the version of Christian republicanism described in his work on civil religion.

First, Bellah judged these movements to be the "successor movements to
the counterculture," which itself he judged a product of Americans' encounter with the "irrationalities and horrors of modern history."[36] Bellah
credited the counterculture with drawing attention to the diseases plaguing
American society, but he also worried that it was less a cure than a symptom.
Bellah could come across as strikingly vituperative when he characterized
the counterculture as claiming "the answer to our present need is no control
at all, let the impulses run free, natural man is at heart innocent and good."
The Berkeley Free Speech Movement had degenerated into the "Filthy
Speech Movement," Bellah worried, and to it and like-minded organizations
he quoted Melville: "Well, well, one hears the kettledrums of hell." He was
quite serious; he believed that America's productive tension between "utili-
tarian individualism" and "Biblical religion"—the one promoting a restless
quest for personal improvement and the other tempering the first with moral
stricture—had been overturned in the 1960s, and the counterculture at its
worst revealed American culture was sinking into a "cynical privatism" or
selfishness.[37]

Second, Bellah worried that because the "counterculture's deepest influences came from Asia," new religious movements were providing for "an
erosion of the legitimacy of the American way of life." This is not to say that
Bellah believed that Asian religious ideas were inherently destructive, but it
did mean that he believed that new religious movements ignored or assailed
the values that supported American institutions. Bellah's students consistently reported to him that, as one put it about those who joined the Healthy-
Happy-Holy Organization, members were "experienced with drugs and
demonstrations" and "have not fully made the transition from the fluid lifestyle of the counterculture."[38] As did countercult evangelicals, Bellah concluded that these groups were "survival units" for the counterculture, preying
on young people suffering from its ills. But, he warned, all such movements
"have withdrawn fundamentally from contemporary American society, see
it as corrupt and illegitimate, and place their hope in a radically different
vision." To the extent such movements flourished in the United States, the
American social order would have to be drastically rewritten to accommodate new social values. This might not be catastrophic, but Bellah offered
several worrying options, ranging from "mindless rationalization of means
and the lack of concern with ends" that would accompany a vast national
commitment to the accumulation of wealth and power, to (on the other end
of the spectrum) "a relapse into traditional authoritarianism." In both situ-

ations he saw little hope for the survival of new religious movements—which would be squelched by a repressive regime or the mighty engine of capitalism—but also little hope for the endurance of liberal Protestant Christian republicanism.[39]

By the late 1970s the notion of civil religion was becoming increasingly controversial. Jimmy Carter's inability to please either secular critics or full-throated evangelicals indicated as much. Bellah's own proposals also met increasing criticism. Some other academics assailed the notion of "civil religion" as Bellah described it as incoherent, or argued that it was simply one version of many, or maintained that Bellah was less observing American life than promoting his particular vision of it. And yet, Bellah's concept of "civil religion" drew supporters from liberal Protestant Americans who felt American society drifting away from them. Richard Philbrick, religion columnist for the *Chicago Tribune*, observed, "I suspect that some critics of civil religion are really offended by it because . . . they don't like the values which in their view it supports." Philbrick claimed that many of Robert Bellah's critics were upset that the rhetoric of civil religion was "bulldozing differences" in a diverse nation.[40] While the columnist was defensive of Bellah, his crankiness revealed that growing numbers of Americans were less and less sympathetic to the very notion of a common cultural consensus, let alone one based upon the historic tendencies of Christian republicanism.

The Theological Mandate of the Religious Right

The ambivalent relationship Bellah and his supporters held with religious diversity was possible because they drew on the ecumenical Cold War consensus which privileged good citizenship over theological orthodoxy. They put little weight on commanding the title of "Christian." For conservative evangelicals, however, the word was critical. Beginning in the mid-1970s, a number of Christian political groups began to lobby government officers and influence voting behavior in favor of their version of Christian politics. Such groups, which have been collectively called the "Religious Right," should be understood as more than just lobbying agencies. The Religious Right was a theological movement that defended a version of Christian republicanism—and though its supporters shared an ethical emphasis with advocates of civil religion, as their confrontation with the cults illustrated they would insist also upon the word "Christian."

As did civil religion advocates, the Religious Right emphasized the importance of moral behavior to the preservation of American democracy, but their immersion in the notion of worldview convinced them that only adherence to conservative Protestant theology could truly foster it. The idea of Western civilization that they inherited from the midcentury Christian consensus as translated through partisans like Francis Schaeffer primed them to believe that the health of an evangelical Christian worldview was the health of the nation, and that the rise of pluralism of belief led to the decay of American culture. As Schaeffer put it in his 1981 battle cry, *A Christian Manifesto,* the great problem with American Christians was that they "have seen things in bits and pieces instead of totals." The sexual revolution, rising divorce rates, Watergate, strife over Vietnam: "each thing is a part, a symptom, of a much larger problem."[41]

Given their belief in worldview ideology and worry about orthodoxy, it is no surprise that the evangelicals who would lead the Religious Right drew on the language of the countercult movement to paint their political opponents as believers in a false religion, a non-Christian materialist philosophy suborning American society. They understood their disagreements with political opponents as simply another iteration of Christian civilization's long battle with cults. The southern California evangelical power couple Tim and Beverly LaHaye, who ran a large Christian ministry and published a number of books, taught that Greece and Rome, which had abandoned their traditional religions to pursue strange new mystery cults, were a warning that "departure from their original religious beliefs" was a sure "sign of moral collapse" in any culture. Indeed the LaHayes warned that there were really only "two kinds of religion today . . . Biblical" religion on the one hand, and "pagan" religion on the other.[42] The young and charismatic Dallas televangelist James Robison also saw the cult movement as a microcosm of a broader social problem. "The upsurge of cults stands as the most obvious evidence today of those who turn to teachers who speak what people want to hear rather than what they need to hear," Robison said.[43]

The threat many of these evangelicals saw looming behind the cults was "secular humanism," a phrase *Christianity Today* credited Francis Schaeffer with popularizing.[44] For Schaeffer, secular humanism was itself a long-standing heresy—indeed, even a pagan religion, as cults were. Evangelicals did not call secular humanism a religion simply as a rhetorical device. Schaeffer clarified that he used the word because religions offered "total world view," a way of understanding humanity and human beings' relationship to God and to each other. Many other conservative evangelicals agreed. James Robison, for instance, described secular humanism as "essentially a religion which worships the mind of man."[45] Like the cults, secular humanism was materialist, in that it conceived of humanity as the product of blind nature rather than of divine intention and believed that the end of human beings lay in material success. Like cults, secular humanism was utopian, promising that through rational reform society could be perfected. Like cults, despite such promises, secular humanism ended up promoting chaos, and, finally, like cults, secular humanism would decay into totalitarianism.

Evangelicals' strident assault on the popular 1980 television series *Cosmos*, hosted by the astrophysicist Carl Sagan, illustrates the ways they saw secular humanism infiltrating popular culture. In his *Christian Manifesto* Schaeffer repeated no fewer than three times his incredulity at Sagan's declaration that, as Schaeffer put it, "the impersonal cosmos is all there is or ever was or will be." Sagan managed to "indoctrinate millions of unsuspecting viewers with this humanistic final view of reality," Schaeffer mourned.[46] Sagan was destructive, the evangelical scientist Richard A. Baer explained in an article in *Christianity Today*, because he offered "virtually all the key terms of the Judeo-Christian drama of creation and salvation"—but stripped of divinity, and instead in service to "a form of nature mysticism" which was, essentially, "philosophical materialism or atheism."[47]

Further, evangelicals were suspicious of Sagan's command of television. They associated the vast majority of television programs with amoral technical mastery, believing the medium was easily used to promote secular humanist aims. Tim LaHaye complained that the media rarely took flattering photographs of Christian activist Phyllis Schlafly, but rather waited until she stood with "mouth open or in an uncomplimentary pose." This was not simple grousing. LaHaye was comfortable arguing that television was "the most powerful vehicle in controlling the minds of a generation." Through repetition, use of light and color, and subtle demonization of opposition, LaHaye believed that secular humanists had "gained such mind control that only a few thousand of them can literally govern 216 million people." LaHaye's theories drew on an old Christian fear that a technocratic elite could subvert minds through scientific mastery; from the Germans in World War I to Communists in the Cold War to secular humanists in the United States, the threat was always the same. LaHaye explained that "Hollywood uses immoral or amoral stories and plays not because they make good art, but because they offer a tremendous vehicle for assaulting the minds of our citizens with their humanistic beliefs." Many evangelicals agreed. (Of course many also mastered television themselves.)[48]

Their hostility to television reflected a broader evangelical ambivalence with the culture of consumer capitalism. Some conservative evangelicals associated capitalism with greed, materialism, and a lack of values. Americans loved "the ritual of religion while at the same time bathing and basking in the glory of worldliness and materialism," James Robison said, warning that "the driving force behind one's desire for success is often for none other than what the Bible calls filthy lucre."[49] Jerry Falwell likewise compared Americans to Adam and Eve in the Garden of Eden, observing, "We may have plenty to eat from the heavily laden trees around us, but we are restless and unhappy."[50]

Many leaders of the Religious Right spoke with such vehemence because they were particularly troubled by the great publicity the prosperity-gospel movement gained in the 1980s. The prosperity gospel derived from the same nineteenth-century New Thought movements that inspired Norman Vincent Peale. Its ideas gained popularity through the channels of mid-twentieth century Pentecostal revivalism, where, aided by the Cold War's emphasis on Christianity's consonance with individualism and capitalism, biblical promises of abundance and healing through faith in Christ became linked to economic and social success. By the 1970s and 1980s, preachers like Oral Roberts and Jim Bakker had audiences of millions who found the links that they drew between Christianity and success in the American marketplace entirely in line with their assumption that Christianity underlay the structures of American life. Such preachers flourished in the modern media environment that evangelicals found suspect Christianizing the medium in ways LaHaye approved of. For instance, Jim Bakker's theme park, Heritage USA, presented an overtly Christian vision of American history and Western civilization. It featured a meticulously maintained façade of a small American town enlivened with regular dramatic performances of scenes from the American past and the life of Jesus on the same stage, intertwining the two with each other in the midst of a shopping center. It was the very image of what the prosperity gospel believed America to be. As one supporter of Bakker claimed, "I've been to Heritage USA and I felt like I was in heaven."[51]

Many advocates of the prosperity gospel supported the Religious Right, but divisions between them and Christians like Falwell and LaHaye who rejected the theology reveal how broad a coalition the Religious Right was. To conservative Christians like Jerry Falwell, the prosperity gospel was simply materialism. Falwell bluntly labeled it "bad doctrine" and stated,

"God hasn't called all saints to be healthy and wealthy."[52] Rather, he and other Christian opponents of the doctrine believed that it inappropriately exalted desire, advancing no higher goal than pleasure and shallow self-expression rather than the divine destiny that religious discipline offered. Beverly LaHaye counseled evangelical women that "desire for things such as a better home, a newer car, [and] many clothes . . . draw[s] the homemaker into a discontented and covetous position."[53] Her warnings signaled that evangelical fears about unrestrained desire could creep into the home and corrupt the essential unit of American society: the family.

The Perilous Transformation of the American Family

The connection evangelicals drew between secular humanism's rejection of Christian teaching and the social breakdown they saw around them was best exemplified in the ways evangelicals explained the era's turbulent shifts in familial and gender roles. They linked secular humanism to the breakdown of these roles and linked that breakdown to social chaos, which in turn would lead to the rise of authoritarianism. By contrast, a truly Christian understanding of history revealed a natural "gendered order," premised on a true understanding of what men and women were like and consisting of a right relationship between men, women, and children. Abiding by this gendered order would promote the democratic freedom Americans enjoyed. In 1988, a group of Religious Right organizations released a "Family Manifesto" that declared, "We proclaim that sexual differentiation extends to psychological traits which set natural constraints on gender roles." Hence, the nuclear family was "an immutable structure established by our Creator," providing necessary "social and psychological functions" for the maintenance of a good society. As Jerry Falwell succinctly put it, "Families reared in the correct way contribute significantly to the success of a constitutional government."[54]

Peter Marshall and David Manuel's 1977 *The Light and the Glory* was an extremely popular retelling of American history from an evangelical perspective; it emphasized that the family was the primary vehicle through which American society was structured according to God's will. Like Bellah, the authors praised the Puritans, but while Bellah emphasized Puritan communalism and self-restraint, Marshall and Manuel praised Puritan adherence to the gendered order. They warned, "The biggest single cause of the breakdown of the American family is that so much of what we could call *love*, the Puritans would have another name for: *idolatry*." Modern families indulged their children and failed to teach discipline and virtue. But Puritans understood the divine origin of gender hierarchy: "Unlike most modern parents, the Puritans knew that their children did not belong to them; they belonged to God." Marshall and Manuel attributed Puritan self-governance to Puritans' understanding of themselves as "a big family. This was as God intended, and was one of the fruits of the horizontal aspect of the covenant."[55]

As Carl Sagan was evangelicals' bête noire on the issue of secular humanism, Benjamin Spock represented the apotheosis of humanist self-gratification in the realm of the family. In 1946, Spock, a pediatrician, had published *Baby and Child Care*, which quickly became one of the best-selling American books of the twentieth century. By the 1960s Spock was marching in demonstrations against the Vietnam War, and in 1972 he accepted the presidential nomination of the People's Party, which called for universal health care, withdrawal of American troops around the world, a guaranteed minimum income, and the legalization of marijuana. By the mid-1970s, conservative Christians were linking Spock's political activism to his ideas about child rearing, which encouraged parents to avoid strict discipline and allow children self-expression. The columnist Stewart Alsop grumped that too many children were "Spocked when they should have been spanked," and Norman Vincent Peale accused him of encouraging "instant gratification of needs." The connection between this reputation for laxity and the social turmoil of the 1960s and 1970s was irresistible to many observers. A journalist with the *Chicago Tribune* reported that when a young mother was advised to read Spock's manual, she snapped, "Absolutely not. I'm not interested in raising revolutionaries."[56]

For evangelicals the doctor began from a false, materialist premise—that children's physical desires should be indulged—and the result was unsurprising: a generation of children plagued with moral and psychological incapacity. Tim and Beverly LaHaye assailed "the nonbiblical child-raising concepts of Dr. Benjamin Spock and his followers—who announced that permissivism encouraged creativity." According to the LaHayes, Spock had "produced a whole generation of selfish, inconsiderate, undisciplined adults." Jerry Falwell declared that "the problem with our youth must trace back to their upbringing. . . . For the past two decades psychologists have told parents not to spank their children. The result has been the most rebellious and irresponsible generation of young people who have ever lived in America." Phyllis Schlafly, the conservative Catholic activist, declared that Spock's degenerate philosophy had even ruined the doctor's own life, tartly observing, "Spock bought the whole bag of liberation. He walked out on his faithful wife Jane."[57]

The generally preferred alternative for evangelicals was James Dobson, a University of Southern California psychology professor and conservative Christian, whose 1970 *Dare to Discipline* was premised on the same notion of Christian worldview that guided many conservative evangelicals. Dobson professed admiration for Spock but argued that the doctor's work had led to "an unworkable, illogical philosophy of child management" that had resulted in social breakdown. "In an age of widespread drug usage, immorality, civil disobedience, vandalism and violence," Dobson claimed, "permissiveness has not just been a failure; it's been a disaster." Instead, Dobson argued that children needed not only discipline from their parents—from time-outs to light physical punishment like spanking (and, memorably, squeezing the carotid artery)—but a sense of themselves as beings possessed of "personal strength" and hence a need for "the art of self control." This was of course evangelical Protestant theology, which taught that human beings were simultaneously divinely created but also sinners. It countered materialist philosophy with republican moral restraint.[58]

Just as American Christians worried that their fellow citizens wandered into materialist philosophies like communism and cults because they unknowingly hungered for Christianity, Dobson argued that much bad behavior in modern children stemmed not from willful maliciousness but from the psychological strain of living in a materialist society. Dobson demonstrated the fluidity with which evangelicals had adopted the language of psychology as he described the problem. "Many of the youngsters who are behaving in such antisocial and self-destructive ways are actually lost, aimless, and valueless individuals," Dobson said. Youth were acting on the "inner emptiness" they experienced because they did not understand their true nature. For Dobson, moral decadence was a self-reinforcing problem that emerged only when children were not taught that "God's spiritual laws are as inflexible as His physical laws." If one jumped off a high roof, one would die, Dobson pointed out. Similarly, God's moral laws were constructed to guard human nature. That was why, he quoted the Bible, "the wages of sin is death," and why America's children who did not know those laws were spiraling out of control for lack of them.[59]

While Protestants like Dobson used psychology to describe the concept of a gendered order, Catholics had long believed that gendered order derived from natural law. In the 1970s Catholics began publicly employing the same language to define gendered order that John Ryan had used to describe the nation's economic order and ex-communists had used to condemn the deleterious effects of communism. Phyllis Schlafly organized a number of lobbying groups designed to stop the Equal Rights Amendment and promote the cause of the traditional family, and she argued that God had manifestly instituted gender roles into the very physical design of the universe. "The female body with its baby producing organs was not designed by a conspiracy of men but by the Divine Architect of the human race," she maintained. Hence, Schlafly declared, even the most apparently mundane distinctions between the genders were rooted in the natural law of the universe. The "differences between men and women are also emotional and psychological. Without women's innate maternal instinct the human race would have died out," she wrote. "Men are philosophers and women are practical, and 'twas ever thus." Therefore, according to Schlafly, the "Judeo-Christian ethic" demanded that the "customs and laws" of Western society should be built to support mothers.[60]

Though many evangelicals were skeptical of the salvific power of Schlafly's faith, they embraced her movement for two reasons. First, since the beginning of the Cold War, Catholics had consciously looked for ways to reconcile their distinctively Catholic ideas about democracy, natural law, and human nature with the American commitment to democracy. Catholic writers had proven capable of using Catholic language in ways Protestants might understand and support. Thus, evangelicals were in many ways already prepared to recognize Catholics as potential allies in the struggle against a common enemy. Second, as had Charles Coughlin Schlafly worked hard to put herself in that broader rhetorical tradition. She used terms like *Judeo-Christian* and spoke not of "natural law" but of "Biblical" principles. To Schlafly and others in the 1970s, all "orthodox Christians," as the Catholic writer James Hitchcock put it, shared fundamental principles about human nature that both undergirded their particular policy platforms and also allowed cooperation across denominations.[61]

In 1980, Jimmy Carter convened the White House Conference on Families, which he had promised evangelical leaders since his election but only managed to construct during his bid for reelection. Carter spoke of the conference in the same civil-religious terms he had used in his speech on energy the year before. He emphasized that the family connected the history of the individual to that of the nation, describing a cemetery in his hometown of

Plains, Georgia, where Carters had been buried since the eighteenth century. He emphasized that the family should be a refuge in a modern society in which "people are uprooted" by a "fast-changing, technological world." For Carter, the family was a repository of virtues and structure where "the motivation and the morals and goals of a life are first shaped." He described the family as a "community" rather than emphasizing its gendered structure, recounting the network of relatives and neighbors that raised him and holding up his wife Rosalynn's childhood as an example of a successful single-parent family. For him, ultimately, the family was a source of common virtue in a diverse society: "We can learn how to live in harmony and helpfulness with one another, and nourish the individuality of those who live in the same home; respect one another, even though we're different."[62] His description of the family emphasized the basic notion of Bellah's civil religion: the power of virtuous behavior to bind together an increasingly pluralist nation in a deliberative democracy.[63]

While evangelicals shared with Carter and civil-religion advocates concern that the family faced challenges from materialism, they assailed the president for failing to recognize that the most essential aspect of the family was that it translated into human society a divine order that promoted stability and made democracy possible. Evangelical women particularly condemned Carter's ideas. Beverly LaHaye, who besides authoring books founded the evangelical lobby Concerned Women for America, outlined how the gendered order promoted public good. "The woman who is truly spirit-filled will want to be totally submissive to her husband," she wrote. She hastened to clarify that she did not mean dominated or controlled. "Submissive does not mean that she is owned and operated by her husband but that he is the head or manager," she claimed. "He helps her develop to her greatest potential." She warned of wives who "tend to demasculinize a man by dominating and leading him" and explained that such a disruption would lead only to unhappy families. The LaHayes together explained why. "Her husband has a need for her to submit. This is not something the husband learns or tries to develop. It is a built in need which God designed for him." Only when this balance was properly understood could American society achieve a stable democracy. "The unfortunate women's lib leaders who cry out for more freedom will never experience true liberation until they have first met Jesus Christ and followed his plan for women's freedom," the LaHayes wrote.[64]

Evangelicals invoked a number of evidences that the breakdown of the gendered order was wrecking American society. Concerned Women for

America joined the National Pro-Family Coalition, which aimed to swamp the Conference on Families with delegates and repeatedly invoked cults to warn conference attendees how departing from a Christian worldview would undermine the stability of American society. Beverly LaHaye declared that the conference leaders "distorted the traditional meaning of family to include any kind of living arrangement, from married lesbians raising children to weird hippie communes." Nancy Barcus, an evangelical delegate to the Los Angeles conference, wrote in *Christianity Today* that evangelicals were concerned that the term *family* might be "understood as including colonies of unrelated persons with cultic or homosexual tendencies." As Connie Marsher, director of the Pro-Family Coalition, explained, "Families are not religious cults, families are not Manson families, families are not heterosexual or homosexual liaisons outside of marriage."[65]

In addition to cautioning against cults, the LaHayes warned that the increasing visibility of homosexuality in American culture was a sign of materialism and would lead to the decay of democracy. "Masculine fathers who love and spend time with their sons never saw them become homosexuals until recently," they wrote. "Today there is so much propaganda and encouragement given [to] the practice that many young people experiment with it until it becomes a learned behavior."[66] A weak father would leave his son vulnerable to the corrupting forces of mechanical conditioning of the sort B. F. Skinner had described. Evangelicals saw the AIDS crisis of the 1980s as the natural result of the violation of God's gendered order. Jerry Falwell described the disease as "the gay plague" and warned that AIDS spread because Americans were "embracing what God has condemned: sex outside of marriage." Gay Americans, Falwell said, "are literally killing themselves with their lust." He warned Americans that the cost of caring for those with AIDS would be put upon "normal families like yours and mine," implicitly equating "American" and "normal" with the heterosexual nuclear family.[67]

Similarly, evangelicals interpreted the racial upheavals of the 1950s and 1960s as evidence that materialist strain on the family was undermining the American social order. Many echoed a common interpretation of Daniel Patrick Moynihan's 1965 report *The Negro Family: A Case for National Action*. Moynihan, then an official in the Department of Labor, drew on the work of black academics like Kenneth Clark and E. Franklin Frazier to argue that the lingering effects of slavery and Jim Crow laws had done such damage to the economic prospects of African Americans that black families were coming apart. Moynihan worried that the rising number of black families headed by single mothers was driving "the deterioration of the fabric of Negro society" and would produce more crime and more poverty.[68] He argued that the problem demanded a reform in government aid to African Americans on the economic margins. However, many conservative politicians countered that the report actually demonstrated that poverty in black communities was due to cultural pathology that government aid only exacerbated.[69]

Evangelicals agreed. Many had long suspected that the civil rights movement was in fact a communist ploy to undermine American democracy, so arguing that government aid to African American families encouraged moral decay was not a far step. At the alternative "pro-family conference" that Falwell helped to organize to counter Carter's Conference on Families, organizer Ed McAteer promised panels illustrating that "solutions for family problems will not be found in government programs."[70] In his sermon "America and Work," delivered July 1, 1979, Falwell blamed the rioting that had broken out in African American neighborhoods over the previous decade on single-parent families and government aid. "The first thing that an indigent society finds itself in is lawlessness, riot," he said. Further, Falwell associated that moral decay with a failure of Christianity. "People out of work with a lot of spare time . . . won't serve God." The black evangelical Glandion Carney agreed. "Blacks have not paid enough attention to the quality of family life," Carney told the National Black Evangelical Association. He urged black Americans to abandon the "welfare system . . . beset by a lack of moral consistency and direction," and instead to renew individual moral commitments.[71]

The Fear of a Materialist State

Evangelicals saw as the logical conclusion of the decline of the traditional family the rise of authoritarian materialism in all the forms they had learned to fear it: the insidiousness of psychological brainwashing; the terrifying machinery of the bureaucratic state; the dominance of a commercialized media which played on animal appetites. They argued that all these forces sought to supplant the natural authority parents derived from God-given gender roles—and were using the turmoil of American society to do so. The rise of materialist, secular-humanist philosophy in the United States had enabled a conspiratorial elite to seize control of society and choke off democracy. As with all else, Francis Schaeffer had warned of this. As social morals degenerated due to materialism's promotion of hedonism, chaos would erupt. "An elite, an authoritarianism as such, would gradually force form on a society so that it will not go on to chaos," Schaeffer predicted. That elite would accept the predicates of secular humanism and would use materialist techniques to manipulate American society. He invoked scientists who advocated using pills to calm emotions, psychologists who sought "experiments with brain control," "subliminal influence" through the media, and simple martial law. "And most people will accept it," Schaeffer mourned, for equally materialist reasons: "from the desire for personal peace and affluence, from apathy."[72]

George Gilder, an evangelical intellectual whose 1981 book, *Wealth and Poverty,* was "the bible of the Reagan Administration" (according to *Christianity Today*), connected the rise of secular humanism to the power of the state and the collapse of the traditional family. His 1978 book, *The Visible Man,* traced the fortunes of Sam Brewer, a young, black ex-Marine accused of rape and "belittled by pity and charity and sociology." Separated by the state from his family and his church, Sam became what Gilder believed the government expected of black people: an imprisoned criminal with a wife and family dependent upon government aid. For Gilder the story of Brewer illustrated that "the welfare state attacks the problem of the absence of husbands by rendering husbands entirely superfluous." When Gilder looked at poverty in the African American community, he saw "moral, religious values collapse, as they have to a great extent in inner city society (with crime and illegitimacy rates beyond belief)," and a failure to recognize that "the observance of moral law does greatly increase the possibilities for material achievement."[73] Gilder's work illustrates the ways evangelicals connected their fear of secular humanism to the growing power of the state, and their worry that, as Schaffer put it, "having no Christian consensus to contain it, that freedom leads to chaos or slavery under the state."[74]

Evangelicals thus argued that the growing power of the state reflected the power of secular humanism in American culture. Senator Jesse Helms, an evangelical from North Carolina, declared on the floor of the Senate, "When you have men who no longer believe that God is in charge of human affairs, you have *men attempting to take the place of God by means of the Superstate*."[75] Helms argued that the growth of American government reflected secular humanism's false understanding of human potential. According to Tim LaHaye, America had been long blessed with its "Bible-based form of government and our unique Bible-based education system." But, he argued, as secular humanism made its way into government, "humanist social planners" had begun to establish "a one world socialist state, where Plato's dream of three classes of people would be fulfilled."[76]

Evangelicals feared that secular humanists wanted to expand government in order to replace divinely ordained social structures with their own rationalized, amoral systems of power. The growth of government was for them a process of usurpation of the functions of religion and the family. In 1979, James Robison delivered a sermon on his weekly syndicated television show in which he accused gay men of recruiting children into homosexuality. A station in Dallas pulled his show, citing the Fairness Doctrine, which required television stations to allot equal time to both sides on controversial topics. Robison was furious. "Governments that abridge this freedom do so, not so much because they want to suppress Christian thought but because they want to control all thought," he declared later. It was "tyranny of the mind," he said, "totally at odds with the principles of liberty and dignity on which the American system rests."[77] It was easy for evangelicals to see a similar looming threat in Carter's Conference on Families, which, according to Connie Marshner, sought to supplant the family with its own institution. "The more government, combined with the helping professions establishment, take away the functions family need to perform," she said, "the less purpose there is for the family, per se, to exist."[78]

Since the 1950s, evangelical women had assailed public schools in particular for undermining the authority of Christian, Western parents in order to promote "Eastern" totalitarianism in the guise of diversity and multiculturalism. At a Concerned Women for America symposium in 1986, a speaker warned, "'God's plan has always been' that parents educate their children at home." Another declared that this was so because public schools had become permeated with "Eastern mysticism," which he located in techniques like "calm-down time" and meditation in classes. This Eastern influence would, the speaker warned, lead to "a total totalitarian system."[79] As Mark Albrecht of the Spiritual Counterfeits Project warned, schools sought to teach what he called "an ominous boiling thundercloud rolling in from the East" because "spiritual delusion is a necessary part of conditioning the people for eventual political-economic-religious rule by a mystical elite."[80] In 1984, E. Earle Ellis, a professor at New Brunswick Theological Seminary, warned in the *Wall Street Journal* that the absence of explicit Christianity in America's school curriculum did not leave students religionless;

rather, Ellis claimed, "A religion of secular humanism is clearly established in the public schools with its explicit exclusion of God."[81]

Despite their association of such ideas with the East, many evangelicals followed Schaeffer in laying the beginnings of educational decay at the feet of John Dewey. Schaeffer argued that Dewey's theories of education were centered on the child's will and desires rather than on the information the child was to be inculcated with, a prioritization that was unacceptably humanistic, denying the authority of God. "Those in the universities saw themselves as little computers controlled by the larger computer of the university, which in turn was controlled by the still larger computer of the state," Schaeffer declared. Tim LaHaye went even further, arguing that Dewey changed Columbia University into a "citadel for atheistic humanism," following which "Columbia gradually took over, ideologically, the nation's school system—until today, the Bible, on which it was once founded, is the only thing you cannot study in the public school."[82] So did secular humanism extend its power over the American government.

New Alliances

Evangelicals' growing fixation on the state as the manifestation of secular humanism explains an otherwise boggling event. On July 25, 1984, Tim La-Haye spoke at a rally in Constitution Hall, which stands on the Ellipse in Washington, DC, within sight of the White House. On one side of the stage stood a replica of the Liberty Bell, on the other, the Statue of Liberty. Four thousand people crowded the hall; another two thousand waited outside. Before LaHaye's speech, actors portraying Americans as diverse as George Washington, Harriet Tubman, and Joseph Smith "uttered ringing words about freedom and the costs of winning it and maintaining it." Following the rally, attendees marched from Constitution Hall to the White House for a candlelight vigil, urging the state to respect religious liberty.[83]

The rally was organized by the Coalition for Religious Freedom, of which LaHaye was a cochairman. The coalition and the rally, though, were largely funded by Sun Myung Moon and the Unification Church—evidence of an unexpected alliance between evangelicals and one of the groups they had vigorously denounced. By the time of the pageant, LaHaye was dismissive of the threat of cults. "I'm not concerned about the Unification Church advancing its cause here in America because I'm convinced there are so many people being freed by the truth of the gospel," he said. "What I am concerned about is the spread of religious persecution that will lead to a totalitarian state." Despite LaHaye's cavalier words, not all evangelicals were on board with the new partnership, especially since Moon had formed the Coalition for Religious Freedom soon after his conviction on charges of income tax fraud.[84]

For some, the conviction revealed precisely what they had believed about Moon all along. "Moon does seek economic power; it is a major tenet in his doctrine," declared Walter Martin's *Christian Research Institute Journal*. Moon taught, so the journal said, that "he must restore all earthly things back to God, and that can only be done when all earthly things are under his control." Darrel Malcolm, an Illinois pastor, said he left the rally feeling "a little bit used. . . . I felt like there was a hidden agenda of trying to buy legitimacy within the Christian community."[85] These were traditional fears that if an organization like the Unification Church successfully claimed the Christian label, there would be dire consequences.

To many other American evangelicals, however, the primary manifestation of materialism they saw at work in the 1980s was no longer the cults but the state. Their vision of Western history as a battleground between materialism and Christianity fed their fears that America was sliding toward authoritarianism, and hence informed their willingness to recalibrate the lines of struggle. The rhetoric of evangelical leaders at the pageant transformed cults into legitimate religions because they stood against materialism. When he stepped to the podium at the pageant, Robert Grant, the founder of the Religious Right organization Christian Voice, warned that religious freedom was under attack from "the vast sea of bureaucrats" who had "taken upon themselves to decide what is religion and what is not." Then LaHaye blamed Moon's prosecution on "secular humanist philosophy," which was driving the state to persecute any faith, and warned Americans to be aware of "man's responsibility to God."[86]

The conflicts of the 1970s and 1980s had shifted the ground for these evangelicals. After all, cults themselves were only a single symptom of the deeper problem of American materialism, and their political and social threat paled against the larger challenged posed by the humanist takeover of the American government. Evangelicals now proved willing to make a compromise: to define Christianity in terms of historical narrative rather than of content, and to prioritize defense of a category they called "Christian civilization." The evangelical Robert Webber argued that the Moral Majority was actually secular, that it was fixated on social values rather than on his definition of "Christian": a transcendent relationship with Jesus Christ. At times, the Moral Majority's leaders agreed. According to one of Jerry Falwell's friends, the Baptist "stresses every chance he gets that it [the Moral Majority] is not religious."[87] His definition of the term revealed the Moral Majority's priorities.

In January 1989 Ronald Reagan prepared to leave the presidency. On the eleventh of the month he delivered an address to the nation. "I've spoken of the shining city all my political life," he said, referring to an image often invoked in his campaigns for office. It was the same metaphor Jesus used in Matthew 5:14, when he told his followers, "You are the light of the world. A city that is set on a hill cannot be hidden." Reagan continued, "But in my mind it was a tall, proud city built on rocks stronger than oceans, windswept, God-blessed, and teeming with people of all kinds living in harmony and peace; a city with free ports that hummed with commerce and creativity." The image was an appropriate one for Reagan and for the Christians who supported him. Reagan was divorced and while in office no churchgoer. But he managed in speeches like this to turn Christianity into Christian civilization, identifying what it meant to be Christian with those aspects of American civilization the Religious Right prized. His Christian civilization was built of free enterprise, traditional morality, and imagined racial harmony— and Reagan's skill at rhetoric associated these things with the policies of his administration: military spending, the elimination of government social programs, and a great deal of public piety of the sort exhibited in this speech.[88] Evangelical support of Reagan stemmed in part from his ability to speak the language of Christian civilization, and the same sense of siege which led LaHaye into alliance with Moon led thousands of Christians like him to support Reagan. In a way, Christian civilization had never seemed closer, nor more distant.

Epilogue

IN MID-OCTOBER 2012, Republican presidential candidate Mitt Romney made a pilgrimage to Montreat, North Carolina, to meet with the Reverend Billy Graham, perhaps the most admired evangelical in the country. The ninety-three-year-old Graham welcomed the lifelong Mormon to his home on a ridge overlooking the town, and the two sat by Graham's fireplace, where the pastor offered a prayer for the candidate and for the United States. Romney thanked him and said, "Prayer is the most helpful thing you can do for me."

After the meeting, the Billy Graham Evangelistic Association altered its website to remove language describing Mormonism as a cult. But in an interview, Graham's son Franklin, who had taken up daily management of his father's ministry, was more cautious. Romney, Franklin Graham said, "is a Mormon. Most Christians would not recognize Mormonism. . . . But he would be a good president if he won the nomination." In the same interview, Franklin Graham for the first time repudiated the belief held by many other evangelicals that President Barack Obama, whom Romney was challenging, was not a Christian.[1] Indeed, two years earlier, the Pew Research Center reported that only 34 percent of Americans believed that Obama was a Christian, while 18 percent said the president was a Muslim and 43 percent stated they did not know.[2] This despite the fact that in multiple speeches in his 2008 campaign, in both his books, and even in the 2004 convention speech that had introduced him as a national figure, Obama had declared his Christianity—though he stated that it propelled him to different ideas about American politics than did the faith of the Religious Right. "We worship an awesome God in the blue states," Obama had declared at the Democratic National Convention. Then he paraphrased the Bible, insisting, "I am my brother's keeper. I am my sister's keeper" to defend the Democratic Party's commitment to social welfare programs. Four years later he told *Christianity Today,* "I believe in the redemptive death and resurrection of Jesus Christ," but also, "I believe in the example that Jesus set by feeding the hungry and healing the sick and always prioritizing the least of these over the powerful."[3] And yet, until his father met with Romney, Franklin Graham avoided stating whether he accepted Obama's identification as a Christian.

The 2012 election, in which two self-professed Christians had to find ways to convince other self-professed Christians that they were indeed Christian, dramatically illustrated the variety of Christianities present in American politics: the ways in which various Christian groups had sought to seize control of the term *Christian* and the reasons why the Religious Right had been so successful in forging a link between evangelical Protestantism, traditional social hierarchies, and the notion of Western civilization. The reasons why Americans doubted the Christian faith of both Obama and Romney had as much to do with the particular politics and historical narratives the term had acquired over the course of the twentieth century as they had to do with doctrine or theology. And by the same token, Obama's and Romney's efforts to claim the term for themselves required them to grapple with its genealogy.

Both Obama and Romney sought to identify their faith with the old notion of American Christian republicanism, emphasizing that Christianity for them meant moral rectitude and civic virtue. But they met resistance. In November and December of 2007 Romney was campaigning for the presidency for the first time and was locked in a tight battle for support in Iowa with Arkansas governor and Baptist minister Mike Huckabee, who had, thirty years earlier, worked for evangelical James Robison. In his campaign memoir, *Character Makes a Difference,* Huckabee denied wanting to "impose our religion" upon the United States. Rather, he explained, "It's that we want to shape the culture and laws by using a worldview we believe has value."[4] This language firmly rooted Huckabee in the tradition of the Religious Right, which believed that American democracy depended upon citizens' possession of an evangelical Christian worldview. As his struggle with

Romney intensified, Huckabee began insinuating that Romney did not share these beliefs. In November Huckabee implicitly contrasted himself with Romney in a television commercial that claimed Huckabee was a "Christian leader." In December he "innocently" asked a reporter whether Mormons believed "that Jesus and the devil are brothers." When the reporter asked whether Huckabee thought Mormonism was a cult, Huckabee replied, "I don't know much about it."[5]

Huckabee's attempt to invalidate Romney's claim to the word *Christian* was evident in his use of the term to describe his own faith while pinpointing particular esoteric doctrines of Romney's. Huckabee sought to root Romney in the world of cults, which the American Christian consensus had long found suspicious. Romney's response was to claim Christian republicanism's moral language for himself. In a December 2007 speech addressing the role of his, and others', faith in American politics, Romney sounded a great deal like the framers of Columbia's Contemporary Civilization course, or like Robert Bellah. "Freedom requires religion just as religion requires freedom," the governor argued. He meant that it was only through religious belief that human beings could understand their divine origins and hence properly value the importance of freedom. Romney explicitly asserted that any religious faith might meet these demands, praising Jewish tradition and Muslim devotion: "Differences in theology exist between the churches in America, [but] we share a common creed of moral convictions." The Contemporary Civilization course had sought to describe religion as something separate from any specific Christian theology, and Robert Bellah differentiated "civil religion" from any particular faith; however, both ended up taking for granted the expectations and norms of liberal Protestantism. Romney similarly privileged Christian republicanism in his speech, professing faith in Jesus Christ and arguing that any "person of faith" who sought political office should affirm "the equality of humankind, the obligation to serve one another, and a steadfast commitment to liberty."[6] This version of Christianity offered a vision of the United States as the home of the Cold War Christian consensus; a place of vague religious pluralism bound to the ethical commitments of liberal Protestantism.

Unsuccessful in his bid for the presidency in 2008, Romney ran again in 2012 and proved capable in that campaign of embracing a form of Christianity more amenable to conservative evangelicals. That year he aimed to bridge the gap many evangelicals perceived between "cults" and their own vision of a Christian society. In the spring of 2012 Romney delivered the commencement address at Jerry Falwell's Liberty University. He sought to illustrate that a Mormon like himself could share in evangelicals' imagination of what a Christian democracy might look like, even if he did not share in their version of Christianity. "People of different faiths, like yours and mine, sometimes wonder where we can meet in common purpose when there are so many differences in creed and theology," Romney said. "Surely the answer is that we can meet in service, in shared moral convictions about our nation stemming from a common worldview." The term *worldview*, an evangelical catchword, revealed Romney's struggle to show that his Mormonism could produce the same sort of Christian civilization that evangelicals prized. His speech recapitulated the connections between Christian faith and Western democracy that American Christians had long taken for granted. "Central to America's rise to global leadership is our Judeo-Christian tradition, with its vision of the goodness and possibilities of every life," Romney argued. "Culture—what you believe, what you value, how you live—matters." He maintained that an American society that sanctioned the things evangelicals found objectionable, including abortion and same-sex marriage, would in turn degrade American democracy: the same fears the Religious Right entertained.[7]

For many evangelicals, this was enough. Indeed, it mirrored their rapprochement with Sun Myung Moon thirty years before, and with Catholics in the years of the Cold War. Just as Tim LaHaye managed to find common cause with the Unification Church in the 1980s because he believed that Moon could advance evangelicals' vision for Christian democracy, so did a number of evangelicals find that Romney's commitment to the idea of a Christian worldview and culture sufficed to make an alliance. Mark DeMoss, an evangelical public relations strategist who served on the board of Liberty University and numbered the Grahams among his clients, had signed on with Romney during his first presidential campaign in 2007. That year, DeMoss argued, "I am more concerned that a candidate shares my values than he shares my theology"—implicitly accepting Romney's argument that a Christian worldview did not necessarily need to be wed to a particular version of Christianity.[8]

But many other evangelicals did not buy into this compromise. Notably, many Liberty students—less given to political strategy than their university leaders—complained that Romney's speech was inappropriate for students preparing to take a Christian worldview into the world. Sarah Misch asserted, "I would not want to end my studies at a Christian university by being sent into the world at commencement by a Mormon. We came to Liberty because of our faith in Jesus, not for political reasons."[9] More prominently, in October 2011 a Baptist minister named Robert Jeffress introduced Texas governor Rick Perry, one of Romney's primary opponents, at the Values Voter Summit, a major meeting of the Religious Right. Later that day, Jeffress declared that Romney "is not a Christian." Jeffress seemed bemused by the media furor his statement generated. "This isn't news," he told a reporter, citing the long history of the countercult movement. He also affirmed that Romney was "a non-Christian who embraces Biblical values," finding his way toward the compromise evangelicals had been making for thirty years, separating the notion of Christian worldview from strict Christian theology. Jeffress also called Romney's eventual general-election opponent, Barack Obama, "a professing Christian . . . who embraces unbiblical values."[10]

Jeffress and other evangelicals attacked Obama's Christianity for a number of reasons. At the Values Voter Summit, the Texas pastor stated that his paramount reason for doing so was Obama's politics, which he perceived to be detrimental to the sort of Christian democracy the Religious Right believed in. Others felt the same way. In 2008, for instance, the conservative Catholic senator Rick Santorum asserted, "If you look at his [Obama's] actions about what he believes from a public-policy point of view, and how that squares with the faith he says he subscribes to, I see a lot of disconnections." In 2012, as Santorum was mounting his own campaign against Romney in the Republican primary, he expanded on those disconnections. Obama, he claimed, had been subverted by "radical environmentalists" who rejected the idea that "man should be in charge of the earth. . . . We're not here to serve the Earth, the Earth is not the objective. Man is the objective," Santorum explained. He continued to describe how the president's policies on abortion and birth control, in Santorum's opinion, reflected what he called "phony theology," which misunderstood the special nature of humanity in Christian thought.[11]

But to other evangelicals, more threatening than Obama's particular policies was the ominous fact of his identity. Obama, an African American with a name derived from the Luo culture of Kenya, did not seem to them to have a place in the historical narrative that rooted true Christianity in Anglo-Saxon Europe. The so-called birther movement, which spread the falsehood that Obama had been born in Africa and thus was not, as the Constitution required of presidents, a "natural-born citizen," demonstrated how closely Obama's racial and religious identities seemed intertwined. To many Americans it appeared that Obama's race, name, and supposed birthplace precluded him from being a Christian.[12] This movement spread on right-wing internet sites throughout Obama's years as president. Even after the president had produced a birth certificate proving he was born in Hawaii, polls showed that 30 to 40 percent of Republicans believed he was born in Kenya.[13] Two years before the meeting between his father and Romney, in an appearance on a television news show, Franklin Graham stated, "I think the president's problem is that he was born a Muslim. His father was a Muslim. The seed of Islam is passed through the father like the seed of Judaism is passed through the mother. He was born a Muslim." Graham demonstrated the ways in which, for many white American Protestants, race and religion were identical, and hence, Christianity, the whiteness of Western civilization, and American citizenship were inextricably linked. He followed up his initial claims with a concession that Obama "renounced Islam and he has accepted Jesus Christ. That's what he says he has done. I cannot say that he hasn't."[14] Setting aside the fact that Obama was not in fact raised as a Muslim and thus had nothing to renounce, Graham's skepticism of the president's professed beliefs was evidently based on the president's race.

Even some among Obama's critics who acknowledged that he was not a Muslim had difficulty accepting his Christianity. In March 2008 tapes surfaced of Obama's pastor, Jeremiah Wright of Chicago's Trinity United Church of Christ, preaching sermons which many white Americans found disquieting. But many black Americans took these remarks as a matter of course, a gap that revealed a chasm between how white and black Christians understood the relationship between their faith and American politics.[15] Most incendiary were two sermons preached in the months after the September 11, 2001, terrorist attacks. In both, Wright echoed the language of earlier advocates of black theology who had argued that the Christian republican tradition in the United States assumed that American Christianity was by default white. Like many black theologians, Wright argued that true Christianity was incompatible with the racist democracy the United States had created. The government, he said in his sermon "Confusing God and Government," "wants us to sing 'God Bless America.' No, no, no, not God Bless America. God damn America—that's in the Bible—for killing innocent people. . . . The United States government has failed the vast majority of her citizens of African descent."[16] According to Wright's

Christianity, American democracy fell short of the standards demanded in the Bible, and thus African Americans should separate their faith from their nation.

Many white American Christians and conservatives, not accustomed to thinking of Christianity and American democracy as being in opposition with each other, reacted angrily and denied Wright's Christianity. The standard accusation was that Wright's church was not a "Christian" congregation because it was "a political organization constantly advocating for social change," as Stanley Kurtz wrote in the *Weekly Standard*. Charles C. Johnson contended in the *American Spectator* that "Wright conceived of a Christianity in which black rage and the black power ideology fused with Marxist thought." Conservative provocateur Ann Coulter declared, "It's Obama's church attendance—back in Chicago—that proves he's an atheist," because Wright preached not religion but "hatefilled demagoguery" and "racism."[17] At the same time, Kurtz explained that a real Christian church would not portray America "as a white supremacist nation"; Johnson denounced Wright's "political" claim that American corporations had driven Africa into poverty; and Coulter insisted that "any person sitting in the Rev. Wright's church . . . does not believe in God" because attendance was "borderline racist."[18] All such critics implicitly coded American Christianity as white, just as Columbia University's Contemporary Civilization course and J. Stanley Durkee had decades before. To them, Wright's Afrocentric version of Christianity was de facto irreligious because of the attention it paid to race. All insisted that the acceptable politics of American Christianity could not be racial but should rather focus on issues of reproduction and the family. The first piece of evidence Coulter offered that Obama was no Christian was his "fanatical opposition to allowing Illinois hospitals to save the lives of babies with God-given souls."[19]

Ironically, Obama's own discussions of his Christianity revealed a differing version of the Christian impulse. Obama distanced himself from Wright soon after the pastor's sermons became public. His speech responding to Wright in March 2008 was far closer to Mitt Romney's variety of Christian republicanism than to either the moralism of Obama's critics or Jeremiah Wright's liberation theology. Rather, Obama offered a vision of Christianity that emphasized both ethical behavior and racial reconciliation and that echoed the teachings of Bayard Rustin or Martin Luther King Jr. He had learned at Wright's church "our obligations to love one another; to care for the sick and lift up the poor." That kind of Christianity provided "a single note—hope!" and an ultimately universalist vision of the United States which joined black and white Americans together. As Obama put it in his autobiography, his own Christian experience was to him "at once unique and universal, black and more than black."[20] Indeed, Obama perceived Christianity as a tool by which Americans could be brought into communities of deliberation and mutual respect, even across lines of race or ideology. Obama predicated the need for these communities upon the divinely mandated importance of each individual and, drawing on his often-cited favorite philosopher, Reinhold Niebuhr, upon a simultaneous sense of humility and optimism.[21]

Before Wright's time in the media spotlight, and before Obama ran for the presidency, Obama spoke to a gathering of liberal Christians and echoed many of the complaints of the countercultists. He mused about Americans' "chronic loneliness." Their "work, their possessions, their diversions, their sheer busyness is not enough." These were the same reasons conservative evangelicals gave to explain the rise of the cults and the growth of the materialist state. But Obama offered a different interpretation. He explained that he had felt the emptiness himself in college, and concluded that "without a commitment to a particular community of faith, I would always remain apart, and alone." For him, the meaning of Christianity for American democracy was the community and network of mutual commitments it created. He credited this belief to a number of sources—"the power of the African American religious tradition to spur social change," for one, and Wright's teachings for another. But he also, like Mitt Romney, insisted that religion should speak to "the moral underpinnings of the nation," arguing that issues of poverty and racism and violence required a common moral language to address them. Obama thus embraced liberal Protestant universalism, arguing that these were values "accessible to people of all faiths, including those with no faith at all"[22]

A month before voters chose between Obama and Romney, the Pew Research Center on Religion and Public Life was reporting that the number of "nones" in America, people who professed belonging to no specific religion, had grown to about one in five adults—an all-time high. As the Pew Forum described these people, "they became unaffiliated, at least in part, because they think of religious people as hypocritical, judgmental, or insincere. Large numbers also say they became unaffiliated because they think that religious organizations focus too much on rules and not enough on spirituality."[23] Throughout the 2012 presidential campaign, many of the "nones," as well as many agnostics or atheists, repeated these claims. Christians, they said, were hypocritical, overly focused on issues of personal morality, and willfully neglectful of certain values earlier Christian groups had embraced: the ideal of human equality and a critique of materialism that took on American capitalism as a system. Kenneth Anderson, an ex-Mormon and law professor at American University, argued that Romney's Mormonism—and Christianity in America as a whole—had itself been absorbed by materialism. The regimented world of Mormon mission work, Anderson argued, taught Mormons "that success with God, as with life, is fundamentally a matter of sales. There is always a risk of young Mormons' concluding that packaging is more important than product." From this, Anderson argued that Mitt Romney's "lack of principle" derived from his religion's essentially capitalist underpinnings. The same could be true, he argued, of evangelical Christianity, with its subculture of pop rock and kitschy art, which "resemble nothing so much as the Wal-Mart of the soul on sale."[24] For Anderson, American Christianity was simply shallow consumer capitalism.

Similarly, supporters of marriage equality, abortion rights, and other issues of sexual freedom often had, by the mid-2010s, come to identify American Christianity as their primary opponent. Annie Laurie Gaylor, co-president of the Freedom from Religion Foundation (FFRF), called in 2015 for a "re-Enlightenment" of America in which "reason" would replace "religion." Religion, Gaylor argued, actually hampered the goals Barack Obama ascribed to Christianity: community building, dialogue, and mutual respect. Hence, she claimed, religion inhibited democracy. Christianity "is but a myth and superstition that hardens hearts and enslaves minds," Gaylor wrote in an FFRF press release. In addition, she pointed out "there are no references to 'consent of the governed,' 'civil liberties' or 'democracy' in the bible."[25]

Authors like Gaylor critical of American Christianity experienced something of a renaissance in the early 2000s, when the administration of President George W. Bush again empowered the Religious Right. A number of journalists raised warnings about "dominionism," a relatively small branch of Reformed theology which, according to Chris Hedges, "seeks to redefine traditional democratic and Christian terms and concepts to fit an ideology that calls on the radical church to take political power." The notion that Christianity might influence politics in any sense was a mark of danger for these writers, who instinctively associated the idea with the Religious Right. Hedges presented his own form of faith as much less dangerous, precisely because it disclaimed certainty about the truth of Christianity at all, emphasized "acts of compassion," and repudiated organized political involvement. This was the sort of Christianity that liberal Protestantism, having abandoned the war for the term to the Religious Right, was comfortable with in the years after the rise of Jerry Falwell.[26]

Another cadre of authors were sometimes styled the New Atheists, and warned that Christian convictions hampered democracy as part of a larger crusade they waged against religion in general. "There is no telling what our world would now be like had some great kingdom of Reason emerged at the time of the Crusades and pacified the credulous multitudes of Europe and the Middle East," wrote the neurologist Sam Harris. "We might have had modern democracy and the Internet by the year 1600."[27] Harris offered a counterstory to the historical narratives American Christians of all types had generated: rather than human equality emerging from religious teaching about the divine origin of humanity, Harris rooted equality and democracy in the Enlightenment and the rise of scientific rationality.

Many people sympathetic to arguments like those of Anderson and Harris felt vindicated when, in 2016, television personality Donald Trump won the presidency. Having watched Trump fumble through incorrect biblical references like "Two Corinthians" and admit to sexual abuse of women, many critics of American Christianity took the endorsement of Trump by evangelical leaders like Jerry Falwell Jr. as evidence of Christianity's moral bankruptcy. And yet, conservative evangelical support for Trump was consistent with Tim LaHaye's support for Sun Myung Moon and widespread evangelical support for Ronald Reagan. Falwell frankly confessed that he did not endorse Trump because of the mogul's faith. Instead, he wrote, he and his father had always hired "the best lawyers, accountants and financial management we could find without regard to whether they shared our faith."[28] He took Trump's business success as a sign that the candidate was in tune with the needs of American Christians, a sentiment shared by many advocates of the prosperity gospel who offered Trump their support. Mark Burns, an African American pastor, declared at a Trump rally, "Jesus said, above all things, I pray that you prosper. . . . I think that is what Donald Trump represents." Similarly, other evangelicals understood Trump's determination to stop immigration as "religious nationalism" that would prevent "the Muslims from taking over America," as the Texas pastor Bob Roberts put it.[29] To these varied Christians, Trump's belief or lack thereof in Christian orthodoxy mattered less than his commitment to Christian civilization as they imagined it.

In some sense, Trump's victory thus demonstrated the success of the Religious Right's version of Christian civilization. But to many others, Christian and non-Christian alike, it proved their worst suspicions. In making the case that religion harmed democracy, Annie Laurie Gaylor argued that "religion" was "against equal rights for gays, atheists and women."[30] Trump's victory seemed indeed to offer evidence for the point. But nonetheless, Gaylor's argument accepted the definition of Christianity that Jerry Falwell and Beverly LaHaye offered, overlooking that of Albert Cleage or Dorothy Day. The Religious Right's success in narrowing the capaciousness of Christianity has caused Barack Obama and Jim Wallis frustration, to be sure—but it also means that a wide and fertile field of Christian ideas and language lies ready to harvest.

NOTES

ACKNOWLEDGMENTS

INDEX

NOTES

Prologue

1. Nick Corasanti, "Donald Trump Quotes Scripture, Sort Of, at Liberty University Speech," *New York Times*, January 18, 2016.
2. On Trump and Christianity see Sarah Posner, "Amazing Disgrace: How Donald Trump Hijacked the Religious Right," *New Republic*, April 2017, 34–37; DeMoss quoted in Emma Green, "Liberty University Students Want to Be Christians—Not Republicans," *Atlantic*, October 2016, accessed June 20, 2017, https://www.theatlantic.com/politics/archive/2016/10/liberty -university-trump/505400/.
3. Gregory A. Smith and Jessica Martinez, "How the Faithful Voted: A Preliminary Analysis," Pew Research Center, http://www.pewresearch.org /fact-tank/2016/11/09/how-the-faithful-voted-a-preliminary-2016-analysis/, accessed February 3, 2017. However, other reports had Trump winning 80 percent of white evangelicals. See, for example, http://www.cnn.com /election/results/exit-polls, accessed June 14, 2017.
4. James Dobson, "Why I Am Voting for Donald Trump," *Christianity Today*, October 2016, 58; Michelle Boorstein, "Why Evangelicals Can't Agree on Trump," *Washington Post*, March 19, 2016, B2.
5. Gretel Kauffman, "Are This Iowa Congressman's Views on Immigration Racist?" *Christian Science Monitor*, March 13, 2017, 1; Philip Bump, "Rep. Steve King Warns that 'Our Civilization' Can't Be Restored With 'Somebody Else's Babies," *Washington Post*, March 12, 2017.
6. For some of these successes, see Daniel K. Williams, *God's Own Party: The Making of the Christian Right* (New York: Oxford University Press, 2012), especially 159–187; Darren Dochuck, *From Bible Belt to Sun Belt: Plain Folk*

Religion, Grassroots Politics, and the Rise of Evangelical Conservatism (New York: Norton, 2011), especially 326–397; and Steven P. Miller, *The Age of Evangelicalism: America's Born Again Years* (New York: Oxford University Press, 2014), 3–9, 60–87. On the Religious Right's rhetorical accomplishments, see Susan Friend Harding, *The Book of Jerry Falwell: Fundamentalist Language and Politics* (Princeton, NJ: Princeton University Press, 2000), 61–64, 82–84, particularly; see also James Davison Hunter, *Culture Wars: The Struggle for the Soul of America* (New York: Basic Books, 1992), 39–42. Neil J. Young, *We Gather Together: The Religious Right and the Problem of Interfaith Politics* (New York: Oxford University Press, 2015) explores the theoretical and theological problems inherent in building this rhetorical alliance.

7. Howell Raines, "Reagan Backs Evangelicals in Their Political Activities," *New York Times*, August 23, 1980, 8; and Bruce Bursma, "A New Crusade: Right Wing Christians Gird for Election Day," *Chicago Tribune*, August 31, 1980, 2; see also Matthew Lassiter's discussion of the meeting in "Inventing Family Values," in *Rightward Bound: Making America Conservative in the 1970s*, eds. Bruce J. Schulman and Julian Zelizer (Cambridge, MA: Harvard University Press, 2008), 13–15.

8. W. B. Gallie, "Essentially Contested Concepts," *Proceedings of the Aristotelian Society* 56 (1956), 167–198. See also the introduction to Catherine Brekus and Clark W. Gilpen, eds., *American Christianities: A History of Dominance and Diversity* (Chapel Hill: University of North Carolina Press, 2011), 1–25.

9. David Sehat, *The Myth of American Religious Freedom* (New York: Oxford University Press, 2011), especially 51–73.

10. Alexis de Tocqueville, *Democracy in America*, trans. Harvey C. Mansfield and Delba Winthrop (Chicago: University of Chicago Press, 2002), 275–277. See also 279–280. On Tocqueville's understanding of religion in American democracy, I have relied on Patrick Deneen, *Democratic Faith* (Princeton, NJ: Princeton University Press, 2014), 214–239; on his reading of American gender norms, Laurie Johnson, *Honor in America: Tocqueville on American Enlightenment* (Lanham, MD: Rowman and Littlefield, 2017), 47–71.

11. I draw here on the discussion of Rush in Robert H. Abzug, *Cosmos Crumbling: American Reform and the Religious Imagination* (New York: Oxford University Press, 1994), 25.

12. Mark A. Noll, *America's God: From Jonathan Edwards to Abraham Lincoln* (New York: Oxford University Press, 2005), 2, and Mark A. Noll, "What is 'American' about Christianity in the United States?" in Brekus and Gilpen, *American Christianities*, 382–399. Noll synthesizes a larger historiographical school that links the democratization of American culture and the rise of low-church and evangelical Protestantism in America, such as Nathan O. Hatch, *The Democratization of American Christianity* (New Haven, CT: Yale University Press, 1989), or Noll, Hatch, and George M. Marsden, *The Search for Christian America* (Colorado Springs: Helmers and Howard, 1989).

13. Hugh Heclo, *Christianity and American Democracy* (Cambridge, MA: Harvard University Press, 2007), particularly 140–145; Ross Douthat, *Bad Religion: How We Became a Nation of Heretics* (New York: Free Press, 2012), 79, 285.

14. Lewis Henry Morgan, *Ancient Society: Or, the Lines of Human Progress from Savagery to Civilization* (New York: Henry Holt, 1877), 6–9. On the relation ship of religion and civilization in the late nineteenth century, and on the notion of "civilization" generally, see Brett Bowden, *Empire of Civilization: The Evolution of an Imperial Idea* (Chicago: University of Chicago Press, 2009), 2–42, and Gail Bederman, *Manliness and Civilization: A Cultural History of Gender and Race in the United States, 1880–1917* (Chicago: University of Chicago Press, 1995), 19–27. Sylvester Johnson, *African American Religions, 1500–2000: Colonialism, Democracy and Freedom* (New York: Cambridge University Press, 2015), 59–67, and Tisa Wenger, *Religious Freedom: The Contested History of an America Ideal* (Chapel Hill: University of North Carolina Press, 2017), 1–15 address the ways progressive notions of civilization as manifested in religion led Americans toward imperialism.

15. Robert A. Speer, "The Non-Christian Religions Inadequate to Meet the Needs of Man," in *Students and the Modern Missionary Crusade* (New York: Student Volunteer Movement for Foreign Missions, 1906), 96, 98.

16. "Called to Resist Bigotry," Called to Resist, accessed June 9, 2017, www .calledtoresist.org.

17. Jim Wallis, "Resistance Is Patriotic—and Christian," *Sojourners,* January 5, 2017, https://sojo.net/articles/resistance-patriotic-and-christian, accessed June 9, 2017.

18. Paul A. Djupe, Jacob R. Neiheisel, and Anand Edward Sokhey, "How Fights over Trump Have Led Evangelicals to Leave Their Churches," *Washington Post,* April 11, 2017, https://www.washingtonpost.com/news/monkey-cage/wp /2017/04/11/yes-many-voters-left-their-congregations-over-trump-so-what -else-is-new/, accessed April 11, 2017.

19. Jim Wallis, *God's Politics: Why the Right Gets It Wrong and the Left Doesn't Get It* (New York: HarperCollins, 2005), xx. Tim Rutten, "Walking Away from Christianity," *Los Angeles Times,* August 4, 2010, 5; see also Rice's "My Trust in My Lord," *Washington Post,* March 21, 2008, 5.

20. David Kinnaman and Gabe Lyons, *Unchristian: What a New Generation Really Thinks about Christianity, and Why It Matters* (New York: Baker Books, 2008), 27–32; Adelle Banks, "Youth See Christians as Judgmental, Anti-Gay," *USA Today,* October 10, 2007. See also Robert Jones, *The End of White Christian America* (New York: Simon and Schuster, 2016), 131–132, 227–231.

21. Maria D. Mitchell explores the term *materialism* and its flexibility in *The Origins of Christian Democracy: Politics and Confession in Modern Germany* (Ann Arbor: University of Michigan Press, 2012), 4–5, 77–79. Following Talal Asad, I understand *secular* to have no inherent definition; rather, it is formed through debates over the definition of *religious.* Talal Asad, *Formations of the*

Secular: Christianity, Islam, Modernity (Stanford, CA: Stanford University Press, 2003), especially 8–12, 181–205.

22. On the careers of materialism and naturalism, see Paul K. Moser, "Contemporary Materialism," in *Contemporary Materialism*, eds. Moser and J. D. Trout (New York: Routledge, 2002), 1–34; Michael Eldridge, "Naturalism," in *The Blackwell Guide to American Philosophy*, ed. Armen T. Marsoobian (Malden, MA: Blackwell Publishing, 2004), 53–72.

23. William James, *Pragmatism: A New Name for Some Old Ways of Thinking* (1907; New York: Cambridge University Press, 2014), 93–94; William James, *The Will to Believe* (New York: Longman, Green and Company, 1907), 83. See also Donald A. Crosby, *The Philosophy of William James: Radical Empiricism and Radical Materialism* (Lanham, MD: Rowman and Littlefield, 2013), 131–135.

24. Tocqueville, *Democracy in America*, 519. See also Peter Lawler, "Tocqueville on Pantheism, Materialism and Capitalism," in *Democracy and Its Friendly Critics: Tocqueville and Political Life Today*, ed. Peter Lawler (Lanham, MD: Lexington Books, 2004), 34–36.

25. Joseph LeConte, *Religion and Science* (New York: Appleton and Company, 1880), 274–276; on LeConte, see Ronald L. Numbers, *Science and Christianity in Pulpit and Pew* (New York: Oxford University Press, 2007), 74–78; on materialism and evolution more generally, see Frederick Gregory, "The Impact of Darwinian Evolution on Protestant Theology in the Nineteenth Century," in *God and Nature: Historical Essays on the Encounter between Christianity and Science*, eds. David C. Lindberg and Ronald L. Numbers (Berkeley: University of California Press, 1986), 369–390, and Ronald L. Numbers, *The Creationists* (Berkeley: University of California Press, 1986), 3–20.

26. Karl Marx and Friedrich Engels, *The Communist Manifesto*, trans. Samuel Moore (New York: Pocket Books, 1964), 69–70. Ken Morrison, *Marx, Durkheim, Weber: Formations of Modern Social Thought* (London: Sage Publications, 2006), 37–42, 161–166, 278–281.

27. On Marx's journey to the United States, see Daniel Rodgers, *Atlantic Crossings: Social Politics in a Progressive Age* (Cambridge, MA: Harvard University Press, 1998), 90–92, 140–142; on American reformers' fears of capitalism's reorganization of American society, see Paul Boyer, *Urban Masses and Moral Order in America, 1820–1920* (Cambridge, MA: Harvard University Press, 1978), 45–46, and Robert Wuthnow, "A Good Life and a Good Society: The Debate over Materialism," in *Rethinking Materialism: Perspectives on the Spiritual Dimension of Economic Behavior*, ed. Robert Wuthnow (Grand Rapids, MI: Eerdmans, 1995), 1–24.

28. For these movements, see T. J. Jackson Lears, *No Place of Grace: Anti-Modernism and the Transformation of American Culture* (New York: Oxford University Press, 1981), particularly 203–217 on Cram; on Norton, see James Turner, *The Liberal Education of Charles Eliot Norton* (Baltimore, MD: Johns Hopkins University Press, 1999), 347; on the Knights of Labor, see

William A. Mirola, *Redeeming Time: Protestantism and Chicago's Eight-Hour Movement, 1866–1912* (Urbana: University of Illinois Press, 2015), 93, Robert E. Weir, *Beyond Labor's Veil: The Culture of the Knights of Labor* (University Park: Pennsylvania State University Press, 1996), and Heath Carter, *Union Made: Working People and the Rise of Social Christianity in Chicago* (New York: Oxford University Press, 2015). On Christian Populists, see Michael Kazin, *A Godly Hero: The Life of William Jennings Bryan* (New York: Knopf, 2005).

1. Reconstruction, Spiritualism, and the Shape of an Argument

1. "First Pronunciamiento," in Victoria C. Woodhull, *The Origin, Tendencies and Principles of Government* (New York: Woodhull, Claflin and Company, 1871), 19. On Woodhull's rise, see Barbara Goldsmith, *Other Powers: The Age of Spiritualism, Suffrage and the Scandalous Victoria Woodhull* (New York: Knopf, 1988), especially 187–214; Amanda Frisken, *Victoria Woodhull's Sexual Revolution: Political Theatre and the Popular Press in Nineteenth Century America* (Philadelphia: University of Pennsylvania Press, 2012), 1–23.

2. This letter was anonymously sent to the *Hartford Courant*, November 11, 1871; Emanie Sachs and other scholars have identified the author as Catharine Beecher, noting that Woodhull herself thought Beecher wrote it. Sachs reprints it in *The Terrible Siren: Victoria Woodhull* (New York: Harper, 1928), 124–125. The clash between the two is further explored in Goldsmith, *Other Powers*, 180–182; Woodhull's response is in Victoria Claflin Woodhull and Tennessee Claflin, *The Human Body the Temple of God* (London: Woodhull, Claflin and Company, 1890), 30.

3. Edward J. Blum, *Reforging the White Republic: Race, Religion and American Nationalism, 1865–1898* (Baton Rouge: Louisiana State University Press, 2015), 115; George Julian, *Political Recollections: 1840–1872* (Chicago: Jansen, McClurg and Company, 1884), 323.

4. Victoria C. Woodhull, *A Speech on the Principles of Social Freedom* (New York: Woodhull, Claflin and Company, 1872), 14, 8. Various newspaper accounts, including "Free Lover Lectures on Free Love," *Weekly Argus*, November 22, 1871, and "Died of Free Love: The Women's Suffrage Movement," *Lancaster Gazette*, November 22, 1871, reported on Woodhull's departure from the script and volleys with her audience.

5. Andrew Jackson Davis, *The Present Age and Inner Life: A Sequel to Spiritual Intercourse* (New York: Partridge and Brittan, 1853), 32, 38, 47. On Christian spiritualism and spiritualism's interaction with Christianity more generally, Bret E. Carroll, *Spiritualism in Antebellum America* (Bloomington: Indiana University Press, 1997), 8–9, 71–72; R. Laurence Moore, *In Search of White Crows: Spiritualism, Parapsychology, and American Culture* (New York: Oxford University Press, 1977), 46–59; Robert S. Cox, *Body and Soul: A Sympathetic*

History of American Spiritualism (Charlottesville: University of Virginia Press, 2003).

6. *Detroit Union*, November 17, 1873; reprinted in Woodhull and Claflin, *The Human Body the Temple of God*, 388.

7. Woodhull, *The Origin, Tendencies and Principles of Government*, 226, 229.

8. Davis, *The Present Age and Inner Life*, 24; Andrew Jackson Davis, *The Approaching Crisis* (Boston: William White, 1870), 62.

9. Cari Carpenter, *Selected Writings of Victoria Woodhull* (Lincoln: University of Nebraska-Lincoln Press, 2010), 68. On spiritualism and society in the late nineteenth century, see Molly McGarry, *Ghosts of Futures Past: Spiritualism and the Cultural Politics of the Nineteenth Century* (Berkeley: University of California Press, 2008), especially 94–121; Ann Braude, *Radical Spirits: Spiritualism and Women's Rights in Nineteenth-Century America* (Bloomington: Indiana University Press, 2001), 162–192; and Mark Lause, *Free Spirits: Spiritualism, Republicanism and Radicalism in the Civil War Era* (Urbana: University of Illinois Press, 2016), especially 119–124, 152–159.

10. Victoria Woodhull, *The Garden of Eden: Or Paradise Lost and Found* (New York: Woodhull, Claflin and Company, 1875), 26.

11. Woodhull, *The Origins, Tendencies and Principles of Government*, 246.

12. Ulysses S. Grant, *Personal Memoirs of U.S. Grant* (New York: The Century Company, 1895), 1:4, 53, 83, 201, for instance. On Grant's disputed deathbed baptism, Stefan Lorent, "Baptism of US Grant," *Life*, March 26, 1951, 90–97 and Charles Bracelen Flood, *Grant's Final Victory: Ulysses S. Grant's Heroic Last Year* (Cambridge, MA: Da Capo Press, 2011), 145–146

13. Grant's moral life is discussed and sources cited in Edward Longacre, *General Ulysses S. Grant: The Soldier and the Man* (New York: Da Capo Press, 2006), 11–13.

14. "Christian statesman" cited in Anne Marie Taylor, *Young Charles Sumner and the Legacy of the American Enlightenment* (Boston: University of Massachusetts Press, 2001), 54; statement of belief reprinted in Archibald Henry Grimke, *The Life of Charles Sumner: The Scholar in Politics* (New York: Funk and Wagnalls, 1896), 38.

15. John Sherman, *Recollections of Forty Years in the House, Senate, and Cabinet* (Chicago: Werner Company, 1895), 75; Charles Richard Williams, ed., *The Diary and Letters of Rutherford B. Hayes* (Columbus: Ohio State Archaeological and Historical Society, 1922), 3:39, 642.

16. John Quincy Adams, *Letters of John Quincy Adams to His Son, on the Bible and Its Teachings* (Auburn, NY: Derby, Miller & Co., 1848), 22, 99–101. On Adams's religious life, see Paul Nagel, *John Quincy Adams: A Private Life, a Public Life* (Cambridge, MA: Harvard University Press, 1997), 124, 160–162; Daniel Walker Howe explores faculty philosophy in *The Unitarian Conscience: Harvard Moral Philosophy, 1805–1861* (Cambridge, MA: Harvard University Press, 1970), 44–47, 56–62; and *The Making of the American Self: Jonathan*

Edwards to Abraham Lincoln (New York: Oxford University Press, 2009), 9–13, 131–134.

17. Albert Richardson, *A Personal History of U.S. Grant* (Hartford, CT: American Publishing Company, 1868), 48; see also Henry C. Deming, *The Life of Ulysses S. Grant, General United States Army* (Hartford, CT: Scranton, 1868), 22–3, who quotes Jesse on his wife and praises Grant as "one of a number of illustrious men whose character was shaped by their mothers." The truth of Grant's parentage was, of course, more complex: Edward Longacre offers a mixed assessment of Hannah's mothering in *General Ulysses S. Grant*, 5–11. On the moral establishment, David Sehat, *The Myth of American Religious Freedom* (New York: Oxford University Press, 2011), particularly 51–73.

18. Edward Mansfield, *A Popular and Authentic Life of Ulysses S. Grant* (Cincinnati: R.W. Carroll & Company, 1868), 20.

19. "General Grant: The Country's Candidate for President," *New York Times*, July 4, 1868, 1.

20. *Official Proceedings of the National Republican Conventions of 1868, 1872, 1876, 1880* (Minneapolis: Charles W. Johnson, 1903), 54–56.

21. "The Condition of the South—General Summary of an Observer," *New York Times*, March 22, 1868, 1.

22. Edward Peirce, ed., *Memoir and Letters of Charles Sumner* (Boston: Roberts Brothers, 1893), 4:76. For the Radical efforts in Congress during the war, Allan Bogue, *The Earnest Men: Republicans of the Civil War Senate* (Ithaca, NY: Cornell University Press, 1991), 152–181, 188–196; Herman Belz, *Reconstructing the Union: Theory and Policy During the Civil War* (Ithaca, NY: Cornell University Press, 1966).

23. George Julian, *Speeches on Political Questions* (New York: Hurd and Houghton, 1872), 306. On Julian's religion see Patrick Riddleberger, *George Washington Julian, Radical Republican* (Indianapolis: Indiana Historical Bureau, 1966), 8–11. For Radical Republicans' religion more generally, see Victor Howard, *Religion and the Radical Republican Movement, 1860–1870* (Lexington: University Press of Kentucky, 1990), 168–182.

24. "Speech of the Honorable H. W. Berry," *Congressional Globe: First Session of the Forty-Second Congress, Appendix* (Washington: Office of the Congressional Globe, 1871) , 267.

25. Charles Francis Adams, ed., *Charles Sumner: His Complete Works* (Boston: Lee and Shepherd, 1900), 2:414.

26. Gerard N. Magliocca, *American Founding Son: John Bingham and the Invention of the Fourteenth Amendment* (New York: New York University Press, 2013), 126.

27. Charles Sumner, *The Question of Caste* (Boston: Wright and Potter, 1869), 10; see also Taylor, *Young Charles Sumner*, 276–277.

28. *Speech of the Hon. Henry Wilson of Massachusetts on Representation of Rebel States* (Washington: Office of the Congressional Globe, 1866), 7.

29. Julian, *Political Recollections*, 265–268.

30. Harriet Beecher Stowe, *Palmetto Leaves* (Boston: James Osgood and Company, 1873), 314–315. See also Blum, *Reforging the White Republic*, 88–119 and Alexander Keyssar, *The Right to Vote: The Contested History of Democracy in the United States* (New York: Basic Books, 2005), 77–79.

31. Henry Ward Beecher, *Norwood: Or Village Life in New England* (New York: Scribner's, 1868), 83, 86. See also William McLoughlin, *The Meaning of Henry Ward Beecher: An Essay on the Shifting Values of Mid-Victorian America, 1840–1870* (New York: Knopf, 1970), 228–230.

32. Horace White, "Forgiving Grant," *Chicago Tribune*, August 7, 1872, 4. This interpretation of the Liberal Republicans is in debt to Andrew Slap, *The Doom of Reconstruction: The Liberal Republicans in the Civil War Era* (New York: Fordham University Press, 2006), especially ii–xxv, 88–125.

33. Asa Mahan, "The Voice of Oberlin," *Chicago Tribune*, August 26, 1872, 5.

34. Theodore Parker, *The Slave Power* (Boston: American Unitarian Association, 1858), 157.

35. "The Kansas Question," *Putnam's Review* 6 (October 1855), 431–433; cited in Phillip Shaw Paludan, "Religion and the American Civil War," in *Religion and the American Civil War*, eds. Randall M. Miller, Harry S. Stout, and Charles Reagan Wilson (New York: Oxford University Press, 1998), 24.

36. Henry Wilson, *History of the Rise and Fall of the Slave Power in America* (Boston: Houghton, Osgood and Company, 1879), 150–151.

37. Mahan, "The Voice of Oberlin," 5.

38. Asa Mahan, "The Presidential Canvass," *Chicago Tribune*, September 2, 1872, 4.

39. Ibid. On Greeley's seizure of the Liberal Republican nomination and his choice of platform, see Slap, *The Doom of Reconstruction*, 126–163; Blum, *Reforging the White Republic*, 113–118; Robert C. Williams, *Horace Greeley: Champion of American Freedom* (New York: New York University Press, 2006), 292–304.

40. Horace Greeley, *Recollections of a Busy Life*, 398–399.; *Proceedings of the Liberal Republican Convention in Cincinnati* (New York: Baker and Goodwin, 1872), 40.

41. "A Greeley Reformer," *New York Times*, September 14, 1872, 11.

42. Everett Chamberlain, *The Struggle of '72: Issues and Candidates of the Present Political Campaign* (Chicago: Union Publishing Company, 1872), 441–442, 463, 502.

43. Frederick Douglass, "My Reasons for Opposing Horace Greeley," in *The Frederick Douglass Papers*, eds. John W. Blassingame and John R. McKivigan (New Haven, CT: Yale University Press, 1991), 4:327–328. See also Edward J. Blum, "O God of a Godless Land: Northern African American Challenges to White Christian Nationhood, 1865–1906," in *Vale of Tears: New Essays on Religion and Reconstruction*, eds. Blum and W. Scott Poole (Macon, GA: Mercer University Press, 2005), 93–112; Lawrence Grossman, *The Democratic Party and the Negro: Northern and National Politics, 1868–1892* (Urbana:

University of Illinois Press, 1976), 30–45; Xi Wang, *The Trial of Democracy: Black Suffrage and Northern Republicans, 1860–1910* (Athens: University of Georgia Press, 1997), 106–110; and David Miles Johnson, "Beyond Freedom: The Black North, 1863–1883," PhD Dissertation, University of California, Berkeley, 2007, 99–104.

44. "Back to Slavery," editorial, *San Francisco Elevator,* November 16, 1872, 3.

45. "National Colored Convention," *Weekly Louisianan,* April 14, 1872, 1.

46. See *The Greeley Record* (Washington, DC: Union Republican Congressional Executive Committee, 1872), 99, which pilloried Greeley for saying favorable things about "free love."

47. Walter Rauschenbusch, *Christianity and the Social Crisis* (1907; New York: Macmillan, 2013), 254, 369.

48. Rauschenbusch, *Christianity and the Social Crisis,* 221.

49. Rauschenbusch, *Christianity and the Social Crisis,* 277.

50. Jane Addams, *A New Conscience and an Ancient Evil* (New York: Macmillan, 1912), 56–57, 103. See also Victoria Bissell Brown, "Sex and the City: Jane Addams Confronts Prostitution," in *Feminist Interpretations of Jane Addams,* ed. Maurice Hamington (University Park: Penn State University Press, 2010), 125–149.

51. Carter G. Woodson, *The History of the Negro Church* (Washington, DC: Associated Publishers, 1921), 305–306.

2. Creating Western Civilization at Columbia University

1. Erskine tells the story of his recruitment and decision in John Erskine, *Democracy and Ideals* (New York: George H. Doran, 1920), 120–123, and John Erskine, *The Memory of Certain Persons* (New York: J. B. Lippincott, 1947), 258–259. He recalls his office on 199.

2. Erskine, *Democracy and Ideals,* 71. On Erskine I also draw on Katherine Chaddock, *The Multi-Talented Mr. Erskine: Shaping Mass Culture through Great Books* (New York: Palgrave Macmillan, 2012) and Joan Shelley Rubin, *The Making of Middlebrow Culture* (Chapel Hill: University of North Carolina Press, 1998), 148–209.

3. Erskine, *The Memory of Certain Persons,* 259–261; Erskine, *My Life as a Teacher* (New York: J. B. Lippincott, 1948), 28; Rubin, *The Making of Middlebrow Culture,* 151–152. For liberal Protestant use of the word "materialism" see, for instance, Lyman Abbott, *The Twentieth Century Crusade* (New York: Macmillan, 1918), 104, and the discussion in James C. Turner, *The Liberal Education of Charles Eliot Norton* (Baltimore: Johns Hopkins University Press, 1999), 261–262.

4. William Hutchison, "Protestantism as Establishment," in *Between the Times: The Travail of the Protestant Establishment in America, 1900–1960,* ed. Hutchison (New York: Cambridge University Press, 1990), 3–18; Elesha

Coffman, *The Christian Century and the Rise of the Protestant Mainline* (New York: Oxford University Press, 2013), 12–33.

5. My discussion of Protestant liberalism primarily reflects four sources. Most important are William Hutchison, *The Modernist Impulse in American Protestantism* (Cambridge, MA: Harvard University Press, 1976), especially 4–9, and Amy Kittelstrom, *The Religion of Democracy: Seven Thinkers and the American Liberal Tradition* (New York: Penguin, 2015), 3–11. See also Kathryn Lofton, "The Methodology of the Modernists," *Church History* 75:2 (June 2006), 374–402; and Leigh Eric Schmidt, "The Parameters and Problematics of American Religious Liberalism," in *American Religious Liberalism,* eds. Schmidt and Sally Promey (Indianapolis: Indiana University Press, 2012), 1–17. On the blurriness of liberal Protestant definitions of religion, Richard Wightman Fox, "The Culture of Liberal Protestant Progressivism," *Journal of Interdisciplinary History,* 23:3 (Winter 1993), 639–660 and Tracy Fessenden, *Culture and Redemption: Religion, the Secular, and American Literature* (Princeton, NJ: Princeton University Press, 2007), especially 84–109.

6. John Erskine, *Must Christians Choose Between the Bible and Prohibition?* (New York: New York World, 1922), 7, 9.

7. John J. Coss to his mother, April 6, 1917, John Jacob Coss Papers, series I, box 2, Rare Book and Manuscript Library, Columbia University.

8. George M. Marsden, *The Soul of the American University: From Protestant Establishment to Established Non-Belief* (New York: Oxford University Press, 1994), 123–196 argues that this sort of Christianity was dominant in American universities in the early twentieth century. See also Andrew Jewett, *Science, Democracy and the American University* (New York: Cambridge University Press, 2013), 8–14, 88–90; he calls these people "scientific democrats" and emphasizes their roots in liberal Protestantism, particularly Dewey's; as he claims on page 97, Dewey saw the "Christian ethical canon as uniquely aiding the survival of the species." David Hollinger, in *After Cloven Tongues of Fire: Protestant Liberalism in Modern American History* (Princeton, NJ: Princeton University Press, 2013), describes a phenomenon taking place throughout the twentieth century: liberal Protestants may have discarded the orthodoxies and meta-physics of their faith, but they nonetheless retained many of its assumptions about the moral life, ecumenical commitments, and democracy. See particularly 1–18 and his discussion of William James, 93–117. I draw the term post-Protestants from Robert Crunden, *Ministers of Reform: The Progressive Achievement in American Civilization, 1889–1920* (New York: Basic Books, 1982).

9. John Dewey, *Christianity and Democracy* (Ann Arbor: University of Michigan Press, 1892), 66, 68; and Steven C. Rockefeller, *John Dewey, Religious Faith, and Democratic Humanism* (New York: Columbia University Press, 1994), 133–136, 190–195.

10. Larry Hickman and Thomas Alexander, eds., *The Essential Dewey: Pragmatism, Education, Democracy* (Bloomington: Indiana University Press, 1998),

1:25. Patrick Deneen advances the argument that intellectuals like Dewey developed a generically religious way of talking about democracy in *Democratic Faith* (Princeton, NJ: Princeton University Press, 2005), 178–182.

11. Franklin Giddings, *Democracy and Empire* (New York: Macmillan, 1901), 50–51; and John Louis Recchiuti, *Civic Engagement: Social Science and Progressive Era Reform in New York City* (Philadelphia: University of Pennsylvania Press, 2007), 26–27. For his ideas about "commonality of a kind" and human egalitarianism, see Franklin Giddings, *Principles of Sociology* (New York: Macmillan, 1905), 17, 359–360; and Rosalind Rosenberg, *Beyond Separate Spheres: Intellectual Roots of Modern Feminism* (New Haven, CT: Yale University Press, 1982), 149–152. Robert C. Bannister, *Sociology and Scientism: The American Quest for Objectivity, 1880–1940* (Chapel Hill: University of North Carolina Press, 1987), 79–85, treats Giddings's metaphysical ventures much less sympathetically.

12. Irwin Edman, *A Philosopher's Holiday* (New York: Viking Press, 1938), 277–278.

13. Irwin Edman, *Human Traits and Their Social Significance* (Boston: Houghton Mifflin, 1920), iii, 299, 184–185, 209. *Introduction to Contemporary Civilization: A Syllabus* (New York: Columbia University Press, 1921), 13–15.

14. Kittelstrom, *The Religion of Democracy*, 218–221. On the delicate, and sometimes unsuccessful, attempt to peel religion and ethics apart in American higher education, see Julie Reuben, *The Making of the Modern University: Intellectual Transformation and the Marginalization of Morality* (Chicago: University of Chicago Press, 1996), especially 176–230.

15. John Erskine, *My Life as a Teacher* (New York: Macmillan, 1948), 172–173.

16. John J. Coss, "Religious Organizations," in *National Service Handbook,* ed. George Creel (Washington, DC: Government Printing Office, 1917), 27–28.

17. Elting E. Morison, ed., *The Letters of Theodore Roosevelt* (Cambridge: Harvard University Press, 1954), 8:928. On Roosevelt's views about civilization and Christianity, see Joshua David Hawley, *Theodore Roosevelt: Preacher of Righteousness* (New Haven, CT: Yale University Press, 2008), especially 78–83. See also Matthew McCullough, *The Cross of War: Christian Nationalism and U.S. Expansion in the Spanish American War* (Madison: University of Wisconsin Press, 2014), particularly 37–60.

18. Joseph McCabe, *The Evolution of Civilization* (New York: G. P. Putnam, 1922), 3; Brett Bowden, *Empire of Civilization: The Evolution of an Imperial Idea* (Chicago: University of Chicago Press, 2009), 2–42; and Gail Bederman, *Manliness and Civilization: A Cultural History of Gender and Race in the United States, 1880–1917* (Chicago: University of Chicago Press, 1995), 19–27.

19. James Marcus King, *Facing the Twentieth Century: Our Country; Its Power and Peril* (New York: Eaton and Mains, 1899), 135–136.

20. Theodore Roosevelt, *The Winning of the West: Volume I* (New York: G. P. Putnam, 1889), 4; Josiah Strong, *Our Country: Its Possible Future and Present Crisis* (New York: Baker and Taylor Company, 1885), 175. Reginald Horsman,

Race and Manifest Destiny: The Origins of American Racial Anglo-Saxonism (Cambridge, MA: Harvard University Press, 1981), 2–25, traces this linkage to the English Reformation and British settlement of America, understood as a mandate for first British then American uniqueness. See also Matthew Frye Jacobson, *Whiteness of a Different Color: European Immigrants and the Alchemy of Race* (Cambridge, MA: Harvard University Press, 1998), 39–90, 203–213.

21. Herbert Baxter Adams, *The Germanic Origins of New England Towns* (Baltimore, MD: Johns Hopkins University Press, 1882), 33, 8. On Adams, see Richard Hofstadter, *The Progressive Historians: Turner, Beard, Parrington* (New York: Knopf, 1968), 2–8.

22. Woodrow Wilson, *The State* (New York: D.C. Heath and Company, 1898), 583.

23. For the ways Woodrow Wilson exemplified these ideas, see Cara Lea Burnidge, *A Peaceful Conquest: Woodrow Wilson, Religion, and the New World Order* (Chicago: University of Chicago Press, 2016), 60–61, 91–98.

24. John Erskine, *My Life as a Teacher* (Philadelphia: J. B. Lippincott, 1948), 122–124.

25. Torao Taketomo, *Paulownia: Seven Stories from Contemporary Japanese Writers* (New York: J. B. Lippincott, 1918), 9–10.

26. John Erskine, *The Moral Obligation to Be Intelligent and Other Essays* (New York: Duffield and Company, 1921), 39–41, 15–16, 26, 27, 28.

27. James Freeman Clarke, *Ten Great Religions: An Essay in Comparative Theology* (Boston: James R. Osgood and Company, 1871), 1:2. See also David Mislin, *Saving Faith: Making Religious Pluralism an American Value at the Dawn of the Secular Age* (Ithaca, NY: Cornell University Press, 2015), 41–51; Tomoko Masuzawa, *The Invention of World Religions* (Chicago: University of Chicago Press, 2005), 51–79; and Amanda Porterfield, "Religious Pluralism in Religious Studies," in *Gods in America*, eds. Charles Cohen and Ronald Numbers (New York: Oxford University Press, 2013), 21–43.

28. Erskine, *The Memory of Certain Persons*, 347. Erskine's linking of democracy and Christianity was derived in some measure from his teacher Edward Woodberry, a New Humanist who affirmed the spiritual nature of democracy. "A conception of the soul and its destiny . . . underlies democracy," Woodberry taught his students. "This is why it is the most spiritual government known to man, and therefore the highest reach of man's evolution." Woodberry, *Heart of Man and Other Papers* (New York: Macmillan, 1904), 217–218.

29. Frank Aydelotte, *Final Report of the War Issues Course of the Students' Army Training Corps* (Washington, DC: War Department, 1919), 53–55, 55. Aydelotte himself was a New Humanist who shared Erskine's notions about the relationship between art, religion, and democracy; see Ruth Shoemaker Wood, *Transforming Campus Culture: Frank Aydelotte's Honors Experiment at Swarthmore College* (Lanham, MD: Rowman and Littlefield, 2012), 1–12.

30. Robert J. Hutcheon, *The Causes of Germany's Moral Downfall* (Boston: Beacon Press, 1919), 47, v.

31. "Rooting Out Christianity in Germany," *Literary Digest*, October 13, 1917, 36.
32. Discussed in George M. Marsden, *Fundamentalism and American Culture* (New York: Oxford University Press, 2006), 147–152; quote on 150. See also Matthew Avery Sutton, *American Apocalypse: A History of Modern Evangelicalism* (Cambridge, MA: Harvard University Press, 2014), 58–62.
33. Erskine, *The Memory of Certain Persons*, 262–263.
34. "German Ideas of the State," *Methodist Review* 101 (September 1918), 679.
35. Joseph Crooker, "Reaction Against America's Bondage to the German Spirit," *Current Opinion* 59:3 (September 1915), 184–185.
36. Hutcheon, *The Causes of Germany's Moral Downfall*, 30.
37. Thomas F. A. Smith, *The Soul of Germany: A Twelve Years' Study of the People from Within* (New York: George H. Doran Company, 1915), 27–28, 63–64. The problem of "two Germanys"—one rational and enlightened, the other militaristic and brutal—engaged many American progressives. See Daniel Rodgers, *Atlantic Crossings: Social Politics in a Progressive Age* (Cambridge, MA: Harvard University Press, 1998), 273–277.
38. Smith, *The Soul of Germany*, 62, 65.
39. Alexander Crawford, *Germany's Moral Downfall: The Tragedy of Academic Materialism* (New York: The Abington Press, 1919), 53.
40. Nicholas Murray Butler, *True and False Democracy* (New York: Scribner's, 1915), 14. On Butler's personality, see Thomas Bender, *New York Intellect: A History of Intellectual Life in New York City, from 1750 to the Birth of the Modern Age* (New York: Knopf, 1987), 296–299.
41. William Carnochan, *The Battle of the Curriculum* (Stanford, CA: Stanford University Press, 1993), 60–71. For a case study see also Turner, *The Liberal Education of Charles Eliot Norton*, 346–393.
42. Roscoe Lewis Ashley, *Early European Civilization* (New York: Macmillan, 1915), 343, 328.
43. On the Columbia course Contemporary Civilization, see Carnochan, *The Battleground of the Curriculum*, 69–71; Carol Gruber, *Mars and Minerva: World War I and the Uses of Higher Learning in America* (Baton Rouge: LSU Press, 1975), 240–244; Willis Rudy, *Total War and Twentieth-Century Higher Learning* (Cranbury, NJ: Associated University Press, 1991), 22–31.
44. Harry J. Carman and Louis M. Hacker, "General Education in the Social Sciences in Columbia University," in *Social Sciences in General Education*, ed. Earl J. McGrath (Dubuque, IA: William C. Brown Co., 1948), 16.
45. Robert McCaughey, *Stand, Columbia: A History of Columbia University* (New York: Columbia University Press, 2003), 274–277. For contemporary fears about industrialization's impact on democracy, see Kevin Mattson, *Creating a Democratic Public: The Struggle for Urban Participatory Democracy During the Progressive Era* (University Station: Penn State University Press, 2010), Leon Fink, *Progressive Intellectuals and the Dilemma of Democratic Commitment* (Cambridge: Harvard University Press, 1998).

46. Franklin Giddings, *The Responsible State* (New York: Macmillan, 1918), 3–4, 5, 107. For a broad examination of the work of Columbia academics in the war period, see Bender, *New York Intellect*, 312–313, 88–98.

47. John Dewey, "On Understanding the Mind of Germany," *Atlantic Monthly*, February 1916, 253, 255, 257. See also Dewey, *German Philosophy and Politics* (New York: Holt, 1915), 7, 94–96, and Alan Cywar, "John Dewey in World War I: Patriotism and International Progressivism," *American Quarterly* 21:3 (Autumn 1969), 578–594. Dewey's argument was echoed by others, the sociologist Thorstein Veblen, for instance, in *Imperial Germany and the Industrial Revolution* (New York: Macmillan, 1915), 102–106.

48. James Harvey Robinson, *History of Europe: Our Own Times* (New York: Houghton Mifflin, 1921), 578.

49. James Harvey Robinson, "Conceptions and Methods of History," in *Congress of Arts and Sciences, 1904,* ed. Howard J. Rogers (Boston: Houghton Mifflin, 1906), 2:50; and Robinson, *The New History* (New York: Macmillan, 1912), 5–6. Robinson presented this argument in a number of the textbooks he wrote; see, for instance, Robinson, *Medieval and Modern Times: An Introduction to the History of Western Europe* (Boston: Ginn and Company, 1926), 1. On his ideas, see Ernst Breisach, *American Progressive History* (Chicago: University of Chicago Press, 1993), 31–39.

50. James Harvey Robinson, *Civilization* (London: Britannica, 1929), 19–20.

51. Franz Boas, *Race and Democratic Society* (New York: Biblo and Tannen, 1928), 200. On Boas's democratic thought, see Jewett, *Science, Democracy and the American University*, 259–263.

52. *Introduction to Contemporary Civilization: Third Edition* (New York: Columbia University Press, 1921), viii–ix. In 1919 and 1920 a first and second edition were published in two volumes; the third edition revised both into a longer single volume for the first time. On Coss's leadership, McCaughey, *Stand, Columbia*, 291.

53. Irwin Edman, *Human Traits and Their Social Significance* (Boston: Houghton Mifflin, 1920), iii.

54. Edman, *Human Traits and Their Social Significance*, 279, 285, 289. *Introduction to Contemporary Civilization*, 13; the syllabus cites William James, *Varieties of Religious Experience* (New York: Longmans, Green and Company, 1920), particularly James's discussion of saintliness and equanimity accessible through religion. James defines religion as "the feelings, acts and experiences of individual men in their solitude so far as they apprehend themselves to stand in relation to whatever they may consider the divine," 31.

55. *Introduction to Contemporary Civilization*, 13–14.

56. Edman, *Human Traits and Their Social Significance*, 133, 153–155; the discussion of customary and reflective morality is in pages 193–197. On Boas's influence, 198–200.

57. Carlton J. H. Hayes, *A Political and Social History of Modern Europe* (New York: Macmillan, 1920), xx–xxi, 101–102.

58. John Herman Randall Jr., *The Making of the Modern Mind* (orig. pub. 1926; New York: Columbia University Press, 1976), 4, 38–39.

59. Edman, *Human Traits and Their Social Significance*, 196–197.

60. Randall, *The Making of the Modern Mind*, 143; *Introduction to Contemporary Civilization*, 24, 14.

61. Hayes, *A Political and Social History of Modern Europe*, 102–105. This theory was echoed by a number of other writers on the Contemporary Civilization syllabus; for instance, James Bryce, *Modern Democracies* (New York: Macmillan, 1921), 2:569–571; Veblen, *Imperial Germany and the Industrial Revolution*, 44–46.

62. *Introduction to Contemporary Civilization*, 23–24; Randall, *The Making of the Modern Mind*, 366; *Introduction to Contemporary Civilization*, 23–24.

63. Carlton J. H. Hayes, *A Brief History of the Great War* (New York: Macmillan, 1921), 410–411, 21.

64. Randall, *The Making of the Modern Mind*, 622.

65. Randall, *The Making of the Modern Mind*, 625. On the Christian debates over the League of Nations, see Burnidge, *A Peaceful Conquest*, 106–127; Markku Ruotsila, "Conservative American Protestants in the League of Nations Controversy," *Church History* 72:3 (September 2003): 593–616.

66. Homer Folks, *The Human Cost of the War* (New York: Harper and Brothers, 1921), 23, 27.

67. Bryce, *Modern Democracies*, 2:576–578, 606.

68. Memorandum, Findings of the Personnel Survey Committee, December 1927, John Jacob Coss Papers, Rare Book and Manuscript Library, Columbia University.

69. Memorandum, "Administration of Organized Religious Work at Columbia University," January 26, 1928, John Jacob Coss Papers, series II, box 5, Rare Book and Manuscript Library, Columbia University.

70. Memorandum, "Is Columbia Doing Enough for the Religious Life of Its Students?" John Jacob Coss Papers, series II, box 5, Rare Book and Manuscript Library, Columbia University.

71. Findings of the Personnel Survey Committee, December 1927. On universities embracing voluntary expressions of faith as a means to build good citizenship, see Marsden, *The Soul of the American University*, 236–267.

72. Contemporary Civilization Budget, October 19, November 6, and November 11, 1936, John Jacob Coss Papers, series II, box 5, Rare Book and Manuscript Library, Columbia University. On the influence of Columbia's Contemporary Civilization course, see Gilbert Allardyce, "The Rise and Fall of the Western Civilization Course," *American Historical Review* 87 (1982):695–725.

73. Arthur Sears Henning, "Coolidge Sees Peril in Reform Clamor," *Chicago Tribune*, July 6, 1926, 1. For the conventionality of Coolidge's religious beliefs, see David Greenberg, *Calvin Coolidge* (New York: Henry Holt and Company, 2006), 55–56.

74. "McAdoo Hits Materialism," *New York Times*, May 1, 1924, 9.
75. Charles A. Greathouse, ed., *Official Report of the Proceedings of the Democratic National Convention* (Indianapolis: Bookwalter-Ball-Greathouse Printing, 1929), 126, 172.
76. "Relation of the Klan to American Citizenship," *Union Leader*, June 4, 1925. For this source and links between the Klan and the Reformation, I am indebted to Kelly J. Baker, *The Gospel According to the Klan: The KKK's Appeal to Protestant America, 1915–1930* (Lawrence: University Press of Kansas, 2011), 39–46.
77. Hiram Wesley Evans, *The Menace of Modern Immigration* (Dallas, TX: Knights of the Ku Klux Klan, 1924), 19, 24, 25.
78. Joe Cain, ed., *The Last Message of William Jennings Bryan* (London: Euston Grove Press, 2009), 19, 41–42. On Bryan's faith and its relationship to politics, see Michael Kazin, *A Godly Hero: The Life of William Jennings Bryan* (New York: Knopf, 2006), 262–266.
79. William Jennings Bryan, *In His Image* (New York: Fleming H. Revell, 1922), 123, 185, 213.
80. Robert Lansing, *The Power of Democracy* (Washington, DC: Government Printing Office, 1919), 2, 5, 8, 9. On Lansing's character, see Thomas Henry Hartig, "Robert Lansing: An Interpretive Biography," PhD dissertation, Ohio State University, 1974.Robert Lansing, *Address before the Reserve Officers' Training Corps* (Washington, DC: Government Printing Office, 1917), 9.

3. Challenging Western Civilization at Howard University

1. "Fall 1938—History of Civilization, or Thought and Culture," Alain Locke Papers, series 164, box 163, folder 8, Moorland-Spingarn Research Center, Howard University.
2. "Philosophy I: Introduction to Philosophy" and "The Philosophy of Religion," Alain Locke Papers, series 164, box 163, folder 6. This narrative reflected common theories about the history of religions in the late nineteenth and early twentieth centuries. See Amanda Porterfield, "Religious Pluralism in Religious Studies," in *Gods in America*, eds. Charles Cohen and Ronald Numbers (New York: Oxford University Press, 2013), 21–43.
3. John W. Boyer, *The University of Chicago: A History* (Chicago: University of Chicago Press, 2015), 241–251; David Orlinsky, "Not Very Simple, but Overflowing: A Historical Perspective on General Education at the University of Chicago" in *General Education in the Social Sciences: Centennial Reflections on the College of the University of Chicago*, ed. John J. MacAloon (Chicago: University of Chicago Press, 1992), 42–52; Hayward Keniston, Ferdinand Schevill, and Arthur P. Scott, *Introductory General Course in the Humanities: Syllabus, Seventh Edition* (Chicago: University of Chicago Press, 1937).

4. Keniston, et al., *Introductory General Course in the Humanities*, 107, 110.

5. On civilizationism and uplift, see Kevin K. Gaines, *Uplifting the Race: Black Leadership, Politics and Culture in the Twentieth Century* (Chapel Hill: University of North Carolina Press, 1996), 17, 100–126. The term *civilizationism* was coined by Wilson Jeremiah Moses, *Afrotopia: The Roots of African American Popular History* (New York: Cambridge University Press, 1998), 96, 123–125.

6. Edward E. Curtis, *Islam in Black America: Identity, Liberation and Difference* (Albany: State University of New York Press, 2002), 45–63; Susan Nance, "Mystery of the Moorish Science Temple: Southern Blacks and American Alternative Spirituality in 1920s Chicago," *Religion and American Culture* 12:2 (Summer 2002), 123–166; Edward J. Blyden, *Christianity, Islam and the Negro Race*, Christopher Fyfe, ed. (orig. pub. 1887; Edinburgh: University of Edinburgh Press, 1967).

7. *The Inauguration of J. Stanley Durkee, A.M., PH.D. as President of Howard University November 12, 1919* (Washington, DC: Howard University, 1919), 14.

8. *The Inauguration of J. Stanley Durkee*, 14, 21–22.

9. *The Inauguration of J. Stanley Durkee*, 16.

10. See Sabiyha Prince, *African Americans and Gentrification in Washington, D.C.: Race, Class, and Social Justice in the Nation's Capital* (Burlington, VT: Ashgate Publishing, 2014), 37–55; Jan Voogd, *Race Riots and Resistance: The Red Summer of 1919* (New York: Peter Lang, 2008), 85–88, 100–104. The term *nadir* in reference to African American history was popularized by Rayford Logan, *The Negro in American Life and Thought: The Nadir, 1877–1901* (New York: The Dial Press, 1954).

11. On liberal Protestantism and the African American educational system in the early twentieth century, see Gary Dorrien, *The Making of American Liberal Protestantism: Idealism, Realism and Democracy, 1900–1950* (Louisville, KY: Westminster/John Knox Press, 2003), 356–390, 415–445; Leroy Davis, *A Clashing of the Soul: John Hope and the Dilemma of African American Leadership and Black Higher Education in the Early Twentieth Century* (Athens: University of Georgia Press, 1998), 35–40; and Barbara Dianne Savage, *Your Spirits Walk beside Us: The Politics of Black Religion* (Cambridge, MA: Harvard University Press, 2008), 205–238.

12. "The Fiftieth Anniversary of Morehouse College," *Missions* 8:4 (April 1917), 269. For historically black colleges generally, see James D. Anderson, *The Education of Blacks in the South: 1860–1925* (Chapel Hill: University of North Carolina Press, 1998) and Joe M. Richardson, *Christian Reconstruction: The American Missionary Association and Southern Blacks, 1861–1890* (Tuscaloosa: University of Alabama Press, 1986).

13. On classical education, see Richardson, *Christian Reconstruction*, 125–135; George Marsden, *The Soul of the American University: From Protestant Establishment to Established Nonbelief* (New York: Oxford University Press, 1991), 33–47;

William B. Carnochan, *The Battleground of the Curriculum: Liberal Education and American Experience* (Palo Alto, CA: Stanford University Press, 1994), 22–39. On the debate between industrial and liberal education, see Davis, *A Clashing of the Soul*, 88–97, and Virginia Lantz Denton, *Booker T. Washington and the Adult Education Movement* (Tallahassee: University of Florida Press, 1993). For Washington's support for vocational education at Howard, see Rayford Logan, *Howard University: The First Hundred Years* (Washington, DC: Howard University Press, 1967), 118.

14. Booker T. Washington, "Relation of Industrial Education to National Progress," *Annals of the American Academy of Political and Social Sciences* 33:1 (January 1909), 11–12. On Washington's message to rural African Americans, see Robert Norrell, *Up from History: The Life of Booker T. Washington* (Cambridge, MA: Harvard University Press, 2009), 44–54, 106–109.

15. W. E. B. Du Bois, *The Souls of Black Folk* (orig. pub. 1903; New York: Pocket Books, 2014), 95. See also Edward J. Blum, *W. E. B. Du Bois: American Prophet* (Philadelphia: University of Pennsylvania Press, 2009), 85–91.

16. Kelly Miller, *The Primary Needs of the Negro Race* (Washington, DC: Howard University Press, 1899), 10–11; discussed in Lewis V. Baldwin, *There Is a Balm in Gilead: The Cultural Roots of Martin Luther King, Jr.* (Minneapolis, MN: Fortress Press, 1991), 263. Throughout his career Miller believed that people of African descent had a unique capacity for religious faith, a controversial position that set him apart from some of his colleagues. Curtis J. Evans, *The Burden of Black Religion* (New York: Oxford University Press, 2008), 166–171, 191.

17. Logan, *Howard University*, 160–169, 139.

18. Logan, *Howard University*, 168–169, 152–153.

19. Justus D. Doenecke, *Nothing Less Than War: A New History of America's Entry into World War I* (Lexington: University Press of Kentucky, 2011), 250–278; Logan, *Howard University*, 174–178.

20. "The Semi-Centennial of Howard University," *Howard University Record* 11:7 (December 1917), 14.

21. George Washington Williams, *History of the Negro Race in America from 1619 to 1880* (New York: G. P. Putnam's Sons, 1883), 2:96. On "vindication history" as a genre, see Stephen G. Hall, *A Faithful Account of the Race: African American Historical Writing in Nineteenth-Century America* (Chapel Hill: University of North Carolina Press, 2004), 2–11; John Ernest, *Liberation Historiography: African American Writers and the Challenge of History* (Chapel Hill: University of North Carolina Press, 2004), 54–56.

22. "The Semi-Centennial of Howard University," 21, 23, 24.

23. W. E. B. Du Bois, "What Is Civilization? Africa's Answer," in *W. E. B. Du Bois: A Reader,* ed. Meyer Weinberg (New York: Harper and Row, 1970), 378. See also Wilson J. Moses, "Culture, Civilization and the Decline of the West," in *W. E. B. Du Bois on Race and Culture,* eds. Bernard W. Bell, Emily R. Grosholz, and James B. Stewart (New York: Routledge, 2013), 243–260.

24. Cited in Logan, *Howard University,* 179. The board of trustees was normally made up of between thirteen and twenty individuals, roughly two-thirds of whom were always white. Zachery R. Williams, *In Search of the Talented Tenth: Howard University Public Intellectuals and the Dilemmas of Race, 1926–1970* (Columbia: University of Missouri Press, 2010), 23–24.

25. Logan, *Howard University,* 179–181; on the Student Officer's Training Camps, see Willis Rudy, *Total War and Higher Twentieth-Century Higher Learning: Universities of the Western World in the First and Second World Wars* (Rutherford, NJ: Fairleigh Dickinson Press, 1991), 23–27.

26. See, for instance, Thomas Montgomery Gregory to Woodrow Wilson, May 11, 1917, box 37-1, Thomas Montgomery Gregory Papers, Moorland-Spingarn Research Center, Howard University, Washington, DC. Du Bois is quoted from *Crisis,* April 1917, 270–271, reprinted in Nina Mjagkij, *Loyalty in Time of Trial: The African American Experience During World War I* (Lanham, MD: Rowman and Littlefield Publishers, 2011), 167–168. For context, see Chad L. Williams, *Torchbearers of Democracy: African American Soldiers in the World War I Era* (Chapel Hill: University of North Carolina Press, 2010), 38–47; Adam P. Wilson, *African American Army Officers of World War I: A Vanguard of Equality in War and Beyond* (Jefferson, NC: McFarland and Company, 2015), 29–45.

27. Arthur Schomburg, *Racial Integrity: A Plea for the Establishment of a Chair of Negro History in Our Schools and Colleges* (New York: n.p., 1913), 11.

28. On "race histories" see Laurie F. Maffly-Kipp, *Setting Down the Sacred Past: African-American Race Histories* (Cambridge, MA: Harvard University Press, 2010), especially 33–40.

29. Logan, *Howard University,* 171; Williams, *In Search of the Talented Tenth,* 20–21. See also Ida E. Jones, *The Heart of the Race Problem: The Life of Kelly Miller* (Littleton, MA: Tapestry Press, 2011), 188–208 and Michael Winston, *Howard University Department of History, 1913–1973* (Washington, DC: Howard University Press, 1973), 20; "Syllabus of an Extension Course of Lectures on Race Contacts and Inter-Racial Relations," Alain Locke Papers, collection 164, box 163, folder 12, Moorland-Spingarn Research Library, Howard University, Washington, DC.

30. Williams, *In Search of the Talented Tenth,* 23–24; Logan, *Howard University,* 187–189.

31. Carter G. Woodson, *The Miseducation of the Negro* (Washington, DC: Associated Publishers, 1933), 100.

32. Logan, *Howard University,* 171–173.

33. Carter Woodson to Jesse Moorland, April 23, 1920, box 34, folder 695, Jesse Moorland Papers, Moorland-Spingarn Research Center, Howard University, Washington, DC.

34. Jesse Moorland to Carter Woodson, April 24, 1920, box 34, folder 695, Jesse Moorland Papers.

35. Carter Woodson to Jesse Moorland, May 15, 1920, box 34, folder 695, Jesse Moorland Papers.

36. Kelly Miller to Jesse Moorland, May 2, 1921, box 34, folder 674, Jesse Moorland Papers.

37. Ibid.

38. Carter Woodson to Jesse Moorland, March 10, 1920, box 34, folder 695, Jesse Moorland Papers; on the episode, see Logan, *Howard University*, 208.

39. Logan, *Howard University*, 220; Jacqueline Goggin, *Carter G. Woodson: A Life in Black History* (Baton Rouge: Louisiana State University Press, 1993), 50–52, 204–206.

40. "Alumnus," "Howard Students on Strike, Durkee 500 Miles Away," *Baltimore Afro-American*, May 16, 1925, in J. Stanley Durkee Papers, box 3, folder 43, Moorland-Spingarn Research Center, Howard University, Washington, DC. On the strike, see Logan, *Howard University*, 220–222, Williams, *In Search of the Talented Tenth*, 30–32, and Hayward Farrer, *The Baltimore Afro-American, 1892–1950* (Westport, CT: Greenwood Press, 1998), 45–47.. On Durkee's reported opposition, see "And Durkee 500 Miles Away," *Washington Daily American*, May 8, 1925, and "Durkee Tells Strikers Police May Be Called," *Washington American*, May 12, 1925, in J. Stanley Durkee Papers, box 3, folder 47.

41. "Alumnus," "Favoritism Ascribed to HU Proxy," *Baltimore Afro-American*, June 27, 1925, in J. Stanley Durkee Papers, box 3, folder 43. Williams, *In Search of the Talented Tenth*, 27–32.

42. Raymond Wolters, *The New Negro on Campus: Black College Rebellions of the 1920s* (Princeton, NJ: Princeton University Press, 1975), 89.

43. "HU Alumni Urged to Seek the Intervention of Their Congressmen," *Baltimore Afro-American*, November 21, 1925, in J. Stanley Durkee Papers, box 3, folder 43; *Washington Daily American*, December 11, 1925, in J. Stanley Durkee Papers, box 3, folder 45. Jones, *The Heart of the Race Problem*, 208–233, covers Durkee's uneasy relationship with Miller.

44. "Alumnus," "Durkee Absents Himself as Neval Thomas Talks to HU Students," *Baltimore Afro-American*, November 14, 1925, in J. Stanley Durkee Papers, box 3, folder 43.

45. Maffly-Kipp, *Setting Down the Sacred Past*, 16–65.

46. Alexander Crummell, *The Future of Africa* (New York: Charles Scribner, 1862), 4–5.

47. Leila Amos Pendleton, *A Narrative of the Negro* (Washington, DC: R. L. Pendleton, 1912), 26. Wilson Moses, *The Golden Age of Black Nationalism* (New York: Oxford University Press, 1988), 15–32.

48. Mary Beth Mathews, *Doctrine and Race: African American Evangelicals and Fundamentalism between the Wars* (Tuscaloosa: University of Alabama Press, 2017), 126–131.

49. Evans, *The Burden of Black Religion*, 150–161.

50. "History of Civilization, or Thought and Culture," Alain Locke Papers, collection 164, box 163, folder 8; "Introduction to Philosophy" and "The Philosophy of Religion," Alain Locke Papers, collection 164, box 163, folder 12. On Locke's relationship with pragmatism, see Leonard Harris, *The Philosophy of Alain Locke: Harlem Renaissance and Beyond* (Philadelphia, PA:

Temple University Press, 1989), 17–25. On his religious inclinations, see
Christopher Buck, *Alain Locke: Faith and Philosophy* (Los Angeles: Ka-
limat, 2005); Leonard Harris and Charles Molesworth, *Alain L. Locke:
Biography of a Philosopher* (Chicago: University of Chicago Press, 2008),
206–211.

51. Alain Locke, "Moral Imperatives for World Order," in *The Works of Alain
Locke*, ed. Charles Molesworth (New York: Oxford University Press, 2012),
545, 556.

52. Alain Locke, "Race Contact and Inter-Racial Relations," in *The Works of Alain
Locke*, 258, 261. On Locke's philosophy in conversation with Boas and
pluralists, see Everett Helmut Akam, *Transnational America: Cultural Pluralist
Thought in the Twentieth Century* (Lanham, MD: Rowman and Littlefield,
2002), 139–156; Buck, *Alain Locke: Faith and Philosophy*, 60–64; Harris, *The
Philosophy of Alain Locke*, 51–67.

53. Kelly Miller, "The Negro Sanhedrin," 2, Kelly Miller Papers, collection 164,
box 71-6, folder 155, Moorland-Spingarn Research Library, Howard University, Washington DC.

54. Kelly Miller, "Religion and Race," Kelly Miller Papers, collection 164, box
71–6, folder 160.

55. Carter Woodson, "Why the Negro in History," *The Journal of Negro History*
2 (April 1926), 238. "History as It Is," *Negro History Bulletin* 8 (April 1945),
168. On Woodson's aims for the ASNLH, see Jeffrey Aaron Snyder, "Race,
Nation and Education: Black History During Jim Crow," PhD dissertation,
New York University, 2011, particularly 39–89; Pero Dagbovie, *The Early Black
History Movement, Carter G. Woodson, and Lorenzo Johnston Greene* (Urbana:
University of Illinois Press, 2007), 15–83; Robin D. G. Kelley, "'But a Local
Phase of a World Problem': Black History's Global Vision," *Journal of American
History* 86 (December 1999): 1045–1077. The moral imperative of black history
writing is explored in Maghan Keita, *Race and the Writing of History: Riddling
the Sphinx* (New York: Oxford University Press, 2000), 52–55; the separatist
vision these thinkers embraced is theorized in a later period in Nikhil Pal
Singh, *Black Is a Country: Race and the Unfinished Struggle for Democracy*
(Cambridge, MA: Harvard University Press, 2004), 30–38.

56. Kelly Miller, "Religion and Race," Kelly Miller Papers, collection 164, box
71–6, folder 160.

57. "Negro History Pageant Marked by Good Acting," *St. Louis Herald*, February 22, 1930, Carter Goodwin Woodson Papers, part II, reel I, Library of
Congress.

58. Carter Woodson, "The Negro in Europe," *Journal of the Association for the
Study of Negro Life and History* (December 1940), 51–52; Carter Woodson,
"Europeans and the Negro," *Negro History Bulletin* 4 (October 1941), 51.

59. Carter Woodson, "The Most Romantic of Our History is That of the Negro,"
Negro History Bulletin 1:5 (February 1938), 10. Capitalization original.

60. Arthur Schomburg, "The Negro Digs Up His Past," in *The New Negro*, ed.
Alain Locke (orig. pub. 1925; New York: Touchstone, 1997), 670–673 is a good

statement of this confidence. On Ethiopianism, see John Cullen Gruesser, *Black on Black: Twentieth-Century African American Writing about Africa* (Lexington: University Press of Kentucky, 2000), 20–50.

61. Drusilla Dunjee Houston, *Wonderful Ethiopians of the Ancient Cushite Empire* (Oklahoma City: Universal Publishing Company, 1926), 57–58; Pauline Hopkins, "A Primer of Facts Pertaining to the Early Greatness of the African Race," reprinted in Hanna Wallinger, *Pauline E. Hopkins: A Literary Biography* (Athens: University of Georgia Press, 2005), 293–315; see also discussion on 112–122.

62. *Howard University Record* 17:1 (November 1922), 10. Cited in Michael R. Winston, *The Howard University Department of History, 1913–1973* (Washington, D.C.: Howard University, 1973), 43. Hansberry received an MA from Harvard in 1931. He never finished his PhD, possibly because he had difficulty finding a mentor capable of judging the quality of his work. See Keita, *Race and the Writing of History*, 96. Charles Wesley to Carter Woodson, December 18, 1922, Jesse Moorland Papers, box 34, folder 694.

63. William Hansberry, "The African Civilizations Section of the Department of History of Howard University," Jesse Moorland Papers, box 32, folder 670.

64. Joseph Harris, ed., *The William Leo Hansberry African History Notebook: Pillars in Ethiopian History* (Washington, DC: Howard University Press, 1974), 11. Joseph Harris, ed., *The William Leo Hansberry African History Notebook: Africa and Africans As Seen by Classical Writers* (Washington, DC: Howard University Press, 1981), 81–82. After Hansberry's death, his colleague Joseph Harris collected his many, many lecture notes and edited them into volumes he called "notebooks."

65. Harris, ed., *Africa and Africans*, 22.

66. Harris, ed., *Africa and Africans*, 82.

67. William Hansberry, "Howard's Supreme Opportunity," *Howard University Record* 17:3 (1923), 417.

68. William Hansberry, "Introduction to Ancient and Mediaeval African Civilization," Jesse Moorland Papers, box 32, folder 670, Moorland-Spingarn Research Center, Howard University, Washington, DC.

69. Harris, ed., *Pillars in Ethiopian History*, 66–67, 80, 74.

70. Harris, ed., *Pillars in Ethiopian History*, 85.

71. Harris, ed., *Pillars in Ethiopian History*, 75–76.

72. Harris, ed., *Pillars in Ethiopian History*, 86–87, 93.

73. Harris, ed., *Pillars in Ethiopian History*, 99.

74. Randall Burkett, *Garveyism as a Religious Movement* (Lanham, MD: Scarecrow Press, 1978), 89–98; E. David Cronon, *Black Moses: The Story of Marcus Garvey and the Universal Negro Improvement Association* (Madison: University of Wisconsin Press, 1969), 178–181; quote on 178.

75. Carter Woodson, "Christianity and the Negro," Carter Goodwin Woodson Papers, series I, reel 11.

76. Kelly Miller, "Forty Years of Negro Education," 486, Kelly Miller Papers, collection 164, box 71–6, folder 140. See also Savage, *Your Spirits Walk beside Us,* 13–19, and Evans, *The Burden of Black Religion,* 161–172, for educated African Americans' fears of the "black church."

77. Charles L. Lumpkins, *American Pogrom: The East St. Louis Race Riot and Black Politics* (Athens: Ohio University Press, 2008).

78. Kelly Miller, "The Disgrace of Democracy: An Open Letter to President Woodrow Wilson, August 4, 1917," Kelly Miller Papers, box 71–6, folder 134. The letter was published as a pamphlet and sold more than a quarter million copies. See W. D. Wright, "The Thought and Leadership of Kelly Miller," *Pylon* 39 (June 1978), 180–192.

4. Catholic Community in the Great Depression

1. Samuel Rosenman, ed., *The Public Papers and Addresses of Franklin D. Roosevelt* (New York: Random House, 1938), 1:777–778.

2. John McHugh Stewart to John A. Ryan, October 29, 1932, John A. Ryan Papers, box 35, folder 12, Catholic University of America, Washington, DC. On Ryan's attitude toward the election, see John A. Ryan, *Social Doctrine in Action: A Personal History* (New York: Harper and Brothers, 1941), 246–248.

3. John A. Ryan, "The Present Business Recession: A Speech Delivered in Hartford, December 1937," 7–8, John A. Ryan Papers, box 47, folder 19. The speech was reprinted as *The Present Business Recession* (Washington, DC: Government Printing Office, 1938), and entered into the *Congressional Record* by Congressman Herman Koppelmann of Connecticut.

4. On Catholicism alienated from early twentieth-century American society, see William M. Halsey, *The Survival of American Innocence: Catholicism in an Era of Disillusionment, 1920–1940* (South Bend, IN: Notre Dame University Press, 1980), which describes Ryan's letter on 1 and discusses Thomism on 152–169; James T. Fisher, *The Catholic Counterculture in America, 1933–1962* (Chapel Hill: University of North Carolina Press, 1989). Kenneth J. Heineman, *A Catholic New Deal: Religion and Reform in Depression Pittsburgh* (University Park: Penn State University Press, 1999), 12–23, describes Catholics seeking a middle way between secular socialism and industrial capitalism. Heineman and I follow the earlier argument of Aaron Ignatius Abell, *American Catholicism and Social Action: A Search for Social Justice, 1865–1950* (South Bend, IN: University of Notre Dame Press, 1963), especially 234–264.

5. Editorial, *Commonweal* 17 (November 16, 1932), 58.

6. Ryan, "The Present Business Recession," 7.

7. For Ryan's career before the Great Depression, see Francis L. Broderick, *Right Reverend New Dealer: John A. Ryan* (New York: Macmillan, 1963), especially 200–233; Gary Dorrien, *Social Ethics in the Making: Interpreting an American Tradition* (Malden, MA: Blackwell, 2011), 185–226.

8. John A. Ryan, *Citizen, Church and State* (New York: Paulist Press, 1938), 17.

9. John A. Ryan, *A Living Wage* (New York: Grosset and Dunlap, 1906), 26.

10. John A. Ryan, "The Present Business Recession," 7–8. On Ryan's ideal society, see Thomas E. Woods Jr., *The Church Confronts Modernity: Catholic Intellectuals and the Progressive Era* (New York: Columbia University Press, 2004), 136–141.

11. Ryan, *A Living Wage*, 46. My thanks to Patrick Hayes for pointing out the passage.

12. Peter Guilday, "The Catholic Church in the United States: A Sesquicentennial Essay," *Thought* 1 (June 1926), 3. On Leo and Ryan's interest in Aquinas and the Bellarmine theory, see Philip Gleason, *Contending with Modernity: Catholic Higher Education in the Twentieth Century* (New York: Oxford University Press, 1995), 125–128; and Joseph M. McShane, *"Sufficiently Radical": Catholicism, Progressivism, and the Bishops' Program of 1919* (Washington, DC: Catholic University of America Press, 1986), 31–53. See, for instance, Moorhouse F. X. Millar, "History and Development of the Democratic Theory of Government in Christian Tradition," in *The State and the Church*, eds. Millar and Ryan (New York: Macmillan, 1922), quoted on 120, 113–122; see also Joseph Husslein, "Democracy a 'Popish' Innovation," *America* 21 (July 5, 1919), 338–340.

13. John Clement Rager, *Democracy and Bellarmine* (Shelbyville, IN: Qualityprint, 1926), 3.

14. John A. Ryan, *American Democracy versus Racism, Communism* (New York: Paulist Press, 1939), 6.

15. John A. Ryan, "American Catholics and American Socialism," *Ecclesiastical Review*, December 1932, 586. For a discussion of Ryan's philosophy of democracy, see Christine Firer Hinze, "What Is Enough? Catholic Social Thought, Consumption and Material Sufficiency," in *Having: Property and Possession in Religious and Social Life*, eds. William Schweiker and Charles Mathewes (Grand Rapids, MI: Eerdmans, 2004), 62–89; J. Michael Stebbins, "Toward a Developmental Understanding of the Common Good," in *Religion and Public Life: The Legacy of Monsignor John A. Ryan*, eds. Robert Kennedy et al. (Lanham, MD: University Press of America, 2001), 119–131; and particularly K. Healen Gaston, "Demarcating Democracy: Liberal Catholics, Protestants and the Discourse of Secularism," in *American Religious Liberalism*, eds. Leigh E. Schmidt and Sally M. Promey (Indianapolis: Indiana University Press, 2012), 337–358.

16. John A. Ryan, *The Place of the Negro in American Society*, (Washington, DC: Howard University Press, 1943), 7.

17. Ryan, "American Catholics and American Socialism," 586. The phrase "organic society" was present in the papal encyclicals. See Pius XI, in *Quadragesimo Anno*, which described it as a state of affairs in which "the various occupations, being interdependent, cooperate with and mutually

complete one another, and, what is still more important . . . mind, material things, and work combine and form as it were a single whole." United States Conference of Catholic Bishops, *Compendium of the Social Doctrine of the Church* (Washington, DC: USCCB Publishing, 2004), 121.

18. Ryan, *The Place of the Negro in American Society*, 12.
19. Broderick, *Right Reverend New Dealer*, 261–263; see, for instance, Ryan, *American Democracy versus Racism*, 5–6. For his membership in the NAACP, see Ryan, "N.A.A.C.P.," *The Crisis* 24:1 (May 1922), 71.
20. Ryan, *The Place of the Negro in American Society*, 4, 5, 6, 7, 8.
21. "Mixed Army Endorsed by White Catholic," *The Baltimore Afro-American*, March 6, 1943.
22. Jacob Billikaph to John A. Ryan, March 4, 1943, John A. Ryan papers, box 2, folder 12.
23. John A. Ryan, "After the Depression," *Catholic Action*, January 1932, 6.
24. John A. Ryan, *The Constitution and Catholic Industrial Teaching* (New York: Paulist Press, 1937), 9. On Ryan's austerity, see Eugene McCarraher, *Christian Critics: Religion and the Impasse in Modern American Social Thought* (Ithaca, NY: Cornell University Press, 2000), 43.
25. Francis Haas, "Poverty and Wealth," in *Moral Factors in Economic Life*, ed. John A. Ryan (Washington, DC: National Council of Catholic Men, 1931), 12.
26. John A. Ryan, *The Relationship of Catholicism to Fascism, Socialism, and Democracy* (Washington, DC: National Catholic Welfare Council, 1938), 8–9; Ryan, "American Catholics and American Socialism," *Ecclesiastical Review*, December 1932, 586.
27. John A. Ryan. *The State and the Church* (Washington, DC: National Catholic Welfare Council, 1937), 54–55.
28. Fred O. Seier to John A. Ryan, November 11, 1936, John A. Ryan Papers, box 42, folder 17.
29. John A. Ryan, *Roosevelt Safeguards America* (New York: Democratic National Committee, 1936), 7.
30. "Msgr. Ryan Backs Coughlin's Stand," *New York Times*, December 5, 1933, 85. Cited in *Right Reverend New Dealer*, 223.
31. Charles A. Coughlin, *A Series of Lectures on Social Justice* (Royal Oak, MI: The Radio League of the Little Flower, 1933), 18. On the NUSJ and Coughlin's alienation from Roosevelt, see Sheldon Marcus, *Father Coughlin: The Tumultuous Life of the Priest of the Little Flower* (New York: Little, Brown, 1973), 64–66, 79–81; and Alan Brinkley, *Voices of Protest: Huey Long, Father Coughlin and the Great Depression* (New York: Vintage, 1983), 119–123, 287–288.
32. Coughlin, *A Series of Lectures on Social Justice*, 122–123.
33. Charles A. Coughlin, *The World Court* (Royal Oak, MI: The Radio League of the Little Flower, 1933), 4.
34. John A. Ryan, "Radio Address, January 28, 1935," John A. Ryan papers, box 42, folder 27.

35. "Text of Father Coughlin's Address," *New York Times*, July 17, 1936, 6. On Coughlin's popularity and career, see Brinkley, *Voices of Protest*, 107–124; Marcus, *Father Coughlin*, especially 71–101. For Coughlin as a demagogue and the particular details of the Cleveland address, see David Harry Bennett, *Demagogues in the Depression: American Radicals and the Union Party* (New Brunswick, NJ: Rutgers University Press, 1969), 3–30; and Raymond Gram Swing, *Forerunners of American Fascism* (New York: Julian Messner, 1935), 14–21.

36. "Text of Father Coughlin's Address," 6.

37. Ryan, *Roosevelt Safeguards America*, 6.

38. Ibid., 11–12.

39. Charles Coughlin, *Eight Lectures on Labor, Capital and Justice* (Royal Oak, MI: The Radio League of the Little Flower, 1934), 65. On primitivism, see Mircea Eliade, *Myth and Reality* (New York: Harper and Row, 1963), and Richard T. Hughes and C. Leonard Allen, *Illusions of Innocence: Protestant Primitivism in America, 1630–1875* (Urbana: University of Illinois Press, 1988).

40. Coughlin, *Eight Lectures on Labor, Capital and Justice*, 64. Brinkley, *Voices of Protest*, 99.

41. Charles Coughlin, *Father Coughlin's Radio Discourses* (Royal Oak, MI: The Radio League of the Little Flower, 1932), 83, 85.

42. Susie Kaufman to John A. Ryan, November 9, 1936, John A. Ryan Papers, box 42, folder 16 (capitalization original); Elizabeth Seymour to John A. Ryan, October 12, 1936, John A. Ryan Papers, box 42, folder 4; Ambrose Tenure to John A. Ryan, November 16, 1936, John A. Ryan Papers, box 42, folder 18.

43. Mrs. Frank Lamphear to John A. Ryan, November 9, 1936, John A. Ryan Papers, box 42, folder 16. On anticlericalism from non-Catholics, see John Higham, *Strangers in the Land: Patterns of American Nativism, 1860–1925* (New Brunswick, NJ: Rutgers University Press, 1983), 177–178; on anticlericalism within American Catholicism, see Jay Dolan, *The American Catholic Experience* (New York: Doubleday, 1985), 173–174.

44. "Jim" to John A. Ryan, November 24, 1936, John A. Ryan Papers, box 42, folder 21; Marguerite Frost to John A. Ryan, October 13, 1936, John A. Ryan Papers, box 42, folder 11.

45. Coughlin, *Eight Lectures on Labor, Capital and Justice*, 62, 7–8. Coughlin's religious hostility to Roosevelt was mirrored in many conservative Protestants' similarly conspiratorial thinking. See Matthew Avery Sutton, "Was FDR the Antichrist? The Birth of Fundamentalist Antiliberalism in a Global Age," *Journal of American History* 98:4 (March 2012), 1052–1074.

46. Coughlin, *Driving out the Money-Changers* (Royal Oak, MI: The Radio League of the Little Flower, 1933), 39. On Coughlin's anti-Semitism, see Brinkley, *Voices of Protest*, 269–273.

47. Ryan, *Social Doctrine in Action*, 263–264.

48. "Coughlin Apology Made to Roosevelt," *New York Times*, July 23, 1936, 1.

49. "Two Political Priests," *Catholic Review*, October 16, 1936, 1.

50. J. S. Nelson to John A. Ryan, October 9, 1936, John A. Ryan Papers, box 41, folder 20.

51. Dorothy Day, *The Long Loneliness* (New York: Harper, 1952), 165. On Ryan and Day at the Shrine, see Thomas A. Tweed, *America's Church: The National Shrine and Catholic Presence in the Nation's Capital* (New York: Oxford University Press, 2011), 166–168.

52. Peter Maurin, *Easy Essays* (Eugene, OR: Wipf and Stock, 2003), 7.

53. Rufus Barrow points out that there are "at least a dozen" types of personalism; Rufus Barrow, *Personalism: A Critical Introduction* (St. Louis, MO: Chalice Press, 1999), 12. Jacques Maritain noted wryly that some of them had no more in common than the word *person;* cited in Thomas D. Williams, *Who Is My Neighbor? Personalism and the Foundations of Human Rights* (Washington, DC: Catholic University of America Press, 2005), 138. However, he also argues that the uniqueness and dignity of the individual experience is a useful measuring rod.

54. Dorothy Day, *Peter Maurin: Apostle to the World* (Maryknoll, NY: Orbis Books, 2004), 35–36. On personalism in the Catholic Worker movement, I am indebted to Geoffrey B. Gneuhs, "Peter Maurin's Personalist Democracy," in *A Revolution of the Heart: Essays on the Catholic Worker,* ed. Patrick G. Coy (Philadelphia: Temple University Press, 1988), 47–69; and Marc H. Ellis, *Peter Maurin: Prophet in the Twentieth Century* (Eugene, OR: Wipf and Stock, 2003).

55. Dorothy Day, *Loaves and Fishes* (Maryknoll, NY: Orbis Books, 1997), 22.

56. Maurin, *Easy Essays,* 8.

57. Dorothy Day, "Catholic Worker Celebrates Third Birthday," *Catholic Worker,* May 1936, 1, 6.

58. Ibid., 6.

59. Dorothy Day, *House of Hospitality* (New York: Wipf and Stock, 1939), 265.

60. Dorothy Day, "Co-operative Apartment for Unemployed Women Has Its Start in Parish," *Catholic Worker,* December 1933, 1. Day, *Houses of Hospitality,* 42–49.

61. Dorothy Day, "Letter to our Readers," *Catholic Worker,* May 1947, 3.

62. Dorothy Day, "Aims and Purposes," *Catholic Worker,* February 1940, 7. Fisher explores Day's commitment to the Body of Christ in *The Catholic Counterculture in America,* 11–12, 38–42.

63. Dorothy Day, "Relief and Birth Control," *Catholic Worker,* January 1935, 3. On Day's opinions about social welfare, see also Harry Murray, "Dorothy Day, Welfare Reform, and Personal Responsibility," *St. John's Law Review* 73:3 (Summer 1999), 789–804. For her opinions of the New Deal in particular, see Mel Piehl, *Breaking Bread: The Catholic Worker and the Origin of Catholic Radicalism in America* (Philadelphia: Temple University Press, 1982), 232–242.

64. Dorothy Day, "More about Holy Poverty, Which Is Voluntary Poverty," *Catholic Worker,* February 1945, 1.

65. Dorothy Day, "C. W.'s Position," *Catholic Worker,* July–August 1940, 1. On Day and the draft, see Eileen Egan, "Dorothy Day: Pilgrim of Peace," in *A Revolution of the Heart,* ed. Coy, 69–114.

66. Dorothy Day, "Our Stand," *Catholic Worker,* June 1940, 1.

67. Dorothy Day, "Wars Are Caused by Man's Loss of Faith in Man," *Catholic Worker,* September 1940, 1.

68. On the Catholic revival, see Philip Gleason, "In Search of Unity: American Catholic Thought, 1920–1960," *Catholic Historical Review* 65:2 (April 1979), 185–205.

69. "Apostolic Letter of Pope Pius XI," reproduced in "Preliminary Memorandum: July 25, 1939," Commission on American Citizenship Records, box 1, folder 2, Special Collections, Catholic University of America, Washington, DC. For Pius's anxiety about Nazism, see Claudia Carlen, ed., *The Papal Encyclicals: 1740–1981* (Ann Arbor, MI: Pierien Press, 1990) 3:525–536. For a discussion of the origins of the encyclical, see John Francis Pollard, *The Papacy in the Age of Totalitarianism, 1914–1948* (New York: Oxford University Press, 2014), 265–274; and "A New Basal Reading Series," Commission on American Citizenship Records, box 1, folder 1.

70. Archbishop Dennis Dougherty Press Release, November 21, 1938, Commission on American Citizenship Records, box 1, folder 2.

71. Joseph Corrigan, "Report of the Commission on American Citizenship," [1942], Commission on American Citizenship Records, box 1, folder 1. The careful wording should be noted; it specifies Catholicism only in the United States, for instance. On Americanism, see Scott Appleby, *Church and Age Unite: The Modernist Impulse in American Catholicism* (South Bend, IN: Notre Dame University Press, 1992).

72. Daniel Sargent, "A Word about Maritain," *Commonweal* 19 (March 23, 1934), 567.

73. Jacques Maritain, "The Reconciliation of the Gospel and Democracy," [1944], 22, 21, 19, John A. Ryan Papers, box 50, folder 19. The talk encapsulates many ideas in Maritain, *Christianity and Democracy* (San Francisco: Ignatian Press, 1944). On Maritain in the United States, see John T. McGreevy, *Catholicism and American Freedom: A History* (New York: W.W. Norton, 2003), 194–210; and Gleason, *Contending with Modernity,* 163–164.

74. On the organization of the commission, see C. Joseph Nuesse, *The Catholic University of America: A History* (Washington, DC: Catholic University of America Press, 1990), 297–298; Francis Haas to Patrick McCormick, October 27, 1942, Commission on American Citizenship Records, box 1, folder 1; Robert H. Connery, "Commission on American Citizenship Progress Report, November 14, 1939," Commission on American Citizenship Records, box 1, folder 2.

75. A discussion of the titles of these books is in "Report on the Commission on American Citizenship," November 10, 1942, Commission on American Citizenship Records, box 1, folder 1.

76. Sister Mary Thomas Aquinas and Katherine Keaneally, *Methods and Procedures for This Is Our Land: Fourth Reader* (Boston: Ginn and Company, 1942), 3. On the religious-education movement and its understanding of the relationship among character, democracy, and religion, see David Setran, "Morality and the Democracy of God: George Albert Coe and the Liberal Protestant Critique of American Character Education, 1917–1940," *Religion and American Culture* 15:1 (Winter 2005), particularly 109–113; and Heather Warren, "Character, Public Schooling, and Religious Education," *Church History* 7:1 (Winter 1997), 61–80.

77. George Albert Coe, *A Social Theory of Religious Education* (New York: Scribner's, 1917), 134. On this balance, see John L. Elias, "Education in Time of War: George Johnson and the Commission on American Citizenship of the Catholic University of America," *Religious Education* 104:2 (April 2009), 133–148.

78. Robert Connery, *Americans All: A Student Handbook of the Catholic Civics Clubs* (Washington, DC: Catholic University of America Press, 1940), 3–4.

79. George Johnson, "The Duties of Teachers in the Defense of American Democracy, *Catholic Educational Review* (October 1940), 451, 457–458.

80. *The Teaching of Current Affairs: A Teacher's Manual* (Washington, DC: Catholic University Press, 1940), 4, 7.

81. "Report on the Commission on American Citizenship, 1946," 1, Commission on American Citizenship Records, box 10, folder 18.

82. George Johnson, "The Commission on American Citizenship at the Catholic University of America," *Journal of Educational Sociology* 16:6 (February 1943), 380–385.

83. Mary Thomas Aquinas and Mary Synon, *This Is Our Heritage* (Boston: Ginn and Company, 1943), 54, 163–164.

84. Mary Marguerite, *This Is Our Town* (Boston: Ginn and Company, 1942), 12–15, 100, 178, 289.

85. Marguerite, *This Is Our Town*, 39; Aquinas and Synon, *This Is Our Heritage*, 191–196.

86. Aquinas and Synon, *This Is Our Heritage*, 396–399.

87. Aquinas and Keneally, *Methods and Procedures for This Is Our Land*, 94, 144.

88. Aquinas and Synon, *This Is Our Heritage*, 346.

89. Aquinas and Keaneally, *Methods and Procedures for This Is Our Land*, 63.

5. The Anxiety of Christian Anticommunism

1. Whittaker Chambers, *Witness* (1952; Washington, DC: Regnery Press, 2001), 17–19. See also Sam Tanenhaus, *Whittaker Chambers: A Biography* (New York: Random House, 1997), xx–xxii.

2. Chambers, *Witness*, 8.

3. For a discussion of ex-communists and the literature of witness, see Michael Kimmage, *The Conservative Turn: Lionel Trilling, Whittaker Chambers, and the*

Lessons of Anti-Communism (Cambridge, MA: Harvard University Press, 2009), 142–158, 215–222, 228–229. On Chambers's theory of history, see Hyrum Lewis, "Sacralizing the Right: William F. Buckley Jr., Whittaker Chambers, Will Herberg and the Transformation of Intellectual Conservatism, 1945–1964," PhD dissertation, University of Southern California, 2007, 70–74.

4. Wendy L. Wall, *Inventing the "American Way": The Politics of Consensus from the New Deal to the Civil Rights Movement* (New York: Oxford University Press, 2008), Jonathan P. Herzog, *The Spiritual Industrial Complex* (New York: Oxford University Press, 2011), and Kevin Kruse, *One Nation under God: How Corporate America Invented Christian America* (New York: Basic Books, 2015) argue that national unity around a particular version of Christianity was fomented by anxious elites in the postwar years. Raymond Haberski, in *God and War: American Civil Religion since 1945* (New Brunswick: Rutgers University Press, 2012), 12–13, also discusses the ways in which the notion of a consensus was generated by some American Christians but hardly characterized all.

5. For discussion of Eisenhower's claim, see Patrick Henry, " 'And I Don't Care What It Is': The Tradition-History of a Civil Religion Proof-Text," *Journal of the American Academy of Religion* 49:1 (March 1981), 35–49.

6. For works that emphasize American anxiety, see Robert S. Ellwood, *1950: Crossroads of American Religious Life* (Louisville, KY: Westminster John Knox Press, 2000), 1–3; Stephen Whitfield, *The Culture of the Cold War* (Baltimore, MD: Johns Hopkins University Press, 1996), 77–101; William Inboden, *Religion and American Foreign Policy, 1945–1960: The Soul of Containment* (New York: Cambridge University Press, 2008).

7. Fulton Sheen, *The Cross and the Crisis* (New York: Books for Libraries Press, 1969), viii. Kevin Schultz, *Tri-Faith America: How Catholics and Jews Held Postwar America to Its Protestant Promise* (New York: Oxford University Press, 2011), 56–60.

8. The phrase "theological revival" is Andrew Finstuen's. He explores these two groups in *Original Sin and Everyday Protestants: The Theology of Reinhold Niebuhr, Billy Graham, and Paul Tillich in an Age of Anxiety* (Chapel Hill: University of North Carolina Press, 2009). See especially 13–47; Miller is cited on 34. Finstuen drew the concept from theologian John Bennett's article "Two Revivals," *Christianity and Crisis* (December 28, 1959), 193. The first *Time* article was on Reinhold Niebuhr: "Faith for a Lenten Age," *Time*, March 8, 1948; the second on Fulton Sheen: "Microphone Missionary," *Time*, April 14, 1952. See also Herberg's essay and others in Ben Zion Bokser, *Judaism and Modern Man* (New York: Theological Library, 1957).

9. Ellen Herman, *The Romance of American Psychology: Political Culture in the Age of Experts* (Berkeley: University of California Press, 1995), 2–20.

10. Fulton J. Sheen, *Peace of Soul* (New York: McGraw Hill, 1949), 2. On Sheen's approach to psychology, see Robert Kugelmann, *Psychology and Catholicism: Contested Boundaries* (New York: Cambridge University Press, 2011), 193–197.

11. Fulton J. Sheen, "The Psychology of a Frustrated Soul," January 4, 1948, in Sheen, *The Modern Soul in Search of God: Thirteen Addresses Delivered In The Nationwide Catholic Hour* (Washington DC: National Council of Catholic Men, 1950), 9.; Fulton J. Sheen, *You* (Washington, DC: National Conference of Catholic Men, 1947), 17–20.

12. "Candida: The Audience Was Polite," *Newsweek*, August 20, 1945, 89; *Congressional Record* 91:3 (Washington DC: Government Printing Office, 1945), 4167; Sylvia Jukes Morris, *The Price of Fame: The Honorable Clare Boothe Luce* (New York: Random House, 2012), 133–134, 142–147.

13. Clare Boothe Luce, "The Real Reason," *McCall's*, March 1947, 160; Morris, *The Price of Fame*, 156–157.

14. Norman Vincent Peale, *The Power of Positive Thinking* (New York: Fawcett Crest, 1984), 60. On Peale and the New Thought movement, see Joseph W. Williams, *Spirit Cure: A History of Pentecostal Healing* (New York: Oxford University Press, 2013), 76–78; on Peale's background, see Carol V. R. George, *God's Salesman: Norman Vincent Peale and the Power of Positive Thinking* (New York: Oxford University Press, 1993), 10–12, and Christopher Lane, *Surge of Piety: Norman Vincent Peale and the Remaking of American Religious Life* (New Haven: Yale University Press, 2016), 19–38.

15. Pius XII, "On Psychotherapy and Religion," *Catholic Documents* 11 (May 1953), 15.

16. James A. Pike, *Beyond Anxiety* (New York: Scribner's, 1953), 6; Curtis Cate, "God and Success," *Atlantic Monthly* (April 1957), 75.

17. On the role of publishing in fostering this style of Christianity, see Matthew S. Hedstrom, *The Rise of Liberal Religion: Book Culture and Spirituality in the Twentieth Century* (New York: Oxford University Press, 2012).

18. William Z. Foster, *The Twilight of World Capitalism* (New York: International Publishers, 1949), 56. Noncommunists agreed; see for instance Morris Ernst and David Loth, *Report on the American Communist* (New York: Holt, 1952), 127.

19. Fulton J. Sheen, *Communism and the Conscience of the West* (New York: Macmillan, 1948), 49, 80. My interpretation of Sheen owes a debt to Kathleen Riley, *Fulton J. Sheen: An American Catholic Response to the Twentieth Century* (New York: Alba House, 2004), 16–18.

20. Chambers, *Witness*, 15, 105–107, 185.

21. Bella V. Dodd, *School of Darkness* (New York: Devin-Adair, 1954), 85.

22. Louis Budenz, *This Is My Story* (New York: McGraw Hill, 1947), 39–40, 47, 49, 52, 56. See also Jimmy Randal Grant, "Louis Francis Budenz: The Origins of a Professional Anti-Communist," PhD dissertation, University of South Carolina, 2006, 39–45.

23. Richard Wright, "I Tried to Be a Communist," *Atlantic Monthly*, September 1944, 61–64. See also James Zeigler, *Red Scare Racism and Cold War Radicalism* (Oxford: University of Mississippi Press, 2015), 58–97.

24. Cited in Wayne Cooper, *Claude McKay: Rebel Sojourner in the Harlem Renaissance* (Baton Rouge: Louisiana State University Press, 1996), 65.

25. Claude McKay, "Soviet Russia and the Negro," in *The Crisis Reader: Stories, Poetry and Essays from the NAACP Crisis Magazine,* ed. Sondra Wilson (New York: Modern Library, 1999), 286.

26. Budenz, *This Is My Story,* 115.

27. Wright, "I Tried to be a Communist," 62.

28. Elizabeth Bentley, *Out of Bondage* (New York: Devin-Adair, 1951), 10. Bentley's narrative was heavily shaped by her lover Joseph Brunini, a Catholic who also served on the grand jury that heard her initial testimony. See Kathryn S. Olmstead, *Red Spy Queen: A Biography of Elizabeth Bentley* (Chapel Hill: University of North Carolina Press, 2002), 156–158.

29. Peter C. Kent, *The Lonely Cold War of Pope Pius XII: The Roman Catholic Church and the Division of Europe, 1943–1950* (Montreal: McGill-Queen's University Press, 2002), 114–116, 226–229; Paul Betts, "Religion, Science, and Cold War Communism: The 1949 Cardinal Mindszenty Show Trial," in *Science, Religion and Communism in Cold War Europe,* eds. Betts and Stephen A. Smith (London: Palgrave Macmillan, 2016), 275–305.

30. Betts, "Religion, Science, and Cold War Communism," 295–297; Nicholas Boer, *Cardinal Mindszenty and the Implacable War of Communism against Religion and the Spirit* (Berlin: BUE, 1949), 297.

31. Ferenc Nagy, "Attack on a Soul," *Life,* February 21, 1949, 28, and Susan L. Carruthers, *Cold War Captives: Imprisonment, Escape and Brainwashing* (Berkeley: University of California Press, 2009), 136–139.

32. Carruthers, *Cold War Captives,* 174–217; Ron Robin, *The Making of the Cold War Enemy: Culture and Politics in the Military-Intellectual Complex* (Princeton, NJ: Princeton University Press, 2001), 162–185.

33. B. F. Skinner, *Science and Human Behavior* (New York: The Free Press, 1953), 285. Laura McKenzie Zeiss, "Cold War Fictions of Behaviorism: Theories of Psychological Influence in American Cold War Literature," PhD dissertation, University of California, Irvine, 2008, 1–28, 60–64.

34. B. F. Skinner, *Walden Two* (1948; Saddle River, NJ: Prentice-Hall, 1976), 87, 89. See also Michelle M. Nickerson, *Mothers of Conservatism: Women and the Postwar Right* (Princeton: Princeton University Press, 2012), 103–136, for popular suspicion of the "mental health establishment" and its ability to exert control over the mind.

35. Cleon Skousen, *The Naked Communist* (Salt Lake City: Ensign Publishing, 1960), 1.

36. Edward Hunter, *Brainwashing from Pavlov to Powers* (New York: Bookmaster, 1960), 309; Edward Hunter, *Communist Psychological Warfare* (Washington, DC: Government Printing Office, 1958), 14. Robin, *The Making of the Cold War Enemy,* 94–124; Herman, *The Romance of American Psychology,* 124–153.

37. Edward Hunter, *Brainwashing: The Story of the Men Who Defied It* (New York: Pyramid Books, 1968), 249, 251, 269.

38. William H. Whyte, *The Organization Man* (New York: Simon and Schuster, 1956), 3; C. Wright Mills, *White Collar: The American Middle Classes* (New

York: Oxford University Press, 1951), 187. These fears have generated a
great deal of scholarship; see for instance Elaine Tyler May, *Homeward
Bound: American Families in the Cold War Era* (New York: Basic Books,
1999), especially 124, and George Marsden, *The Twilight of the American
Enlightenment: The 1950s and the Crisis of Liberal Belief* (New York: Basic
Books, 2014), 4–20.

39. Dodd, *School of Darkness*, 222–223.
40. Wright, "I Tried to Be a Communist," 65.
41. Joseph McCarthy, *McCarthyism: The Fight for America* (New York: Devin-
Adair, 1952), 1–2; the book was, in the words of William Walker, "assembled" by McCarthy's assistant Jean Kerr, from McCarthy's speeches.
William T. Walker, *McCarthyism and the Red Scare: A Reference Guide* (Santa
Barbara, CA: ABC-Clio, 2011), 66.
42. "McCarthy Wars on Traitors in American Life," *Chicago Tribune*, July 10,
1952, 5.
43. Elizabeth Bentley, *Out of Bondage*, 184, 188, 173, 196.
44. Dodd, *School of Darkness*, 13, 15, 153, 47.
45. Chambers, *Witness*, 16.
46. Dodd, *School of Darkness*, 209.
47. "Report of Employment of Homosexuals in Government," *Senate Subcom-
mittee on Investigations* (Washington, DC: Government Printing Office,
1950), 4. See also Kyle A. Cuordileone, *Manhood and American Political
Culture in the Cold War* (New York: Routledge, 2005), 67–88; David K.
Johnson, *The Lavender Scare: The Cold War Persecution of Gays and Lesbians
in the Federal Government* (Chicago: University of Chicago Press, 2004),
31–38.
48. House Committee on Un-American Activities, *Hearings Regarding Communism in the United States Government*, 80th Congress, 2nd session (Washington,
DC: Government Printing Office, 1948), 551. These hearings are discussed in
Veronica A. Wilson, "Elizabeth Bentley and Cold War Representation: Some
Masks Not Dropped," *Intelligence and National Security* 14:2 (Summer 1999),
49–69.
49. Claudia Carlen, ed., *The Papal Encyclicals: 1740–1981* (Ann Arbor, MI: Pierien
Press, 1990), 3:525–536. For a discussion of its origins, see John Francis Pollard,
The Papacy in the Age of Totalitarianism, 1914–1958 (New York: Oxford Univer-
sity Press, 2014), 265–274.
50. Universal Declaration of Human Rights, paragraph 1, discussed in Samuel
Moyn, "Personalism, Community and the Origins of Human Rights," in
Human Rights in the Twentieth Century, Stefan Ludwig-Hoffman, ed. (New
York: Cambridge University Press, 2014), 85–106, and Samuel Moyn, *Chris-
tian Human Rights* (Philadelphia: University of Pennsylvania Press, 2015),
especially 25–65.
51. Fulton Sheen, "False Liberty," *The Catholic Hour*, January 8, 1939, 15, 17–18, and
"True Liberty," *The Catholic Hour*, January 15, 1939, 28, Fulton J. Sheen Papers,

box 1, folder 8, American Catholic History Research Center and University Archives, Catholic University of America, Washington DC. On "Judeo-Christianity," see Mark Silk, *Spiritual Politics: Religion and America Since 1945* (New York: Simon and Schuster, 1989), 40–54; for a contemporary advocate, Paul Tillich, "Is There a Judeo-Christian Tradition?" (New York: American Jewish Congress, 1952). Schultz, *Tri-Faith America*, 56–57, 87–89.

52. The essay was originally published in *The Atlantic* in 1957; reprinted in Reinhold Niebuhr, *Pious and Secular America* (New York: Scribner's 1958), 2, 6, 13. Reinhold Niebuhr, "Democracy, Secularism and Christianity," *Christianity and Crisis* 13:3 (March 2, 1953), 19–20; Daniel F. Rice, *Reinhold Niebuhr and John Dewey: An American Odyssey* (Albany: SUNY Press, 1993), 236–240. Niebuhr expresses suspicion about American devotion to democracy in his earlier "Democracy as a Religion," *Christianity and Crisis* 7:8 (August 4, 1947), 1. Niebuhr foreshadows Charles Taylor's second and third definition of the secular: a nonreligious force which creates meaning, and a regime in which religious belief is one option among many. Charles Taylor, *A Secular Age* (Cambridge, MA: Harvard University Press, 2007), 1–5. The gloominess of 1940s and 1950s American religious life is explored in Jason W. Stevens, *God-Fearing and Free: A Spiritual History of America's Cold War* (Cambridge, MA: Harvard University Press, 2010); he argues that the era repudiated the sunnier Protestant optimism of the pre-Depression era.

53. Robert Ashworth, *The Story of the National Conference of Christians and Jews* (Washington, DC: National Conference of Christians and Jews, 1950), 8–9, 81. See also Victoria Barnett, "'Fault Lines': An Analysis of the National Conference of Christians and Jews," PhD Dissertation, George Mason University, 2012, 60–61. Quotation from a 1933 transcript, cited in Barnett, "'Fault Lines,'" 74. Schultz, *Tri-Faith America*, 15–18, explores the NCCJ's notion of religious diversity as a source of democracy.

54. Dodd, *School of Darkness*, 236–237. See also Bella V. Dodd, "I Found Sanctuary," in *Roads to Rome: The Intimate Personal Stories of Converts to the Catholic Faith*, ed. John O'Brien (New York: Macmillan, 1954), 48–50.

55. Bentley, *Out of Bondage*, 197–198; Olmstead, *Red Spy Queen*, 158.

56. Granville Hicks, "Arnold Toynbee's Balance Sheet," *New York Times*, May 2, 1948, 205.

57. Eileen Summers, "Indeed, There Is a Mrs. Toynbee," *Washington Post*, November 14, 1954, S6.

58. Whittaker Chambers, "Historian Arnold J. Toynbee," *Time*, March 17, 1947. For Toynbee's fame, see William H. McNeill, *Arnold J. Toynbee* (New York: Oxford University Press, 1989), 213–216.

59. Will Durant and Ariel Durant, *A Dual Autobiography* (New York: Simon and Schuster, 1977), 277, 17.

60. Will Durant and Ariel Durant, *Lessons of History* (New York: Simon and Schuster, 1968), 51.

61. Arnold Toynbee, *A Historian's Approach to Religion* (New York: Oxford University Press, 1956), 266–267. See also William H. McNeill, "Some

Basic Assumptions of Toynbee's *A Study of History*," in *The Intent of Toynbee's History*, ed. Edward Gargan (Chicago: Loyola University Press, 1961), 35–38.

62. "A Study of History," *Life*, February 23, 1948, 132. See, for instance, "Dr. Toynbee and Mr. Stimson Point the Way to Our Salvation," *Baltimore Sun*, September 22, 1947, 22; McNeill, *Arnold J. Toynbee*, 216–220.

63. "Will Durant Explains Interdependence Aims," *Los Angeles Times*, April 23, 1945, 8; "Durant Leader in Move to Aid World Amity," *Los Angeles Times*, April 11, 1945, 7.

64. "West in Paradox, Toynbee Asserts," *New York Times*, October 30, 1955, 71; Arnold Toynbee, *A Study of History* (New York: Oxford University Press, 1946), 2:339.

65. Durant and Durant, *Lessons of History*, 43, 37, 96.

66. Will Durant, *Our Oriental Heritage* (New York: Simon and Schuster, 1935), viii–ix, 937–938.

67. D.G. Somervell, ed., *Arnold Toynbee's A Study of History* (New York: Oxford University Press, 1988), 1:8, 6–8.

68. Arthur Schlesinger, *The Vital Center: The Politics of Freedom* (1949; New York: Transaction Publishers, 1998), 104, 170, 223. Philip Gorski argues that Schlesinger's enunciation of the Cold War consensus's "middle way" remains valuable for the United States today: *American Covenant: A History of Civil Religion from the Puritans to the Present* (Princeton, NJ: Princeton University Press, 2017), 1–2.

69. The text of the speech and of the question-and-answer session are available at "Speech of Senator John F. Kennedy, Greater Houston Ministerial Association, Rice Hotel, Houston, TX, September 12, 1960," The American Presidency Project, accessed February 13, 2017, http://www.presidency .ucsb.edu/ws/?pid=25773; and "Question and Answer Period Following Speech of Senator John F. Kennedy, Ministerial Association of Greater Houston, Houston, TX, September 12, 1960," The American Presidency Project, accessed February 13, 2017, http://www.presidency.ucsb.edu/ws/ ?pid=25774.

70. John Courtnay Murray, *We Hold These Truths: Catholic Reflections on the American Proposition* (1960; New York: Rowman and Littlefield, 2005), 42, 191–192. John O'Malley, *What Happened at Vatican II* (Cambridge: Harvard University Press, 2010), 211–218.

71. John F. Kennedy, "Remarks at the Dedication Breakfast of International Christian Leadership, Inc., February 9, 1961," The American Presidency Project, accessed February 13, 2017, http://www.presidency.ucsb.edu/ws/?pid =8211.

72. Robert F. Kennedy, *To Seek a Newer World* (New York: Bantam Books, 1967), 24, 18–19.

73. William F. Buckley, "Nihil Obstat," *National Review*, January 28, 1961, 56–57.

74. William F. Buckley, *God and Man at Yale: The Superstitions of Academic Freedom* (New York: Regnery, 1951), lxvi, 7, 29.

75. William F. Buckley, *Up from Liberalism* (New York: McDowell, 1959), 68. Kimmage, *The Conservative Turn*, 228–230, 236–246. Neil J. Young discusses conservative dissent from ecumenism in *We Gather Together: The Religious Right and the Problem of Interfaith Politics* (New York: Oxford University Press, 2015), 3–8.

76. Harold J. Ockenga, "Christ for America," May 1943, 13–14, Harold J. Ockenga Papers, Gordon Conwell Theological Seminary, North Hamilton, MA. Cited in Matthew Avery Sutton, *American Apocalypse: A History of Modern Evangelicalism* (Cambridge, MA: Harvard University Press, 2014), 283.

77. Quoted in Ronald Taylor, *Chavez and the Farm Workers* (Boston: Beacon Press, 1975), 81. On Chavez's immersion in Catholic social teaching, see Marvin Krier Mich, *The Challenge and Spirituality of Catholic Social Teaching* (Maryknoll, NY: Orbis Books, 2011), 188–198.

78. Cesar Chavez, "Peregrinacion, Penitencia, Revolucion," in *The Words of Cesar Chavez*, eds. Richard Jay Jensen and John C. Hammerback (College Station: Texas A&M University Press, 2002), 16–17. On the march, I have used Susan Ferriss and Ricardo Sandoval, *The Fight in the Fields: Cesar Chavez and the Farmworkers Movement* (New York: Harcourt Brace, 1997), 116–119.

6. Global Christianity and Black Freedom

1. Martin Luther King Jr., "'I've Been to the Mountaintop:' Address Delivered at the Bishop Charles Mason Temple, April 3, 1968," in *A Call to Conscience: The Landmark Speeches of Martin Luther King, Jr.*, eds. Clayborne Carson and Kris Shepard (New York: IPM/Warner Books, 2001), 209.

2. The ACOA's Declaration of Conscience is reprinted in Lewis V. Baldwin, *To Make the Wounded Whole: The Cultural Legacy of Martin Luther King, Jr.* (Minneapolis: Augsburg Press, 1992), 205–206.

3. Carson and Shepard, eds., *A Call to Conscience*, 44.

4. Martin Luther King, Jr. *Why We Can't Wait* (New York: Penguin, 1964), 119–120. Tim Lake, "Martin Luther King, Jr.: Toward a Democratic Theory," in *The Liberatory Thought of Martin Luther King, Jr.: Critical Essays on the Philosopher King*, ed. Robert E. Birt (Lanham, MD: Lexington Books, 2012), 177–197, argues that King believed in the "democratizing potential" of the American system, though not uncritically. These two sides to King's thought are related to Michael C. Dawson's notions of "radical egalitarianism" and "disillusioned liberalism," as discussed in *Black Visions: The Roots of Contemporary African-American Political Ideologies* (Chicago: University of Chicago Press, 2001), 15–18.

5. I draw here from Nikhil Pal Singh, *Black is a Country: Race and the Unfinished Struggle for Democracy* (Cambridge, MA: Harvard University Press, 2005), 3–18. On the competing impulses in King's background and education, see James H. Cone, "Martin Luther King—Black Theology, Black Church," *Theology Today* 40:4 (January 1984), 409–420.

6. Alex Haley interview with Malcolm X, in David Gallen, *Malcolm X: As They Knew Him* (New York: Ballantine Books, 1995), 109–130.

7. Gayraud S. Wilmore, *Black Religion and Black Radicalism: An Interpretation of the Religious History of Afro-Americans*, 2nd ed. (Maryknoll, NY: Orbis Books, 1983), 167–191. See also Mark I. Chapman, *Christianity on Trial: African American Religious Thought before and after Black Power* (Maryknoll, NY: Orbis Books, 1996). For scholars who concur with Wilmore, see Charles Marsh, *God's Long Summer: Stories of Faith and Civil Rights* (Princeton, NJ: Princeton University Press, 1997) and Charles M. Payne, *I've Got the Light of Freedom: The Organizing Tradition and the Mississippi Freedom Struggle* (Berkeley: University of California Press, 1995), especially 364–367.

8. For scholars who connect Christianity and the Black Power movement, see Kerry Pimblott, *Faith in Black Power: Religion, Race and Resistance in Cairo, Illinois* (Lexington: University Press of Kentucky, 2017) and Angela D. Dillard, *Faith in the City: Preaching Radical Social Change in Detroit* (Ann Arbor: University of Michigan Press, 2007).

9. Martin Luther King, Jr., "Paul's Letter to American Christians," in *A Knock at Midnight: Inspiration from the Great Sermons of Reverend Martin Luther King, Jr.*, eds. Clayborne Carson and Peter Halloran (New York: Warner Books, 1998), 29–32. Thomas F. Jackson explores the connections King drew between economic injustice and racism in *From Civil Rights to Human Rights: Martin Luther King, Jr. and the Struggle for Economic Justice* (Philadelphia: University of Pennsylvania Press, 2007), 2–5. On King's use of the prophetic style, see David Chappell, *A Stone of Hope: Prophetic Religion and the Death of Jim Crow* (Chapel Hill: University of North Carolina Press, 2009), 44–67, and Lewis V. Baldwin, *There Is a Balm in Gilead: The Cultural Roots of Martin Luther King, Jr.* (Minneapolis, MN: Fortress Press, 1991), 273–337. For the liberal Protestant education of SCLC leaders, see David Garrow, *Bearing the Cross: Martin Luther King and the Southern Christian Leadership Conference* (New York: HarperCollins, 1999), 42–52. Penny von Eschen, *Race against Empire: Black Americans and Anticolonialism* (Ithaca: Cornell University Press, 1997).

10. *Handbook for Freedom Army Recruits*, Records of the Southern Christian Leadership Conference, 1954–1970, Part 4: Records of the Program Department, Series IV, Records of the Voter Registration and Political Education Project 1963–1968, Subseries 2, Box 169:17, Martin Luther King, Jr. Library and Archives, Atlanta, Georgia.

11. Martin Luther King, Jr., to John F. Kennedy, September 1963, Records of the Southern Christian Leadership Conference, 1954–1970, Part 1: Records of the President's Office, Series I: Correspondence, Subseries 2, Primary Correspondents, 1958–1967, Box 4:20, Martin Luther King, Jr. Library and Archives.

12. Cited in Richard Kluger, *Simple Justice: The History of Brown v. Board of Education and Black America's Struggle for Equality* (New York: Vintage Books, 2004), 221. On Marshall's fundraising trips, see Juan Williams, *Thurgood*

Marshall: American Revolutionary (New York: Random House, 1998), 110, 242–246.

13. Williams, *Thurgood Marshall*, 241.

14. Near the end of his life he claimed that his activism "did not spring from being black." Rather, he rooted it in his "Quaker upbringing and the values instilled in me by grandparents who reared me. . . . Those values were based on the concept of a single human family and the belief that all members of that family are equal." Bayard Rustin, *Time on Two Crosses: The Collected Writings of Bayard Rustin* (New York: Simon and Schuster, 2003), 3–4. See also Sebastian Galbo, "The 'Roving Ambassador': Bayard Rustin's Quaker Cosmopolitanism and the Civil Rights Movement," *Inquiries Journal* 6:4 (2014), 1–4, and Jervis Anderson, *Bayard Rustin: Troubles I've Seen* (New York: HarperCollins, 1997), 20–23. On Rustin's marginalization in the SCLC, see Jerald Podair, *Bayard Rustin: American Dreamer* (Lanham, MD: Rowman and Littlefield, 2009), 42–43.

15. Bayard Rustin, "The Nature of the Present Crisis," 3, Articles on Civil Rights, 1940s–1950s, box 39, Bayard Rustin Papers, Library of Congress, Washington, DC. Bayard Rustin, *In Apprehension How Like a God!* (Philadelphia: Young Friends Movement, 1948), 18, 28, Articles on Civil Rights, 1940s–1950s, box 39, Bayard Rustin Papers, Library of Congress, Washington, DC.

16. Bayard Rustin, "General Observations on the Journey of Reconciliation," in Bayard Rustin, *Down the Line: the Collected Writings of Bayard Rustin* (Chicago: Quadrangle Books, 1971), 15, 22–23. On the Journey of Reconciliation and Rustin's part in it, see Derek Charles Catsam, *Freedom's Main Line: The Journey of Reconciliation and the Freedom Rides* (Lexington: University Press of Kentucky, 2009), 18–28. Chappell, *A Stone of Hope*, 105–131.

17. Bayard Rustin, *In Apprehension How Like a God!*, 3, Articles on Civil Rights, 1940s–1950s, box 39, Bayard Rustin Papers.

18. Enlarged Meeting of the Working Committee of the Department on Studies in Evangelism, World Council of Churches Division of Studies, "A Case Study—The Freedom Movement," April 16, 1964, 1–2, Records of the Southern Christian Leadership Conference, 1954–1970, Part 4: Records of the Program Department, Series I, Records of Andrew J. Young, Program Director, 1961–1964, Subseries 1, Office Files, 1961–1964, Box 135:21, Martin Luther King, Jr. Library and Archives. On Young's role in the production of the report and the work of the WCC, see Andrew Young, *An Easy Burden: The Civil Rights Movement and the Transformation of America* (Waco, TX: Baylor University Press, 1994), 410–411; Andrew DeRoche, *Andrew Young: Civil Rights Ambassador* (Wilmington, DE: Scholarly Resources, 2003), 32.

19. "WCC Asks Ghana to Reconsider Expulsion Order, 21 August 1962," Records of the Southern Christian Leadership Conference, 1954–1970, Part 4: Records of the Program Department, Series I, Records of Andrew J. Young, Program Director, 1961–1964, Subseries 1, Office Files, 1961–1964, Box 135:21, Martin Luther King, Jr. Library and Archives.

20. Martin Luther King Jr., "Speech at a Rally, Savannah, Ga.," *The Papers of Martin Luther King, Jr., Volume VII*, eds. Claybourne Carson and Tenisha Armstrong (Berkeley, CA: University of California Press, 2014), 114.

21. On Thurman and these networks, see particularly Sarah Azaransky, *This Worldwide Struggle: Religion and the International Roots of the Civil Rights Movement* (New York: Oxford University Press, 2017), especially 16–50. On debates over the role of Christianity in the global decolonization movement, see Darcie Fontaine, *Decolonizing Christianity: Religion and the End of Empire in France and Algeria* (New York: Cambridge University Press, 2016), especially 172–214.

22. J. A. Rogers, "My Gratitude to My Educational Heritage," *New Pittsburgh Courier*, August 28, 1965, 9; J. A. Rogers, "History Shows," *New Pittsburgh Courier*, October 31, 1964, 8. On this point, see James H. Meriwether, *Proudly We Can Be Africans: Black Americans and Africa, 1935–1961* (Chapel Hill: University of North Carolina Press, 2002), particularly 15–19.

23. Robert Buis, *Religious Belief and White Prejudice* (Johannesburg: Raven Press, 1975), 11. See the discussion of Buis in Ronald Nicolson, "Other Times and Other Customs," in *The Eye of the Storm: Bishop John William Colenso and the Crisis of Biblical Interpretation*, ed. Jonathan A. Draper (London: T&T Clark, 2003), 178–181.

24. D. F. Malan, letter to John Piersma, reprinted in Malan, *Apartheid: South Africa's Answer to a Great Problem* (Pretoria: State International Publishing, 1954), 81; translated in Lindie Koorts, "An Unlikely Charismatic Leader: D. F. Malan in a Weberian Light," in *Charismatic Leaders and Social Movements: The Revolutionary Power of Ordinary Men and Women*, ed. Jan Willem Stutje (New York: Berghahn Books, 2012), 59; see also Lindie Koorts, *D. F. Malan and the Rise of Afrikaner Nationalism* (Cape Town: Tafelberg, 2014).

25. American Nazi Party, "Smash the Black Revolution Now," August 10, 1963, files on March on Washington, 1963, Bayard Rustin Papers, box 27.

26. Bowers quoted and discussed in Charles Marsh, *God's Long Summer*, 49–82.

27. J. W. Long to Martin Luther King Jr., November 1965, records of the Southern Christian Leadership Conference, 1954–1970, Part 1: Records of the President's Office, Series I: Correspondence, 1958–1968, Subseries 3: Secondary Correspondence, Box 18:28, Martin Luther King, Jr. Library and Archives.

28. Levi Reynolds to Martin Luther King Jr., August 14, 1964, Records of the Southern Christian Leadership Conference, 1954–1970, Part 1: Records of the President's Office, Series I: Correspondence, 1958–1968, Subseries 3: Secondary Correspondence, Box 12:20, Martin Luther King, Jr. Library and Archives.

29. Benjamin E. Mays, *Born to Rebel: An Autobiography* (Athens: University of Georgia Press, 2011), 355. On Mays's involvement with the council and his vision of a racially blind Christian civilization, see Lawrence E. Carter Sr.,

Walking Integrity: Benjamin Elijah Mays, Mentor to Martin Luther King (Macon, GA: Mercer University Press, 1998), 103–107; Randal Maurice Jenks, *Benjamin Elijah Mays: Schoolmaster of the Movement* (Chapel Hill: University of North Carolina Press, 2012), 196–200; Barbara Dianne Savage, *Your Spirits Walk Beside Us: The Politics of Black Religion* (Cambridge: Harvard University Press, 2009), 205–237, especially 218–220.

30. Savage, *Your Spirits Walk Beside Us*, 145–146.

31. A. Philip Randolph, "A. Philip Randolph Looks at Labor," *New Pittsburgh Courier* (April 16, 1960), 4.

32. Ibid.

33. A. Philip Randolph, "The World of Color in Revolution," 3, papers of A. Philip Randolph, Speeches and Writings File, series 4, box 37, Library of Congress, Washington, DC.

34. Meriwether, *Proudly We Can Be Africans*, 97.

35. A. Philip Randolph, "Africa—Challenge and Crisis," 7, papers of A. Philip Randolph, Speeches and Writings File, series 4, box 37. This passage is a close paraphrase of W. E. B. Du Bois's *The World and Africa: An Inquiry into the Part Which Africa Has Played in World History* (New York: Viking, 1947), 43. Randolph adds the word *Western,* emphasizing that he is speaking of the same civilization Malan and others claimed to be defending. In Randolph's speech manuscript, he does not credit Du Bois for the passage, though he praises the book elsewhere in the speech, on page 11. Randolph's speech is also reprinted in Andrew Edmund Kersten and David Lucander, eds., *For Jobs and Freedom: Selected Speeches and Writings of A. Philip Randolph* (Amherst: University of Massachusetts Press, 2014), 345–351.

36. "Whites Arrested in Campaign," *Bulletin of Americans for South African Resistance* 10 (January 14, 1953), 2.

37. "Our Conference on Africa," *Washington Afro-American*, September 8, 1962. On the impact of Negritude on African Americans, see Kevin K. Gaines, *American Africans in Ghana: Black Expatriates and the Civil Rights Era* (Chapel Hill: University of North Carolina Press, 2014), 30–33.

38. Martin Luther King Jr., "Defense and Aid Fund," Records of the Southern Christian Leadership Conference, 1954–1970, Part 1: Records of the President's Office, Series I: Correspondence, 1958–1968, Subseries 3: Secondary Correspondence, Box 15:85, Martin Luther King, Jr. Library and Archives. Martin Luther King Jr., *Call for an International Boycott of Apartheid South Africa, December 10, 1965* (New Orleans: New Orleans Anti-Apartheid Coalition, 1965), 3.

39. Martin Luther King Jr., "Statement at the American Negro Leadership Conference on Africa, November 24, 1962," Records of the Southern Christian Leadership Conference, 1954–1970, Part 3: Records of the Public Relations Department, Series IX: Publications, Subseries 1: Press Releases, Box 120:12, Martin Luther King, Jr. Library and Archives. At the same time, as Brenda Gayle Plummer notes, African Americans involved in groups like the

ACOA faced the delicate task of not appearing subversive to their own government, presenting themselves as an interest group rather than politically radical separatists. Plummer, *In Search of Power: African Americans in the Era of Decolonization, 1956–1974* (New York: Cambridge University Press, 2014), 121–125.

40. Martin Luther King Jr., "Call for an International Boycott of Apartheid South Africa, December 10, 1965," 1–3.

41. Harry Levette, "Says Ucano Disgraced Ghana with Loud Boastings and Ill Feeling," Associated Negro Press, April 17, 1957, The Claude A. Barnett Papers: The Associated Negro Press, 1918–1967, Part 1: Associated Negro Press News Releases, 1928–1964, Series C: 1956–1964, Chicago Historical Society.

42. A. Philip Randolph, "The World Challenge of Ghana," in *For Jobs and Freedom*, eds. Kersten and Lucander, 340–342.

43. Melanie Jane Wright, *Moses in America: The Cultural Uses of Biblical Narrative* (New York: Oxford University Press, 2003), 105–111; Bruce Feiler, *America's Prophet: How the Story of Moses Shaped America* (New York: William Morrow, 2009), 208–241.

44. Martin Luther King Jr., "The Birth of a New Nation," in *The Papers of Martin Luther King, Jr., Volume IV*, eds. Claybourne Carson and Peteron Holloran (Berkeley: University of California Press, 2000), 156. See also Gaines, *African Americans in Ghana*, 78–79, and Gary S. Selby, *Martin Luther King and the Rhetoric of Freedom: The Exodus Narrative in America's Struggle for Civil Rights* (Waco, TX: Baylor University Press, 1998), 91–114.

45. King, "The Birth of a New Nation," 157, 160–161.

46. Jane Bond to Deborah Barnett, April 11, 1963, Records of the Southern Christian Leadership Conference, 1954–1970, Part 3: Records of the Public Relations Department, Series III: Records of Jane M. Bond, Research Assistant, Subseries I: Correspondence, Box 116:16, April 1963, Martin Luther King., Jr. Library and Archives.

47. On the Freedom Schools, see Jon N. Hale, *The Freedom Schools: Student Activists in the Mississippi Civil Rights Movement* (New York: Columbia University Press, 2016), especially 90–91, on the notion of Christianity and civilization; Russell Rickford, *We Are an African People: Independent Education, Black Power, and the Radical Imagination* (New York: Oxford University Press, 2016), 79–82; Featherstone is quoted on page 80.

48. This syllabus was submitted for consideration by Barbara Jones of the Student Non-Violent Coordinating Committee and Beatrice Young of the Amistad Society. "African American History Curriculum Outline Records of the Citizenship Education Program, 1956–1967," Records of the Southern Christian Leadership Conference, 1954–1970, Part 4: Records of the Program Department, Subseries 4: Records of Annell Ponder, 1962–1964, Box 155:32, Martin Luther King, Jr. Library and Archives.

49. Septima P. Clark, "Citizenship Education Proposal for 1965–1970," Records of the Southern Christian Leadership Conference, 1954–1970, Part 4: Records of

the Program Department, Series III, Records of the Citizenship Education Program, Subseries 3: Records of Septima P. Clark, Box 154:14, 1963–1968, Martin Luther King, Jr. Library and Archives. For an overview of the Citizenship Education Program and the Highlander schools, see John M. Glen, *Highlander: No Ordinary School, 1932–1962* (Lexington: University Press of Kentucky, 1988), especially 155–173; I have also consulted Dorothy F. Cotton, *If Your Back's Not Bent: The Role of the Citizenship Education Program in the Civil Rights Movement* (New York: Simon and Schuster, 2012), especially 98–107.

50. Eugene Kayden, "Statement for the Legislative Committee on Highlander Folk School, February 26, 1959," Part 4: Records of the Program Department, Series III, Records of the Citizenship Education Program, Subseries 3: Records of Septima P. Clark, Box 154:9, Martin Luther King, Jr. Library and Archives.

51. Septima Poinsette Clark and LeGette Blythe, *Echo in My Soul* (New York: Dutton, 1962), 68.

52. Clark and Blythe, *Echo in My Soul*, 31. For Clark's religious upbringing I have relied on Rosetta E. Ross, *Witnessing and Testifying: Black Women, Religion, and Civil Rights* (Philadelphia: Fortress Press, 2003), 52–61, and Katherine Mellen Charron, *Freedom's Teacher: The Life of Septima Clark* (Chapel Hill: University of North Carolina Press, 2009), 13–50. On uplift, Kevin K. Gaines, *Uplifting the Race: Black Leadership, Politics, and Culture in the Twentieth Century* (Chapel Hill: University of North Carolina Press, 1998). On Clark's vision for the CEP, see Donna Gillespie, "First Class Citizenship Education in the Mississippi Delta, 1961–65," *Journal of Southern History* 80:1 (February 2014), 109–142.

53. Jacquelyn Hall interview with Septima Poinsette Clark, July 25, 1976, 9, Southern Oral History Program Collection #4007, University Library, University of North Carolina at Chapel Hill.

54. Jacquelyn Hall interview with Septima Poinsette Clark, 47.

55. "Highlander Folk School Reading Booklet," 3–4, Records of the Southern Christian Leadership Conference, 1954–1970, Part 4: Records of the Program Department, Series III, Records of the Citizenship Education Program, Subseries 3: Records of Dorothy Cotton, Box 153:27, Martin Luther King, Jr. Library and Archives.

56. Septima Clark, "Report from the Field: Telfair County, Jacksonville, Georgia," Records of the Southern Christian Leadership Conference, 1954–1970, Part 4: Records of the Program Department, Series III: Records of the Citizenship Education Program, Subseries 5: School Reports, Box 160:49, Martin Luther King, Jr. Library and Archives.

57. *Citizenship Clinic Manual for Voter Registration* (Atlanta: Southern Christian Leadership Conference, 1963), 24, Records of the Southern Christian Leadership Conference, 1954–1970, Part 4: Records of the Program Department, Series III, Records of the Citizenship Education Program, Subseries 3: Records of Dorothy Cotton, Box 153:24, Martin Luther King, Jr. Library and Archives.

58. Annell Ponder, "Background Report, Citizenship Education Program, Albany, Georgia," Part 4: Records of the Program Department, Series III: Records of the Citizenship Education Program, Subseries 5: School Reports, Box 158:11, Martin Luther King, Jr. Library and Archives.

59. Septima Clark, "South Carolina: A New Sound in the Air," September 21, 1964, Series I, Records of Andrew Young, Program Director, 1961–1964, Subseries 2, Records of the Citizenship Education Program, 1961–1964, Subseries iii, Alphabetical File, Box 137:2, Martin Luther King, Jr. Library and Archives.

60. Dorothy Cotton to George Young, September 7, 1962, Records of the Southern Christian Leadership Conference, 1954–1970, Series III, Records of the Citizenship Education Program, 1956–1967, Subseries 2, Records of Dorothy Cotton, 1960–1969, Subseries i, Correspondence, 1960–1969, Box 153:7, Martin Luther King, Jr. Library and Archives.

61. Clark's recollections are discussed in Charron, *Freedom's Teacher*, 315–316. On the paradoxes surrounding King's engagement with gender, see Linda T. Wynn, "Beyond Patriarchy: The Meaning of Martin Luther King, Jr., for the Women of the World," in *"In An Inescapable Network of Mutuality": Martin Luther King, Jr. and the Globalization of an Ethical Ideal*, eds. Lewis V. Baldwin and Paul R. Dekar (Eugene, OR: Wipf and Stock, 2013), 55–89.

62. "WCC Asks Ghana to Reconsider Expulsion." On Nkrumah's actions, *Ghana Evening News*, October 23, 1961. Quoted in Ebenezer Obiri Addo, *Kwame Nkrumah: A Case Study of Religion and Politics in Ghana* (Lanham, MD: University Press of America, 1997), 139–152; quotations from 144 and 145.

63. Kwame Nkrumah, *The Autobiography of Kwame Nkrumah* (London: Thomas Nelson and Sons, 1957), 122. See also Addo, *Kwame Nkrumah*, 139–140.

64. Kwame Nkrumah, *Consciencism: Philosophy and Ideology for De-Colonization* (New York: Modern Reader, 1970), 50, 70, 79. This book was to some degree ghostwritten; see Trevor Jones, *Ghana's First Republic* (London: Methuen & Co., 1976), 297–298. On "consciencism," see also D. Zizwe Poe, *Kwame Nkrumah's Contribution to Pan-Africanism: An Afrocentric Analysis* (New York: Routledge, 2001), 4–7. The notion of the "African personality" was articulated earlier by Edward Blyden, who argued that each "race" manifested certain aspects of God's character. Robert July, *The Origins of Modern African Thought: Its Development in West Africa during the Nineteenth and Twentieth Centuries* (New York: Praeger, 1967), 208–234.

65. Steve Biko, "Black Consciousness and the Quest for a True Humanity," *Ufahamu: A Journal of African Studies* 11:1 (1981), 136, 137–138.

66. Biko, "Black Consciousness and the Quest for True Humanity," 138. On black consciousness and Christianity generally, I have used Lyn S. Graybill, *Religion and Resistance Politics in South Africa* (New York: Praeger, 1995), 83–85; Daniel R. Magaziner, *The Law and the Prophets: Black Consciousness in South Africa, 1968–1977* (Athens: Ohio University Press, 2010), 15–34, quoted on 56; and Josiah Ulysses Young, *African Theology: A Critical Analysis and Annotated Bibliography* (Westport, CT: Greenwood Press, 1993), especially 3–7.

67. James H. Cone, "Black and African Theologies: A Consultation," *Christianity and Crisis* (March 3, 1975), 50–51; James H. Cone, "Content and Method of Black Theology," *Journal of Religious Thought* 32:2 (Fall–Winter 1975), 90–103; Kwesi Dickson, "African Theology: Origins, Methodology, and Content," *Journal of Religious Thought* 32:2 (Fall–Winter 1975), 39, 40, 45. See also Dwight N. Hopkins, "A Transatlantic Comparison of a Black Theology of Liberation," in *Freedom's Distant Shores: American Protestants and Post-Colonial Alliances with Africa*, ed. R. Drew Smith (Waco, TX: Baylor University Press, 2006), 84–105.

68. Gayraud Wilmore, "African and Black Theology—Ghana Consultation: A Summary Report," *Journal of Religious Thought* 32:2 (Fall–Winter 1975), 104–111; Cone, "Black and African Theologies," 51.

69. Stokely Carmichael, *Ready for Revolution: the Life and Struggles of Stokely Carmichael (Kwame Ture)* (New York: Scribner, 2003), 290. Savage, *Your Spirits Walk Beside Us*, 259–271. I have also used Dwight N. Hopkins, *Black Theology USA and South Africa: Politics, Culture and Liberation* (Eugene, OR: Wipf and Stock, 1989), particularly 147–167.

70. Pauli Murray, "Black Theology and Feminist Theology: A Comparative View," *Anglican Theological Review* 60 (January 1978), 3–24; reprinted in Gayraud Wilmore and James Cone, eds., *Black Theology: A Documentary History* (Maryknoll, NY: Orbis Books, 1979), 305. See also Sarah Azaransky, *The Dream is Freedom: Pauli Murray and American Democratic Faith* (New York: Oxford University Press, 2011), 92–96. For womanist thought that echoed Murray's critique of Cone, see Stacey M. Floyd-Thomas, *Deeper Shades of Purple: Womanism in Religion and Society* (New York: New York University Press, 2006), 1–17.

71. Pauli Murray, "Healing and Reconciliation," in *Pauli Murray: Selected Sermons and Writings* (Maryknoll, NY: Orbis Books, 2007), 87.

72. Albert Cleage, *Black Christian Nationalism* (New York: William Morrow, 1972), 30, 32, 37, 242. On Cleage, I have relied on Dillard, *Faith in the City*, 237–286; Chapman, *Christianity on Trial*, 69–100; and Raphael G. Warnock, *The Divided Mind of the Black Church: Theology, Piety and Public Witness* (New York: NYU Press, 2014), 104–107.

73. Cleage, *Black Christian Nationalism*, xxxiv, 3–6; Cleage, *The Black Messiah* (New York: Sheed and Ward, 1968), 24; see also Yosef ben-Jochannan, *African Origins of the Major "Western Religions"* (New York: Alkebu-Ian Books, 1970); Yaacov Shavit, *History in Black: African Americans in Search of an Ancient Past* (New York: Routledge, 2013), 187–199.

74. Cleage, *Black Christian Nationalism*, 15.

7. Cult and Countercult

1. "President Lights New Tree, Notes Crisis-Dimmed Glow," *Chicago Tribune*, December 15, 1973, B12; Sue Cronkite, "Cheering, Chanting Youths Prove Spirit

of America Still Alive; Support Nixon," *Birmingham News,* December 24, 1973, 1; Michael L. Mickler, *A History of the Unification Church in America, 1959–1974: Emergence of a National Movement* (New York: Garland Press, 1993), 204–205.

2. Laurence Stern and William R. MacKaye, "Rev. Moon: Nixon Backer," *Washington Post,* February 15, 1974, A1. Moon's close disciple Bo Hi Pak describes the meeting in *Messiah: My Testimony to Reverend Sun Myung Moon* (Lanham, MD: University Press of America, 2000), 331–344.

3. Alec Gallup, *The Gallup Poll* (Lanham, MD: Rowman and Littlefield, 2005), 24–25.

4. Edward B. Fiske, "The Closest Thing to a White House Chaplain," *New York Times,* June 8, 1969, 108, 110. On Graham and Nixon's relationship, see Steven P. Miller, *Billy Graham and the Rise of the Republican South* (Philadelphia: University of Pennsylvania Press, 2009), 136–158, and Raymond Haberski, *God and War: American Civil Religion since 1945* (New Brunswick, NJ: Rutgers University Press, 2012), 85–86.

5. Billy Graham, "Watergate," *Christianity Today,* August 8, 1974, 9. On evangelicals' fears about Watergate, see Steven P. Miller, *The Age of Evangelicalism: America's Born Again Years* (New York: Oxford University Press, 2014), 11–14.

6. Mae M. Ngai, "The Unlovely Residue of Outworn Prejudices: The Hart-Celler Act and the Politics of Immigration Reform, 1945–1965," in *Americanism: New Perspectives on the History of an Ideal,* eds. Michael Kazin and Joseph McCartin (Chapel Hill: University of North Carolina Press, 2006), 108–127, and David Reimers, *Still the Golden Door: The Third World Comes to America* (New York: Columbia University Press, 1992), 92–123.

7. Charles Lippy, *Pluralism Comes of Age: American Religious Culture in the Twentieth Century* (London: Taylor and Francis, 2000), 114–115.

8. On this formulation, see Ann Gleig and Lola Wiliamson, *Homegrown Gurus: From Hinduism in America to American Hinduism* (Albany: State University of New York Press, 2013), 2–4, and Lola Williamson, *Transcendent in America: Hindu-Inspired Meditation Movements as New Religion* (New York: New York University Press, 2010), 26–55.

9. Carol Ascher, "The Return of Jewish Mysticism," *Present Tense* 7–8 (Spring 1980), 37. See also Lola Williamson, *Transcendent in America,* 43–44, and Philip Goldberg, *American Veda: From Emerson and the Beatles to Yoga and Meditation* (New York: Random House, 2010), 130–151.

10. Charles Babcock, "Moon Sect Support of Nixon Derailed," *Washington Post,* November 10, 1977, A1; *New Hope News,* August 20, 1974, cited in Anson Shupe and David Bromley, *"Moonies" in America: Cult, Church and Crusade* (Berkeley: Sage Publications, 1979), 162; Marjorie Hyer, "Korean Cult Chief Sun Myung Moon Beset by Troubles," *Washington Post,* October 16, 1974, C8.

11. Eileen Barker, *The Making of a Moonie: Brainwashing or Choice?* (New York: Blackwell, 1984), 47–49, and John Lofland, *Doomsday Cult: A Study of Conversion, Proselytization and Maintenance of Faith* (New York: Irvington Publishers, 1977), 257–259. See also Mickler, *History of the Unification Church*, 87.

12. Virginia Brandt Berg, *The Hem of His Garment: The Life Story of Virginia Brandt* (Zurich: World Services, 1981), 20. On Berg's history, see William Sims Bainbridge, *The Endtime Family: Children of God* (Albany: State University of New York Press, 2002), 3–7, and Larry Eskridge, *God's Forever Family: The Jesus People Movement in America* (New York: Oxford University Press, 2013), 63–68.

13. David Berg, "Millions of Miles of Miracles," 118, The New Religious Movements Vertical Files Collection, box 7, folder 12, Graduate Theological Union Archives and Special Collections, Berkeley, California.

14. Jim Wallis, *Revive Us Again: A Sojourner's Story* (Nashville: Abingdon Press, 1983), 16, 79. See also David Swartz, *Moral Minority: The Evangelical Left in an Age of Conservatism* (Philadelphia: Pennsylvania University Press, 2012), 47–68, and Brantley Gasaway, *Progressive Evangelicals and the Pursuit of Social Justice* (Chapel Hill: University of North Carolina Press, 2014), 37–39, 53–75.

15. David Berg, "Warning," 6, The New Religious Movements Vertical Files Collection, box 7, folder 12.

16. David Berg, "Millions of Miles of Miracles," 118, box 7, folder 12, The New Religious Movements Vertical Files Collection.

17. Lester Kinsolving, "The Children of God Stamp Up a Storm," *San Francisco Examiner*, March 26, 1972, B6; Michael Lonergan to Arthur Piepkorn, November 5, 1969, The New Religious Movements Vertical Files Collection, box 7, folder 12. Ronald M. Enroth, Edward E. Ericson Jr., and C. Breckenridge Peters, *The Jesus People: Old-Time Religion in the Age of Aquarius* (Grand Rapids, MI: Eerdmans, 1972), 21–41.

18. On the organization and reorganization of the Children of God, see Roy Wallis, "Yesterday's Children: Cultural and Structural Change in a New Religious Movement," in *The Social Impact of New Religious Movements*, ed. Bryan Wilson (New York: Rose of Sharon Press, 1981), 97–133.

19. Berg, "Warning," 1, The New Religious Movements Vertical Files Collection, box 7, folder 12; "Mo Himself" [David Berg], *Survival: The True Story of Moses and the Children of God* (Dallas: Children of God Publications, 1972), 14.

20. Untitled letter, The New Religious Movements Vertical Files Collection, box 7, folder 12; Berg, *Survival*, 24, 14. On the Children's economic arrangements, see Bainbridge, *Endtime Family*, 29–37, and James D. Chancellor, *Life in the Family: An Oral History of the Children of God* (Syracuse, NY: Syracuse University Press, 2000), 177–205.

21. Faith David, "Thank You!—You Are Changing the World!" 64, 67, 69, The New Religious Movements Vertical Files Collection, box 7, folder 13.

22. Sara, "Expecting a Miracle," 282, The New Religious Movements Vertical Files Collection, box 7, folder 12.

23. David Berg, *Our Answers for the Daily News* (London: The Children of God, 1977), 2, 12.

24. David Berg, *Old Love, New Love, The Old Church And The New Church* (London: The Children of God, 1969), 2; David Berg, "The Flirty Little Fishy!" in *The Basic Mo Letters* (London: The Children of God, 1974), 527–534. On the Law of Love and sexuality in the Children of God, see James Lewis and J. Gordon Melton, "Sexuality and the Maturation of the Family," in *Sex, Slander, and Salvation: Investigating the Family/Children of God*, eds. Lewis and Melton (Stanford, CA: Center for Academic Publication, 1994), 71–94.

25. David Berg, "Happy Rebirthday," 1978, The New Religious Movements Vertical Files Collection, box 7, folder 12.

26. Berg, *Survival*, 25.

27. Hosea David, "Bible Studies with Dad!," 72, The New Religious Movements Vertical Files Collection, box 7, folder 12. See also "Recommended Curriculum and Slides," *Family News International*, March 1, 1982, 24.

28. "Loveville University" and "A Children's Singing Tour," *Family News International*, March 1, 1982, 4, 10.

29. "A Children's Singing Tour," *Family News International*, 9.

30. David Berg, "40 Days! And Nineveh Shall Be Destroyed!," 2, The New Religious Movements Vertical Files Collection, box 7, folder 13.

31. On conservative evangelical and fundamentalist end-times prophecy, see Paul Boyer, *When Time Shall Be No More: Prophecy Belief in Modern America* (Cambridge, MA: Harvard University Press, 1994), particularly 80–115 and 152–181. On its influence on the Jesus People more broadly, see Eskridge, *God's Forever Family*, 72–74, and Enroth et al., *The Jesus People*, 31. In "40 Days! And Nineveh Shall Be Destroyed!," 1, Berg predicted that the United States would be destroyed in January 1974.

32. Berg, *Survival*, 35–36, 12.

33. John Dart, "Children of God Sect Resurrects Doom Prophecy," *Los Angeles Times*, August 2, 1970, B1. See also Berg, *Survival*, 20.

34. Berg, *Survival*, 14.

35. Ibid.

36. A number of scholars of Unificationism have made this observation, including Shupe and Bromley, *"Moonies" in America*, 100–101; Barker, *Making of a Moonie*, 43, 74–75; Frederick Sontag, *Sun Myung Moon and the Unification Church* (Nashville: Abingdon Press, 1977), 73–77.

37. Sun Myung Moon, *Divine Principle: Four Hour Lecture* (New York: Holy Spirit Association for the Unification of World Christianity, 1977), 17–18; Sun Myung Moon, *America in God's Providence: Two Speeches by the Reverend Sun Myung Moon* (New York: Bicentennial God Bless America Committee, 1976), 6–7.

38. Moon, *Divine Principle*, 6–7, 10–11, 1–4.

39. Moon, *America in God's Providence*, 6, 8; James Edgerly, "America in Search of a New Ethics," *World Student Times*, March 1980, 9; "The Unification Church," *Sunrise*, July 1, 1978, 1.

40. Moon, *America in God's Providence*, 3–5, 9, 23; see also 18–19.
41. Edgerly, "America in Search of a New Ethics," 9; Moon, *America in God's Providence*, 11; "Re-Education Center: Sixth Training Session, 1970," The New Religious Movements Vertical Files Collection, box 38, folder 15.
42. Russell Chandler, "Wants to Unify the World," *Los Angeles Times,* January 30, 1974, C1. On Unification's economic and living practices, see Lofland, *Doomsday Cult,* 54; Barker, *Making of a Moonie,* 234–236; Jonathan Gullery, *The Early Days of Reverend Sun Myung Moon and the Unification Church: The Path of a Pioneer* (New York: HSA Publications, 1986), 57–69.
43. "Report on the Oakland *Tribune* Articles on the Unification Church and the New Education Development, published November 6–11, 1977," 16, 12, 10, The New Religious Movements Vertical Files Collection, box 38, folder 15.
44. Scott Armstrong and Maxine Cheshire, "Korean CIA Tied to Moon Rally," *Washington Post,* November 7, 1976, A1; Moon Conviction Is Upheld by Court," *New York Times,* September 14, 1983, B4. Bernadette Kenny discusses protests of the conviction in *Exclusively Religious: The Unification Church v. the Tax Commission: A Case Study of the Indivisibility of Religion, Politics, and Economics* (New York: National Conference of Christians and Jews, 1983).
45. Russell Chandler, "Korean Evangelist Ends 21-City Day of Hope Speaking Tour," *Los Angeles Times,* January 30, 1974, A1.
46. William Claiborne, "Rev. Moon Is Denounced by Three Major Faiths," *Washington Post,* December 29, 1976, A1; Ira Pearlstein, "Rev. Moon and His Army of Mesmerized Moonies," *Baltimore Sun,* May 23, 1976, K2. See also Sean McCloud, *Making the American Religious Fringe: Exotics, Subversives, and Journalists, 1955–1993* (Chapel Hill: University of North Carolina Press, 2004), 145–151.
47. Moon, *America in God's Providence*, 11, 16, 21–22.
48. Robert Mason, "US Foreign Policy: From Containment to Aggressive Defense," *World Student Times,* February 1980, 4.
49. "Papasan Speaks at Family Meeting," *New Epoch Times,* 1970, 129. Cited in Barker, *Making of a Moonie,* 52.
50. See, for instance, *The Fundamentals* (Chicago: Testimony Publishing Company, 1909–1917), 5:112–113. Another early work is William Irvine's 1917 treatise *Heresies Exposed,* 10th ed. (New York: Loizeaux Brothers, 1964), 1, 8, which does not use the word *cult* but argues that a variety of "heresies" were deceived by the myth of "progress" and as such erected "a veil between needy man and a waiting God." This observation is echoed in Philip Jenkins, *Mystics and Messiahs: Cults and New Religious Movements in American History* (New York: Oxford University Press, 2000), 46–47, and Anson Shupe, David G. Bromley, and D. L. Olive, *The Anti-Cult Movement in America* (New York: Garland, 1984), 10–11. An important exception was Mormonism, which, during the nineteenth century, attracted sharp criticism for its practice of polygamy and its theocratic control of the Utah Territory; see J. Spencer Fluhman, *A Peculiar People: Anti-Mormonism and the Making of Religion in Nineteenth Century America*

(Chapel Hill: University of North Carolina Press, 2012), 103–127. Throughout, in a concession to those whose ideas I am discussing, I will use *cult* to describe the groups targeted by countercultists. I do not intend the pejorative meaning of the term.

51. Russell P. Spittler, *Cults and Isms* (Grand Rapids, MI: Baker Book House, 1962), 12. See, for other such works, the Baptist minister Herbert Wyrick's *Seven Religious Isms: An Historical and Scriptural Review* (Grand Rapids, MI: Zondervan, 1940), 5, and Jan van Baalen, *The Gist of the Cults* (Grand Rapids, MI: Eerdmans, 1938, 1944), 5. See also Sean McCloud's discussion of definitions in *Making the American Religious Fringe*, 45–47. On definitions of *cult* and evangelicals' use of the term, see Douglas Cowen, "Bearing False Witness: Propaganda, Reality Maintenance, and Christian Anti-Cult Apologetics," PhD dissertation, University of Calgary, 2000, 29–31.

52. The term *evangelical* may mean, broadly speaking, Protestants who promote a born-again experience. It may also refer more specifically to a group of theologically conservative Protestants who self-consciously mobilized in rejection of separatist fundamentalists and sought renewed public engagement in the 1940s and 1950s. In this section, when I use the term, it is those whom I mean. See, for instance, George Marsden, *Reforming Fundamentalism: Fuller Seminary and the New Evangelicalism* (Grand Rapids, MI: Eerdmans, 1987), 3–11, and Joel A. Carpenter, *Revive Us Again: The Reawakening of American Fundamentalism* (New York: Oxford University Press, 1997), 3–13.

53. Edward J. Tanis, *What the Sects Teach* (Grand Rapids, MI: Baker Books, 1958), 12, 54.

54. Edwin W. Bishop, "Congregationalism and Christian Science," *Congregationalist and Christian World*, October 8, 1904, 499. Similarly, evangelicals organized missions to such groups, encouraging theological engagement with them. By the 1890s, Baptists, Methodists, and Presbyterians had erected home missions targeting Mormons and warned that, as one Baptist teacher cautioned, missionaries must master scripture because Mormons knew it thoroughly. Mary G. Burdette, ed., *Twenty-Two Years' Work among Mormons* (Chicago: Woman's Baptist Home Mission Society, 1905), 25. Jana K. Riess, "Heathen in Our Fair Land: Anti-Polygamy and Protestant Women's Missions to Utah, 1869–1910," PhD dissertation, Columbia University, 2000, 213–214, 145–147.

55. Anthony Hoekema, *The Four Major Cults: Christian Science, Jehovah's Witnesses, Mormonism, Seventh-Day Adventism* (Grand Rapids, MI: Eerdmans, 1963), xi, 374–375, 376, 379.

56. Walter R. Martin, "Christian Research Institute," *The Christian Librarian* 14:1 (October 1970), 15–18. Some scholars have distinguished between "countercult" and "anticult" activities; the second term is usually applied to secular critics of new religious movements, who assail them for restricting civil liberties, "brainwashing," and so on. Most of these critics were concerned academics, parents who wanted their children out of such

movements, and "deprogrammers," who would, for a fee, kidnap those children and convince them under pressure to leave the movement. The "countercult" movement, on the other hand, is normally identified with Protestant Christians' distinctively religious and philosophical critique of many of these same groups. There were, of course, overlaps between the differing groups. Ted Patrick, the most famous deprogrammer, was a practicing Baptist, for instance, and often parent groups were made up of churchgoers. Not infrequently, though, different branches of the anticult movement might find themselves working at cross purposes derived from their different objections to these groups, which makes the distinction valuable. See Cowan, "Bearing False Witness," 15–20, and George D. Chryssides, *Exploring New Religions* (London: Cassell, 1999), 345–351. The Protestant sociologists Ronald M. Enroth and J. Gordon Melton were among the first to insist on this distinction, in their *Why Cults Succeed Where the Church Fails* (Elgin, IL: Brethren Press, 1985), 25–26. Shupe et al. use *anti-cult* to describe all such movements; see Shupe, Bromley, and Olive, *The Anti-Cult Movement in America*, vii–viii.

57. Nancy Friedman, "Born Again to Raise Hell," *Bay Area Journal*, July 22, 1984. On the origins of the SCP, see Eskridge, *God's Forever Family*, 262–263, and "Dear Friends" fundraising letter, October 25, 1983, The New Religious Movements Vertical Files Collection, box 34, folder 2.

58. Carl Henry, *Remaking the Modern Mind* (Grand Rapids, MI: Eerdmans, 1946), 8, 26. On "worldview," see Molly Worthen, *Apostles of Reason: The Crisis of Authority in American Evangelicalism* (New York: Oxford University Press, 2014), 24–32, and David K. Naugle, *Worldview: The History of a Concept* (Grand Rapids, MI; Eerdmans, 2002), 5–31. On the Religious Right as an intellectual movement that emphasized Christian epistemology and declension, see Andrew Hartman, *A War for the Soul of America: A History of the Culture Wars* (Chicago: University of Chicago Press, 2015), 38–40, 86–87.

59. Francis Schaeffer, *How Should We Then Live? L'Abri Fiftieth Anniversary Edition* (Wheaton, IL: Crossway Books, 2005), 19. On Schaeffer, see Worthen, *Apostles of Reason*, 209–219, and Barry Hankins, *Francis Schaeffer and the Shaping of Evangelical America* (Grand Rapids, MI: Eerdmans, 2008), especially 160–192.

60. Schaeffer, *How Should We Then Live?*, 48, 98, 110. Despite his oversimplifications, Schaeffer was honest enough to acknowledge the diverse religious views of the American Founders, but he argued that each was "Christian" in the sense that each was in "the circle of that which a Christian consensus brings forth, even though he himself is not a Christian in the first sense."

61. Schaeffer, *How Should We Then Live?*, 51, 22, 227.

62. Hildreth Cross, *Introduction to Psychology: An Evangelical Approach* (Grand Rapids, MI: Eerdmans, 1952), 11; Clyde M. Narramore, *Psychology of Counseling: Professional Techniques for Pastors, Teachers, Youth Leaders and All Who*

Are Engaged in the Incomparable Art of Counseling (Grand Rapids, MI: Zondervan, 1960), 197, 301. For a discussion of the competing impulses toward secular training and spiritual mission in conservative evangelical counseling in this period, see Susan E. Myers-Shirk, *Helping the Good Shepherd: Pastoral Counselors in a Psychotherapeutic Culture, 1925–1975* (Baltimore: Johns Hopkins University Press, 2010), 206–234.

63. David Harrington Watt, *A Transforming Faith: Explorations of Twentieth-Century American Evangelicalism* (New Brunswick, NJ: Rutgers University Press, 1991), 137–154, and Randall J. Stephens and Karl W. Giberson, *The Anointed: Evangelical Truth in a Secular Age* (Cambridge, MA: Harvard University Press, 2012), 101–112.

64. Narramore, *Psychology of Counseling*, 118, 146.

65. Witness Lee, *The Practical Expression of the Church* (Anaheim, CA: Living Stream Ministries, 1970), 139; "Leafletting the Local Church," 3. "Dear Friend" fundraising letter, April 1982, The New Religious Movements Vertical Files Collection, box 34, folder 3. See also Russell Chandler, "Jesus Movement Still Going Strong," *Los Angeles Times*, December 13, 1975, 34. Later, the SCP became embroiled in a lawsuit with Witness Lee and the Local Church that nearly bankrupted the SCP. "Bankruptcy Halts Trial of Religious Group," *San Francisco Chronicle*, March 5, 1985, 53.

66. "Dear Friend" fundraising letter, April 1982, The New Religious Movements Vertical Files Collection, box 34, folder 3.

67. Schaeffer, *How Should We Then Live?*, 208; Nadine W. Scott, "Seminars End Today," *Honolulu Star-Bulletin*, December 28, 1980; *Cutting through the Spiritual Counterfeits*, (Berkeley, CA: Spiritual Counterfeits Project, 1975), 3. The New Religious Movements Vertical Files Collection, box 34, folder 2.

68. Ronald Enroth, *Youth, Brainwashing and the Extremist Cults* (Grand Rapids, MI: Zondervan, 1977), 149–151. For "anticult," nonevangelical, and academic critiques that expressed this sort of fear, see, for instance, Florence W. Kaslow and Lita Linzer Schwartz, "The Cult Phenomenon: Historical, Sociological, and Familial Factors Contributing to Their Appeal," in *Cults and the Family*, eds. Kaslow and Marvin B. Sussman (New York: Howarth Press, 1982), 3–5; for an anticult but nonevangelical assessment directed at a general audience, see Carroll Stoner and Jo Anne Parke, *All God's Children: The Cult Experience, Salvation or Slavery?* (Radnor, PA: Chilton Books, 1977), xiii–xv. Both works follow a widely accepted hypothesis that explained the appeal of new religious movements with deprivation theory: people joined such movements because of lack, dislocation, or psychological disturbance in other aspects of their lives. McCloud, *Making the American Religious Fringe*, 113–126, explores this reading of new religious movements more generally.

69. Walter Martin, *The Kingdom of the Cults* (Minneapolis, MN: Bethany House, 1965), 11, 345, 25–26, 28, 30–31; "Leafletting the Local Church," 3.

70. *Information Hearing on the Cult Phenomenon in the United States, February 5, 1979* (Washington, DC: Government Printing Office, 1979), 39–41. See also Marjorie Hyer, "Cult Hearings Noisy, Tense," *Washington Post,* February 6, 1979, A14, reporting that witnesses described "cult members as victims of mind control." On the broad coverage of cults practicing "brainwashing" in the 1970s, see Philip Jenkins, *Mystics and Messiahs: Cults and New Religions in American History* (New York: Oxford University Press, 2008), 187–208, McCloud, *Making the American Religious Fringe,* 127–160, and Anson D. Shupe and David G. Bromley, eds., *A Documentary History of the Anti-Cult Movement* (Arlington, TX: Center for Social Research, 1985), chapter 4.

71. "Seven Steps to Slavery," *Religious Research Digest* 1:1 (January 1961), 23; Enroth, *Youth, Brainwashing and the Extremist Cults,* 163.

72. "Hanoi's Pavlovians," *Time,* April 14, 1967, 33.

73. Friedman, "Born Again to Raise Hell."

74. Reuben Baerwald, "The Cults: A Research Packet," The New Religious Movements Vertical Files Collection, box 7, folder 29.

75. Ted Patrick and Tom Dulick, *Let Our Children Go!* (New York: E. P. Dutton and Company, 1976), 20.

76. David Fechto, "Rationalism, Mysticism and the Fallen Human Consciousness," *Spiritual Counterfeits Project Newsletter* 6 (September/October 1975), 2–3; "Right On," Christian World Liberation Front, September 1972, The New Religious Movements Vertical Files Collection, box 5, folder 13.

77. Hal Lindsay, *The Late Great Planet Earth* (Grand Rapids, MI: Zondervan, 1970), 115, 116. The distinction between Christianity and religion was common among conservative evangelicals; see Susan Friend Harding, *The Book of Jerry Falwell: Fundamentalist Language and Politics* (Princeton, NJ: Princeton University Press, 2000), 133–141.

78. "Seminars End Today."

79. John Charles Cooper, *Religion in the Age of Aquarius* (Philadelphia: Westminster Press, 1973), 22–23; Enroth et al., *The Jesus People,* 169, 174; Enroth, *Youth, Brainwashing and the Extremist Cults,* 15, 187, 197; Enroth, *Youth, Brainwashing and the Extremist Cults,* 166.

80. Douglas Sturm, "You Shall Have No Poor Among You," in *The Legacy of Billy Graham: Critical Reflections on America's Greatest Evangelist,* ed. Michael G. Long (Louisville, KY: Westminster/John Knox, 2013), 67–68; Darren Grem, *The Blessings of Business: How Corporations Shaped Conservative Christianity* (New York: Oxford University Press, 2016), 49–82, especially 54–55. "Scriptural Proof for the Free Enterprise System," undated typescript, National Association of Evangelicals Archives, box 40, Billy Graham Center, Wheaton College, Wheaton, IL. See also Darren Dochuk, *From Bible Belt to Sun Belt: Plain Folk Religion, Grassroots Politics, and the Rise of Evangelical Conservatism* (New York: W. W. Norton, 2011), 182–194.

8. Civil Religion, the Religious Right, and the
Fracturing of Christian Republicanism

1. My discussion of these cases is shaped by Daniel K. Williams, *God's Own Party: The Making of the Christian Right* (New York: Oxford University Press, 2010), 63–65 and Kevin M. Kruse, *One Nation under God: How Corporate America Invented Christian America* (New York: Basic Books, 2015), 170–201.
2. Erwin Griswold, "Notable and Quotable," *Wall Street Journal*, September 12, 1963, 12; Kruse, *One Nation under God*, 188–189.
3. "Supreme Court Prayer Ban—Where Will It Lead?" *Christianity Today*, July 20, 1962, 25–26. See also George Dugan, "Churches Divided, with Most in Favor," *New York Times*, June 18, 1963, 1.
4. Conference Notes, No. 142, March 1, 1963, William O. Douglas Papers, box 1295, Library of Congress, Washington, DC.
5. Adam Clymer, "City Urges Supreme Court to Uphold Bible in Schools," *Baltimore Sun*, February 28, 1963, 52.
6. Robert N. Bellah, "Civil Religion in America," *Dædalus, Journal of the American Academy of Arts and Sciences*, 96:1 (Winter 1967), 2; reprinted in Bellah, ed., *Beyond Belief: Essays on Religion in a Post-Traditionalist World* (New York: Harper and Row, 1970), 168. On the long history of various types of "civil religion," in the modern United States, see Ray Haberski, *God and War: American Civil Religion Since 1945* (New Brunswick, NJ: Rutgers University Press, 2012).
7. Bellah's interactions with Carter are discussed in Kevin Mattson, *"What the Heck Are You Up To, Mr. President?": Jimmy Carter, America's "Malaise," and the Speech That Should Have Changed the Country* (New York: Bloomsbury, 2010), 142–144, and Kenneth Morris, *Jimmy Carter, American Moralist* (Athens: University of Georgia Press, 1996), 3–4, 261–262.
8. Robert N. Bellah, *The Broken Covenant: American Civil Religion in a Time of Trial* (New York: Seabury Books, 1975), 52. David A. Hollinger, *After Cloven Tongues of Fire: Protestant Liberalism in Modern American History* (Princeton, NJ: Princeton University Press, 2013), 18–56, explores the ways in which liberal Protestant ideas became, for many Americans, the unrecognized water they swam in, as does Wade Clark Roof, *Spiritual Marketplace: Baby Boomers and the Remaking of American Religion* (Princeton, NJ: Princeton University Press, 1999). Nicholas J. Demerath III and Rhys H. Williams, "Civil Religion in an Uncivil Society," *The Annals of the American Academy of Political and Social Science* (1985): 154–166, maintained that Bellah's version of civil religion was an attempt to reinvigorate traditional Christian social values. Philip Gorski, *American Covenant: A History of Civil Religion from the Puritans to the Present* (Princeton, NJ: Princeton University Press, 2017), 1–9, argues that this tradition is best called "prophetic republicanism."
9. Bellah, "Civil Religion in America," 168; Bellah, *The Broken Covenant*, 84; Bellah, "Religious Evolution," *Beyond Belief*, 29–32. Ronald Beiner argues that the very notion of "civil religion" is an attempt to bring religious

language into the service of a political regime in *Civil Religion: A Dialogue in the History of Philosophy* (New York: Cambridge, 2010), 2.

10. Bellah, "Civil Religion in America," 3.

11. Bellah, "Preface," *Beyond Belief*, xiv–xvii.

12. Phillip E. Hammond, "Civility and Civil Religion," and "Pluralism and Law in the Formation of American Religion," in *Varieties of Civil Religion*, eds. Robert N. Bellah and Hammond (New York: Harper and Row, 1980), 142–144, 204–205.

13. Harvey Cox, *The Secular City: Secularization and Urbanization in Theological Perspective* (New York: Macmillan, 1965), 85. See also David A. Hollinger, "The Realist-Pacifist Summit Meeting of March 1942 and the Political Reorientation of Ecumenical Protestantism in the United States," *Church History* 79 (September 2010), 654–677.

14. Bellah, *Broken Covenant*, 149; Bellah, *Beyond Belief*, 187; Robert N. Bellah, "Religion and the Legitimation of the American Republic," in Bellah and Hammond, *Varieties of Civil Religion*, 5.

15. J. W. Fulbright, "The Fatal Arrogance of Power," *New York Times*, May 15, 1966, 15; J. William Fulbright, *The Arrogance of Power* (New York: Random House, 1966), 249. On Fulbright and "Western civilization," see Randall Bennett Woods, "Dixie's Dove: J. William Fulbright, the Vietnam War, and the American South," *Journal of Southern History* 60:3 (August 1994), 533–552. On the network of Protestants in Congress, see Steven P. Miller, *The Age of Evangelicalism: America's Born Again Years* (New York: Oxford University Press, 2011), 38–40.

16. "Lasting Peace a Fragile Matter, Nixon Warns," *Washington Post*, February 2, 1973, A2; "Nixon Stresses Peace at Prayer Breakfast," *Baptist Press*, February 1, 1973.

17. Hatfield's speech reprinted in *Between a Rock and a Hard Place* (Waco, TX: The Word Press, 1974), 94–95; see also "Lasting Peace a Fragile Matter;" Hatfield's letter in Mark Hatfield, *Not Quite So Simple* (New York: Harper and Row, 1968), 153–154; Mark Hatfield, *Conflict and Conscience* (Waco, TX: Word Books, 1971), 66–67, 74, 39. Hatfield's policy tactics on Vietnam are discussed in Lon Fendall, *Stand Alone or Come Home: Mark Hatfield as an Evangelical and Progressive* (Newberg, OR: Barclay Press, 2008), 110–129, and David R. Swartz, *Moral Minority: The Evangelical Left in an Age of Conservatism* (Philadelphia: University of Pennsylvania Press, 2012), 68–84. Bellah invokes Fulbright in "Civil Religion in America," *Beyond Belief*, 189.

18. Bellah, *The Broken Covenant*, xiii–xiv, 152–153. Robert N. Bellah, "American Civil Religion in the 1970s," in *American Civil Religion*, eds Russell B. Richey and Donald G. Jones (New York: Harper and Row, 1974), 260.

19. Charles Henderson, *The Nixon Theology* (New York: Harper and Row, 1972), 13, 170, 208. Haberski, *God and War*, 85–87.

20. Paul Starr, "Rebels after the Cause," *New York Times*, October 13, 1974, 31.

21. Christopher Lasch, *The Culture of Narcissism: American Life in an Age of Diminishing Expectations* (New York: W. W. Norton, 1979), xv, 14–15. Lasch's

biographer Eric Miller connects Lasch and Bellah in *Hope in a Scattering Time: A Life of Christopher Lasch* (Grand Rapids: Eerdmans, 2010), 325, 358.

22. Bellah, "Preface," *Beyond Belief,* xiv–xvii.

23. Bellah, "Introduction," in Bellah and Hammond, *Varieties of American Civil Religion,* xiii; and Bellah, "Religion and the Legitimation of the American Republic," in Bellah and Hammond, *Varieties of American Civil Religion,* 15.

24. Bellah, *The Broken Covenant,* 56; Jimmy Carter, "Remarks Accepting the Martin Luther King, Jr. Nonviolent Peace Prize," *Public Papers of the Presidents of the United States: Jimmy Carter, 1979* (Washington, DC: Government Printing Office, 1990), 1:27.

25. Bellah, "Civil Religion and the New Religious Movements," in Bellah and Hammond, *Varieties of American Civil Religion,* 175.

26. Hammond, "Civility and Civil Religion: The Emergence of Cults," in Bellah and Hammond, *Varieties of American Civil Religion,* 194. Lewis V. Baldwin offers a similar interpretation of King using the "prophetic" model in *The Voice of Conscience: The Church in the Mind of Martin Luther King, Jr.* (New York: Oxford University Press, 2010), 3–4, 86–87. There is a large amount of writing on the various uses that King in particular and the civil rights movement in general have been put to since his death; with particular reference to civil religion, I have found useful George R. Seay Jr., "A Prophet with Honor? The Martin Luther King Holiday and the Making of a National Icon," in *The Domestication of Martin Luther King, Jr.: Clarence B. Jones, Right-Wing Conservatism, and the Manipulation of the King Legacy,* eds. Lewis V. Baldwin and Rufus Burrow (Eugene, OR: Wipf and Stock, 2013), 213–236.

27. Bellah, "Civil Religion in America," in *Beyond Belief,* 185–186; Lasch, *The Culture of Narcissism,* 54–55; see also his *The True and Only Heaven: Progress and Its Critics* (New York: W. W. Norton, 1991), 233–236. On the role of the Puritans in America's imagined past see Donald E. Pease, *The New American Exceptionalism* (Minneapolis: University of Minnesota Press, 2009), 75–78; Steven K. Green, *Inventing a Christian America: The Myth of the Religious Founding* (New York: Oxford University Press, 2015), 234–235.

28. John Herman Randall, Jr., *The Making of the Modern Mind* (1926; New York: Oxford University Press, 1976), 159–160. On the rehabilitation of the Puritans in the middle twentieth century, see Francis T. Butts, "The Myth of Perry Miller," *American Historical Review,* 87:3 (1982), 665–694, and Michael McGiffert, "American Puritan Studies in the 1960s," *The William and Mary Quarterly* 27:1 (January 1970), 36–67.

29. Martin Marty, "Two Kinds of Two Kinds of Civil Religion," in *American Civil Religion,* eds. Russell E. Richey and Donald G. Jones (New York: Harper and Row, 1974), 144–156. Marty distinguished as well between a "transcendent" form of civil religion, which placed the nation under the judgment of divine authority, and a "self-transcendent" type, which treated

the nation itself as the ultimate source of divinity. See also Marty, *A Nation of Behavers* (Chicago: University of Chicago Press, 1976), 180–203.

30. Sacvan Bercovitch, *The American Jeremiad* (1978; Madison: University of Wisconsin Press, 2012), xli–xlii, xi, xiii.

31. See, for instance, Bellah, *Beyond Belief,* 186; Hammond, "The Civil Religion Proposal," in Bellah and Hammond, *Varieties of Civil Religion,* 201. Abraham J. Heschel, *The Prophets* (New York: Harper and Row, 1962); David W. Noble, "Robert Bellah, Civil Religion, and the American Jeremiad," *Soundings* 65:1 (Spring 1982), 88–102.

32. James A. Henretta, Kevin J. Fernlund, Melvin Yazawa, eds., *Documents for America's History, Volume 2: Since 1865* (Boston: Bedford/St. Martin's, 2011), 409.

33. Art Buchwald, "They Had a Hot Time in Washington This Summer," *Washington Post,* September 2, 1979, B2.

34. Jim Wallis, "The Outsider in the White House," *Sojourners,* January 1978, 6. For more critics, see Randall Balmer, *Redeemer: The Life of Jimmy Carter* (New York: Basic Books, 2014), 130–135.

35. Hammond, "Civility and Civil Religion: The Emergence of Cults," in Bellah and Hammond, *Varieties of American Civil Religion,* 197.

36. Robert N. Bellah, "The New Consciousness and the Crisis in Modernity," in *The New Religious Consciousness,* eds. Robert N. Bellah and Charles Y. Glock (Berkeley: University of California Press, 1976), 333–334. On Bellah's relationship with "civil religion," Matteo Bortolini, "The Trap of Intellectual Success: Robert N. Bellah, the American Civil Religion Debate, and the Sociology of Knowledge," *Theory and Society* 41:2 (March 2012), 187–210.

37. Bellah, *Broken Covenant,* 84. "Filthy Speech Movement," in Bellah, "The New Consciousness and the Berkeley New Left," in Bellah and Glock, *The New Religious Consciousness,* 79; Bellah, "The New Consciousness and the Crisis in Modernity," in Bellah and Glock, *The New Religious Consciousness,* 334, 342.

38. Alan Tobey, "The Summer Solstice of the Healthy-Happy-Holy Organization," in Bellah and Glock, *The New Religious Consciousness,* 21, 23.

39. Bellah, "The New Consciousness and the Crisis in Modernity," in Bellah and Glock, *The New Religious Consciousness,* 344, 349, 351.

40. James A. Mathisen, "Twenty Years After Bellah: Whatever Happened to American Civil Religion?" *Sociological Analysis* 50:2 (Summer 1989), 129–146; John F. Wilson, in *Public Religion in American Culture* (Philadelphia: Temple University Press, 1979), 3–23, 169–177, expressed frustration with the vague nature of precisely what Bellah and others meant by the term *civil religion* and suggested that the proposal represented a "revitalization movement" of white American Protestantism. Marty, "Two Kinds of Two Kinds of Civil Religion," argued that Bellah overly limited what "civil religion" might be. Richard Philbrick, "Worship Has Place in the World Outside the Confines of Churches," *Chicago Tribune,* November 11, 1972, A13.

41. Francis A. Schaeffer, *A Christian Manifesto* (Wheaton, IL: Crossways Books, 1981), 17.

42. Tim LaHaye and Beverly LaHaye, *Spirit-Controlled Family Living* (New York: Fleming H. Revell, 1978), 28; Tim LaHaye, *The Battle for the Mind: A Subtle Warfare* (Old Tappen, NJ: Fleming H. Revell Company, 1980), 133.

43. James Robison, *Save America to Save the World* (Wheaton, IL: Tyndale House, 1980), 66; see also James Robison, *America: Garden of the Gods* (Atlanta: Cross Roads Publications, 1976), 10.

44. Stephen Board, "An Evangelical Thinker Who Left His Mark," *Christianity Today*, June 15, 1984, 60.

45. Robison, *Save America to Save the World*, 75. For repetition of Schaeffer, see, for instance, James Hitchcock, *What Is Secular Humanism?* (Ann Arbor, MI: Servant Books, 1982), 7–8, 11–13, which repeats Schaeffer's citation of various Supreme Court cases and his denunciation of the "Humanist Manifestos" issued in 1933 and 1976 by various American intellectuals. LaHaye, *Battle for the Mind*, 27–46, paraphrases (with credit) Schaeffer's history of the West and invokes Schaeffer's denunciations of the Humanist Manifestos. Schaeffer's specific points, tropes, and fixations on particular events were widely repeated across the conservative Christian community.

46. Schaeffer, *Christian Manifesto*, 43, 53, 58.

47. Richard A. Baer, "They Are Teaching Religion in the Public Schools," *Christianity Today*, February 17, 1984, 12, 13, 14.

48. LaHaye, *Battle for the Mind*, 152, 147–149, 83.

49. Robison, *Garden of the Gods*, 28; *Save America to Save the World*, 88. Robison here is paraphrasing Schaeffer, *How Should We Then Live? L'Abri Fiftieth Anniversary Edition* (Wheaton, IL: Crossway Books, 2005), 205.

50. Jerry Falwell, *Strength for the Journey: An Autobiography* (New York: Simon and Schuster, 1987), 362, 26.

51. Quoted in Frances Fitzgerald, *The Evangelicals: The Struggle to Shape America* (New York: Simon and Schuster, 2017), 401; Heritage USA is discussed on 339–402. See also John Wigger, *PTL: The Rise and Fall of Jim and Tammy Faye Bakker's Evangelical Empire* (New York: Oxford University Press, 2017), 126–138, 222–225. On the prosperity gospel, see Kate Bowler, *Blessed: A History of the American Prosperity Gospel* (New York: Oxford University Press, 2013), especially 11–41, and Philip Luke Sintiere, *Salvation with a Smile: Joel Osteen, Lakewood Church, and American Christianity* (New York: New York University Press, 2015), especially 107–137.

52. "Falwell Shuns Prosperity Theology," *Fredericksburg (VA) Free Lance Star*, June 6, 1987, 27.

53. Beverly LaHaye, *The Spirit-Controlled Woman* (Eugene, OR: Harvest House, 1976), 94. This distrust of wealth extended to left-leaning evangelicals as well; see Ronald J. Sider, *Rich Christians in an Age of Hunger* (New York: Thomas Nelson Publishing, 1978), 112. On Sider and other progressive evangelicals, see Brantley Gasaway, *Progressive Evangelicals and the Pursuit of Social Justice* (Chapel Hill: University of North Carolina Press, 2014), especially 200–235, and Swartz, *Moral Minority*, 153–170.

54. "Family Manifesto," The General Records of the Moral Majority, 1:1–4, box 1, Archives, Guillermin Library, Liberty University, Lynchburg, Virginia; Jerry Falwell, *Listen, America!* (New York: Bantam Books, 1981), 112. Seth Dowland, *Family Values and the Rise of the Christian Right* (Philadelphia: University of Pennsylvania Press, 2015), 11–12, Jason C. Bivins, *The Fracture of Good Order: Christian Anti-Liberalism and the Challenge to American Politics* (Chapel Hill: University of North Carolina Press, 2003), and Sally K. Gallagher, *Evangelical Identity and Gendered Family Life* (New Brunswick, NJ: Rutgers University Press, 2003) all discuss the notion of a gendered order. See also Robert Self, *All in the Family: The Realignment of American Democracy since the 1960s* (New York: Hill and Wang, 2012), 3–17.

55. Peter Marshall Jr. and David Manuel, *The Light and the Glory* (Old Tappan, NJ: Fleming H. Revell Company, 1977), 178, 180.

56. On Spock's activism and reputation, see Thomas Maier, *Dr. Spock: An American Life* (New York: Basic Books, 2003), 347–358, and Richard Cohen, "Spock Is Still Fighting for America's Kids," *Washington Post,* June 4, 1981, C1; Edwin McDowell, "Don't Blame Everything on Dr. Spock," *Wall Street Journal,* August 17, 1972, 10. Alsop and Peale are quoted in Ann Hulbert, *Raising America: Experts, Parents, and a Century of Advice about Children* (New York: Knopf, 2011), 258–260. Minnie Wartell, "Confessions of a Former Spock Mother," *Chicago Tribune,* November 26, 1972, E1.

57. LaHaye and LaHaye, *Spirit-Controlled Family Living,* 31; Falwell, *Listen, America!,* 121; Phyllis Schlafly, *The Power of the Positive Woman* (New Rochelle, NY: Arlington House, 1977), 27.

58. James Dobson, *Dare to Discipline* (Wheaton, IL: Tyndale House, 1970), 12, 13–14, 19, 179. Dobson expresses respect for Spock in "Snatching the Family from Its Grave," *Christianity Today,* May 7, 1982, 16.

59. Dobson, *Dare to Discipline,* 19, 179. A good exploration of the ways in which evangelicals adopted the psychological language surrounding the notion of the traditional family is Margaret Lamberts Bendroth, "Fundamentalism and the Family: Gender, Culture, and the American Pro-family Movement," *Journal of Women's History* 10:4 (1999), 35–54.

60. Schlafly, *Power of the Positive Woman,* 12, 17, 19, 70–71. On Catholic activism against abortion before *Roe v. Wade,* see Daniel K. Williams, *Defenders of the Unborn: The Pro-Life Movement Before Roe v. Wade* (New York: Oxford University Press, 2016), particularly 10–39.

61. Schlafly, *Power of the Positive Woman,* 33, 144. James Hitchcock, *What Is Secular Humanism?* (Ann Arbor: Servant Books, 1982), 116–118. Neil J. Young describes Schlafly's efforts as part of the broader attempt by activist Catholic, evangelical, and Mormon leaders to reconcile their diverse traditions behind political activism in *We Gather Together: The Religious Right and the Problem of Interfaith Politics* (New York: Oxford University Press, 2015), especially 155–158.

62. Jimmy Carter, "Remarks at the Opening Session of the White House Conference on Families," *Public Papers of the Presidents of the United States: Jimmy Carter, 1980–1981* (Washington, DC: Government Printing Office,

1990), 2:1033–1034. On Carter's involvement with the Conference, see J. Brooks Flippen, *Jimmy Carter, the Politics of Family, and the Rise of the Religious Right* (Athens: University of Georgia Press, 2011), 219–220, 268–272.

63. These ideas were developed in Robert Bellah, Richard Madsen, William M. Sullivan, Ann Swidler, and Steven M. Tipton, *Habits of the Heart: Individualism and Commitment in American Life* (Berkeley: University of California Press, 1985), 86–90.

64. Beverly LaHaye, *The Spirit-Controlled Woman*, 71, 130; LaHaye and LaHaye, *Spirit-Controlled Family Living*, 87, 83.

65. Beverly LaHaye, *Who But a Woman?* (New York: Thomas Nelson, 1984), 45, 13; Nancy Barcus, "Families under Stress," *Christianity Today*, September 19, 1980, 24; see also John Maust, "The White House Feud on the Family," *Christianity Today*, May 2, 1980, 47; Interview with William Martin, in *With God on Our Side: The Rise of the Religious Right in America* (New York: Broadway Books, 2005), 182.

66. LaHaye and LaHaye, *Spirit-Controlled Family Living*, 23.

67. "AIDS: The Gay Plague," The General Records of the Moral Majority, MOR 1-2-3 folder 1, 1:1–4, box 1. Martin, *With God on our Side*, 200–207; "AIDS Insurance Letter," The General Records of the Moral Majority, MOR 1-2-3 folder 4; MOR 1:1–4, box 1.

68. Daniel Patrick Moynihan, *The Negro Family: A Case for National Action* (Washington, DC: Office of Policy, Planning and Research, Department of Labor, 1965), 5. For a discussion of the writing and argument of the report, see James Patterson, *Freedom Is Not Enough: The Moynihan Report and America's Struggle over Black Family Life from LBJ to Obama* (New York: Basic Books, 2010), 47–65.

69. For instance, see the libertarian Charles Murray's *Losing Ground: American Social Policy 1950–1980* (New York: Basic Books, 1984), 29–33; see also Ellen Reese, *Backlash against Welfare Mothers Past and Present* (Berkeley: University of California Press, 2005), particularly 158–161, 187–191.

70. "America's Pro-Family Conference," The General Records of the Moral Majority, MOR 1-4-1, folder 4; MOR 1:1–4, box 1. On the Religious Right's suspicion of the civil rights movement, see Williams, *God's Own Party*, 46–48.

71. Jerry Falwell, "America and Work," July 1, 1979. This sermon is excerpted and discussed extensively in Vernon Ray, "A Rhetorical Analysis of the Political Preaching of the Reverend Jerry Falwell: The Moral Majority Sermons, 1979," PhD dissertation, Louisiana State University, 1985, 110–111 and passim; Glandion Carney, "Black Americans: Still Looking for the Promised Land," *Christianity Today*, April 10, 1981, 32–33.

72. Schaeffer, *How Should We Then Live?*, 237–243, 245.

73. George Gilder, *The Visible Man: A True Story of Post-Racist America* (Ithaca, NY: ICS Press, 1978), 22, xx; Rodney Clapp, "Where Capitalism and Christianity Meet," *Christianity Today*, February 4, 1983, 24–26. See also Bethany Moreton, *To Serve God and Wal-Mart: The Making of Christian Free Enterprise* (Cambridge, MA: Harvard University Press, 2009), passim.

74. Schaeffer, *Christian Manifesto*, 29.

75. Jesse Helms, *When Free Men Shall Stand* (Grand Rapids, MI: Zondervan, 1976), 27.

76. LaHaye, *Battle for the Mind*, 37–38.

77. Robison, *Save America to Save the World*, 73. On the controversy, see Flippen, *Jimmy Carter*, 209–210.

78. Interview with William Martin, in *With God on Our Side*, 182.

79. "Christian Lobbyists Boost Conservatism," *Los Angeles Times*, June 25, 1986, D1. On evangelical women's collision with public schools, see James Moffett, *Storm in the Mountains: A Case Study of Censorship, Conflict, and Consciousness* (Carbondale: Southern Illinois University Press, 1982), and Michelle M. Nickerson, *Mothers of Conservatism: Women and the Postwar Right* (Princeton, NJ: Princeton University Press, 2012), 69–103.

80. Mark Albrecht, "The Sellout of Science," *Spiritual Counterfeits Project Journal*, August 1978, 27, 19, 5.

81. E. Earle Ellis, "If Only a Secular Religion Is Taught," *Wall Street Journal*, March 27, 1984, 1.

82. Schaeffer, *How Should We Then Live?*, 164–169, 206; LaHaye, *Battle for the Mind*, 29.

83. "Let Freedom Ring," *Today's World*, August / September 1984, 57–58; Beth Spring, "With Their Leader in Prison, Moonies Pursue Legitimacy," *Christianity Today*, September 7, 1984, 56–58.

84. Spring, "With Their Leader in Prison, Moonies Pursue Legitimacy," 62; "Moon Conviction Is Upheld by Court," *New York Times*, September 14, 1983, 3.

85. Isamu Yamamoto and Paul Carden, "A Summary Critique," *Christian Research Institute Journal*, Fall 1992, 32; "With Their Leader in Prison, Moonies Pursue Legitimacy," 57. See also Massimo Introvigne, *The Unification Church* (Salt Lake City: Signature Books, 2000), 7–9, and Carlton Sherwood, *Inquisition: The Persecution and Prosecution of the Reverend Sun Myung Moon* (New York: Regnery, 1991), 375–379.

86. "Let Freedom Ring," 57–58.

87. Webber, *The Moral Majority: Right or Wrong?* (Wheaton, IL: Crossway Books, 1981), 12–13; Tom Minnerty, "The Man behind the Mask: Bandit or Crusader," *Christianity Today*, September 4, 1981, 28.

88. Richard M. Gamble, *In Search of the City Upon a Hill: The Making and Unmaking of an American Myth* (New York: Continuum, 2012), 141–165; see also Tracy Fessenden, "Christianity, National Identity, and the Contours of Religious Pluralism," in Brekus and Gilpin, *American Christianities*, 399–427.

Epilogue

1. On Romney's meeting with Graham and its aftermath, see Daniel Burke, "After Romney Meeting, Billy Graham Website Scrubs Mormon Cult

Reference," *Washington Post*, October 17, 2012; Melina Mara, "Billy Graham Prays with Mitt Romney," *Washington Post*, October 11, 2012; Neil J. Young, *We Gather Together: The Religious Right and the Problem of Interfaith Politics* (New York: Oxford University Press, 2016), 291–294.

2. Nicole Allen, "Does the Muslim Myth Threaten Obama?," *The Atlantic*, August 19, 2010. By 2015, the number of Americans who believed Obama was a Muslim had climbed to 29 percent, according to a CNN/ORC poll. Sarah Pulliam Bailey, "A Startling Number of Americans Still Believe President Obama Is a Muslim," *Washington Post*, September 14, 2015.

3. Sarah Pulliam Bailey and Ted Olsen, "Q&A: Barack Obama," *Christianity Today*, January 23, 2008; "Barack Obama's Remarks at the Democratic Convention," *USA Today*, July 27, 2004. On the link between Obama's faith and politics, see R. Ward Holder and Peter Josephson, *The Irony of Barack Obama: Barack Obama, Reinhold Niebuhr, and the Problem of Christian State- craft* (New York: Routledge, 2016), especially 45–87; and Kelefa Sanneh, "Project Trinity: The Perilous Mission of Obama's Church," in *The Best African American Essays 2010*, ed. Randall Kennedy (New York: Random House, 2010), 83–96.

4. Mike Huckabee and John Perry, *Character Makes a Difference: Where I'm From, Where I've Been, and What I Believe* (Nashville: B&H Publishing, 2007), 174.

5. Zev Chafets, "The Huckabee Factor," *New York Times*, December 16, 2007, 1. See also Mike Allen and Jonathan Martin, "Romney Speech on Faith Brings Risk," *USA Today*, December 5, 2007, A2.

6. "Romney's Faith in America Address," *New York Times*, December 6, 2007. A useful comparison of Romney's and Huckabee's contrasting ideas about religion and politics in the 2008 campaign is Daniel DiSalvo and Jerome E. Copulsky, "Faith in the Primaries," *Perspectives on Political Science* 38:2 (Spring 2009), 99–106. I also found useful the following analyses of Romney's speech: Richard Benjamin Crosby, "Mitt Romney's Paralipsis: (Un)Veiling Jesus in 'Faith in America,'" *Rhetoric Review* 32:2 (March 2013), 119–136; and Brian Kaylor, "No Jack Kennedy: Mitt Romney's 'Faith in America' Speech and the Changing Religious-Political Environment," *Communication Studies* 62:5 (November/December 2011), 491–507.

7. Philip Rucker, "Romney Delivers Spiritual Address at Liberty University," *Washington Post*, May 12, 2012, 1; Ashley Parker, "Romney Assures Evangeli- cals that Their Values Are His, Too," *New York Times*, May 13, 2012, 1.

8. Michael Luo, "Letter Urges Conservative Christians to Support Romney," *New York Times*, October 11, 2007, A28.

9. Laura Bernardini and Dan Merica, "Romney's Mormonism Leads to Angry Student Response," *Indianapolis Recorder*, April 27, 2012, B2.

10. Richard A. Oppel Jr., "Prominent Pastor Calls Romney's Church a Cult," *New York Times*, October 8, 2011, A10.

11. Justin Sink, "Santorum Explains 'Phony Theology' Comment, Says Obama Is a Christian," *The Hill*, February 19, 2012.

12. On the birther movement and its ties to conservative evangelicalism, see Matthew Hughey, "Show Me Your Papers!: Obama's Birth and the Whiteness of Belonging," *Qualitative Sociology* 35:2 (June 2012), 163–181; Simone Brown and Ben Carrington, "The Obamas and the New Politics of Race," *Qualitative Sociology* 35:2 (June 2012), 113–121; and Ruth Rosen, "The Tea Party and Angry White Women," *Dissent* 59:1 (Winter 2012), 61–65.

13. Eric Zorn, "Polls Reveal Sobering Extent of Nation's Fact Crisis," *Chicago Tribune*, January 5, 2017, C1. See also Jonathan Mahler, "Search Party," *New York Times Magazine*, January 1, 2017, 9–11.

14. Leslie Savan, "The False and Seedy Claim that Obama Is Muslim," *The Nation*, August 24, 2010; Bankole Thompson, "Obama's Jesus Factor," *Michigan Chronicle*, February 9, 2011, A1. See also Rebecca Anne Goetz, "Barack Hussein Obama: America's First Muslim President?," in *Faith in the New Millennium: The Future of Religion and American Politics*, eds. Matthew Avery Sutton and Darren Dochuk (New York: Oxford University Press, 2015), 74–91.

15. This point is made in Anthea Butler, "The Black Church: From Prophecy to Prosperity," *Dissent* 61:1 (Winter 2014), 38–41; and Jeffrey Weiss, "Obama Pastor Jeremiah Wright's Incendiary Quotes Illuminate Chasm Between Races," *McClatchy-Tribune Business News*, April 8, 2008; as well as in Michael Eric Dyson, *The Black Presidency: Barack Obama and the Politics of Race in America* (Boston: Houghton Mifflin, 2016), 86–89.

16. Jeremiah Wright, "The Day of Jerusalem's Fall," sermon, September 16, 2001, and Jeremiah Wright, "Confusing God and Government," sermon, April 13, 2003, both accessed April 15, 2017 at ABC website, http://abcnews.go.com /Blotter/story?id4719157&page1.

17. Stanley Kurtz, "Jeremiah Wright's Trumpet," *Weekly Standard* 13:34 (May 19, 2008), 32, 33; Charles C. Johnson, "The Gospel According to Wright," *American Spectator* 44:10 (December 2011/January 2012), 25–26; Ann Coulter, "Obama Is Not a Muslim," *Human Events* 66:31 (September 6, 2010), 5.

18. Kurtz, "Jeremiah Wright's Trumpet," 32; Johnson, "The Gospel According to Wright," 36; Coulter, "Obama Is Not a Muslim," 5.

19. Coulter, "Obama Is Not a Muslim," 5.

20. Catherine Ellis and Stephen Drury Smith, eds., *Say It Loud!: Great Speeches on Civil Rights and African American Identity* (New York: Perseus Books, 2010), 264–265; see also Barack Obama, *Dreams from My Father: A Story of Race and Inheritance* (New York: Random House, 2007), 294.

21. On Obama's Christian republicanism, I draw on James Kloppenberg, *Reading Obama: Dreams, Hope, and the American Political Tradition* (Princeton, NJ: Princeton University Press, 2011), especially 118–112 and 141–143; Holder and Josephson, *The Irony of Barack Obama*, 45–50; and David Brooks, "A Man on a Gray Horse," *Atlantic Monthly* (September 2002), 24–25.

22. Barack Obama, "We Cannot Abandon the Field of Religious Discourse," in Natalie Goldstein, *Religion and the State* (New York: Facts on File, 2010),

167–169; see also David Espo, "Obama: Democrats Must Court Evangelicals," *Washington Post*, June 28, 2006, A12.

23. Kimberly Winston, "The Rise of the 'Nones,'" *Christian Century*, October 31, 2012, 14. On the "Nones," see Robert D. Putnam and David E. Campbell, *American Grace: How Religion Divides and Unites Us* (New York: Simon and Schuster, 2012), 120–132; "Faith in Flux," Pew Research Center, April 27, 2009, accessed February 10, 2017, www.pewforum.org/2009/04/27/faith-in-flux/.

24. Kenneth Anderson, "Mormons, Muslims, and Multiculturalism," *Weekly Standard* 13:15 (December 24, 2007), 18–19. Elements of Anderson's critique have been echoed by scholars; see, for instance, R. Laurence Moore, *Selling God: American Religion in the Marketplace of Culture* (New York: Oxford University Press, 1995); Leigh Eric Schmidt, *Consumer Rites: The Buying and Selling of American Holidays* (Princeton, NJ: Princeton University Press, 1997), especially 19–32; and Timothy Gloege, *Guaranteed Pure: The Moody Bible Institute, Business, and the Making of Modern Evangelicalism* (Chapel Hill: University of North Carolina Press, 2015), especially 138–162.

25. Ann Grauvogl, "Happily God Free," *Isthmus*, December 18, 2009, 14; Annie Laurie Gaylor, "Secularists Are on the March," *Targeted News Service*, May 19, 2015, 1; Annie Laurie Gaylor, "Pennsylvania Bible Resolution Is Sinfully Unconstitutional," *Targeted News Service*, January 27, 2012, 1. Capitalization original. The argument that Christianity inhibited democracy has a history that goes back to the nineteenth century; see Leigh Eric Schmidt, *Village Atheists: How America's Unbelievers Made Their Way in a Godly Nation* (Princeton, NJ: Princeton University Press, 2016), 55–56.

26. Chris Hedges, *American Fascists: The Christian Right and the War on America* (New York: The Free Press, 2006), 11, 8; see also Michelle Goldberg, *Kingdom Coming: The Rise of Christian Nationalism* (New York: Norton, 2006).

27. Sam Harris, *The End of Faith: Religion, Terror, and the Future of Reason* (New York: Norton, 2004), 109. Similar arguments are made by other "new atheists" in A. C. Grayling, *The God Argument: The Case against Religion and for Humanism* (New York: Bloomsbury, 2013), 244–245; and Christopher Hitchens, *God Is Not Great: How Religion Poisons Everything* (New York: McClelland and Stewart, 2008), 28. Stephen LeDrew offers a rebuttal in *The Evolution of Atheism: The Politics of a Modern Movement* (New York: Oxford University Press, 2016), 87–89.

28. Jerry Falwell Jr., "Why I Endorsed Donald Trump," *Washington Post*, January 27, 2016, accessed February 10, 2017, https://www.washingtonpost.com/news/acts-of-faith/wp/2016/01/27/jerry-falwell-jr-heres-the-backstory-of-why-i-endorsed-donald-trump/.

29. Elizabeth Dias, "Donald Trump's Prosperity Preachers," *Time*, April 14, 2016, accessed May 15, 2017, http://time.com/donald-trump-prosperity-preachers/; Harry Bruinius, "Why Evangelicals Are Trump's Strongest Travel-Ban Supporters," *Christian Science Monitor*, March 3, 2017, 1.

30. "FFRF Debuts Atheist Marquee," *Freethought Today*, November 1, 2015, 3.

ACKNOWLEDGMENTS

Much credit for this book goes to a number of scholars and friends—so many that as I write their names I realize how lucky I am to possess such a constellation—who offered aid, review, and commentary that made this book stronger. The idea germinated in conversations with Richard Bushman and Jana Reiss. Jana's expert pen took the first draft through an editing triathlon and made it far stronger. Kelley Blewster and Louise Robbins did the same for a later draft. Mark Edwards, Michael Kazin, and John Turner, bless them, read the entire manuscript before I submitted it to the press. The writers' group at Henderson State University—Angela Boswell, Travis Langley, Suzanne Tarta-mella, and Michael Taylor, in particular—gamely plowed through many chapters, and Katrina Rogers in the Huie Library's interlibrary loan office is a miracle worker. Patrick Hayes, Amanda Hendrix-Komoto, Christopher Jones, Hannah Jung, Laurie Maffly-Kipp, Maria Mazzenga, Cristy Meiners, Ben Park, Kerry Pimblott, Jonathan Stapley, and Michael Utzinger all read a chapter or two. Joseph Stuart provided a final reading and an index. Elesha Coffman, Ray Haberski, Elizabeth Jemison, Brendan Pietsch, and Ethan Schrum offered insightful comments at various conferences where I presented portions of the work, and Ethan graciously agreed to read an extended portion afterward. Sharon Harris, Debby Pettit, Laura Thomas, and Taylor Parsell offered valuable research assistance. Timothy Meagher and Maria Mazzenga at the Catholic University of America University Archives, David Stiver at Special Collections in the Graduate Theological Union's Flora Lamson Hewlett Library, the staff of the Rare Books and Manuscripts Library at Columbia University, and that of the Moorland-Spingarn Research Center at Howard University deserve particular thanks for their accommodation of my work. Paul Harvey and the anonymous reviewers for the press also offered extensive and thoughtful comments, and Joyce Seltzer, Kathi Drummy, and Angela Piliouras have been invaluable in the manuscript's preparation.

But beyond academia, I want to thank my family: Kent, Winnie, Rosanne, Maurice, John, and Amy, all of whom offered far more love and support than I deserve. If any are Christian, it is truly them.

INDEX